MARKETING GLOBAL JUSTICE

Marketing Global Justice is a critical study of efforts to 'sell' global justice. The book offers a new reading of the rise of international criminal law as the dominant institutional expression of global justice, linking it to the rise of branding. The political economy analysis employed highlights that a global elite benefit from marketised global justice whilst those who tend to be the 'faces' of global injustice - particularly victims of conflict - are instrumentalised and ultimately commodified. The book is an invitation to critically consider the predominance of market values in global justice, suggesting an 'occupying' of global justice as an avenue for drawing out social values.

Christine Schwöbel-Patel is Associate Professor at Warwick Law School and Co-Director of the Centre for Critical Legal Studies. She is the author of *Global Constitutionalism in International Legal Perspective* (2011) and editor of *Critical Approaches to International Criminal Law: An Introduction* (2014).

CAMBRIDGE STUDIES IN INTERNATIONAL AND COMPARATIVE LAW: 152

Established in 1946, this series produces high quality, reflective and innovative scholarship in the field of public international law. It publishes works on international law that are of a theoretical, historical, cross-disciplinary or doctrinal nature. The series also welcomes books providing insights from private international law, comparative law and transnational studies which inform international legal thought and practice more generally.

The series seeks to publish views from diverse legal traditions and perspectives, and of any geographical origin. In this respect it invites studies offering regional perspectives on core *problématiques* of international law, and in the same vein, it appreciates contrasts and debates between diverging approaches. Accordingly, books offering new or less orthodox perspectives are very much welcome. Works of a generalist character are greatly valued and the series is also open to studies on specific areas, institutions or problems. Translations of the most outstanding works published in other languages are also considered.

After seventy years, Cambridge Studies in International and Comparative Law sets the standard for international legal scholarship and will continue to define the discipline as it evolves in the years to come.

Series Editors
Larissa van den Herik
Professor of Public International Law, Grotius Centre for International Legal Studies, Leiden University
Jean d'Aspremont
Professor of International Law, University of Manchester and Sciences Po Law School

A list of books in the series can be found at the end of this volume.

MARKETING GLOBAL JUSTICE

The Political Economy of International Criminal Law

CHRISTINE SCHWÖBEL-PATEL

University of Warwick

To Charlotte,

Knowing that you are part
of the next generation of critical
legal researchers fills me with
pride and hope for our discipline!
From Cunshine x

CAMBRIDGE
UNIVERSITY PRESS

CAMBRIDGE
UNIVERSITY PRESS

University Printing House, Cambridge CB2 8BS, United Kingdom

One Liberty Plaza, 20th Floor, New York, NY 10006, USA

477 Williamstown Road, Port Melbourne, VIC 3207, Australia

314–321, 3rd Floor, Plot 3, Splendor Forum, Jasola District Centre, New Delhi – 110025, India

79 Anson Road, #06-04/06, Singapore 079906

Cambridge University Press is part of the University of Cambridge.

It furthers the University's mission by disseminating knowledge in the pursuit of education, learning, and research at the highest international levels of excellence.

www.cambridge.org
Information on this title: www.cambridge.org/9781108482752
DOI: 10.1017/9781108697651

© Christine Schwöbel-Patel 2021

First published 2021

A catalogue record for this publication is available from the British Library.

Library of Congress Cataloging-in-Publication Data
Names: Schwöbel-Patel, Christine, author.
Title: Marketing global justice : the political economy of international criminal law / Christine Schwöbel-Patel.
Description: Cambridge, United Kingdom ; New York, NY : Cambridge University Press, 2021. | Series: Cambridge studies in international and comparative law | Includes bibliographical references and index.
Identifiers: LCCN 2021002441 (print) | LCCN 2021002442 (ebook) | ISBN 9781108482752 (hardback) | ISBN 9781108710909 (paperback) | ISBN 9781108697651 (epub)
Subjects: LCSH: International criminal law–Public opinion. | International criminal law–Marketing. | Branding (Marketing) | Mass media and criminal justice.
Classification: LCC KZ7235 .S39 2021 (print) | LCC KZ7235 (ebook) | DDC 345–dc23
LC record available at https://lccn.loc.gov/2021002441
LC ebook record available at https://lccn.loc.gov/2021002442

ISBN 978-1-108-48275-2 Hardback

CONTENTS

FIGURES

ACKNOWLEDGEMENTS

Many people had a hand in helping this book ripen from idea to manuscript and I am deeply indebted to them. I am particularly indebted to the immense intellectual labour from which I draw in my quotations and references. I have tried, where possible, to rely on female thinkers in this book – an amazing array of wonderful spirit, defiance, and brain power.

I am thankful to the people who have given me the space to write. And – while acknowledging the privilege of being able to write in a warm room, on a nice computer and with a fully belly, a supportive husband and family – in a genre-breaking move, I also want to acknowledge the pressures and struggles. When reading the acknowledgements of other authors, I am struck with a deep envy of extended peaceful research periods, generous grants, exceptional editors, formidable colleagues, friends, and families. Oh, I am lucky to have formidable colleagues, friends, and family, and an exceptional editor, and had two periods of research leave, but much of my working time remains hard-fought, compromised, and negotiated. This book was written between school runs and meetings, during long and bank-balance-busting commutes, between bedtime battles and sleep-deprived nights, between travels to conferences after arranging a military-style operation of childcare, between rudimentary house cleans and cooking basic dinners, in snatched moments of having hooked the kids onto the television. It was written between teaching preparations, lectures and seminars, and meeting student demands; it was written between writing reviews and responding to emails. And then there is the restlessness that comes with a keen sense that the wonderful work which is in progress at the same time must also be 'The Competition'. Despite the admiration, there is a worrying sense that this competition never sleeps, is always one step ahead, doing a project more valuable, more captivating. Thousands of women and their families, of course, do the same. We muddle through: Never quite achieving everything on the to-do list; never getting to that illusive place promised as 'things will get better *when* . . .'; never seeing the bottom of that insatiable washing basket. So, it is heartening to know that the academic nirvana exists in some people's acknowledgements, but it does not exist in mine. This book, then, is a product of the neoliberal order in which we live. Ironically, I realise that a book engaging with neoliberalism has perhaps come about *because* of this and not *despite* of it. But, neoliberalism is not the hero in this story. Rather, the heroes are those who fight it with their politics, their solidarity, their activism, and their kindness.

So I soften when I think of the amazing network of solidarity without which this book would not have come about. Intellectual co-travellers, who generously gave up some of their precious time to read draft chapters include Kate Grady, who found the time to comment on a draft just as her own book was coming close to completion; Jessie Hohmann, a co-traveller not only in common research questions but also in the exhausting course of being a working academic mum of young children; Robert Knox, who is wise and witty, and whose feedback is so on-point that it generates the greatest admiration and envy; Mavluda Sattorova, my brilliant friend who is my gracious SOS contact for many international law questions; Ntina Tzouvala, whose unfathomably extensive knowledge of international law and political economy helped bring loose ends of the argument together; Latha Varadarajan, who reminds me not to get distracted from the most important questions; Illan Wall, whose energy can move the most obstinate of obstacles, from conceptual doubt to departmental policies; and my dad, Christoph Schwöbel, whose ability to immediately pick up the core of an argument has been a lifelong object of my admiration. I am lucky to have friends who are marketing professionals, who sent me literature recommendations and read drafts. Sarah and James O'Connor remind me that marketing is often driven by smart, generous, and kind people (too). The exchange with my mum, Marlene Schwöbel-Hug, was one of the most valuable aspects of the writing process. I sent her each chapter via email, which she then printed out at her home in Germany, read and marked up, and sent in the post back to the UK. She became more and more outraged by the injustice of marketised global justice, which spurred me on. My husband and partner, Axit, grudgingly read drafts and listened to my monologues on the other side of the childcare, house-care, career-care squeeze (which he begrudges far less than the reading of drafts) and despite believing that he would not be able to give me any useful feedback, gave me the best. After a perhaps unforgiveable reduction of these wonderful people to a few adjectives, there are others who also helped this project along, through commenting on drafts, discussions of ideas, creating opportunities to present work in progress, or through their own research. Many thanks to Marina Aksenova, Kelly-Jo Bluen, Lianne Boer, Adam Branch, Ruth Buchanan, Michelle Burgis-Kasthala, Kirsten Campbell, Richard Clements, Randle DeFalco, Mark Drumbl, Maria Elander, Michelle Farrell, Matt Fisher, Jo Frank, Geoff Gordon, Alexandre Haines, John Haskell, Daniel Joyce, David Kennedy, Emily Kidd-White, Tor Krever, Dino Kritsiotis, Heidi Matthews, Padraig McAuliffe, Frédéric Mégret, Liz Moor, Gabe Mythen, Kate Nash, Vasuki Nesiah, Anne Neylon, Alan Norrie, Sarah Nouwen, Deger Ozkaramanli, Charlie Peevers, Sophie Rigney, Gerry Simpson, Maja Spanu, Sofia Stolk, Victor Tadros, Immi Tallgren, and Wouter Werner. Despite this great collaborative effort, I, of course, take sole responsibility for any errors.

I had the opportunity to present work in progress at many conferences and workshops over the years. I am grateful for those who organised, attended, and commented at these events. They include Warwick Law School's Centre for Critical Legal Studies reading group; the Narration and Aesthetics in Transnational Law and Politics Workshop, Centre for Global Cooperation, University of Duisburg-Essen; Law, Arts, Culture Seminar, Osgoode Hall Law School, York University; ReVisions Seminar Series, University of Glasgow; Art and International Courts Workshop, iCourts, University of Copenhagen; International Humanitarian Law Unit, University of Nottingham; Unit for Global Justice, Goldsmiths, University of London; International Law and the Media Workshop, Queen Mary University of London; Third World Approaches to International Law: On Praxis and the Intellectual Conference, The American University Cairo; Seminar Series, Warwick Law School; Institute for Global Law and Policy, June events, Harvard Law School; Visiting Fellows' Seminar, Lauterpacht Centre for International Law, University of Cambridge; and the Law and Boundaries Conference, Sciences Po. I also owe thanks to the series editors Jean d'Aspremont and Larissa van den Herik for their enthusiasm for this rather unusual international law book. Tom Randall has been an exceptionally engaged, patient, and reassuring editor.

Earlier conceptualisations of the themes in this book appeared in 'The Rule of Law as a Marketing Tool: The International Criminal Court and the Brand of Global Justice', in Christopher May and Adam Winchester (eds.), *Research Handbook on the Rule of Law* (Edward Elgar 2018) 434–452 and 'The Market and Marketing Culture of International

Criminal Law', in Christine Schwöbel (ed.), *Critical Approaches to International Criminal Law – An Introduction* (Routledge 2014) 264–280. An earlier version of Chapter 5 'Working It: The Brand of the Ideal Victim' appeared as 'The Ideal Victim of International Criminal Law' (2018) 29(3) *European Journal of International Law* 703–724. I am grateful for permission to reproduce this material here.

This book, whose beginnings predate them both, is for Nilu and Ayla, with gratitude that they always make me laugh, and in the hope that they might be less enthralled by marketised global justice than my generation.

1

Introduction

The Prosecutor has to be a bit of a salesman: He has to persuade people to accept a new idea: Global Justice.[1]

1.1 Selling Global Justice

Why is it unremarkable for the prosecutor of the world's first permanent International Criminal Court (ICC) to be described as a *salesman*? Why does it appear normal for the last surviving prosecutor of the Nuremberg trials, Benjamin Ferencz, to use marketing terminology to state 'my *slogan* has always been "law not war"'.[2] Equally unremarkable is the claim of the second chief prosecutor of the ICC that '[t]he *return on our investment* for what others may today consider to be a huge cost for justice is effective deterrence and saving millions of victims' lives'.[3] And, it seems entirely ordinary – if rather comical – that a poster for a documentary on the ICC should depict a judge, the chief prosecutor, and the deputy prosecutor standing resolutely against a black background, half turned sideways to the viewer – a scene reminiscent of a movie poster of a John Grisham-meets-Goodfellas adaptation.[4]

This book is a critical study of the marketing practices adopted to 'sell' global justice, and the attendant primacy of market values over social values. Taking note of marketing practices, I suggest, presents a so far under-explored view onto the deeply structuring features of marketing

[1] Film trailer of *Prosecutor*. Directed by Barry Stevens, White Pine Pictures 2010.
[2] Nadia Khmomami, '"It was as if I had peered into hell": the man who brought the Nazi death squads to justice', *The Guardian*, 7 February 2017.
[3] Fatou Bensouda, 'Statement', Ceremony for the solemn undertaking of the prosecutor of the International Criminal Court, International Criminal Court (15 June 2012).
[4] *The Court*. Directed by Marcus Vetter and Michele Gentile, Filmperspektive GmbH 2012, movie poster at www.thecourt-movie.com/. Some versions of the poster include the movie star Angeline Jolie and Benjamin Ferencz alongside the Court officials www.marcus vetter .com/de/filme

1

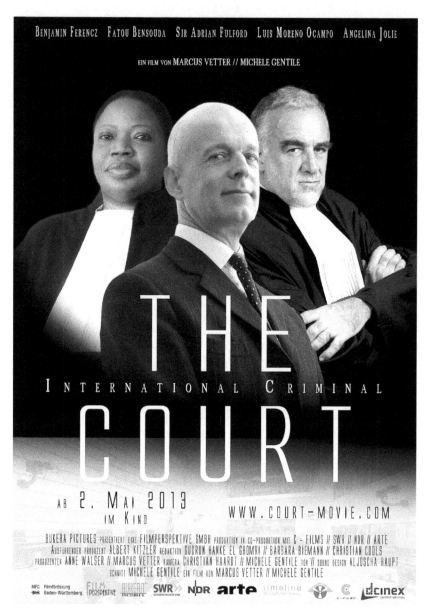

Figure 1.1   *The Court*, movie poster.
© Filmperspektive GmbH

for global justice. *Marketing Global Justice*, therefore, examines the following questions: In what ways are ideas of global justice (re)defined when they are made marketable? Who benefits and who loses when global justice is marketised? What are the constraints and opportunities of marketised global justice for individuals and organisations that act in the name of global justice? And, what is the political, economic, social, and cultural context of marketing global justice?

In order to answer these questions, this book examines international criminal law (ICL) as the dominant global justice project of the early twenty-first century. The practice and discipline of ICL, which seeks to fight the impunity of mass crimes, has successfully fought off competition from other challengers of global justice. The shift from the dominance of the human rights movement, which emerged in the 1970s with a strong grassroots element, to the dominance of the anti-impunity movement, which emerged in the 1990s with a strong institutional element, was by no means natural or obvious. Many alternative ideas of global justice were excluded or marginalised as anti-impunity and its ideas of punitive justice became popular. In particular, ideas about global justice that seek to address redistribution in the context of a deeply unequal world have been marginalised in the ascent of the anti-impunity movement. ICL's visual and discursive attention to distinguishing between 'good' and 'evil' play a central role in its dominance. This sub-discipline of international law, which gives expression to some of the core ideas of neoliberalism such as individualism and the separation of law and politics, has acted as a mechanism through which competing actors configure global justice for capital growth.[5]

The actors competing for resources in the name of global justice operate in, what I call, the *global justice sector*. The terminology of a 'sector' takes heed of the fact that market values (such as eliminating the competition and stimulating growth), and marketing practices (such as branding), are central to the formation and functioning of the dominant understandings of global justice. An analysis of the shaping of global justice, therefore, requires a deeper analysis of what

---

[5] Capital growth refers here to the increase in value of an asset or investment over time as a financial return. I do not distinguish between economic, cultural, social, or symbolic capital as per Pierre Bourdieu, 'The Forms of Capital' in John G. Richardson (ed.), *Handbook of Theory and Research for the Sociology of Education* (Greenwood Press 1986) 241–258.

constitutes 'value' in the typically non-profit areas of global justice. By examining how non-governmental organisations (NGOs), international organisations, individuals, and even nation states are exploiting global justice for capital growth, the receding of social values in favour of market values emerges – not only in the global justice sector, but in the neoliberal order as a whole. Of note is particualrly the prominent role of spectacle. Global justice actors tend to prefer a spectacularised version of justice. The ordering function that spectacle has betrays the coloniality behind notions of 'good' and 'evil' propping up a global market system. In its affinity with spectacle, marketised global justice is implicated in the continuing inequality between the Global North and the Global South. The marketisation of global justice is therefore placed at the intersection between international law, neoliberalism, and empire.

The critique is animated on a more granular level by the concern that marketised global justice is harmful to those who should benefit from global justice projects. At its most acute, marketised global justice is harmful to victims of global injustice. The visual and textual aesthetics of marketised global justice studied is deemed as problematically simplifying complexities of victimhood. A marketised understanding of global justice is shown to build on and sustain stereotypes of a feminised, infantilised, and racialised notion of what an 'ideal' victim (for fundraising purposes) would be. The placing of both perpetrators and victims in the Global South is illustrated as being the most 'on brand' version of marketised global justice. Briefly, on terminology: the Global South refers in some measure to that part of the world, also known as the Third World, which came to be seen as the 'non-aligned' states – neither part of the Western 'First' World, nor part of the communist 'Second' World. However, for this study it is important to note that the Global South does not only refer to a geographical terrain; in Luis Eslava's words, it is 'that expansive and usually subordinated socio-political geography', which includes a 'proliferation of Souths in the North and Norths in the South'.[6] The global justice sector sustains this divide by imagining and constructing a seeing, knowing, and giving audience from the Global North and a seen, unknowing, and receiving 'other' from the Global South. Such narrowing of the benefactors and patrons of global justice projects on

---

[6] Luis Eslava, 'TWAIL Coordinates'(Critical Legal Thinking, 2 April 2019), available at: http://criticallegalthinking.com/2019/04/02/twail-coordinates/#fn-27281-2.

the one hand and the beneficiaries of global justice on the other hand has profound de-historicising and de-politicising effects. It edits out a history of exploitation of the Global South and a continuing dependency of the Global North on the value extraction of the former. Marketing practices actively distract from these inequalities, ultimately transforming political actors into consumers.

In its illumination of the marketised understanding of global justice, this book aims 'to learn to see the frame that blinds us to what we see'.[7] A historical-materialist perspective helps to explain why it is that despite a plethora of global justice actors, inequality continues to grow. Bringing together the political and the economic in a critique that builds on the Marxist tradition, centres the distributive (and lack of redistributive) faculties of dominant global justice projects. This critique enables the analysis of inequalities as rooted in historically specific and changing power relations, which are competitive social processes. It does not, however, concern the figure of the top-hat-adorned capitalist in the form of profit-seeking managers who have infiltrated good faith institutions in their bad faith (although some version of this might also exist). Rather, this is a study of the naturalised conscious and unconscious use of market practices in global justice institutions and projects, its origins, its symptoms, and – crucially – resistance to it.

1.2 Global Justice in Competition

The stakes for the universally accepted meaning of global justice are high. Nothing less than being on the right side of moral (and legal) history is in the balance when invoking global justice as the reason behind a project, an intervention, or a new institution.[8] The material benefits of this right side of moral and legal history are substantial, and sometimes existential. I dispense with a definition of global justice in favour of understanding the term as indeterminate, a term for whose determinacy there is competition. There are, in other words, competing understandings of global justice, all of which claim universality or at the very least supremacy over

---

[7] Judith Butler, *Frames of War: When is Life Grievable* (Verso 2010) 100.

[8] Brad Evans and Simona Forti present a similar argument about dubbing certain violence as 'evil', that is, denoting the violence of, for example, the Islamic State as 'evil' places 'us' on the right side of moral history. Brad Evans and Simona Forti, 'Who is "Evil", and Who Is the Victim?', *New York Times*, 16 September 2016.

other meanings. ICL, borne of the idea of fighting impunity of individuals who have committed heinous crimes, is presented as the current dominant, but also contested, iteration of global justice. This competition for global justice is not simply one of morals or of the supremacy of intellectual thought; it is a material competition. As I will demonstrate in the following chapters, the competition for the meaning of global justice is simultaneously the competition for institutions, donations, (fee-paying) students, recruitment of activists, officials, policy-makers, and book deals. The competition over the meaning of global justice is a competition over resources. Marketing is employed as a tool to increase competitiveness (and ultimately, to eliminate the competition). Competitors in the same sector – that is, those aiming to sell similar products and services – use marketing to gain revenue, profits, and increase market share over others. The vital function of marketing in the global justice sector is perhaps best demonstrated by this quotation: 'The game isn't who can make the biggest difference or is fighting for the most important cause. It's he who has the best marketing wins.'[9] These words, uttered by the CEO of the non-profit rating website Charity Navigator, about the success of the viral advocacy video *Kony 2012*, suggest that *selling* a particular cause is more important than the cause itself. That is, if the aim is to 'win'.

Several global justice actors are analysed in this book, from multinational corporations that employ 'brand activism' to nation states that aim to shape national identity through a brand strategy. As one of the primary global justice actors in this competitive sector, the ICC will be scrutinised in depth. Even before its formal establishment with the Rome Statute of 1998, the court was described as an institution for global justice.[10] A year prior to the conference in Rome, UN Secretary General Kofi Annan described the establishment of a permanent international criminal court as the 'final step toward global justice'.[11] Ten years later, the chief prosecutor of the ICC, Luis Moreno Ocampo, titled a talk: 'The International Criminal Court: Seeking Global Justice'. In the talk, he proclaimed the commencement of a 'new legal era', built by the

---

[9] Ken Berger, quoted in Claire Suddath, '"Kony 2012": Guerrilla Marketing', Bloomberg, 31 August 2012.

[10] Rome Statute of the International Criminal Court (signed 17 July 1998, entered into force 1 July 2002) A/CONF.189/9.

[11] Kofi Annan, 'Advocating for an International Criminal Court' (1997) 21(2) *Fordham International Law Journal* 363–366.

ICC.[12] When, in 2012, the new Chief Prosecutor Fatou Bensouda took office, *Time Magazine* enthusiastically ran the headline 'Gambia's Fatou Bensouda. The New Face of Global Justice'.[13] On the occasion of twenty-one years since the signing of the Rome Statute, the NGO Coalition for the ICC used the headline 'Fighting for Global Justice: International Justice Day'.[14] The fight for global justice, however, transgressed what former President of the International Criminal Court Sang-Hyun Song called an 'audacious plan to create a global justice system' of individual accountability;[15] the far more audacious plan was the integration of a global trade law and global criminal law system. In its enabling of and simultaneous 'encasing' of the market, the ICC is a key global institution of the neoliberal order.[16] A switch from actor to audience reveals the constitution of a global justice consumer: a spectator of spectacle, donor to and supporter of the market, and a de-politicised subject.

More generally, a focus on competition between global justice actors provides some insight into the constitution and re-constitution between the *market* as socially and politically constituted and *justice* as socially and politically constituted. The use of marketing practices in traditionally non-market spaces, and the accompanying focus on competition and growth, is typical of shifts towards deregulation, liberalisation, and privatisation associated with neoliberalism. The purpose of the market, according to supporters of a 'free market', is to achieve both financial success (growth/profits) and individual self-actualisation (freedom).[17] Neoliberalism in this sense is also a project of justice. In neoliberalism,

---

[12] Luis Moreno Ocampo, 'The International Criminal Court: Seeking Global Justice' (2007) 40(1) *Case Western Reserve Journal of International Law* 215–225, at 224.

[13] Gillian Parker and Alex Perry, 'Gambia's Fatou Bensouda: The New Face of Global Justice', *Time Magazine*, 18 June 2012.

[14] 'Fighting for Global Justice: International Justice Day' Coalition for the ICC, 16 July 2019, available at: www.coalitionfortheicc.org/news/20190716/fighting-for-global-justice-ijd.

[15] Sang-Hyun Song, 'Statement from the President: International Criminal Justice Day', Presidency of the International Criminal Court, 15 July 2013, available at: www.icc-cpi .int/iccdocs/presidency/ICJ-Day-ICC-President-Statement-Eng.pdf.

[16] 'Encasing' of the market is a short-hand borrowed from Quinn Slobodian, *Globalists: The End of Empire and the Birth of Neoliberalism* (Harvard University Press 2018).

[17] These traditions, and their intellectual histories (often relying on Adam Smith's *Wealth of Nations* [1776] (Penguin 1982) or Friedrich Hayek's *The Road to Serfdom* [1944] (Routledge 2001) will be explained in more depth in the coming chapters. In the US context, these freedoms are often referred to as individual liberties. For example, the 'Index of Economic Freedom', annually published by The Heritage Foundation and the *Wall Street Journal*, which associates economic freedom with 'healthier societies, cleaner

competition means choice and choice means freedom. Competition is therefore already intimately entwined with a sense of what is just. Great faith is placed in the market. Such faith in the market from an international justice perspective is particularly evident in a – now somewhat notorious – speech by Carla Del Ponte (then-chief prosecutor of the International Criminal Tribunal for the former Yugoslavia) at investment bank Goldman Sachs in 2005. In this speech, she stated: 'Investing in justice will bring the best dividends.' She gave five reasons: first, the work of justice alleviates the cost of human suffering; second, justice prevents new costly wars; third, the work of international justice prevents costly post-conflict reconstruction projects; fourth, justice enhances governance that creates a better environment for doing business; fifth, and finally, Del Ponte explains:

> [i]nternational justice is cheap. The cost of the Tribunal [ICTY] is less than one day of US military presence in Iraq. Let me dare another risky comparison: Our annual budget is well under the 10% of Goldman Sachs' profit during the last quarter. See, I can offer you high dividends for a low investment.[18]

The statement is not only striking for its overt use of market terminology and normalisation of the role of the market, but particularly for the role of ICL in creating a space for the market to flourish. I return to the speech several times throughout the book. Del Ponte's statement is illustrative of how to approach neoliberalism and law. ICL in this account is a mechanism employed to enable the market, while a stable state is placed in the position of protecting the market. This corresponds with neoliberalism as a legal-institutional mechanism of ordering, in contrast to how it is often understood as concerning market fundamentalism, or *laissez faire*. The newly stabilised state is therefore placed in the position of protecting the market from popular contestation. In the words of historian Quinn Slobodian, the market is 'encased'.[19] International legal norms and institutions do not, therefore, exist separately from the market; rather, they stabilise (enable and encase) it.

---

environments, greater per capita wealth, human development, democracy, and poverty elimination', www.heritage.org/index/about.

[18] Carla Del Ponte, 'The Dividends of International Criminal Justice', Goldman Sachs, London, 6 October 2005, available at: www.icty.org/x/file/Press/PR_attachments/cdp-goldmansachs-050610-e.htm.

[19] Slobodian, 'Globalists'.

'[T]he law', as Claire Cutler put it succinctly, 'is not an objective force that exists out "there", impacting neutrally on society, economy and polity, but is in "here", both constituting and constituted by social, economic and political forces.'[20] While this constitutive role of law has been examined by critical scholars in international economic law, international investment law, and in international human rights law,[21] it is as yet under-researched in ICL's interpretation of global justice, which is preoccupied with the idea of fighting impunity.[22] As shall be uncovered in the coming chapters, global justice actors' contribution to neoliberalism as a legal-institutional order lies in the enabling of the market and a moralistic structuring of 'good' and 'evil'. This alliance between marketing and anti-impunity has uniquely persuasive and distracting properties, particularly through the prevalence of spectacle. Relatedly, the alliance between marketing and anti-impunity enables illusions about social values and processes of renewal. Marketised global justice frames competition as a mechanism to order social relations; and finally marketing and the fight against impunity elevate property rights on a global scale through the commodification of social values. This alliance has become so normalised that 'the issue is not *whether* or not to brand, but *how* to manage and market the brand.'[23] It follows that this study does not subscribe to neoliberalism as a 'logic' or 'reason', even if these may be a part of the broader project of neoliberalism.[24] The critique aligned with

[20] Claire Cutler, *Private Power and Global Authority: Transnational Merchant Law in the Global Political Economy* (Cambridge University Press 2003) 6.

[21] On international economic law, see, in addition to Cutler, also for example Ntina Tzouvala, 'Neoliberalism as Legalism: International Economic Law and the Rise of the Judiciary' in Ben Golder and Daniel McLoughlin (eds.), *The Politics of Legality in a Neoliberal Age* (Routledge 2017) 116–133. On international investment law, see for example David Schneiderman, 'Investment Arbitration As Constitutional Law: Constitutional Analogies, Linkages and Absences' in Thomas Schultz and Federico Ortino (eds.), *The Oxford Handbook of International Arbitration* (Oxford University Press 2020). On international human rights law, see for example Jessica Whyte,'The Morals of the Market': Human Rights and the Rise of Neoliberalism* (Verso 2019); Susan Marks, 'Human Rights and the Bottom Billion' (2009) 1 *European Human Rights Law Review* 37–49.

[22] Although, see importantly on ICL and accountability of the corporation Grietje Baars, *The Corporation, Law and Capitalism* (Brill 2019).

[23] Charles Skuba, 'Branding America' (2002) 3 *Georgetown Journal of International Affairs* 105–114, at 106. Emphases added.

[24] Neoliberalism as 'logic' is described, for example, by Wendy Brown when she opens her book on neoliberalism by explaining that it is 'a peculiar form of reason that configures all aspects of existence in economic terms'. Wendy Brown, *Undoing the Demos: Neoliberalism's Stealth Revolution* (Zone Books 2017) 17.

the logic line of argument often uses market terminology in quotation marks, as in 'investments' and 'shareholders'.[25] Notably, Del Ponte is not so hesitant. Carla Del Ponte's reference to dividends is not a metaphor, but rather to be read literally, and therefore materially.

1.3   New Branding and New Tribunalism in the 1990s

In this book, the marketisation of global justice is largely placed within the recent historical context of the consolidation of neoliberalism in its legal-institutional form in the 1990s. The period analysed begins roughly around the time of the perceived triumph of Western liberal democracy at the end of the Cold War and the widespread use of market techniques to incorporate former Soviet states into a global capitalist economy. The declared aim of former Soviet state transition to functioning legal and democratic systems was invariably accompanied by policies of economic liberalisation.

Two seemingly unrelated fields were attracting a lot of attention and resources in the 1990s, fields that are revealed as being deeply connected in marketised global justice. First, the 1990s saw the emergence of 'new branding'. Branding was no longer simply about creating a logo; instead, the new perspective of the 1990s was that products and companies should embody relationships, values, and feelings.[26] The idea of associations with a corporation and its products and services as making up 'a brand' emerged at this time. Selling lifestyle rather than selling products became the new branding mantra. The consumer in this move to branding was seen as a global consumer. The idea of a global consumer allowed products and services to be marketed in the same way worldwide.[27] The new ideas and practices of branding were accompanied by an attention to the brand as private property – an asset to be measured, which could be quite distinct from the physical (tangible) assets of a corporation. For consumers, marketing was presented as a way of increasing competition as well as choice. In seeming contradiction of greater choice, however, the 1990s also saw the emergence of

---

[25] See, for example, Sara Kendall, 'Commodifying Global Justice: Economies of Accountability at the International Criminal Court' (2015) 13(1) *Journal of International Criminal Justice* 113–134.

[26] Liz Moor, *The Rise of Brands* (Bloomsbury 2007) 6.

[27] In transnational businesses 'strategic business units' took over responsibility from the individual country managers. John Quelch, 'Global Brands: Taking Stock' (1999) 10(1) *Business Strategy Review* 1–14.

superbrands such as Nike, Marlboro, Coca-Cola, and Levi's. As can be gleaned from these brands, the 1990s was part of the cultural apex of all things American. Brand USA dominated.

The second notable field attracting substantial resources was the anti-impunity movement, which gained support amid an enthusiasm for international institutions. Brand United Nations – with support from the USA – was on the rise. Western states engaged in a 'new intervention-ism' by articulating an alignment between humanitarianism and military power; and a consolidated international economic order began to take shape, with the contours being defined by international financial insti-tutions.[28] The enthusiasm for establishing institutions was particularly prominent in the 'new tribunalism' of the anti-impunity movement.[29] The anti-impunity movement, made up of an alliance of NGOs, interested individuals and states, lobbied hard for their institutional dreams. It began with the garnering of broad-based support for tribunals as the setting for international war crimes prosecutions for crimes committed in the former Yugoslavia and Rwanda, and reached its climax through the establishment of the ICC. New tribunalism and new branding converged in the global justice sector where institutions were built on the understanding that marketing practices were productively transposed from the corporate to the public sphere and where brands increasingly saw the value of global justice themes as a message to sell to consumers.

As these new ideas and practices assumed dominance in marketing and international law respectively, the 1990s was also a time of increas-ingly sustained critique. In 1999, Naomi Klein published her searing critique of branding in *No Logo*.[30] The movement against corporatisa-tion, notably under the name Global Justice Movement, employed pro-test and civil disobedience to force changes to the terms of the nascent World Trade Organization (WTO). Most famously, the clashes between protesters and the police were documented as the 1999 'Battle of Seattle'.[31] In international law, meanwhile, some of the most important

---

[28] The term 'new interventionism' is borrowed here from Anne Orford, 'Muscular Humanitarianism: Reading the Narratives of the New Interventionism' (1999) 10 *European Journal of International Law* 679–711.

[29] Thomas Skouteris, 'The New Tribunalism: Strategies of De-Legitimation in the Era of International Adjudication' (2008) 17 *Finnish Yearbook of International Law* 307–356.

[30] Naomi Klein, *No Logo* (10th anniversary edition, Fourth Estate, 2010).

[31] For an account of the Global Justice Movement after the Seattle protests, see Donatella Della Porta (ed.), *The Global Justice Movement. Cross national And Transnational Perspectives* (Paradigm 2006).

critique around gender, class, and race was being articulated. Anne Orford's iconic piece 'Muscular Humanitarianism: Reading the Narratives of the New Interventionism' was published in 1999, paving the way for a gender and class critique of international law. New Approaches to International Law, a project largely driven by Harvard professor David Kennedy, whose purpose it was to critique assumptions around the liberal-legal project, had not only taken on momentum but was already declared 'done' by 1998.[32] And, for the first time in 1996, another group of Harvard graduates congregated around the abbreviation of TWAIL, Third World Approaches to International Law, consequently producing some of the most salient critiques of international law's imperialism and complicity in the exploitation of the Global South.[33]

Despite a focus on the 1990s, the history of marketised global justice stands in a far longer tradition of the entwinement of the economy and justice institutions, a history of mutual support as well as reinvention. Whether it is the legitimation of colonialism and the impetus for decolonisation, the legitimation of the slave trade and abolitionism, or the legitimation of war and post-war reconstructionism, the marketisation of global justice is situated in a history of mutual profiteering between international legal institutions and the market. Indeed, backlashes have often deepened the grip of the market by other means. The persisting separation of the 'haves' from the 'have-nots' across race, class, and gender lines is built on a material appropriation of value and on epistemological domination.

1.4   Pro Logo or No Logo?

Even to the most casual reader, it will already have become clear that this study is critical of marketised global justice. But, there is also a different side of the story, one that is far more optimistic about neoliberalism and marketing practices. This story is often underpinned by comments pointing out the advances of neoliberalism as creating wealth, generating income, and contributing to higher standards of living. A common supporting argument of this view is the invocation of the higher life

---

[32] 'In the spring of 1998, we celebrated the end of this institutional project at a conference in Cambridge which we called: "Fin de NAIL: A Celebration."' David Kennedy, 'When Renewal Repeats: Thinking against the Box', 32 *New York University Journal of International Law and Politics* (1999–2000) 335–500, at 490.

[33] James Thuo Gathi, 'TWAIL: A Brief History of its Origins, its Decentralized Network, and a Tentative Bibliography' (2011) 3(1) *Trade, Law and Development* 26–64.

expectancy attached to capitalist states; often, this will be contrasted with traditionally socialist states and their trailing life expectancy statistics. This argument is based on the idea that social justice will follow neoliberalism if markets are integrated further and if one waits sufficiently long. It is a version of the 'trickle-down' argument, which claims that wealth generated initially with the elites will trickle down to the less fortunate.

The 'trickle-down' argument is, against the background of growing inequality (not to mention climate catastrophe), rapidly losing credibility. Despite the continued faith in the market, it is now common for analyses of inequalities of wealth, health, education, leisure, and a clean environment to be explained as symptomatic of neoliberalism, even if some uncertainty as to its definition continues to prevail. A defining moment was undoubtedly the International Monetary Fund's (IMF) 2016 report acknowledging that neoliberal policies have increased inequality.[34] Indeed, the IMF described privatisation, deregulation, and liberalisation in the marketing language as having been 'oversold'. And yet, does the growing scepticism about neoliberalism extend to marketing practices such as branding? One might wonder: what is wrong with using marketing to attract attention to global injustices? Posing this question follows the reasoning that instruments of market growth are themselves benign, that they are misunderstood or have simply been in the wrong hands. Following the success of Naomi Klein's critique of branding in *No Logo*, *The Economist* printed a special 'Pro Logo: Why brands are good for you' issue.[35] Brands are only absent in the world's poorest places, begins the lead article. And besides, brand recognition means that large companies become accountable to consumers as brands provide reliability and quality.[36] Simon Anholt, author of *Brand New Justice: The Upside of Global Branding*, argues that marketing is a powerful tool for economic development. Branding can make a 'worthwhile contribution to the fairer distribution of global wealth' if we learn to transfer the branding knowledge of global brands to those who need it:

---

[34] This article was also defining for its explicit use of the term 'neoliberalism', up until then often deemed a figment of the radical left's imagination. Jonathan D. Ostry, Prakash Loungani, and Davide Furceri, 'Neoliberalism: Oversold?' (2016) 53(2) *Finance & Development*, available at: www.imf.org/external/pubs/ft/fandd/2016/06/ostry.htm.

[35] 'Pro Logo: Why brands are good for you', *The Economist*, 8 September 2001.

[36] 'The case for brands', *The Economist*, 8 September 2001.

like it or not, rich and poor, we all live in a money-based global economy, and the lack of money is a primary cause of suffering: so it makes sense to take a closer look at how these brands multiply money, and see whether their genius for doing so might be transferable to some of the people and the places which *really* need it.[37]

I seek to demonstrate that marketised global justice is not just about the cosmetic aspects of employing symbols; the use of branding is symptomatic of the primacy of market values, entrenches these, and reproduces them. The employment of branding, therefore, tends to hinder transformative change.

1.5   The Ideal and Material Worlds of Global Justice

There is a notable dissonance between philosophers of global justice on the one hand and global justice actors analysed in this book on the other hand. An influential body of literature on global justice exists, which is spearheaded by philosophers Thomas Pogge, Amartya Sen, Charles Beitz, and others.[38] This literature largely operates in the sphere of 'the ideal', meaning that it is concerned with notions of fairness under the assumption that all people and institutions could act according to certain moral rules. Moral and ethical conceptions of global justice are considered. That is not to say that the literature misses distributive justice; it does not. Indeed, it focuses largely on questions of equality and the elimination of poverty. It does so by asking where the moral obligations lie towards other people in a globalised world. This includes questions concerning obligations of a wealthy person towards a poor person,[39] and whether tyrannical and dictatorial regimes should be accepted as members in good standing of a reasonable society of peoples.[40] International criminal justice – the interpretation of global justice that is in this book referred to as the most competitive understanding of global justice – ironically does not feature at all, or only features marginally, in the key philosophical

---

[37] Simon Anholt, *Brand New Justice: The Upside of Global Branding* (Butterworth Heinemann 2003) 2.

[38] Thomas Pogge and Darrel Moellendorf (eds.), *The Global Justice Reader: Seminal Essays, Volumes I and II* (Paragon House 2008).

[39] See, for example, Onora O'Neill, 'Lifeboat Earth' in Pogge and Moellendorf, The Global Justice Reader, 1–20 and Charles R. Beitz, 'Justice and International Relations' in Pogge and Moellendorf, The Global Justice Reader, 21–48.

[40] See, for example, John Rawls, 'The Law of People' in Pogge and Moellendorf, The Global Justice Reader, 421–460.

global justice literature.[41] The mighty collection of two volumes and over forty leading names of philosophy and jurisprudence titled *Global Justice: Seminal Essays* does not mention ICL even once. There are several possibilities of how to interpret this. First, ICL described as the most competitive type of global justice may be a straw man argument: the very absence of ICL in philosophical deliberations proves that the project has not been so successful after all. Second, it may simply be that 'the ideal' precludes 'real' institutional manifestations. Frédéric Mégret points out that those thinking philosophically about global justice are simply less likely to consider *existing* institutions of international law.[42] Finally, a disciplinary self-referential myopia may be at play. Philosophers simply do not consider what the lawyers say and vice versa. Despite the philosophers' silence on ICL as global justice,[43] it cannot be denied that ICL has gained a status as the measure for global justice in the dominant institutional framework as well as in the public imagination. Whether it is the television drama *Crossing Lines* based on fictional stories of investigators at the ICC, the many documentaries on international tribunals, the non-fiction genre books on themes of international criminal justice such as *East West Street*[44] and *A Problem from Hell: America in the Age of Genocide*,[45] the op-eds written about the ICC and its tensions with Africa, the NGO demands to send Tony Blair or George Bush to The Hague,[46] UN endorsement, celebrity endorsement, or the repeated call for international criminal justice mechanisms to operate effectively in Syria – anti-impunity is certainly a popular form of global justice.

The marketisation lens focuses the critique on the material conditions and implications of global justice rather than the ideal. It considers the

---

[41] International criminal justice is to be understood as a slightly broader field than ICL. The latter relates more specifically to the institutions and norms of anti-impunity.

[42] Frédéric Mégret, 'What Sort of Global Justice is "International Criminal Justice"' (2015) 13(1) *Journal of International Criminal Justice* 77–96 at 78.

[43] International criminal lawyers and criminal lawyers, on the other hand, have engaged with the justice philosophy. See, for example, Morten Bergsmo and Emiliano J. Buis (eds.), *Philosophical Foundations of International Criminal Law: Foundational Concepts* (Torkel Opsahl Academic EPublisher 2019).

[44] Philippe Sands, *East West Street: On the Origins of "Genocide" and "Crimes against Humanity"* (Alfred Knopf 2016).

[45] Samantha Power, *A Problem from Hell: America and the Age of Genocide* (Flamingo 2010).

[46] A crowd-funded website managed to raise thousands of pounds to pay as bounties for anyone who attempted a peaceful citizen's arrest of Tony Blair, with one of the purposes being to pressure UK authorities to deliver Tony Blair to the ICC, see: www.arrestblair .org.

actions of NGOs, international institutions, individuals and states to be set against the background of political, economic, cultural, and social contexts, which are historically determined. Actors are not discussed as abstract entities with obligations, but in the context of the constraints and possibilities available to them. More specifically, the book considers 'global justice projects' as those that invoke global justice in the context of the dominant political, economic and social order. Therefore, global justice actors are examined in regard to their actions that seek capital growth. That is not to say that utopian ideas of global justice are outside of the frame of the inquiry, and relatedly that *ideas* have little to contribute to transformative change. Not at all.[47] Indeed, the final chapter titled 'Occupying Global Justice' considers this very question, namely whether there is a space for global justice that is not marketised. There is, I suggest, something worth rescuing about global justice, particularly since it has in the past served as a rallying cry for internationalism against corporatisation. Considering histories of resistance based on solidarity and internationalism provides an opening for imagining and implementing an anti-imperial global justice.

1.6 The Aesthetics of Global Justice

'We live in a visual age' is the truism with which the contemporary attraction to spectacular events is often explained.[48] There is a growing recognition in international law of the importance of the visual and the material world, including a new interest in international law's objects.[49] And yet, this is an area that is as yet under-theorised. Why is it that images are increasingly used to convey ideas about some global justice projects (and not others), and why are these images so often catastrophic

---

[47] The charge of economic determinism of Marxism often operates here. Clearly, explains Susan Marks, Marx cannot have doubted the potential of ideas, '[o]therwise, he would not have expended his own energies in the way he did'. Susan Marks, *The Riddle of All Constitutions* (Oxford University Press 2000) 123.

[48] See Roland Bleiker (ed.), *Visual Global Politics* (Routledge 2018). 'We live in a visual age' states the blurb of the collection. Bleiker and the contributors go into much depth on the complexities of this visual age.

[49] Jessie Hohmann and Daniel Joyce (eds.), *International Law's Objects* (Oxford University Press 2018); Amanda Perry-Kessaris, 'The Pop-Up Museum of Legal Objects Project: An Experiment in "Sociolegal Design"' (2017) 68(2) *Northern Ireland Legal Quarterly*, Special Issue on the Pop Museum of Legal Objects, 225–244; Madelaine Chiam et al., 'History, Anthropology and the Archive of International Law' (2017) 5(1) *London Review of International Law* 3–5 (introducing a special issue on artefacts).

images? Why does the good/evil dichotomy of international criminal justice have such wide visual appeal? To make sense of this, we must go beyond the simple observation that 'a picture says more than a thousand words' and that complicated messages need to be communicated in a comprehensive manner. In this book, I suggest that the emphasis on the visual as a form of communicating ideas about justice emanates itself from a sense of acting within a competitive market, 'the attention economy'. An analysis of global justice in the attention economy makes sense of the aesthetics of marketised global justice, an aesthetics that frequently relies on spectacular images of death and suffering. What do these two terms, aesthetics and the attention economy, mean? Aesthetics as I use it in this book is not just about beauty or decoration. Building on Jacques Rancière's definition of aesthetics, aesthetics is employed to describe the sense-experience that accumulates through dominant forms of presentation and representation to constitute that which is deemed to be 'common sense'.[50] What is *seen* in society is part of a political battle, a battle over the distribution of the sensible.[51] The attention economy takes heed of the information (and visual) age in which we live, and transforms attention into a commodity: attention is regarded as a scarce resource for which there is continuous competition. Consequently, 'extreme [is rewarded] at the expense of the erudite, the controversial over the considered'.[52] The self-perception of operating in the attention economy turns catastrophic images and simplified narratives into valuable currencies – means employed to capture 'flickering attention'.[53] In the attention economy, the spectacular images and narratives both *attract* the attention, and have an *ordering* function, introducing hierarchies on what is worthy of attention.

The lens of marketing, and particularly its reductive images and narratives, throws light on the racialised distribution of the sensible. Mostly, suffering is visualised through stereotypes of suffering in the Global South. Global justice actors tend to raise awareness through images and narratives of victims in the Global South, whether an African child's face that appears to appeal for help to the viewer, or the

---

[50] Jacques Rancière, *The Politics of Aesthetics*, trans. Gabriel Rockhill (Bloomsbury 2004).
[51] Rancière, 'Politics of Aesthetics', 7–14.
[52] Patricia McDonald, 'The Attention Economy and the Demise of the Middle Ground', *The Guardian*, 6 July 2016.
[53] Rob Nixon, *Slow Violence and the Environmentalism of the Poor* (Harvard University Press 2013) 6.

women standing in front of makeshift shelters, or the portrayal of the dangerous, seemingly non-repentant, war criminal. Stereotyping is introduced in my analysis as a communicative tool that has distributive properties. Particular attention is given to stereotypes of victims of conflict. In marketised global justice, the victim of conflict is, I argue, condensed to a marketable stereotype, constructed on the basis of assumptions about purchasing power. Much like fundraising campaigns that foreground a 'flies in their eyes' image of victimhood, the victim of global injustice is tailored to the tastes of a Western donor and patronage community. As I will set out, rather than helping the victims of injustice themselves, dominant marketised global justice exploits them. The significance of international law within this aestheticisation of marketised global justice is immense: law offers the means by which such frames are institutionalised and legitimised. To be sure, spectacle and stereotypes of the main protagonists of humanitarianism existed prior to ICL's ascendance, but ICL has provided both a stage and a global audience for a legally institutionalised and marketable version of this frame.

1.7   The Erasure of the Political

Marketised global justice has a de-historicising and de-politicising effect. It not only emphasises marketable stereotypes; it also emphasises marketable events (say, the transitioning of a state to global justice as an indication of its good governance environment), and renders invisible the less marketable historical moments (say, the exploitation of histories of empire). Due to the prioritisation of marketable histories, accompanied by measurement through indexes, reports, and statistics, marketisation causes the marginalisation of political contestation and debate. Spectacularised images and narratives blind the spectator to longer histories of exploitation and resistance. The spectacularised courtroom drama hides context and root causes, the modernistic (de-spectacularised) architecture of international organisations hides the complicities of certain member states in suffering. The normalisation of distractions of spectacle have dulled resistance to its ordering functions. Meanwhile, the market is de-spectacularised, presented as more or less above human action. The marketised idea of global justice is consequently displacing the opportunity for political action. As Achille Mbembe remarked:

> In a world set on objectifying everybody and every living thing in the name of profit, the erasure of the political by capital is the real threat.

The transformation of the political into business raises the risk of the elimination of the very possibility of politics.[54]

And yet, the intensified assault on social values of the neoliberal order has also intensified both backlash and resistance. In this book, I make a distinction between market-based and ultimately market-strengthening backlashes on the one hand and historically rooted resistance on the other hand. Backlashes are indicative of the fact that the taken-for-granted benevolence of the market for global justice is being questioned. But backlashes are also often lodged in market-thinking; this includes demands for transparency, accountability, and efficiency of global justice actors. Backlashes have typically been unable to connect with political movements, fading away as quickly as they arise. This realisation leads at different times and to different degrees to disenchantment and disengagement. Resistance, on the other hand, is rooted in the consciousness of imperialism as the continuing force of accumulation in the global justice sector. This more radical form of response to marketised global justice insists on *re*-politicisation and *re*-historicisation. Rather than being directed solely against global justice actors, resistance is also directed against the neoliberal order, recognising that marketised global justice is both symptomatic and constitutive of neoliberalism.

1.8 'Occupying' Global Justice

The critical perspective on global justice is adopted not simply out of academic curiosity, but with a view to considering possibilities for its radical transformation. Marketised justice is not inevitable; it is the dominant way of understanding global justice, but not the only way. Where there is a space for 'occupying' global justice, there is a space for resistance; moments of solidarity with the exploited and downtrodden; movements of emancipation. For the analysis of 'occupying' global justice, I take inspiration from the eponymous post-financial crisis movements that drew attention to the gap between the 1 per cent and the 99 per cent.[55] In particular, 'occupied' global justice is about resurfacing the undermined anti-imperial origins of global justice movements.[56] Ideas for *unplugged* global justice, *de-spectacularised* global justice,

---

[54] Achille Mbembe, 'The Age of Humanism is Ending', *The Mail & Guardian*, 22 December 2016.

[55] For example, Noam Chomsky, *Occupy* (Penguin 2012).

[56] Adom Getachew, *Worldmaking after Empire: The Rise and Fall of Self-Determination* (Princeton University Press 2019) 175.

unmasked global justice and *resistance* global justice are put forward. These tactics for anti-marketised global justice all have certain historical precendents, and all encounter limitations. But, in Donna Haraway's words: 'We need the power of modern critical theories of how meaning and bodies get made, not in order to deny meanings and bodies, but in order to build meanings and bodies that have a chance for life.'[57]

1.9   A Structure by Way of Key Points

The six key organising terms of marketised global justice I identify in this book are (a) ICL, (b) neoliberalism, (c) the attention economy, (d) spectacle, (e) branding, and (f) neo-colonialism. They are introduced and analysed in the coming chapters in the following way:

- Marketing is not only practised in the for-profit corporate sector but also in a sector, both for-profit and non-profit, referred to here as the 'global justice sector'. ICL's principles and institutions constitute the dominant framing of global justice. This success can in part be attributed to the employment of market-friendly spectacularising of a binary of 'good' and 'evil'. Spectacle, often constituted through stereotypes, has a distributive function in that it tends to prop up the status quo.
- The rise of the new anti-impunity movement coincided with new branding practices in the 1990s. In the wake of global trade liberalisation following the end of the Cold War, both marketing and the global justice sector moved away from *things and products* to *image*. It was a shift towards symbolism. Large corporations switched their focus from commodities to the brand as experience and lifestyle. For global justice, the shift towards image meant the abandonment of human rights defence activism in favour of symbolic criminal prosecutions.
- Neoliberalism's success as legal-institutional order depends on a value shift in favour of market values. As spectacle is foregrounded, a visual market economy gives primacy to exchange value over use-value, a distinction made by Karl Marx in his exposition of value theory.[58] I illustrate the primacy of exchange value (and therefore also market values) through following the circulation of a particular photograph. I argue that the ICC and its supporters circulated the chosen image

---

[57] Donna Haraway, 'Situated Knowledges: The Science Question in Feminism and the Privilege of Partial Perspective' (1988) 14(3) *Feminist Studies* 575–599, at 580.
[58] Karl Marx, *Das Kapital* [1867] (Regnery Publishing 2009).

of Thomas Lubanga Dyilo as a form of publicity. The circulation of the image served the purpose not of information (the photograph's use-value), but of recruitment (the photograph's exchange value).

- The critique of marketised global justice requires a clear understanding of who benefits and who loses. Victims of conflict are most likely to be invoked rhetorically and visually to justify global justice projects. Whether they benefit or lose is therefore particularly important. Highlighting the feminised, infantilised, and racialised stereotype of victimhood is a means to demonstrate their invocation as marketable brands. The critique warns of the dangers of exploitation and alienation prompted by the construction of this 'ideal' victim.

- Different emphases of marketised global justice are illustrated through case studies. The aim of the NGO Invisible Children to make Joseph Kony *famous* exposes links between marketised global justice and military interventionism, racial capitalism, and the elevating of private property (Chapter 6); a closer look at the ICC's practices, and in particular the inclusion of Rome Statute provisions in a treaty between the European Union and its former colonial states, exposes the technicalities employed in the integration of a global criminal law system with a global trade system (Chapter 7); and finally, the use of global justice for place branding purposes, exposes profound de-politicising and de-historicising features of global justice when used as a resource for capital growth by cities and nations. The use of global justice and global injustice for the purposes of place branding is illustrated through three 'mini' case studies of the city of The Hague, and the nation states of South Africa and Cambodia (Chapter 8). The case studies also forcefully reveal both backlashes and resistance to marketised global justice.

- A marketing critique draws attention to the urgency of devising tactics of resistance against marketised global justice. Four tactics are suggested that aim to dislodge global justice from the six key themes mentioned. These tactics, which can be employed by different groups and movements at different times, are: unplugged global justice, despectacularised global justice, unmasked global justice, and resistance global justice. The tactics are presented as means to suggest an 'occupying' of global justice.

1.10   Global Justice Discontents and Alternatives

This book aims to respond to two main areas of growing dissatisfaction: a dissatisfaction with the project of neoliberalism and a fracturing of the international criminal justice project. The advantages of neoliberalism have proved to be grossly unequal, with an undisputed growth of income and social inequality. More than ten years since the financial crisis of 2008 we look back on a period of austerity politics, which shifted the burden of the crash onto normal people rather than the institutions and individuals responsible. Although the financial crisis and more recently the coronavirus pandemic revealed the weaknesses of the dominant system, we are experiencing the 'strange non-death of neoliberalism'.[59] The concerns about neoliberalism, only recently described as 'The Left's Eternal Boogeyman',[60] are now discussed in party politics, in public debate, and in scholarly discussions.[61] Grassroots movements, too, have problematised open markets, free trade agreements and financialisation, relating these to inequalities of wealth, health, education, leisure, and a clean and diverse environment. The internationalism of the Black Lives Matter movement, which is questioning structural racial inequalities, or the Extinction Rebellion, which is creating awareness around a global climate emergency, are examples of movements fighting against market values and for social values.

Like the project of neoliberalism, the international criminal justice project is also under pressure. A common charge against the ICC has concerned its anti-African bias. Looking back on over twenty years of the court's operation, we find that all four of the defendants convicted are Africans;[62] all situations that have reached trial stage are in Africa;[63] and

---

[59] Colin Crouch, *The Strange Non-Death of Neoliberalism* (2011 Polity).

[60] Corey Iacono, 'Neoliberalism: The Left's Eternal Boogeyman', *Foundation for Economic Education* (13 May 2016).

[61] These include Slobodian, 'Globalists'; Wolfang Streek, 'The Return of the Repressed' (2017) 104 *New Left Review* 5–18; Brown, 'Undoing the Demos'; David Harvey, *A Brief History of Neoliberalism* (Oxford University Press 2007). On international law and neoliberalism, see for example, Honor Brabazon (ed.), *Neoliberal Legality: Understanding the Role of Law in the Neoliberal Project* (Routledge 2016); Andrew Lang, *World Trade after Neoliberalism: Reimagining the Global Economic Order* (Oxford University Press 2011).

[62] *The Prosecutor v. Ahmad Al Faqi Al Mahdi* (Judgment and Sentence) ICC-01/12-01/15 (Trial Chamber VIII, 27 September 2016); *The Prosecutor v. Jean-Pierre Bemba Gombo, Aimé Kilolo Musamba, Jean-Jacques Mangenda Kabongo, Fidèle Babala Wandu and Narcisse Arido.* (Judgment) ICC-01/05-01/13-1989-Red (Trial Chamber VII, 19 October 2016); *The Prosecutor v. Germain Katanga* (Judgment) ICC-01/04-01/07-3436-tENG (Trial Chamber II, 7 March 2014); *The Prosecutor v. Thomas Lubanga Dyilo* (Judgment) ICC-01/04-01/06-2842 (14 March 2012).

[63] Central African Republic, Côte d'Ivoire, Darfur, Democratic Republic of the Congo, Kenya, Libya, Mali, and Uganda.

all defendants currently before the ICC are African.[64] After several years of discussions in the African Union and warnings about a mass withdrawal, South Africa, Burundi, and The Gambia announced their withdrawal from the ICC in late 2016. Although each state had its own motivations for the rejection of the court's jurisdiction, the common ground between them was that they considered the ICC a neo-colonial institution.[65] The Gambian information minister even provocatively referred to the court as 'an International Caucasian Court for the persecution and humiliation of people of colour, especially Africans'.[66] Of the three states, only Burundi eventually withdrew, but the withdrawal announcements and subsequent debates nevertheless opened the floor to more sustained critiques of the anti-impunity movement and its coloniality.

Among the many features shared by the two projects of neoliberalism and ICL is the seeming unavailability of alternatives. Alternatives tend to be thought of as binaries: either neoliberalism or communism; either individual criminal accountability or genocide; either marketing or obscurity. This book rejects such binary thinking as itself symptomatic of the de-historicisation and de-politicisation of marketisation – and instead suggests new ways of understanding the shortcomings of contemporary global justice in order to move towards an anti-marketised global justice based on internationalism and solidarity.

[64] The only situation outside of Africa at the time of writing is the investigations in the situation in Georgia, which is before the Pre-Trial Chamber.

[65] The call for anti-imperialism was repeated at the African Union summit in Addis Ababa in January 2017, at which a 'mass withdrawal strategy' was discussed. Here, the chairperson of the African Union Commission paid tribute to the recently deceased Fidel Castro, who 'played a critical role in the global struggle against colonialism and imperialism'. 'The 28th ordinary session of the assembly of the African Union', African Union (30 January 2017) link available at: https://au.int/web/en/newsevents/20170130/28th-ordinary-session-assembly-african-union

[66] 'Gambia withdraws from International Criminal Court', Al Jazeera (26 October 2016).

Ad-Vocacy

What Is Marketing in Global Justice?

> From our beginnings as a single store nearly forty years ago, in every place that we've been, and every place that we touch, we've tried to make it a little better than we found it.[1]

> The willingness to submit to impartial, unbiased scrutiny, is [...] the trademark of law-abiding persons and institutions ....[2]

2.1 Introduction

'Judges, Slobodan Praljak is not a war criminal. With disdain, I reject this verdict', states the former Bosnian Croat general in court when his twenty-year sentence for war crimes is upheld. He subequently drinks from a small bottle. He speaks again, the voice is slightly muffled. 'I have taken poison', the court translator's voice states clearly.

In November 2017, Slobodan Praljak committed suicide in full view of the courtroom cameras. The judges had just delivered their final decision at the International Criminal Tribunal for the former Yugoslavia (ICTY) on the case of Praljak and others accused.[3] Praljak chose the courtroom as the setting for this dramatic act. He also chose the murder mystery classic cyanide as the toxin. Praljak knew that he would grab the attention of an international audience, not only in the courtroom but also in the media covering the case. The former general, who was a producer of theatre, film, and television before his military career, knew what people would pay attention to on an otherwise fairly mundane courtroom day. Media outlets from across the world reported on the events in The Hague, seemingly delighting in the spectacle. The English tabloid newspaper

---

[1] Starbuck website, www.starbucks.co.uk/about-us.

[2] 'Introductory Statement by Justice Louise Arbour, prosecutor ICTY and ICTR at the Launch of the ICC Coalition's Global Ratification Campaign' (Press Release) JL/PIU/401-0E (13 May 1999), available at: www.icty.org/en/press/introductory-statement-just ice-louise-arbour-prosecutor-icty-and-ictr-launch-icc-coalitions.

[3] *Prosecutor v Jadranko Prlić et al. (Judgment)* ICTY-IT-04-74-A (29 November 2017).

Express published eleven 'shock stills as Bosnian war commander dies after drinking poison in courtroom'.[4] It is a moment by moment visual record of the suicide. The headline of the preceding article includes shouty capitalisations: 'Bosnian war commander DIES after drinking POISON in UN courtroom.'[5] International criminal law commentators, meanwhile, were frustrated at the diversion of attention away from the technicalities of the appeals judgment of the *Prlic et al.* ruling.[6] Apart from the technicalities of the case, there were extensive discussions on how Praljak could have smuggled the vial into the courtroom and, more generally, courtroom security was discussed for months following the event.[7] In Croatia, Praljak was celebrated as a martyr.[8] The concern by international criminal lawyers about the attention of the media being diverted is ironic, for it is international criminal lawyers who deal frequently in the currency of spectacle. Spectacle is used to attract attention in a competitive sector in which different actors vie for loyalty for their brand of global justice. It is used as a marketing tool. Praljak's suicide is an episode in which the perpetrator employed this marketing tool for his own ends.

This chapter sets the scene for an understanding of marketised global justice. We are accustomed to corporations such as Coca-Cola, Nike, and Starbucks employing marketing to sell their products, less so legal actors. When analysing the marketing practices of, say, Starbucks, one would ask the following questions: Who are the actual and potential customers? Who has purchasing power? How can the market and consumer base be expanded? What 'sells'? This book invites these questions of global justice

---

[4] Simon Osborne, 'Bosnia war commander DIES after drinking POISON in United Nations courtroom', *Express*, 29 November 2017.

[5] Ibid.

[6] Marko Milanovic, 'An Eventful Day in The Hague: Channelling Socrates and Goering', EJIL: *Talk!*, 30 November 2017.

[7] Marlise Simons and Alan Cowell, 'A War Criminal Drank Poison in Court, and Died. How Could This Happen?', *The New York Times*, 1 December 2017; 'Mechanism Releases to the Public the Report of the Independent Expert Review into Slobodan Praljak's Death', United Nations Residual Mechanism for Criminal Tribunals, 9 March 2018, available at: www.irmct.org/en/news/mechanism-releases-public-report-independent-expert-review-slobodan-praljak%E2%80%99s-death; An independent review was also undertaken: 'Dutch Authorities Conclude Criminal Investigation into Slobodan Praljak's Death', United Nations Residual Mechanism for Criminal Tribunals (Press Release) 2 November 2018, available at: www.irmct.org/en/news/dutch-authorities-conclude-criminal-investigation-slobodan-praljak%E2%80%99s-death

[8] 'War criminal in the Hague but still a war hero in Croatia', Euronews, 1 December 2017, available at: www.euronews.com/2017/12/01/war-criminal-in-the-hague-but-still-a-war-hero-in-croatia

actors, not in order to perpetuate or generate a corporate viewpoint within the global justice sector, but as a form of critique. To pose these questions in the global justice sector aims to elucidate the employment of commercial practices for issues that are often deemed to fulfil a higher moral purpose, and therefore fall outside of the scope of financial returns.

These questions are, moreover, an entry point into a more general reflection on marketisation of justice in the neoliberal order. The following, therefore, aims to sensitise the reader to the fact that it is not simply *fashionable* to employ market(ing) terminology, for example, to casually deem accusations of committing war crimes as 'bad publicity'.[9] Rather, the use of marketing practices and terminology tells us something important about the way in which global justice is understood. The marketing viewpoint provides an insight into what the defendant Praljak grasped about the international criminal law courtroom: global justice is performed on a global stage, a space to sell and perform spectacle, which breaks from the more mundane forms of judicial performance.[10]

Apart from introducing the extension of marketing beyond the commercial space, this chapter seeks to illustrate the market-friendly nature of international criminal justice. The legally universalised notions of 'good' versus 'evil', individualised guilt, and the visceral construction of mass atrocity crimes are particularly suitable for a market-friendly sensationalised aesthetics. Beyond that, I begin to highlight the distributive features of marketised global justice. Delving beyond the use of marketing practices in the global justice sector reveals not only a penchant for corporate thinking, but a deep-seated constitution and affirmation of neoliberalism in its legal-institutional form. The textual and visual competition for the meaning of global justice is, therefore, not an open competition at which all interpretations may claim equal validity. In its international legal guise, which builds on an anti-impunity movement, global justice has been framed to correspond with the power alliances of the dominant international institutions. As spectacle and neoliberalism begin to claim a central position in our understanding of dominant global justice projects, important historical connections between imperialism, international law, and aesthetics emerge.

---

[9] David Luban, 'Carl Schmitt and the Critique of Lawfare' (2010) 43 *Case Western Reserve Journal of International Law*, 457–471, at 457.

[10] Note in this context that the judgment which confirmed Praljak's guilt was no less than 1,400 pages long *Prosecutor v Jadranko Prlić* (Judgment) ICTY-IT-04-74-A (29 November 2017).

We can only understand marketised global justice by accounting for the specific marketing practices employed. I begin, therefore, with an overview of five promotional practices of marketing: branding, advertising, public relations, public diplomacy/place branding, and propaganda. This is followed by an overview of the political, economic, social, and cultural context in which global justice has become marketised: the attention economy, neoliberalism, and legalised morality. The background information on marketing practices specifically and the market more generally culminate in a first overview of the features of the global justice sector.

2.2 What Is Marketing?

Marketing is the practice of promoting and selling products as well as the exploitation of new business opportunities. Marketing has long been a feature of private enterprise. It took on its contemporary meaning with the nineteenth-century industrial revolution, first in Great Britain, then in the USA, and other countries of the Global North. New technologies of production and transportation allowed for the manufacture of mass produced goods that could be widely distributed. With a growing media industry, and new printing and distribution technologies, manufacturers had a new medium at their disposal to advertise their goods but were equally faced with new challenges. One of the new challenges of mass production was to distinguish one product from the other – competitors in the market needed to attract consumers to *their* product. Prior to the industrial revolution, most goods were made locally with the consumer knowing the relevant worker, farmer, or artisan. The greater distances between production and consumer meant that a relationship of trust had to be created to sway purchasing decisions. In the decades that followed, persuasion to sell a good or service became established as a key business practice.[11] Competition is at the heart of marketing as profits can only be achieved if the relevant product or service attracts more attention than similar products or services.

Conventionally, contemporary marketers refer to 'the four Ps': product, price, place, and promotional strategy. Marketers identify the

---

[11] On the different historical narratives of marketing, see for example Michael Enright, 'Marketing and Conflicting Dates for its Emergence: Hotchkiss, Bartels, the "Fifties School" and Alternative Accounts' (2002) 10(5–6) Journal of Marketing Management 445–461.

product, pick a price, choose a place to sell, and finally decide on how to sell the product. The five marketing practices described here – focusing on the last of 'the four Ps' – are identified as sharing important features. Such overlaps are pertinent for an analysis of global justice in the neoliberal order as they reveal common underlying assumptions about how best to persuade individuals to make purchasing and lifestyle decisions. The 'best marketing', therefore, has pertinence for anyone who believes that they have something to sell, whether that is global justice or coffee.

2.2.1 Branding

A 2017 *New York Times* article criticises Serbia for embracing those convicted as war criminals after the Yugoslav Wars by describing this practice as 'Serbia's Brand of Reconciliation'.[12] What does it mean to describe a nation state as having a brand, let alone a brand of reconciliation? Branding is the practice of building loyalty for one product, service, or organisation among similar competing products, services, or organisations.[13] A widely used definition of a successful brand is that of 'a name, symbol, design or some combination, which identifies the "product" of a particular organisation as having a sustainable differential advantage.'[14] Branding is a means of creating the impression that there is something about the brand that sets it apart from its competitors.[15] The emphasis on imagery and emotion serves the purpose of creating so-called 'brand awareness': the image and association in the mind of (target) consumers. And, yes, even nation states can have brands. More

---

[12] Matthew Brunwasser, 'Serbia's Brand of Reconciliation: Embracing Old War Criminals', *The New York Times*, 23 November 2017.

[13] Michael Johnson sets out seven groupings of possible definitions for branding: (1) defined by visual identity, symbol or trademark, (2) defined by the tangible and intangible, (3) defined by customer perceptions, (4) defined as a holistic system, (5) defined by a promise or contract, (6) defined by vision, values and actions, and (7) defined by a sense of social grouping. Michael Johnson, *Branding in Five and a Half Steps* (Thames & Hudson 2016) 16–17.

[14] Peter Doyle, 'Branding' in Michael J. Baker, *The Marketing Book* (Butterworth-Heinemann 1989) 78.

[15] Branding and marketing are often employed synonymously. However, a difference is worth noting: marketing regards the selling of the product and branding concerns the identity of the product. The two are, on a more practical level, interdependent. Branding a product will be with a view to marketing it; marketing without branding is almost impossible.

specifically, a nation's brand can relate to where they are positioned on a global justice/injustice scale.[16]

Branding is moreover the practice of creating trusted icons attached to the promise of a 'better life'. The product or service will not only serve the purpose of, for example, getting you from A to B, quenching your thirst or providing comfortable clothing for exercise; it will also add to a better life more generally. Parallels have, therefore, been drawn between branding and organised faiths. Theodore MacManus, credited with building brands such as Cadillac, Chrysler, and General Electric, is quoted as not simply wishing to persuade customers but rather *converting* them.[17] The brand message is communicated through all manner of outlets, from the product or service's website, to the logo, to annual reports, to social media hashtags. Instant recognisability and associations are the desired reaction. Employees, volunteers, and consumers are all encouraged to promote the brand message within and outside of the organisation. The building of a culture around that promise for employees is also referred to as internal branding. The blurring of lines between employee and consumer channels the idea of 'living the brand'. Branding is not about a product or service; it is about the life lived with and through the product or service. Starbucks, for example, has as its mission not only to sell coffee, but something more: a sense of community. The Starbucks website even states ambitiously its aim of making the world a better place: 'we've tried to make it a little better than we found it'. An enduring example of lifestyle branding is the sports brand Nike, which switched focus from clothing and shoe production to producing big ideas – *transcending* the product in the 1990s. Scott Bedbury, who was head of marketing at Nike and later became Starbucks' Vice President of Marketing, explained that Nike is 'leveraging the deep emotional connection that people have with sports and fitness'.[18] The brand became an experience.

A critical analysis of branding that stands out as particularly penetrating is Naomi Klein's book *No Logo*.[19] In the book, Klein traced the unfolding preference of image over product that became dominant in

---

[16] Discussed in depth in Chapter 8.
[17] Tim Wu, *Attention Merchants: The Epic Scramble to Get Inside Our Heads* (Vintage Books 2016) 58.
[18] Naomi Klein, *No Logo* (10th anniversary edition, Fourth Estate, 2010) 21, quoting Scott Bedbury interviewed by Alan M. Webber, 'What Great Brands Do', *Fast Company*, 31 August 1997.
[19] Klein, 'No Logo'.

the 1990s, and took place alongside the closure of factories in their original place of production and the outsourcing of production to complicated supply chains. Clothes production was outsourced to cheap labour countries (causing or exacerbating the proliferation of and exploitation in sweatshops) and workers' pay and safety were substituted with high investments in a few brand managers.[20] What was left was a 'hollow corporation'.[21]

In the 10th anniversary edition of *No Logo*, Klein reflects on two shifts that had emerged in the decade since publication, shifts that play a key role in the development of marketised global justice: first, the move from branding in predominantly the corporate sphere to branding in the public sphere[22] and second, the branding trend of corporations going 'no logo', attempting to escape their own brand.[23] Branding in the public sphere, the first shift, is illustrated at the very top of public life – the government. Klein claims that the Bush administration of the 2000s 'hollowed out' government similarly to how corporations were hollowed out,[24] handing over essential governing functions to the private sector.[25] The prime position of branding was sealed with the election of Barack Obama as president, the first US president to himself be a 'superbrand'.[26] Klein quotes Desiree Rogers, the White House's social secretary as stating to *The Wall Street Journal*: 'We have the best brand on earth: The Obama brand, our possibilities are endless'.[27] The mass produced and repro-duced pop-art-inspired posters from the 2008 presidential campaign, including the single word 'hope', 'change' or 'progress', are particularly memorable.[28]

---

[20] Ibid.

[21] Ibid xvii.

[22] Ibid xix.

[23] Ibid xv.

[24] The Bush administration continued what the Clinton administration had begun with the defeat of universal health care and the rollback of remaining welfare state provisions, the idea of the government as market actor, and the expansion of freedoms of financial services. See Jodi Dean, *Democracy and Other Neoliberal Fantasies: Communicative Capitalism and Left Politics* (2009 Duke University Press) 3.

[25] Klein, 'No Logo' xix.

[26] Ibid xix.

[27] Ibid xxv.

[28] There are further variations of the poster. The artist Shepard Fairey had them printed independently of the campaign initially. The posters were finally approved, and commis-sioned by the Obama campaign.

Figure 2.1   Obama campaign poster, Shepard Fairey

The corporate sphere, meanwhile, was battling with brand fatigue. As brands became omni-present, consumers started pushing back. They no longer wanted logos everywhere – on their clothing, at their workplace, in their homes, at their favourite coffee shops. Some brands simplified their logos, and new brands minimalised their logos. One example of the minimal brand is the online marketplace Etsy, which launched in 2005 and has such a simple logo (white letters against an orange back-ground) that it does not qualify for copyright protection.[29] In 2009, Starbucks opened its first unbranded, or de-branded, coffee shop in Seattle without the logo or colour scheme. Instead, it had original furni-ture, customers could bring in their own music to be played on the stereo system, and social causes could be amplified. 'After spending two decades blasting its logo onto 16,000 stores worldwide, Starbucks was now trying

---

[29] Alex Bigman, 'Three cool companies join the "No Logo" movement', 99 Designs (2013), at https://99designs.co.uk/blog/trends/beyond-branding-3-awesome-companies-with no logos/.

to escape its own brand.'[30] These no logo Starbucks stores became known as 'Stealth Starbucks'.

By the 20th anniversary of *No Logo*, both of these shifts seem rather unremarkable, indicating the normalisation of branding beyond the corporate sphere, as well as the normalisation of backlashes *within* and not outside of neoliberalism. For as the trend to be 'authentic' has boomed, say in the 'woke' hipster trend of the 2010s, or – more to the point – the activist trend, many counter-cultural trends have become folded into the market rather than existing outside of them.

'They used to say sex sells; now, evidently, it's activism.'[31] This comment – made in response to the call to delete the Uber app and instead to download its competitor Lyft – and the consequent spike in downloads of Lyft, tells us something important about marketing in the twenty-first century. Uber, a transportation network company, had undermined a New York taxi strike at JFK airport in the wake of newly elected President Trump's executive order to ban refugees from entering the US. #Deleteuber started trending on Twitter. Mega-companies such as Starbucks and Airbnb pledged to hire refugees and provide accommodation. All of this was communicated via tweets and highly publicised open letters. These companies could 'see that allocating their marketing budget to good causes has a better reach than spending that money elsewhere right now.'[32] Feel-good can be bought.[33]

Nike, always ahead of the game in mega corporate branding strategies, has famously used the social ideal of racial justice in one of its recent campaigns. In 2018, Nike invited the Black American football quarterback Colin Kaepernick to head up its new campaign. Kaepernick had caused a stir through taking a knee during the American national anthem in protest against social injustice and the institutional racism apparent through police treatment of black people. Nike recruited Kaepernick for the campaign, which was simultaneously the 30th anniversary of its 'Just Do It' tagline. The slogan for the campaign: 'Believe in something, even if it means sacrificing everything.' The campaign

---

[30] Klein, 'No Logo' xv.
[31] Alex Holder, 'Sex doesn't sell any more, activism does. And don't the big brands know it', *The Guardian*, 3 February 2017.
[32] Ibid.
[33] See critically on this: Lisa Ann Richey and Stefano Ponte, *Brand Aid: Shopping Well to Save the World* (University of Minnesota Press 2011)

turned out to be a major marketing success for Nike. Racial justice was monetisable in the same way as a new line of trainers.[34] Nike founder Phil Knight told the business magazine *Fast Company*: 'You can't try and go down the middle of the road. You have to take a stand on something, which is ultimately I think why the Kaepernick ad worked.'[35] The campaign – using the facilities of marketing to distract – also conveniently turned the gaze away from different forms of injustice that Nike was implicated in. In the same summer in which the Kaepernick campaign was conceptualised, civil society organisations were again drawing attention to Nike's failure to implement living wages in its Asian factories, the repression of unionisation of workers, and the troubling working conditions for those at the production end of the business.[36] All of this is important for the construction of global justice. Because Nike was not only shaping its campaigns about global justice, it was also dialectically shaping the political sphere in which racial justice would normally be tackled. While siding with racial justice for their marketing campaign, Nike was simultaneously contributing to value extraction of the Global South.

Tellingly, Philip Kotler, the so-called 'father of modern marketing', has in recent years turned to the study and promotion of what he calls 'brand activism'.[37] According to Kotler, market-driven cause marketing was superseded by corporate-driven corporate social responsibility, which is being superseded by societal-driven brand activism.[38] Whereas in the past, brands chose the issues that they engaged in, Kotler believes that now it is 'stakeholders', that is, employees, customers, society.

---

[34] Nike, Inc.'s fiscal reports for the second quarter of the 2019 financial year (December 2018) showed increased revenues by 10 per cent to US$9.4 billion. See Nike News at: https://news.nike.com/news/nike-inc-reports-fiscal-2019-second-quarter-results.

[35] Bill Snyder, 'Nike co-founder: Why I approved the controversial Colin Kaepernick ad', *Fast Company*, 6 March 2019, available at: www.fastcompany.com/90314699/nike-cofoun der-why-i-approved-the-controversial-colin-kaepernick-ad

[36] 'Adidas and Nike pay record-breaking amounts to footballers, but deny decent wages to women stitching their shirts', Clean Clothes Company news, 11 June 2018, available at: https://cleanclothes.org/news/2018/06/11/adidas-and-nike-pay-record-breaking-amounts-to-footballers-but-deny-decent-wages-to-women-stitching-their-shirts

[37] Christian Sarkar and Philip Kotler, *Brand Activism: From Purpose to Action* (IDEA BITE PRESS 2018).

[38] '"The Case for Brand Activism" – A Discussion with Philip Kotler and Christian Sarkar', *Marketing Journal*, 15 November 2018, available at: www.marketingjournal.org/the case for-brand-activism-a-discussion-with-philip-kotler-and-christian-sarkar/

2.2.2   Advertising

A media advisory statement from the Special Tribunal for Lebanon (STL) stated in October 2013: 'STL requests that the Lebanese authorities take further steps to advertise new accused'.[39] The text on the tribunal website then goes on to explain that posters of one of the accused, Hassan Habib Mehri, had been delivered to the Lebanese authorities 'for the purpose of public advertisement'.[40] The website of the tribunal notes: 'A high resolution of the poster can be found on the STL Flickr account.' Staying with the poster theme, the International Criminal Court launched a social media campaign in 2014 around the hashtag '#Justice Matters #17July', where it called on participants to share the 'campaign poster' on the occasion of 17 July, International Criminal Justice Day.[41] 'Take your photograph holding this sign', the poster urges potential participants.

Advertising is a practice typically used by businesses to attract the attention of potential consumers to their product or service, traditionally through newspaper advertisements and billboards. Advertising employs many of the same tools as branding, including its attention-grabbing tactics. A common distinction between advertising and branding is that the former is short-term, a sales tactic for a new line of products, for example; branding, in contrast, concerns a more long-term view to loyalty.[42] Advertising and branding nevertheless intersect in that advertising is ideally intended to work towards refreshing positive associations with the brand.[43] Advertising often uses means to direct attention in a space where a consumer would not typically have sought out the information on a product or service; it must *distract* a potential consumer from what they were doing. It has, therefore, been described as aiming to

---

[39] 'STL requests that the Lebanese authorities take further steps to advertise new accused', Special Tribunal for Lebanon (Press Release) (11 October 2013), available at: www.stl-tsl .org/en/media/press-releases/2549-media-advisory-stl-requests-that-the-lebanese-author ities-take-further-steps-to-advertise-new-accused.

[40] Ibid.

[41] 'Justice Matters social media campaign launched to commemorate 17 July: International Criminal Justice Day' (Press release), ICC-CPI-20140619-PR1018 (19 June 2014).

[42] At the same time, advertising campaigns are also intended to have long-term benefits. See Les Binet and Peter Field, *The Long and Short of it: Balancing Short and Long-Term Marketing Strategies* (Institute of Practitioners in Advertising 2013).

[43] Byron Sharp, *How Brands Grow: What Marketers Don't Know* (Oxford University Press 2010) xiv.

appeal to the audience's 'baser instincts'.[44] Attention is typically gained through bright colours and through storytelling.

It is no secret that digital technologies have significantly changed the landscape of advertising. Digital information, collected on the web and through applications, is purchased by advertisers. Platforms that collect personal data (such as Google and Facebook) fiercely compete over the quantity and quality of data to sell to businesses that use this data to advertise.[45] Advertising is therefore increasingly personalised, tailored to the digital footprint of an individual's needs and desires. The new frontier is to capture 'commercial intent' right at the moment of its formation. Based on algorithms and potential commerce-driven experiences, a pop-up button appears on your smart device presenting a purchasing opportunity just at the right time.[46]

Advertisers realised the profitability of social justice far earlier than social justice actors discovered advertising. Indeed, advertisers understood the appeal of social justice as early as the suffragette movement. Recognising that women were making purchasing decisions and at the same time recognising a growing women's movement, Old Dutch Cleanser claimed in advertisements of the early twentieth century that its floor cleaner was 'A Champion of Woman's Rights', 'the right to freedom from household drudgery', and 'the right to spotless floors and walls, shining pots and pans'. The suffragettes must have been delighted. Tim Wu, author of *The Attention Merchants*, pithily describes the advertising campaign as 'a commercial cause in social-activist clothing'.[47]

Social justice lifestyle advertising has been particularly *en vogue* since the late 2010s, encapsulating debates on gender, environmental, and racial justice. Recent examples of social justice advertising – alongside the already named Nike campaign – include women's hygiene brand *Always*, which tackles gender stereotyping in its 'Like a Girl' campaign, and beauty brand *Dove*, which tackles body image stereotypes with its 'Real Beauty' campaign. Consumers are eager for social justice content.[48]

---

[44] Wu, 'Attention Merchants' 13.

[45] Bernard E. Harcourt, *Exposed: Desire and Disobedience in the Digital Age* (Harvard University Press 2015).

[46] On capturing 'commercial intent', see, critically, Shoshana Zuboff, *The Age of Surveillance Capitalism: The Fight for a Human Future at the New Frontier of Power* (Profile Books 2019) 259f.

[47] Wu, 'Attention Merchants' 67.

[48] On 'sadvertising' see Oliver Balch, 'The Rise of "Sadvertising": Why Social Good Marketing Works', *The Guardian*, 18 July 2014.

Let us switch register briefly from the marketing perspective to the market, allowing a first glimpse at a structural perspective. Advertising is interesting from a structural viewpoint as it is a means to stimulate economies. Advertising is not only employed to create demand for new products and services (stuff we might need); it is also employed when there is under-consumption, when capital is in danger of slowing or even stopping (for stuff we don't need). Modern capitalist societies generally experience over-production. It is one of the key contradictions of capitalism that there is a rush to achieve greater production but then once it is achieved, there is simply insufficient demand.[49] In order to avoid the collapse of the system, which depends on capital circulating, advertising helps stimulate consumption. Advertising actively creates a lack that can be filled with the consumer product. But it never fully fulfils on the promise, so that consumers continue to buy. This constant renewal relies on the distractedness of the consumer from a final goal (which might be achieved), focusing instead on the process (which is always underway). This structural perspective becomes key for global justice actors and the impossibility of achieving global justice; there are always more campaigns, more projects, more rights to support, but never any closure. This opens a possibility of reflection on how injustice is key for global justice accumulation, just as new markets are key for capital accumulation.

2.2.3   Public Relations and Publicity

In August 2015, when the 'Kosovo Specialist Chambers' (KSC) were established as a hybrid court to investigate crimes committed by the Kosovo Liberation Army, the effort was widely described as a 'public relations campaign'.[50] Given the public opposition from within Kosovo on the one hand and the pressure by the UN and the European Union (EU) on the other hand, the Court was considered as a means to improve Kosovo's bid to accede to the EU and gain wider international recognition.[51] Significantly, the KSC, located in The Hague but a part

---

[49] David Harvey, *Seventeen Contradictions and the End of Capitalism* (Profile Books 2014) 81.

[50] Aidan Hehir, 'Step towards Justice or Potential Timebomb?', *Report: Kosovo Specialist Chambers* (Balkan Investigative Reporting Network 2018).

[51] Anita McKinna, 'Haradinaj's Resignation 2.0: The Continued Politicisation of Transitional Justice in Kosovo', *Balkanist Magazine*, 31 July 2019.

of Kosovo's judiciary, is funded by the EU and staffed exclusively with non-Kosovo citizens.[52] Public relations (PR) is the practice of managing reputations through building relationships and maintaining a positive image (also, ultimately, for the purposes of brand loyalty). Organisations employ PR managers in order to manage relationships between the organisation and its stakeholders, namely employees, media, government officials, and investors. Again, there is some overlap between branding and PR. On a practical level, the PR machinery will act as a medium that communicates the brand identity to stakeholders. But while branding is about creating an identity, PR is about the creation and maintenance of good relationships; this also often includes crisis management. In large businesses and organisations, PR is often a specifically dedicated in-house department. Publicity, a sub-field of PR, is concerned with media presence. Publicity in the corporate sphere is generally sought in order to gain media attention for a project or an aspect of the larger corporation.

2.2.4 Public Diplomacy and Place Branding

Public diplomacy is the communication by public organs to a foreign audience. It is a practice of foreign policy.[53] One would speak of public diplomacy when a public organ wishes to communicate an initiative or positive message – or to counter a negative message – to a foreign public. It is the 'public' equivalent of 'private' PR. The Encyclopaedia Britannica uses the following example to explain public diplomacy: during the Cold War, the United States employed means to persuade European audiences that the foundations of democratic government and capitalist enterprise were superior to Soviet alternatives. The US government's radio broadcasting network, the Voice of America, broadcast into Eastern European nations to dispel myths about the West.[54] In addition, the US State Department built reading rooms in Allied countries, housing books about American culture and history in order to reinforce broad support for US policies.[55] The Information Center Service (ICS) planned and

---

[52] Aidan Hehir, 'Lessons Learned? The Kosovo Specialist Chambers' Lack of Local Legitimacy and Its Implications' (2019) 20(3) *Human Rights Review* 267–287.
[53] Baeta Ociepka, 'Public Diplomacy as Political Communication: Lessons from Case Studies' (2018) 33(3) *European Journal of Communication* 290–303.
[54] 'Public Diplomacy' in *Encyclopaedia Britannica*, see: www.britannica.com/topic/public-diplomacy.
[55] Ibid.

supported programmes for the dissemination of information overseas. Information centres, libraries, distribution and publication of books, English teaching, and exhibitions were part of the programme.[56] Orwell's *Animal Farm* and *Nineteen-Eighty-Four* were widely translated, encouraged, and disseminated for their dystopian takes on communism.[57] More recently, the idea of 'New Public Diplomacy' has emerged, which places the accent on dialogue and engagement rather than 'selling messages'.[58]

Place branding has emerged as a sister discipline and practice to public diplomacy, whereby place branding concerns the marketability of the relevant place (nation state, region, or city) for tourism, trade, or investment. This form of branding highlights the marketable features of the place and hides the less marketable ones. Simon Anholt, a central figure of place branding, suggests that one can distinguish between public diplomacy and place branding in that the former is about ideology and the latter is about commercialisation.[59] However, the United States' efforts to publicise capitalism illustrate that the distinction between the two is perhaps not as clear-cut as Anholt makes it out to be.[60] Indeed, one way of distinguishing between public diplomacy and nation branding is that the former is the US-centric version of selling a nation and the latter the UK-centric version.[61] British marketing and branding agencies have established market dominance for nation branding contracts.[62] Practices that blur the lines between ideology and commercialisation are of particular interest to the study of the marketisation of global justice. Global justice place branding is particularly explicit in The Hague's city brand 'City of International Peace and Justice'.[63]

---

[56] 'Records of the United States Information Agency (RG 306)', USA National Archives, available at: www.archives.gov/research/foreign-policy/related-records/rg-306.

[57] Often, the dissemination of information was outsourced to private businesses.

[58] Jan Melissen (ed.), *The New Public Diplomacy: Soft Power in International Relations* (Palgrave Macmillan 2005).

[59] Simon Anholt, 'Public Diplomacy and Place Branding: Where's the Link? (2006) 2(4) *Place Branding* 271–275.

[60] Indeed, Ministries of Foreign Affairs regularly direct substantial resources to place branding campaigns. See for example: Bengt-Arne B. F. Hulleman, and Robert Govers, 'The Hague, International City of Peace and Justice: A Relational Network Brand' in Keith Dinnie (ed.), *City Branding: Theory and Cases* (Palgrave 2011) 150–156.

[61] György Szondi, 'Public Diplomacy and Nation Branding: Conceptual Similarities and Differences' (2008) *Discussion papers in Diplomacy, Netherlands Institute of International Relations 'Clingendael'* 1.

[62] Ibid.

[63] The Brand The Hague, at: www.brandthehague.nl. Discussed in more depth in Chapter 8.

2.2.5 Propaganda

In 2012, shortly before Fatou Bensouda was to step up from deputy prosecutor of the International Criminal Court (ICC) to chief prosecutor of the ICC, she addressed a George Soros foundation-sponsored forum in South Africa:

> With due respect, what offends me most when I hear criticisms about the so-called African bias is how quick we are to focus on the words and propaganda of a few powerful, influential individuals and to forget about the millions of anonymous people that suffer from these crimes ... because all the victims are African victims.[64]

Bensouda was responding to growing concerns about neo-colonialism, expressed at this time mostly by African leaders and commentators. Her choice of wording – *propaganda* – is noteworthy. The nexus between communication, persuasion, and ideology is particularly prominent in relation to propaganda. Propaganda is, as is well-known, a form of persuasion through mass communication. But of course, this definition applies to all of the above promotional marketing practices too. Today, propaganda is mostly associated with persuasion through the state, particularly for the purposes of garnering public support for war. In the public imagination, propaganda is firmly associated with (former) Soviet states. However, it was in fact the UK and the USA who were the first to use propaganda in the way it is understood today, at a time of increasing militarisation and commercialisation in the 1910s. As there had been no tradition of conscription in the UK, Lord Kitchener, Secretary of State for War, decided to mobilise enthusiasm for militarism through volunteering. The government appealed to recruits through all available media, institutionalised through a special Parliamentary Recruiting Committee. One of the most ubiquitous forms of drawing attention to the state's need for bodies was the image of Kitchener himself, determined look, impressive moustache, and finger pointing out at the viewer claiming variations of 'Your country needs YOU' or 'BRITONS [Lord Kitchener] WANTS YOU'.[65] The image has since been reproduced hundreds of times, memorably in the US context with Uncle Sam pointing a finger at potential recruits. More trivially, it has been reproduced to enlist all sorts of

---

[64] Quoted in: David Smith, 'New chief prosecutor defends international criminal court', The Guardian, 23 May 2012.

[65] On the history of persuasion for volunteering for the war effort, see Wu, 'Attention Merchants' 40.

activities, including school bake sales and Star Wars merchandise. In a state bureaucracy, propaganda is typically practised through a monopoly on the media and other channels of mass communication, often in combination with various means of censorship. While this remains the dominant interpretation, there have at the same time been consistent calls to consider the propagandistic functions of the corporate media in liberal-democratic states. Edward S. Herman and Noam Chomsky labelled the process of persuasion in the 'free world' as 'manufacturing consent'.[66] The line between state propaganda and corporate propaganda is becoming more opaque, despite the seeming diversification of news and contributors to news through social media. Indeed, the stronger corporate connection between social media and communication, say, with Facebook being one of the main news sources in the Western world, arguably aligns information even closer with business interests.

It was notably Sigmund Freud's nephew, Edward Bernays, who first considered propaganda in the context of consumer culture, as we must too for an understanding of marketised global justice. Writing in the 1920s, Bernays claimed that the manipulation of organised habits of the masses constitutes an 'invisible government'.[67] Both elected representatives of government as well as those entities who narrow purchasing choices of commodities (advertisers for example) practice propaganda. Foretelling the conceptualisation of the attention economy, Bernays observed a difference between the theory of everybody buying the best and cheapest commodities offered on the market, and the practice of choosing. 'In practice, if every one went around pricing, and chemically testing before purchasing, the dozens of soaps or fabrics or brands of bread which are for sale, economic life would become hopelessly jammed.'[68] For Bernays, propaganda is a necessary feature of democracy underpinned by a free market. He sees the attendant 'manipulation of the news, the inflation of personality, and the general ballyhoo by which politicians and commercial products and social ideas are brought to the consciousness of the masses' as a necessary evil.[69] Bernays's view on

---

[66] Borrowing from Walter Lippmann, who coined the term. Edward S. Herman and Noam Chomsky, *Manufacturing Consent: The Political Economy of the Mass Media* (Vintage Books 1994).
[67] Edward L. Bernays, *Propaganda* [1928] (IG Publishing 2004) 9.
[68] Ibid 11.
[69] Ibid 12.

propaganda, in short, links political communications of social ideas with consumerism. Both are, according to Bernays, governed by the same mechanisms of persuasion. Incidentally, it was Bernays, who was engaged for one of the first instances of nation branding, namely for Lithuania.[70] The Lithuanian National Council approached Bernays to generate support for Lithuania in the USA. He subsequently contacted the relevant US sports fans, fashion enthusiasts, music lovers, and more, to campaign for Lithuanian athletics, clothes and jewellery, and tunes.[71]

In a swift stocktaking exercise, we see that there are two common themes which span all the named marketing practices: persuasion and distraction. Persuasion to buy or consume is evident in lifestyle branding, where consumption introduces meaning and values; it is present in advertising in the form of creating unexpected needs and consumption opportunities; public relations and publicity cast the web of persuasion slightly narrower in their aims to persuade stakeholders to form positive relationships with the respective organisation; public diplomacy and place branding focus persuasion on citizens and investors; while propaganda takes advantage of a captive audience and streamlined means of communication. The persuasion practiced is on one level always about distraction in that it aims to focus the attention of the consumer on that particular brand, product, service, or communication. The element of distraction also runs deeper. This is perhaps most evident when we speak about propaganda - which is simply a pejorative form of speaking about mass communication and mass distraction. Here, we realise that attention to one message is the channelling of attention at the expense of broader structural issues which implicate the source of the communication.

2.3   Marketing Practices at the International Criminal Court

The employment of marketing practices in the global justice sector can be demonstrated through investigating the ICC's practices of persuasion and distraction. The employment of marketing practices illustrates that marketing is not merely metaphorical but is a practice to be taken seriously. We begin our investigation with branding at the ICC: The brand is conceptualised and promoted within the Assembly of State

---

[70] Labelled as such by Szondi, 'Public Diplomacy and Nation Branding' 3, 4.
[71] Edward L. Bernays, *Public Relations* [1945] (Kessinger Publishing 2002) 80.

Parties, the Presidency, the Office of the Prosecutor, and outreach programmes.[72] The brand of global justice (under which fall variations such as the international rule of law, fighting impunity, and Justice Matters) is associated with a promise for the future: a better world through fighting impunity.

The logo of the ICC sticks to the familiar symbols of global justice: the justice-themed set of scales, the peace-themed olive branch, and the blue colour favoured by international organisations. The *Visual Identity* document of the ICC, which offers guidance on the use of its images, sets out that the colour to be used for the logo is 'ICC Blue: Pantone 541'. Pantone is a US-based company that specialises in colour identities for brands. 'The Pantone Color Institute can guide you through the development of color strategy that fits your company's unique needs', states the website.[73] The colour blue was no doubt chosen to create an association with the slightly lighter and brighter UN Blue, which, incidentally, is Pantone PMS 279. The UN guidelines on the use of the UN emblems remark bluntly 'Blue represents peace in opposition to red, for war.'[74] The visual identity document of the ICC reads: 'An organisation and its logo – these two elements form an inseparable whole.'[75] The ICC logo, it states, is designed to be 'modern, dynamic, simple'. The importance of dissemination is also made clear: 'The logo serves as our signature and should therefore appear on nearly all applications of the Visual Identity.' The logo is registered as Intellectual Property (a trademark) with the World Intellectual Property Organization,[76] meaning that written permission is required for its use. I was unable to attain permission for use in this book. Unauthorised use could mean litigation, the prohibition of its use, and potentially a fine. In 2004, the ICC's Assembly of State Parties even adopted a resolution, named 'Strengthening the International Criminal Court and the Assembly of State Parties' in which the court and state parties are advised to take measures to prevent the use of the

---

[72] The ICC's practices of branding are discussed in greater depth in Chapter 7.

[73] Pantone Color Institute, at: www.pantone.com/color-consulting/about-pantone-color-institute.

[74] 'United Nations Guidelines on the use of the UN emblem', Publications Board Secretariat New York, June 2007. The association of socialism and communism with red – seen most prominently in China's flag (where red is a lucky colour) – is undoubtedly relevant in the UN's colour associations.

[75] 'ICC Visual Identity Website', ICC, 12.

[76] Ibid, 55, under the rubric 'Protection'.

logo for commercial purposes.[77] In the commercial sphere, logos are mostly trademarked so that competing companies can be distinguished. The use of another company's logo is not permitted as it would confuse or deceive consumers. Apart from the more general propertisation at play, it is noteworthy that the ICC is using the same means and channels as a corporation would to protect its brand.

As is common for an international organisation, the ICC has a spokesperson and public affairs unit to deal with public relations. This unit is also tasked with the traditional crisis management issues, such as withdrawal announcements from member states.[78] In 2007, an 'Integrated Strategy for External Relations, Public Information and Outreach' was devised and published.[79] 'Integrated' meant, according to the summary document, an approach shared by the Presidency, Office of the Prosecutor, and the Registry, in order to support a 'common strategy, with mutually reinforcing messages, activities and goals'.[80] The strategy included the creation of a permanent working group, defining short- and medium-term objectives and the establishment of 'performance indicators now reflected in the Court's budget'.[81] Performance indicators are commonly used in the corporate sphere to establish how effectively the company is achieving key business objectives.

Publicity, meanwhile, is not only reserved for spectacular campaigns but also for routine legal processes. For example, it is notable that the opening statements in the ICC case of *Prosecutor v Germain Katanga and Mathieu Ngudjolo Chui* begin with reference to a photo opportunity:

> PRESIDING JUDGE COTTE: (Interpretation) The Court is now in session. Please be seated. Photographer, if you would like to take some photographs of the participants at this hearing, you have a minute in which to do so.
> (Pause in proceedings)
> So the taking of these photographs does contribute to the publicity that there is in the public nature of this hearing. Thank you for that,

---

[77] ICC Assembly of States Parties Resolution, 'Strengthening the International Criminal Court and the Assembly of States Parties', ICC-ASP/3/Res.3 (10 September 2004). Section 2.

[78] 'ICC Statement on the Philippines' notice of withdrawal: State participation in Rome Statute system essential to international rule of law' (Press Release), ICC-CPI-20180320-PR1371 (20 March 2018).

[79] 'Integrated Strategy for External Relations, Public Information and Outreach', ICC Registry (18 April 2007).

[80] Ibid.

[81] Ibid 1.

particularly for the discretion with which you have carried out this taking
of photographs.[82]

Photographs of the courtroom are perceived as an important part of the
publicity of the Court, indicating the imagined audience of publicity,
which is informed by photographs. This may appear obvious, but it is
worth noting that the 'making public' of publicity is both given such a
prime slot in the proceedings, and is conducted with such seriousness.

Even with a brief engagement, we see, then, the ICC using a variety of
marketing practices: it employs branding, advertising, PR, and publicity.
The connections to place branding and propaganda will be discussed in
more depth in the coming chapters. Next, we move on from the analysis
of specific marketing practices to consider the wider social, economic,
and political context in which marketing global justice occurs.

2.4   Global Justice in the Attention Economy

We recall the attention-grabbing faculties of Praljak's televised suicide:
were it not for the live suicide by poison, the confirmation of Praljak's
sentencing – alongside five other defendants – would not have made
headline news. Slobodan Praljak was arguably keenly aware of the staging
of his final performance and the attention it would garner within a
perceived attention economy. Both Praljak's suicide and the ICC's
marketing practices just outlined share the desire for attention, persuad-
ing imagined audiences to engage in their messages, and simultaneously
distracting from structural issues of injustice – including their complicity
in injustices.

The American economist and cognitive psychologist Herbert A. Simon
was one of the first to use the term 'attention economy'. As early as the
1970s, he wrote that 'a wealth of information creates a poverty of
attention'.[83] Simon framed information-overload as an economic problem, where attention is a finite resource. As more and more systems were
being designed to create information, the problem was not *information*-
scarcity, but rather *attention*-scarcity. The term 'attention economy' has

---

[82]   *The Prosecutor v Germain Katanga and Mathieu Ngudjolo Chui* (Trial Hearing) ICC-01/
04-01/07 (24 November 2009), transcript available at: www.icc-cpi.int/Transcripts/
CR2009_08585.PDF.

[83]   H. A. Simon, 'Designing Organizations for an Information-Rich World' in Martin
Greenberger (ed.), *Computers, Communication, and the Public Interest* (The John
Hopkins Press 1971) 40–41.

since been adopted by business strategists, first by Davenport and Beck in 2002,[84] and many more since who seek the solution to the economically framed issue of information overload and attention scarcity in the market.

The story according to Tim Wu begins with the first newspaper sellers who sold advertising space. In 1833, Benjamin Day printed the first one-penny newspaper in the United States, the *New York Sun*. 'What Day understood – more firmly, more clearly than anyone before him – was that while his readers may have thought themselves his customers, they were in fact his *product*.'[85] Day dared to sell the paper at a loss, thereby widening his potential market, and instead selling attention to corporations who wanted to advertise their products. Understanding attention as a commodity to be sold, increased the profits to be gained. Maintaining this new broad readership (and the associated profit from advertising) required stories that grabbed the attention: murder, suicide, conspiracy, theft, prostitution.[86] Soon, the *New York Sun* had competition. And with this competition came not only the need to grab the attention, but to hold it too. Wu explains that in such a situation a race to the bottom ensues: under competition, 'attention will almost invariably gravitate to the more garish, lurid, outrageous alternative. [. . .]'.[87] The coupling of attention and profit thereby led to the truncating and sensationalising of the stories that were circulated.

The attention economy has changed significantly since the days of the one-penny newspaper, although some things also remain unchanged. Among the most profound changes are those prompted by digital technologies. Enormous amounts of complex data are generated daily. Information has become (even more) abundant. The persuasion industry has adapted with new knowledge about human psychology and decision-making.[88] In *Stand Out of Our Light*, James Williams focuses on the de-politicising distraction that transpires with the attention economy in the digital technology age. The individualisation, short-term gains, and pettiness, prompted by the competition for attention threatens 'our

---

[84] Thomas H. Davenport and John C. Beck, *Attention Economy: Understanding the New Currency of Business* (Harvard Business Review Press 2002).
[85] Wu, 'Attention Merchants' 12.
[86] Ibid 13.
[87] Ibid 16.
[88] James Williams, *Stand Out of Our Light: Freedom and Resistance in the Attention Economy* (Cambridge University Press 2018) 28.

collective ability to pursue any politics worth having'.[89] Williams illustrates the inability to mobilise and organise with reference to research that suggests that exposure to repeated notifications (say from a smartphone), can create mental habits of interruption, even in the absence of that technology.[90] Such *dis*tractions can mean interruptions from close scrutiny of political content, through the *at*traction to non-political types of information or clickbait political content.[91] Strategic distractions may come from politicians themselves; here Williams refers to US President Donald Trump's use of Twitter to deflect attention from an important political issue to something inane.[92] It is therefore not simply the consumer who is affected by the attention economy, but the citizen as political subject. The tools of persuasion themselves often remain opaque. Williams notes: 'We've kept our eye on coercive, as opposed to persuasive, designs.'[93] We know when an Orwellian-type of censorship inhibits our freedom, but we are less attuned to the type which we are subjected to as 'free' citizens.

Understanding the means by which attention is directed – and diverted – is key to grasping the effects of the attention economy on priorities in the global justice sector. There are too many injustices to fathom or capture. In the abundance of information on global injustices, and an economised mindset that sees attention as a commodity, the attention economy effects the channelling of attention to particular causes and organisations. Certain causes get what Williams refers to as the 'spotlight' while others are obscured. The attention economy, then, is not only about grabbing the attention *towards* a particular matter; it is also about grabbing the attention *away* from something else. When it comes to global justice, it is often spectacle that grabs attention away from structural harms. But spectacle does even more than that; it also has an ordering function, giving meaning to some iterations of global justice and depleting others.

2.4.1   Spectacle

In common usage, spectacle is mostly used as an adjective that can be attached to positive or negative events: as in 'a spectacular performance',

---

[89] Ibid 47.
[90] Gloria Mark, Daniela Gudith and Ulrich Klocke, 'The Cost of Interrupted Work: More Speed and Stress' (Proceedings of the SIGCHI Conference on Human Factors in Computing Systems 2008).
[91] Williams, 'Stand Out of Our Light'.
[92] Ibid 52.
[93] Ibid 28.

or 'a spectacular failure'. Spectacle as a noun refers mostly to a show: 'The fireworks display was a spectacle'. Spectacle as it is used in this book, as an analytic, often (but not always) loses its preceding article, which indicates that we are no longer referring to a particular event or performance 'the spectacle', but rather a broader relationship. Spectacle is a social relationship mediated by images. This relational aspect of spectacle is what Guy Debord was emphasising when he stated that spectacle is more than simply a collection of images, but rather a 'world vision' constituted through domination.[94] Domination occurs through the commodity under capitalism.

Let us take a step back to consider the relationship between spectacle and commodity. A world vision of social relationships mediated by commodities relates to what Karl Marx termed 'commodity fetishism'.[95] When Marx wrote about commodity fetishism he was trying to capture a fundamental shift to what we today refer to as the consumer society. Commodities were no longer simply about what they could be used for (what is the stuff good for), or the mundane act of exchange (the tradability of stuff we do not need for stuff we do need); commodities were about their representation (what does this stuff mean to you?).[96] For Marx, this had the effect of alienating people from their labour and from each other. Debord takes this a step further, moving beyond the relationship to the commodity as a *thing* to image. 'In all its specific forms, as information or propaganda, as advertisement or direct entertainment consumption, the spectacle is the present model of socially dominant life' states Debord.[97] On account of this, Debord views social life as de-graded through a process of *being* to *having*, and then from *having* to *appearing*.[98] According to Debord, spectacle alienates human relationships as appearance conceals true social relationships. This reaches beyond mass media, which is merely the spectacle's 'most glaring superficial manifestation'.[99]

'Celebrity humanitarianism' is arguably the most glaring superficial manifestation of conceptions of justice and spectacle colliding – or colluding. In the context of humanitarianism, celebrities (the spectacular

---

[94] Guy Debord, *Society of the Spectacle* [1967] (Black & Red 1984) para. 4
[95] Karl Marx, *Das Kapital* [1867] (Regnery Publishing 2009), the commodity abounds 'in metaphysical subtleties and theological niceties', 37.
[96] Thomas Richards, *The Commodity Culture of Victorian England: Advertising and Spectacle* 1851–1914 (Stanford University Press 1991), 4.
[97] Ibid para. 6.
[98] Debord, 'Society of the Spectacle' para. 17
[99] Ibid para. 24.

representation of people) mediate the relationship between individuals and social justice. Hollywood stars, singers, and the more photogenic politicians – generally individuals from the Global North – support a range of causes. The UN has whole-heartedly embraced celebrity humanitarianism with its own celebrity outreach programme of UN Goodwill Ambassadors. Popstar Bono's humanitarian work is well-known, as is Bob Geldof's work for Band Aid. Hollywood actor Angelina Jolie has equally attained the label of 'humanitarian'. Global justice actors in turn can also become celebrities. Nuremberg Prosecutor Benjamin Ferencz, for example, has appeared in at least half a dozen documentaries on international criminal justice,[100] and barrister Amal Clooney is just as well known for her human rights practice as for being the wife of Hollywood star George Clooney. Practising international law is considered to be glamorous. As early as the 1980s, international law was adopting a new image, from dry diplomacy and legalism to something more exciting and adventurous. Writing in 1985, David Kennedy described the institutional environment of international law as imbued both with a 'special dignity' and 'glamor'.[101] Already at university it is engrained in the teaching practices that the study and practice of global justice does not only include a confrontation with global ills, but that it is also something exciting.[102]

A strong critic, Ilan Kapoor, argues that celebrity humanitarianism 'advances consumerism and corporate capitalism, and rationalizes the very global inequality it seeks to redress'.[103] It must be acknowledged that the mockery of celebrity humanitarianism is almost as prevalent as the admiration, beginning with the subversion of Band Aid to *Brand* Aid.[104] Kapoor pushes further than mockery in his critique, articulating the de-politicising features of celebrity humanitarianism, in particular when 'the spectacle of humanitarian relief focuses on the "show"'; on these occasions the outwardly visible and photogenic aspects are valued at the expense of public attention to structural causes.[105] Questions on

---

[100] A recent documentary tells Ferencz's story: *Prosecuting Evil: The Extraordinary World of Ben Ferencz*. Directed by Barry Avrich, Melbar Entertainment Group 2019.
[101] David Kennedy, 'International Legal Education' (1985) 26(2) *Harvard International Law Journal* 361–384, at 366.
[102] Ibid 367.
[103] Ilan Kapoor, *Celebrity Humanitarianism: The Ideology of Global Charity* (Routledge 2013).
[104] Richey and Ponte, 'Brand Aid'.
[105] Kapoor, 'Celebrity Humanitarianism' 3.

redistribution, debt, trade, the environment, poverty reduction, and emergency relief, which should be part and parcel of a public debate, are appropriated. Celebrity take-over of functions that would normally be a state or public function deepens the pervasiveness of market thinking as celebrities choose which issues are debated and which are ignored.[106]

There is often a racialised undertone to humanitarian celebrity culture, with celebrities rightly accused of performing the 'white saviour' role. The photo of the white celebrity among black children is the visual trope of celebrity humanitarianism. As Gayatri Spivak has observed, '[t]here is always a fascination with the picture-perfect idea of poverty; children playing in open sewers'.[107] This implies that the imagined audience of celebrity humanitarianism are white donors in the Global North observing a distant disaster-spectacle. A social justice movement prompted by picture-perfect-poverty remains uncertain; 'only instant celebrity for the philanthropist' is certain.[108] This not only constitutes commodification of poverty, but of *death*.

With his spectacular suicide in the courtroom, Praljak also arguably performed the commodification of death. The life of a 'war hero' is perhaps best celebrated through a martyr's death. Praljak's suicide came only a few months after filming began on a feature film in Croatia titled *General*. The film depicts the 'long-awaited life story of Croatia's much-loved 'war hero' General Ante Gotovina'.[109] Gotovina was indicted for war crimes by the ICTY and was acquitted on appeal in 2012.[110] As can be expected in the celebrity cult of war heroes, the films that Praljak himself directed were aired in Croatia in tribute to his life – and death.[111] Meanwhile, a Croatian artist has painted the suicide scene of the courtroom. The painting was exhibited in the town library in the Croatian

---

[106] George Monbiot, 'Celebrity Isn't Just Harmless Fun – It's the Smiling Face of the Corporate Machine', *The Guardian*, 20 December 2016.

[107] Brad Evans and Gayatri Chakravorty Spivak, 'When Law is Not Justice', *The New York Times*, 13 July 2016.

[108] Ibid.

[109] *General*. Directed by Antun Vrdoljak, Kiklop film and Croatian Television 2019.

[110] *Prosecutor v Ante Gotovina and Mladen Markač* (Appeals Judgment) ICTY-IT-06-90-A (16 November 2012).

[111] Sven Milekic, 'War Criminal Praljak's Death Commemorated in Croatia', *Balkan Insight*, 11 December 2017; 'Croatian TV Broadcasts War Criminal Praljak's Film in Tribute', *The Jakarta Post*, 2 December 2017.

town Zadar.[112] On the anniversary of Praljak's death, a play premiered in Zagreb titled 'I Slobodan Praljak'.[113]

In the context of the attention economy, spectacle not only draws the attention, it also has an ordering function, which in turn has distinct distributive effects. When overloaded with information, a selection must take place on what demands attention. The circulation of images of mass graves, for example, immediately sends out a warning signal about a possible return to fascism and ethnic cleansing in combination with narratives of a past unwillingness to intervene. Action as a response to such images is not only framed in terms of urgency in the attention economy, but also in terms of efficiency of resources. Finite attentional resources find their equivalence in finite resources for action. What to *pay attention to* must be qualified through efficiency reasoning. Visceral and abbreviated narratives and images, which omit social, political, and economic context, often employ stereotypes as an economical (efficient) means of communication.

2.4.2   Stereotypes

According to the Oxford dictionary definition, a stereotype is 'a widely held but fixed and oversimplified image or idea of a particular type of person or thing'.[114] To be sure, we do not require a definition to know what stereotypes are. But, the distributional effects of stereotypes may be less familiar. The political economy analysis of the use of stereotypes in the global sphere is perhaps best introduced through the life and work of Walter Lippmann. Lippmann was an influential US journalist and author in the early to mid-twentieth century. In the early twentieth century, Lippmann was an enthusiast for the United States joining World War I, gaining some influence with President Wilson.[115] During the war, Lippmann worked for the Committee on Public Information, the first official 'US propaganda agency'. The agency produced pamphlets, speeches, books, broadcasts – and a sceptical Lippmann.[116] After the

---

[112] Sven Milekic, 'Poison-Drinking War Criminal's Portrait Exhibited in Croatia', *Balkan Insight*, 27 August 2018.

[113] Anja Vladisavljevic, 'Praljak's Courtroom Suicide Anniversary Marked in Croatia', *Balkan Insight*, 29 November 2018.

[114] 'Stereotype', Oxford Dictionary, available at: www.lexico.com/en/definition/stereotype.

[115] Ronald Steel, *Walter Lippmann and the American Century* (Bodley Head 1981).

[116] 'Before World War One he was a radical socialist. He dropped that for muckraking journalism', explains Edward Said in his review of Ronald Steel's biography of Lippmann. Edward Said, 'Grey Eminence' (1981) 4(4) *London Review of Books* 7.

war, Lippmann would publish the influential book *Public Opinion*, a study of the pictures inside the heads of people that (mis)lead them in their dealings with the world.[117] Lippman coined a term to capture the creation of the simplified images inside people's heads, stripped of all complexity: 'stereotype'. Stereotypes can, according to his thesis, be employed in order to manufacture the consent of the governed; his terminology of 'manufacturing consent' was later adopted by Herman and Chomsky. The manipulation of masses is, according to Lippmann's thesis, created through symbols.[118] Images held in the mind can be used to manipulate individuals to act in a certain way, to support war or to depart with money for things they do not need. In the scepticism of an easily manipulated public, we find a link between stereotypes, neoliberalism, and law. For it was at the Walter Lippmann Colloquium in Paris (so-named because his work was studied there), that the term 'neoliberalism' was first coined to denote a particular way of thinking. At the Colloquium in 1938, Lippmann's *An Inquiry into the Principles of the Good Society* was read and discussed by the likes of Austrian economists Friedrich von Hayek and Wilhelm Röpke. Lippmann emphasised the social aspects of the global economy, going beyond the economists' usual tools of statistics and graphs. 'The social' as a political entity was generally met with suspicion by Lippmann, as well as the other colloquium attendees.[119] Expanding on what he had already identified as mass information and a manipulable public in *Public Opinion*, Lippmann began considering the role of *law* in the creation of a global order that reigned in the manipulability of a public.[120] Quinn Slobodian summarises this approach as 'a synthesis of the Austrian perspective on the subjectivity of value with a new attention to the rule of law'.[121] Lippmann's thinking, along with other neoliberals who saw the public as a potential *problem* for the market, led to considerations on the separation of the market from public opinion.

When Lippmann was writing, racialised stereotypes were pervasive both socially and in law. In his classic book *Orientalism*, Edward Said

---

[117] Walter Lippmann, *Public Opinion* [1922] (Greenbook Publications 2010).
[118] Walter Lippmann, 'Public Opinion' 94.
[119] Edward Said describes Lippmann as 'a man whose view of the mass audience he wrote for was patronising at best, contemptuous at worst'. Said, 'Grey Eminence'.
[120] Walter Lippmann, *An Enquiry into the Principles of the Good Society* (Little Brown 1937).
[121] Quinn Slobodian, *Globalists: The End of Empire and the Birth of Neoliberalism* (Harvard University Press 2018) 81.

drew on an extensive catalogue of formal and literary writing, from speeches in the House of Commons to novels, to demonstrate how stereotypes are constructed, circulated, and perpetuated. Stereotypes of the 'Oriental' as irrational, depraved, childlike are, according to Said, constructed through essentialism that is repeated, accepted, and legitimised. Said argued that the Orient is best understood as a construction of the European Western imagination, as one of Europe's 'deepest and most recurring images of the Other'.[122] Racialised stereotypes that perpetuate the divide between the Global North and the Global South, we begin to see, have distributive functions. This is particularly evident in the stereotypes of people as 'helpless', 'corrupt', 'lazy', or as violent 'monsters'. The stereotyping of ordinary people as helpless, leaders as corrupt, workers as lazy, and black people as prone to become violent monsters, provides a basis for justifying the absence of redistribution. Instead, (white mediated) market techniques in combination with interventionism are emphasised. This racialised coding continues to exist, as Robert Knox has argued, in international law, and in international criminal law (ICL) too. For it is only on the basis of 'racial stereotypes about the propensity of black people towards violence' that the definition of black people as 'monsters' can take hold.[123] We find that as a particular iteration of spectacle, stereotypes direct resources and attention to some issues at the expense of other issues.

With this section, we have peeled back the layers of the attention economy to reveal the distributive effects of spectacle, and in particular stereotypes (a favoured tool of spectacle). Attention, of course, is not a commodity. It can only be construed as a commodity in the context of a global world organised around commodification processes in which social values are transformed into market values.

2.5   Global Justice in a Globalised (and Neoliberal) World

Although the term 'attention economy' was first coined in the 1970s, its penetration increased with the further 'globalisation' of the world, particularly in the 1990s. The collapse of the Soviet Union and its socialist ideology, prompted notions of a 'global village'. Globalisation appeared to hold all kinds of promises, and to a lesser extent, challenges. The

---

[122] Edward Said, *Orientalism* [1978] (Penguin 2003) 1.
[123] Robert Knox, 'Valuing Race? Stretched Marxism and the Logic of Imperialism' (2016) 4 (1) *London Review of International Law* 81–126, at 99.

promises appeared vast, from the more technical promises of connected-ness and communication, to the dazzling excitement of international travel, exploration, and cheaper consumer goods. The greatest challenge was how to 'capture' it. In the international legal academy, this spurred various sub-fields dedicated to 'capturing' globalisation, including global administrative law and transnational private law. Globalisation was largely viewed as benign at worst, and democratising at best. One part of globalisation's story was to describe it as spontaneous processes that came about through technological advances. The other part of the story was globalisation's pacifying and democratising effect through market integration.[124] In international law, this appeared to be producing the 'post-Westphalian' era, where states were slowly disappearing, making way for new transnational actors and networks.

Despite declarations of the disappearing state, the state did not disap-pear. 'The ongoing process of globalization', observed B. S. Chimni in 2001, 'contrary to popular understanding, is not a spontaneous process. There has been decisive state intervention in favour of globalization.'[125] Instead of the state creating the conditions of its own disappearance act, it took on a new role: privileging the protection of the flow of capital. As Martin Carnoy and Manuel Castells note,

> without decisive state intervention, globalization could not have taken place. Deregulation, liberalization, and privatization, both domestically, and internationally were the institutional basis that paved the way for new business strategies with a global reach.[126]

With the consolidation of neoliberal forms of global order – the lifting of trade barriers, growing financialisation, and a new interventionist mili-tarism – disquiet began to grow about institutional globalisation and its potential for reproducing hierarchy. Sceptics of globalisation, such as Chantal Thomas, indeed anticipated – even before the financial crisis – 'increased socioeconomic inequality and economic volatility' as well as

---

[124] John M. Owen, 'How Liberalism Produces Democratic Peace' (1994) 19(2) *International Security* 87–125; Michael Mandlebaum, *The Ideas that Conquered the World: Peace, Democracy, and Free Markets in the Twenty-first Century* (Public Affairs 2002).

[125] B. S. Chimni, 'Teaching, Research and Promotion of International Law in India: Past, Present and Future' (2001) 5 *Singapore Journal of International & Comparative Law* 368–387, at 368.

[126] Martin Carnoy and Manuel Castells, 'Globalisation, the knowledge society, and the Network State: Poulantzas at the millennium' (2001) 1(1) *Global Networks* 1–19, at 5.

the racialised forms of inequality which this includes.[127] Despite some scepticism, including anti-globalisation protests, optimism about the market however prevailed. The market was (at least from an institutional perspective) considered to be the realm of freedom and equality. Any failings leading to 'unfreedom' and inequality remain, in this view (often denoted as 'libertarianism' in the US context), *individual* failings and imperfect realisations of the rule of the market. Such optimism about the (global) market, alongside a paranoia about democratic contestation, is reflected in the neoliberal project.

Neoliberalism is understood in multiple ways. It can be viewed as a contemporary form of capitalism,[128] as an ideology,[129] as an intellectual tradition,[130] as a project,[131] as a model of governmentality,[132] or as a 'normative order of reason'.[133] Different scholars place an emphasis on different twentieth- century periods to consider the origins of neoliberalism. Slobodian invites us to consider the early twentieth century, after World War I, when a group of Austrian economists and lawyers began thinking about a global economic order in the 'ashes of the Habsburg Empire'.[134] A further period commonly referenced is the emergence of the 'Chicago School' at the Department of Economics, University of Chicago in the 1940s. In contrast to the aforementioned Austrian School, the Chicago School is mostly associated with *laissez faire* economics. According to David Harvey, who has written extensively on neoliberalism from a Marxist perspective, the late 1970s are most illustrative for an understanding of the origins of neoliberalism due to the proliferation of market-friendly policies.[135] In the early 1970s, the Bretton Woods era collapsed, largely due to the end of the US dollar's

---

[127] Chantal Thomas, 'Globalization and the Reproduction of Hierarchy' (2000) 33 *University of California, Davis Law Review* 1451–1501, at 1451.

[128] Neoliberalism as 'capitalism in its millennial manifestations', see Jean and John Comaroff, 'Millennial Capitalism: First Thoughts on a Second Coming' (2000) 12(2) *Public Culture* 291–343, at 298.

[129] For example, Vincente Navarro, 'Neoliberalism as Class Ideology; Or, the Political Causes of the Growth of Inequalities' (2007) 37(1) *International Journal of Health Services* 47–62.

[130] Slobodian, 'Globalists'.

[131] David Harvey, *A Brief History of Neoliberalism* (Oxford University Press 2005).

[132] Pierre Dardot and Christian Laval, (Gregory Elliott, trans.) *The New Way of the World: On Neoliberal Society* (Verso 2017).

[133] Wendy Brown, *Undoing the Demos: Neoliberalism's Stealth Revolution* (Zone Books 2015) 9.

[134] Slobodian, 'Globalists', book sleeve.

[135] Harvey, 'A Brief History of Neoliberalism'.

convertibility into gold. Currencies floated on the market.[136] With the collapse of the fixed exchange rate, the Keynesian version of social democracy – one built on a strong state that protects the public good and has redistributive capacities – also collapsed. At the international financial institutions based in Washington DC, the so-called Washington Consensus emerged. These policy prescriptions, initially for countries in the Global South in crisis, included instructions on opening up of markets and the privatisation of public services. Regardless of the periodisation of neoliberalism, what all of these origins stories share is the attempt to come to grips with the extension of the market into various aspects of social life.

As will be discussed in further depth in Chapter 3 'A Brand New Justice', I consider a more recent past of neoliberalism, namely the 1990s, although I do not make a claim to neoliberalism originating then. Instead, this was a period in which neoliberalism *consolidated,* and at the same time was beginning to show its weaknesses. The 1990s are interesting as the decade when liberalism became dominant globally (although not exclusively of course). The international legal currency of 'universality' took on a new meaning as the liberal-legal nation state marked the 'End of History'.[137] The role of international organisations increasingly translated this into a role of protecting capital flow, stabilising, internationalising, and legitimating capitalism.[138] Privatisation is a main tenet of neoliberalism as it creates new means by which capital can circulate. Whether transport, energy, communication, health or education provisions, a global wave of privatisation ensued. The public sector is either minimised or collapsed into the private entirely. The role of the state is reduced, but is no less important: it ensures the protection of the market.

Neoliberalism as a legal-political project is in competition with other projects, projects of community, socialism, and solidarity. They are alternative forms of internationalism that stand in tension with, and challenge, neoliberalism. Neoliberalism's influence varies depending on the context. Often, it reveals weaknesses and requires means to uphold its structures. In the 1990s, the so-called anti-globalisation protests, which

---

[136] 'The end of the Bretton Woods System (1972–1981), International Monetary Fund, History, available at: www.imf.org/external/about/histend.htm.

[137] Francis Fukuyama, 'The End of History?' (1989) 16 *The National Interest* 3–18.

[138] Thomas Biebricher termed the nexus between law and neoliberalism 'juridical neoliberalism'. Thomas Biebricher, 'Neoliberalism and Law: The Case of the Constitutional Balanced-Budget Amendment' 17(5) *German Law Journal* 835–856.

shut down negotiations for the fledgling World Trade Organization as an international organisation set up to benefit private actors, marked a moment of weakness for neoliberalism: its anti-democratic faculties prompted protest instead of acceptance. With international legal institutions on the side of neoliberalism in the form of marketised global justice, however, protest can quickly be delegitimised.

2.6   Global Justice in a World of Legalised Morality

Law's moral authority is an essential condition of global justice claims. In the international sphere, law has adopted a moral higher ground through its claim to bring about peace, security, justice, and development. Political theorist Judith Shklar famously aimed to draw attention to the constructed and naturalised nature of law's moral authority in her analysis of legalism. 'The court of law and the trial according to law are the social paradigms, the perfection, the very epitome, of legalistic morality.'[139] Law is deemed to be the correcting influence on excesses of power. What this legalistic morality obscures are the biases inherent in legalism, some of which have already been gestured towards, for example, the idea that redistribution is outside of the scope of legalistic morality and the biases in favour of the (legalism of the) Global North. After all, legalism's 'most nearly complete expression is in the great legal systems of the European world'.[140] The myth that is carried forward in contemporary interpretations of global justice is of the neutrality of the law. Law, as rational and non-political, is regarded as speaking reason to politics. The strength of the global justice association with *law* is precisely this sense of a reasoned and rational force for good. Justice Jackson of the Nuremberg International Military Tribunal famously subscribed to the victory of law over politics narrative, when he wrote in his concluding report to President Truman:

> The importance of this case is not measurable in terms of the personal fate of any of the defendants who were already broken and discredited men . . . the Four Powers have given the example of submitting their grievances against these men to a dispassionate inquiry on legal evidence.[141]

---

[139] Judith Shklar, *Legalism: Law, Morals, and Political Trials* (Harvard University Press 1986) 2.

[140] Ibid.

[141] 'International Conference on Military Trials: London 1945, Report to the President by Mr. Justice Jackson, October 7, 1946', available at: http://avalon.law.yale.edu/imt/jack63.asp.

At the ICC, this form of legalism is frequently performed and reaffirmed, even internalised. Such internalisation is demonstrated in the wording of an Office of the Prosecutor policy paper, which states that 'the issue is no longer about whether we agree or disagree with the pursuit of justice in moral or practical terms: it is the law'.[142] However, such enormous moral burdens also seemingly burst the seam of what law is capable of. ICL as an expression of this idea of legalism, although dominant, has been contested in various ways. Karl Jaspers famously wrote prior to the trial of senior Nazi Adolf Eichmann in Jerusalem: 'Something other than law is at stake here – and to address it in legal terms is a mistake.'[143] The overreach of the promise of law's moral authority in post-conflict situations led Thomas Skouteris to quip: 'The lawyers are back, primed by a persuasive story about how law can perform a catalytic role in fostering peace and justice.'[144]

2.7 The Global Justice Sector

We have seen in the above that there are many different actors who legitimise their work through referencing global justice. This includes states, international organisations including international courts and tribunals, NGOs, individuals, and of course corporations. The book focuses mostly on the non-profit part of the sector, but acknowledges the mutual influencing of the for-profit limb of the sector and the not-for-profit limb of the sector. We have also learned that the global justice sector is not an open space in which every and any interpretation of global justice has equal validity. Certain interpretations of global justice are dominant. Some global justice actors are able to compete in the sector and influence the circulation of ideas of global justice while others are not. The anti-impunity movement has proven successful in institutional-ising its idea of global justice, therefore outstripping the competition.

---

[142] ICC Office of the Prosecutor, 'Policy Paper on the Interests of Justice' (September 2007), available at: www.icc-cpi.int/NR/rdonlyres/772C95C9-F54D-4321-BF09-73422BB23528/143640/ICCOTPInterestsOfJustice.pdf

[143] Lotte Kohler and Hans Saner (eds.), Robert Kimber and Rita Kimber (trans.), *Hannah Arendt – Karl Jaspers, Correspondence 1926–1969* (Harcourt Brace Jovanovich 1992) 410, a line quoted by several commentators and critics of international criminal justice, including Martti Koskenniemi 'Between Impunity and Show Trials' (2002) 6 *Max Planck United Nations Yearbook* 1–35, at 2, and Lawrence Douglas, *The Memory of Judgment: Making Law and History in the Trials of the Holocaust* (Yale University Press 2001) 174–175.

[144] Thomas Skouteris, *The Notion of Progress in International Law Discourse* (T M C Asser Press 2010) 163.

The ICC takes on a special place in this competitive sector as the main institutional manifestation of the anti-impunity movement. Sarah Nouwen and Wouter Werner's language about the ICC 'monopolising' global justice illustrates the submission to the market:

> The real issue is not whether both restorative justice and distributive justice, as well as equality before the law and retributive justice can be pursued – which is obviously possible – but which conception of justice prevails in times of clashes or limited resources. In a world of horrific constraint, conceptions of justice compete for their realization.[145]

Although a consciousness of the competition compels global justice actors to highlight how far they differ, the dominant actors in the global justice sector share some important features. The study of these shared features provides an insight into which practices, and aesthetics, are deemed most effective. It also indicates the *narrowing* of the idea and practices of global justice.

Through analysis of market practices from the perspective of global justice actors, the prominence of the market in the global justice sector has become apparent in at least three ways: (a) in the adoption of marketing *practices* by the not-for-profit limb of the global justice sector; (b) in the focus on market-friendly global justice *issues*, constructed on the basis of spectacular stereotypes, over other issues; (c) in the construction of an *audience* for global (in)justice issues on the basis of purchasing power. Whilst the market is prioritised in different ways, another feature of global justice in its contemporary form is that it is simultaneously *absent*. Curiously, while there is frequent reference to 'stakeholders' of global justice and commitments to 'efficiency' of using funds, questions of redistribution and structural questions of inequality are very rarely part of the global justice debate.

The absence of the economy is notable also in at least three ways in contemporary global justice projects: (a) absences are created in the attention economy in the form of a focus on the spectacular at the expense of structural issues; (b) absences are created through moral legalism in the international, which hides the biases and decision-making in the name of the law; (c) absences are created through the distributive functions of global justice, which precludes global justice as a redistributive force.

How can the market in the global justice sector be so visible and simultaneously decidedly absent? From the above, we begin to glean

---

[145] Sarah Nouwen and Wouter Werner, 'Monopolizing Global Justice: International Criminal Law as Challenge to Human Diversity' (2015) 13 *Journal of International Criminal Justice* 157–176, at 174.

the persuasive and distracting faculties of marketised global justice. Distractions from structural injustices come hand in hand with attention to the spectacular, which is comprised of a simplified means of communication through stereotypes, images, and slogans. The global justice sector, we begin to see, is a space of mass distraction.

2.8 Conclusion

Let us briefly return to that moment in the courtroom in which the defendant Praljak took the vial of poison. The suicide in the courtroom shocked many observers and commentators, prompting an initial searching for its meaning, which, in a typical analytic turn to the mundane at the expense of the structural, morphed into a debate around courtroom security. The spectacle had an ordering function in that it directed attention away from the causes of violence, away from questions about the composition of the courtroom, away from questions about how to achieve peace. For international lawyers critical of the theatrics, it strengthened their resolve to pay attention to positive law: attention had to be directed to legal technicalities, not politics. Their exclusive position as legal experts separated from politics was reaffirmed. For the media, the spectacle provided a dramatic headline to create clicks, to appease and please advertisers. For supporters of Praljak, the suicide provided a means to celebrate his life, to pay tribute. For his detractors, it provided cause to criticise his self-righteousness and to question the intricacies of courtroom security. Law has of course historically frequently used spectacular events for legitimacy; we can think, for example, of public hangings or show trials. What Slobodan Praljak had understood, however, was the machinery of marketised global justice: a marketing stunt is structurally supported by the system. It was an episode of marketised global justice working exactly as it is set up to work.

Recognising the use of marketing practices opens the door to a broader study of the political economy of global justice. The study of global justice through a political economy method considers the role of markets, profits, competition, and growth to be crucial for political decision-making in government, in law, and in society at large. Moreover, a particular element of the neoliberal order crystallises, namely, the transformation of political actors into consumers. The result appears to be that marketised global justice in its legalised and punitive form not only uses marketing practices, but also helps stabilise and legitimise the protection of the market from democratic contestation. The question that follows is: how did we get here?

3

A Brand New Justice

How Global Justice Became Marketable in the 1990s

> There is now no aspect of our lives which is not open to being used for this theatre of the brand.[1]

3.1 Introduction

Chapter 2 highlighted some prominent features of marketised global justice in the twenty-first century: defendants accused of international crimes can be cast as famous, individuals fighting for impunity can be perceived as glamourous, judges can be concerned about publicity, and cities can use global justice to attract tourism, trade, and investment. This chapter considers the history of the marketisation of global justice. The guiding question is this: When did the marketised expression of global justice consolidate to become the dominant expression of global justice? Specifically, what were the social, economic, and political conditions that allowed the *institutionalisation* of marketised global justice?

The hypothesis is that there is some significance to be gleaned from the intersection between the rise of branding on the one hand and the rise of international criminal law, as the institutionalised form of 'anti-impunity as global justice', on the other hand. These phenomena have been treated as entirely separate, but I suggest that the connection between them is key for understanding the marketisation of global justice. From the centres of power, the 1990s was both designated as 'The End of History' and the beginning of the 'New World Order'. While the Cold War period was marked by competing leadership claims between the United States – self-defined as the 'free world' – and the USSR – self-defined as the socialist and anti-imperialist camp – the 1990s was imagined as a period of unification under liberal democracy.[2] Singling out a specific decade is somewhat

---

[1] Interview with Naomi Klein in *No Logo: Brands, Globalization and Resistance*. Directed by Sut Jhally, Media Education Foundation, 2003. Transcript available at: www.mediaed.org/transcripts/No-Logo-Transcript.pdf.

[2] Francis Fukuyama, 'The End of History?' (1989) 16 *The National Interest* 3–18.

arbitrary, not least given the connections between the preceding and succeeding years. And yet, the breakdown of Soviet communism in combination with the closing of the millennium heightened the expansionism and optimism of certain Western liberal voices, forces, and institutions, making this decade particularly worthy of historical analysis from today's vantage point.

It is rather unsurprising that the marketing world of the 1990s experienced a period of euphoria. As the formerly planned economies of the Soviet bloc rushed to transition to market systems, they opened their borders to trade and investment. This opening caused a vast expansion of markets for goods and services. In addition, new technologies, and particularly the Internet, provided more spaces for advertising (beyond the traditional print media, television, and big-screen commercials), and a more precise targeting of consumers. Branding, previously a practice very much attached to the product or service, completed the transition to *ideas*. With this shift, from product to symbolism, branding became the biggest marketing trend of the decade.[3] The focus on ideas and values is often referred to as lifestyle branding. The product or service faded into the background whilst the brand as idea moved into the spotlight. What follows focuses both on this shift towards lifestyle branding as well as on another important shift in the 1990s, namely, the use of branding beyond the corporate sphere. The aspiration of brands to transcend the product and to market values on the one hand, and the aspiration of global justice actors to use marketing practices for the communication and circulation of their ideas on the other hand, is where marketing and global justice intersect and cross-fertilise.

For international law, the 1990s was an equally ambitious – perhaps even euphoric – period. It was certainly a time of great consolidation and expansionism. It will be illustrated that the decade's 'new interventionism' came about through a powerful alignment between humanitarianism and military power. Interventionism was not only practised in the form of military power; it also appeared in the shape of global economic programmes facilitated and enforced by international financial institutions. The United States as global hegemon simultaneously drove this 'new' order and also resisted it. The ambivalent position of both driving and resisting internationalism is no more clear than in the United States' position towards the International

---

[3] Liz Moor, *The Rise of Brands* (Bloomsbury 2007).

Criminal Court (ICC) in Rome in 1998 – supporting it only in so far as it did not apply to US citizens. As the pendulum swung towards a defined internationalism of the powerful, human rights law took on a new guise, namely, as an instrument *of* state power rather than an instrument *against* state power.[4] The alignment with state power was to prompt a marked shift from state responsibility to individual accountability – at the very least, rhetorically. The following analyses these three shifts (new interventionism, a new ordering of the international economic sphere, and the evolution from state responsibility to individual accountability) as critical for an understanding of the history of marketised global justice.

Not all was new and different in what President George Bush Senior proclaimed as a 'new world order' in a 1990 televised speech to inform Americans about the invasion of Iraq.[5] There were many continuations. A significant continuation was the structural undermining of the economic, political, and cultural influence of the Global South. From the 1950s to the 1970s, the Third World had made efforts to distinguish itself politically from both the West and the Soviet bloc by attempting to build a Non-Aligned Movement after decolonisation.[6] By the early 1990s, however, the economic and political movements were almost entirely repressed.[7] The United States and its Western allies consolidated their power militarily, economically, epistemologically, culturally, and legally over most parts of the world.[8] The repeated repression of the Global South's power and the management of its resistance movements displays new mechanisms of repression by the former imperial powers of the formerly colonised, despite the formal period of decolonisation in the 1950s and 1960s. It follows that, notwithstanding the focus of this

---

[4] Stephen Hopgood, *The Endtimes of Human Rights* (Cornell University Press 2013).

[5] 'Remarks by the President to the Joint Session of Congress', Washington, DC (11 September 1990). https://millercenter.org/the-presidency/presidential-speeches/september-11-1990-address-joint-session-congress

[6] At the same time, many of the new independent governments had strong ties to the Soviet Union, where they united over the fight against imperialism.

[7] That is not to say that Europe and the USA are conceived here as the permanent 'core' and 'prime mover' of history, a historicisation which is criticised by Alexander Anievas and Kerem Nisanciolglu in *How the West Came to Rule: The Geopolitical Origins of Capitalism* (Pluto Press 2015).

[8] On the history of the USA as the twentieth-century superpower, beginning with US involvement in World War I, and the economic dependencies this entailed, see Adam Tooze, *The Deluge: The Great War and the Remaking of Global Order 1916–1931* (Penguin 2015).

chapter being on the 1990s, important connections to other eras and decades are made, including in particular continuations between the 1990s and nineteenth-century economic liberalism and imperialism.

3.2 History and the Questions Asked

But first, a note on methodology. Every historical analysis comes with a choice, and this is not simply the more obvious choice of where or when to begin. The choice also relates to the type of historical methodology: as we are interested in the history of the marketisation of global justice and how it relates to the new demands for anti-impunity, one starting point might be a history of international criminal law (ICL) as a field. The history of ICL is often presented as one beginning with the post–World War II Nuremberg trials leading to the establishment of the ICC in 1998.[9] What Immi Tallgren and Thomas Skouteris call the traditional 'Whig historiography' of ICL typically presumes historical progress and linear development.[10] The Nuremberg and Tokyo trials of 1945 were, according to the dominant narrative, of great significance because this was the first time that individuals were held to account for committing mass crimes. Then, according to this narrative, came a period in which nothing much happened whilst the big powers were embroiled in their Cold War antics of arms racing.[11] In the 1990s, the story then continues with the United Nations (UN) Security Council's establishment of the ad hoc tribunals for Yugoslavia (ICTY) and Rwanda (ICTR). These efforts finally led to the establishment of the ICC, the first permanent court to adjudicate over mass crimes. In this narrative, each project is presented as overcoming some of the difficulties of its predecessor, each project carrying humanity to a better understanding of the requirements of justice. There are numerous attempts at unsettling this traditional

---

[9] Beth van Schaak and Ron Slye, 'A Concise History of International Criminal Law' in Beth van Schaak and Ron Slye (eds.), *International Criminal Law: Essentials* (Aspen Publishers 2009) 27.

[10] Immi Tallgren and Thomas Skouteris, 'Editors' Introduction' in Immi Tallgren and Thomas Skouteris (eds.), *The New Histories of International Criminal Law: Retrials* (Oxford University Press 2019) 1.

[11] 'The Cold War Freeze', according to van Schaak and Slye, 'A Concise History of International Criminal Law'.

narrative, including efforts to offer more 'complete' histories[12] and expose 'hidden histories',[13] forgotten histories,[14] or 'shadow histories'.[15] The approach to the history of global justice that is proposed in this book is, in contrast to the above, one which traces history through material conditions. Questions of economic activity as mapped onto political structures are foregrounded, in particular the distributive effects of international legal institutions.[16] Whiggish history-writing is understood as reflecting those whose material interests have been foregrounded. Put differently, a material approach to history challenges an approach to history that is reductively ideational. An ideational approach might, for example, track the history of global justice through Enlightenment ideas of liberty and progress. This would involve investigating the course of the anti-impunity idea through the decades as progressively culminating in today's idea of anti-impunity. However, such an approach often misses an engagement with the historical context, including questions as to why certain ideas find prominence at a certain time, which ideas were able to circulate and gain purchase, and which ideas were not. The political economy of the circulation of ideas – through privileged publications, patrons, and networks – tends to be blended out in favour of an analysis of the abstract idea. A historical materialist approach therefore assumes that it was not solely due to 'outrage of ongoing impunity' that international criminal law came to prominence in the 1990s.[17] Although, of course, certain key actors may have been inspired by such an outrage, the question of materiality asks why and how the idea of global justice became inflected by anti-impunity demands in the places it did, in which ways these ideas were allowed to circulate, and to whose benefit they were conceptualised.[18]

---

[12] Immi Tallgren, "'Voglio una donna!'": On Rewriting the History of International Criminal Justice with the Help of Women Who Perpetrated International Crimes' in Tallgren and Skouteris, 'New Histories', 110–129.

[13] Kevin Jon Heller and Gerry Simpson (eds.), *The Hidden Histories of War Crimes Trials* (Oxford University Press 2013).

[14] In Christine Schwöbel-Patel, 'The Core Crimes of International Criminal Law' in Kevin Jon Heller et al. (eds.) *The Oxford Handbook of International Criminal Law* (Oxford University Press 2020). I highlight the forgotten history of drug trafficking as an international crime.

[15] Gerry Simpson, 'Unprecedents' in Tallgren and Skouteris, 'New Histories', 12–29.

[16] At the same time, this analysis does not subscribe to a strict economic determinism.

[17] Samuel Moyn, 'On a Self-Deconstructing Symposium' (2016) 110 *AJIL Unbound* 258–262, at 258.

[18] Adapted from Moyn, ibid.

Although this chapter separates branding and the anti-impunity movement for ease of narration, it is worth stating again that it is the *intersection* of branding and the anti-impunity movement that is key for an analysis of marketised global justice. I explain in the following that they both successfully incorporated and helped define new demands for (a) individualism, (b) technologies of visibility, (c) new notions of global ordering, and (d) the consolidation and concentration of structures of power. These are not coincidental intersections. The 1990s saw a mutually influencing relationship emerge between marketing and global justice. Global brands were looking enviously towards NGOs and other civil society formations because they had *meaning* readily available.[19] So while global justice actors were increasingly relying on marketing practices in order to compete in the global justice sector, marketing itself was being defined by global justice.

3.3 Marketing in the 1990s

When the ideological conflict between a liberal-democratic West and a socialist-autocratic East was decided in favour of the former, a major impetus for market expansionism began. The former socialist states, with varying degrees of planned economies and state-owned means of production, became open to privatisation and free trade. For multinational corporations based in the West, the new markets provided new consumers as well as cheaper means of production in terms of labour and materials. Large businesses from the affluent West, both in manufacturing and in services, began to outsource parts of their production to the new low-wage economies. This had, and still has, a profound effect on competition, often leading to a 'race to the bottom', with commodity prices and wages being undercut. Marketing practices changed, adapting to the larger and more fiercely competitive markets. Importantly for our analysis, branding as a discipline and 'science' began in this time.[20] Two main shifts in the practice of branding crystallised in the 1990s: the shift to branding as concerning lifestyle, and the use of branding by non-commercial organisations and actors. These shifts will be discussed in turn.

---

[19] Susannah Hart, 'The Future for Brands' in Susannah Hart and John Murphy (eds.), *Brands: The New Wealth Creators* (Palgrave Macmillan 1998) 206–214.

[20] Michael Johnson, *Branding in Five and a Half Steps* (Thames & Hudson 2016) 15.

3.3.1   Branding Lifestyle

Liz Moor explains in *The Rise of Brands* that it was not until the 1990s that a 'previously diffuse set of practices – product design, retail design, point-of-purchase marketing, among others – became consolidated into an integrated approach to marketing and business strategy known as branding'.[21] Branding consultancies and 'brand management' positions concentrated the previously fractured industry under the term 'branding'.[22] At the same time, business and marketing texts disseminated the language and principles of branding, so that branding emerged as something to be studied as well as practiced.[23] The texts were written mostly by employees of business schools and new branding consultancies in Europe and North America, 'for whom these texts often served as a type of promotional material'.[24] The new practice of branding incorporated more strongly the notion, which had its origins in the nineteenth century, that commodities embodied 'relationships', 'values', and 'feelings'.[25] This is the idea behind the transition from product to brand. What Naomi Klein made sensationally explicit in *No Logo* were the profound societal implications of such new branding principles. In the 1990s, according to Klein, a handful of corporations understood that branding had a potentially larger role to play than the simple cosmetic forms of branding; they began selling lifestyle and ideas instead of products. Klein uses, among other well-known brands, Starbucks as an example, quoting Starbucks CEO Howard Shultz as commenting on the 'Starbucks Experience': People do not simply queue up for coffee, but for 'the romance of the coffee experience, the feeling of warmth and

---

[21] Moor, 'Rise of Brands' 3.
[22] Ibid.
[23] Texts published included John Murphy, *Brand Strategy* (Prentice Hall 1990); David Aaker *Managing Brand Equity: Capitalizing on the Value of a Brand Name* (Jossey Bass 1991); Jean-Noël Kapferer, *Strategic Brand Management: New Approaches to Creating and Evaluating Brand Equity* (Kogan Page 1992); Lynn Upshaw, *Building Brand Identity: A Strategy for Success in a Hostile Marketplace* (Wiley 1995); and Susannah Hart and John Murphy, *Brands: The New Wealth Creators* (New York University Press 1998).
[24] Moor, 'Rise of Brands' 5.
[25] Ibid 6. Diagnosed by Marx in his account of commodity fetishism, Karl Marx, *Das Kapital* [1867] (Regnery Publishing 2009) 37. For a description of the emergence of the 'voyeuristic panorama of surplus as spectacle' in the nineteenth century, see Anne Mcclintock, *Imperial Leather: Race, Gender and Sexuality* (Routledge 1995).

community people get in Starbucks stores'.[26] With the coffee, consumers are also buying into an idea of community. The brand expectation transcends the commodity and expands into the immaterial. Individuals could buy, and buy *into*, a Starbucks community. The industry turned towards means, including sounds and shapes, by which to appeal to the feelings of consumers, rather than basing its marketing strategy on 'logical' propositions.[27] Subtle, and increasingly psychologically determined, means of persuasion emerged. The idea of stepping inside the brand in lifestyle branding was taken to new levels with jeans brand Diesel and sportswear brand Nike opening brand experience stores in 1996 (Diesel flagship stores) and 1999 (NikeTown) respectively.

But the idea of branding was to expand even further, as another new way of doing branding in the 1990s was, according to Klein, to go 'where your brand idea lives' and try to own that.[28] Music festivals for the music industry, sporting events for sports companies – the ambition was to eventually make the space the same as the brand. Technological advancements, particularly the advent of the Internet, enabled this expansion beyond the traditional advertising spaces of billboards, TV, and print media. The brand experience was designed to become the 'authentic' experience. Those brands that did this successfully became the superbrands of the day. The expansionism and consolidation of the superbrands is in keeping with the mergers and acquisitions boom of the 1990s. In short, corporate power became more far-reaching than ever before.

3.3.2 Commercialisation from Individualism to Socialism

As consumerism took centre-stage, so did individualism, in turn spurring consumer demands for expressions of individuality. Paradoxically, individuality became a huge consumer trend in the 1990s. The Levi's brand, for example, used cowboy and Wild West imagery to create associations with rebellion, youthfulness, originality, and excitement. In its uniform properties for a particular generation, it presented the 'ultimate

---

[26] Naomi Klein, *No Logo* (10th anniversary edition, Fourth Estate 2010), 20 citing Howard Shultz, *Pour Your Heart Into It* (Hyperion 1997) 5.

[27] Frank Mort, *Cultures of Consumption: Masculinities and Social Space in Late Twentieth Century Britain* (Routledge 1996) 96; Alan Tomlinson, 'Introduction: Consumer Culture and the Aura of the Commodity' in Alan Tomlinson (ed.), *Consumption, Identity and Style. Marketing, Meanings and the Packaging of Pleasure* (Routledge 1990) 1–40.

[28] Quote from Klein 'No Logo video', Transcript 5.

consumer paradoxical positioning': the mass-production of individuality.[29] While individualism experienced a boom, so did the commercialisation of social goods – such as the commercialisation of community already mentioned above. Flatpack furniture chain IKEA branded its do-it-yourself approach to furniture assemblage and home wares as 'democracy'. Benetton co-opted 'diversity' in its controversial clothing campaigns. Apple used civil rights icons such as Martin Luther King in its campaign of 'Think different'. Society's strongest ideas – community, democracy, diversity, civil rights – became appropriated by brands. In the early 1990s, corporate interest in what was then soberly referred to as 'point-of-purchase politics' grew, with more controversial topics such as gun control or AIDS prevention also finding corporate support.[30] Advertising columnist for the New York Times, Stuart Elliott, wrote in 1992: 'Companies are finding that their politics can be good for business'.[31] The advertising industry became increasingly interested in the 'ethical consumer', a consumer who was concerned about fair trade, peace, the environment, and sustainability. Ice-cream company Ben & Jerry's, a forerunner of this trend, was already selling ice-cream flavours for causes in the late 1980s. A percentage of Peace Pops sales went to pacifist groups,[32] a percentage of Rainforest Crunch sales went to rainforest preservation groups, and a percentage of Wild Maine Blueberry ice-cream sales went to Maine's blueberry-growing Passamaquoddy Native American community. The possibility of commercialising global justice became, cause by cause, a reality.[33]

The Internet, as the new technology of the time, became the main facilitator of brand expansionism. Overwhelmingly, the Internet was a new technology of visibility for brands. While visibility had mattered before, the Internet provided the key means of technology for heightened visibility. Despite the contemporary form of the Internet as a marketplace, the counter-cultural and communitarian roots of the Internet are worth mentioning. The Internet began, as is widely known, as a project of

---

[29] Micael Dahlén, Fredrik Lange, and Terry Smith, Marketing Communications: A Brand Narrative Approach (Wiley 2010) 233.
[30] Stuart Elliott, 'When Products Are Tied to Causes', New York Times, 18 April 1992.
[31] Ibid.
[32] 'Peace Pops' were launched in 1988 to mark the end of the Cold War.
[33] Although from 2008, not from the 1990s, this seems like a good place to mention Ben & Jerry's Imagine Whirled Peace flavour.

connectivity. In the early days, it was seen as a space of participation and diversification.[34] Towards the end of the 1990s, the first social media sites and blogging sites emerged. Social media's technology networks largely began around the Northern Californian Bay area, the hub of the tech industry as well as the United States' centre of counter-culture.[35] Social media, too, was generally associated with liberation, participation, and empowerment.[36] From counter-culture emerged, in a short space of time, a dominant culture based on the marketability of visibility – and a highly profitable one at that.

3.3.3 Intellectual Property Protection and Value

The marketability of visibility is protected from a legal perspective by the field of intellectual property (IP) law. Indeed, IP protection is pivotal for branding and for building a brand image. The IP law regime protects intangible assets of knowledge, information, and creativity. The primary forms of IP rights, in a rather sweeping generalisation, are patents (for inventions), copyright (for literary or artistic forms of expression), and trademarks (for distinctive qualities).[37] Trademarks and industrial designs are registered to protect signs, which assist with differentiation in the marketplace, such as colours, shapes, and sounds (mostly logos). As corporations began to outsource the manufacturing parts of their business to low-wage economies, going from product to image, bundles of intellectual property rights became the major assets held, and the protection of these became more important than ever. Indeed, intellectual property rights can be understood as the greatest contributors to the profitability of a business as they protect the business from competition.[38] It was in the 1990s, with the growing commercial significance of intangible assets, that the multilateral agreement on Trade-Related Aspects of Intellectual Property Rights (the TRIPS agreement) was

---

[34] See, for example, Charles Ess, 'The Political Computer: Democracy, CMC, and Habermas' in Charles Ess (ed.), *Philosophical Perspectives on Computer-Mediated Communication* (State University of New York Press 1996) 197–230.

[35] Ibid. The San Francisco Bay Area is today the home of social media corporations Instagram, Facebook, Twitter, and Academia.edu.

[36] Alice E. Marwick, *Status Update: Celebrity, Publicity & Branding in the Social Media Age* (Yale University Press 2013) 4.

[37] For a critical take, see Christopher May, *A Global Political Economy of Intellectual Property Rights. The New Enclosures?* (Routledge 2000).

[38] Moor, 'Rise of Brands' 91.

signed. IP rights were brought within the trade regime overseen by the World Trade Organization. The TRIPS Preamble states that the agreement is designed to 'reduce distortions and impediments to international trade.'[39] States became the official guarantors of intellectual property rights, enacting and enforcing stricter monitoring measures such as border controls, while at the same time ensuring that such measures themselves would not become impediments to trade. The TRIPS agreement entrenched the *economic motivation* for protecting intellectual property. A widely debated example of the material inequality prompted by the economic focus of intellectual property is the patenting of antiretroviral drugs for patients with HIV.[40] Patents have facilitated unnaturally high prices, particularly for complex chronic conditions, making certain drugs unavailable for less wealthy states and individuals – often those who need them most. In addition, the litigiousness of the pharmaceuticals industry prohibits competitors from investing in new research.[41] The circle of the prioritisation of marketing (image over product) is closed by the fact that pharmaceutical companies spend far more on marketing than they do on research.[42]

The practice of branding, and its legal protection, was in the 1990s beginning to significantly change the market. In the words of Celia Lury, the brand was emerging 'as a key locus for the reconfiguring of contemporary processes of production'.[43] The concept of economic 'value' becomes important here because two interconnected shifts occurred in the late 1980s through to the late 1990s. First, brand value was made measurable; and second, value was separated from the product and attached primarily to the brand. Brands are intangible assets but nevertheless unequivocally regarded as 'multipliers of value'.[44] The problem was: how to measure brand value as an asset? Global brand consultancy Interbrand designed a methodology in the late 1980s to value the

[39] Agreement on Trade-related Aspects of Intellectual Property Rights, Annex 1C Marrakesh Agreement (15 April 1994) 319–350.

[40] Moor, 'Rise of Brands' 98; Amy Kapczynski, 'The Right to Medicines in an Age of Neoliberalism' (2019), 10(1) *Humanity Journal* 79–107; Mariana Mazzucato, *The Value of Everything: Making and Taking in the Global Economy* (Puffin 2018) 207–212.

[41] Mazzucato, 'Value of Everything' 207.

[42] Richard Anderson, 'Pharmaceutical Industry Gets High on Fat Profits', BBC News, 6 November 2014, data compiled by GlobalData.

[43] Celia Lury, *Brands: The Logos of the Global Economy* (Routledge 2004) 17.

[44] Simon Anholt, *Brand New Justice. The Upside of Global Branding* (Butterworth Heinemann 2003) 2.

intangible assets associated with a brand name, alongside the more traditional valuation method of valuing the tangible assets (production facilities, equipment).[45] This first valuation set in motion a change in valuation across a wide range of industries. Today, 'intellectual capital has emerged as the leading asset class'.[46] Klein suggests that the key moment for this paradigm shift was when the tobacco company Philip Morris bought the grocery manufacturing and processing company Kraft for US$ 12.6 billion, a figure six times higher than what the company was worth on paper.[47] With this purchase, 'a huge dollar value had been assigned to something that had previously been abstract and unquantifiable – a brand name'.[48] Value was no longer determined by the cost of material and labour but was almost exclusively associated with image. Towards the mid-1990s, many major corporations no longer understood their central business to be production. With large brands you were not buying a product, you were buying an idea or a lifestyle. At the same time as brands started to move their logos into the foreground, the brand itself became productive. In the 1990s, the brand became a medium for the co-construction of supply and demand.[49] This is not only a shift in valuation; it is a shift in *value*. In other words, the way in which (market) value was measured had an impact on social values.[50]

3.3.4 Branding Beyond the Corporate Space

Despite having origins in the corporate space, 'the theory and practice of branding is now as applicable to a city or a country as it is to a charity or organisation'.[51] Let us take one step back though to recall the change in the 1980s and early 1990s from branding products to corporate branding. The move from product to brand meant that multiple products could fall

---

[45] For Interbrand's self-narration of this history, see Mike Rocha, 'An Exceedingly Good Solution: Looking Back on Thirty Years of Brand Valuation', available at: www.interbrand.com/views/exceedingly-good-solution-30-years-brand-valuation/

[46] Equity research firm Ocean Tomo publishes an annual Intangible Asset Market Value Study (IAMVS). One graph shows intangible assets of the S&P 500 growing from 17 per cent in 1975 to 84 per cent in 2015, available at: www.oceantomo.com/intangible-asset-market-value-study/.

[47] Klein, 'No Logo' 7, 8.

[48] Ibid.

[49] Lury, 'Logos' 27, 28.

[50] Chapter 4 on 'The Value of Global Justice' explores this in more depth through an analysis of exchange value and use value.

[51] Johnson, 'Branding' 13.

under one corporate brand, for example, Virgin's air and rail travel services, financial services, media, and fashion, alongside its original music business.[52] The values of a brand (with value here referring to its distinct attributes and advantages) were considered as extending 'across a plethora of different products and services'.[53] This meant that marketing became increasingly central to the internal organisation of corporations. In the words of Lury, 'brands come to have a dual role: in organising relations between producers and consumers, and in organising relations within the company itself, between employers and employees'.[54] These internal and external properties of branding concern a certain level of socialisation and therefore reduce the leap from the corporate sphere to the public sector to a small hop.

It is well known that corporate interests have pervaded non-corporate spheres for decades, even centuries. The Dutch East India company and the English East India Company are cases in point. During the seventeenth and eighteenth centuries, mercantilist practices determined European power politics. In her discussions of 'Transnational Merchant Law', Claire Cutler explains that the mercantilism of the European powers that sought overseas expansionism varied, some being more protectionist (Portugal and Spain), some more focused on industrial production at home (England). But the European colonial powers were all united in 'the increased recognition of the role that economic matters played in the determination of national power'.[55] Mercantilist policies and the juridification of commercial relations have long been used as means to enable states' accumulation of wealth.[56] It was, however, with the increasing separation of the public and the private that the former became associated with wealth extraction and the latter with wealth creation.[57] As the private sphere was increasingly insulated from political or social regulation and contestation in the late nineteenth and early

---

[52] Lury, 'Logos' 32.

[53] Hart, 'The Future for Brands' 208.

[54] Lury, 'Logos' 33.

[55] A. Claire Cutler, *Private Power and Global Authority: Transnational Merchant Law in the Global Political Economy* (Cambridge University Press 2003) 149.

[56] Robert Cox, *Production, Power, and World Order: Social Forces in the Making of History* (Columbia University Press 1987) 111.

[57] To use the distinction suggested by Mazzucato, 'Value of Everything'.

twentieth centuries, it became infused with an organic and natural character.[58] This led to associations with a certain dynamism, embodied by the figure of the entrepreneur. The belief became pervasive that corporate practices are more efficient, forward-thinking, and better at problem-solving.

Against this background, it is instructive to return to the 1990s and consider the British Labour party and its (re)branding to New Labour. Critical observers of the time cast the party's stance as presenting the party as 'a new, modernised "saleable product"'.[59] This placed publicity at the forefront of its strategy.[60] New Labour's branding strategy included the traditional exercises of updating the party's logo and visual identity as well as the party's 'style' in general, which was to be aligned with 'Cool Britannia'.[61] A photograph of Tony Blair, then-Prime Minister, and Noel Gallagher, lead guitarist of the rock band Oasis, at a reception at No. 10 Downing Street, became the iconic image of the new cool politics.

But the image campaign also had substantive implications, demon-strating the *internal* effect of branding.[62] During the mid-1990s, a new communications strategy was devised around the consistent emphasis on the importance of a unified message, 'one developed through a series of common themes through which all party actors speak with one voice'.[63] From leadership speeches to policy launches to the private lives of leading party figures, they all became 'public events', scripted and curated.[64] When Tony Blair became prime minister in 1997, a new ministerial handbook was published, which stated that 'all major inter-views and media appearances, both print and broadcast, should be agreed with the No 10 Press Office before any commitments are entered into'.[65] The communications team not only influenced how Labour's policy was communicated but also the policies themselves, giving them very real political power. Perhaps the most notable policy amendment, one

---

[58] Cutler, 'Private Power and Global Authority' 152. See also terms that relay this idea of the market as a sphere of nature such as business 'ecosystems'. John Patrick Leary, *Keywords: The New Language of Capitalism* (Haymarket Books 2018), 72–76.

[59] Richard Heffernan, 'Media Management: Labour's Political Communications Strategy' in Gerald R. Taylor (ed.), *The Impact of New Labour* (Palgrave Macmillan 1999) 51.

[60] Ibid 52.

[61] Ibid.

[62] Moor, 'Rise of Brands' 4, referencing Taylor, 'Impact of New Labour'.

[63] Ibid.

[64] Ibid.

[65] UK Cabinet Office, *Ministerial Code. A Code of Conduct and Guidance on Procedures for Ministers*, July 1997, 88.

striking to the heart of the party's values, was the reformation of the party constitution's Clause Four.[66] Clause Four contained the commitment to 'common ownership of the means of production, distribution, and exchange'. This constitutional clause had defined the socialist and working-class interests in party politics, particularly in the early twentieth century when the party was founded (the original version was drafted in 1917 by Sidney Webb). In 1995, as freshly elected party leader, Tony Blair won a vote to amend Clause Four. With its marketing practices, the Labour Party was turning away from social(ist) values and towards market values. The example of the Labour Party illustrates the more general societal move from social value to market value that was becoming normalised during the decade.

Marketing practices beyond the corporate sphere are today taken for granted 'from charity fundraising and "human resources" management to the design of tax forms and the coordination of Olympic bids'.[67] What I have tried to highlight in the above is that this corporate move is not simply cosmetic; it marks a shift in the most fundamental aims and values of the relevant actor.

3.3.5   Contradictions and Backlashes

Although (or perhaps *because*) the 1990s marked the 'height of consumerism' in a timeline of branding,[68] anti-capitalist movements were gaining strength towards the late 1990s. On a consumer level, a distrust towards (super)brands such as Nike emerged. This distrust took on a political flavour, as documented in Klein's *No Logo*. Klein's critique of branding had an explicit political motive, namely to fuel a fledgling grassroots movement, 'a vast wave of opposition squarely targeting transnational corporations'.[69] This call for a movement coincided with the so-called Battle of Seattle. In 1999, protesters gathered in Seattle, where the WTO Ministerial Conference was held. As with most movements of this kind, the protesters' motivations varied, from those concerned about consumer rights, to climate activists, to anti-capitalists. A unifying theme of the protesters was a worry about growing corporate power and its global juridification. There was one point, however, at

---

[66] Michael White, 'Blair defines new Labour', *The Guardian*, 5 October 1994.
[67] Moor, 'Rise of Brands' 5.
[68] Johnson, 'Branding' 15.
[69] Klein, 'No Logo' xviii.

which both adversaries of and advocates for the WTO converged. In the words of Ruth Buchanan, there was 'a considerable degree of consensus about the nature of the "global" and the need for a certain type of legal regime to govern it'.[70] This convergence of the imagination of the global and the promise of the law for ordering the global was ultimately what allowed for the reformism that followed. Buchanan (prophetically) expresses concern about the global justice movement's proceduralist reforms, focusing on accountability and transparency, a preoccupation that could undermine substantive change.[71] The subsequent negotiations, the 'Doha Development Round', met some of the proceduralist reform demands, and also proclaimed the need for a 'humanising globalisation'. Even from its very centre, this idea was acknowledged as a blatant act of marketing. WTO director-general at the time, Mike Moore, is quoted as declaring 'We've got to rebrand!'.[72] The anti-globalisation movement from below lost momentum, while only minor concessions were made by the WTO.[73] The diminished enthusiasm for a demand for global justice from below may also in no small part be due to the unifying politics of the war on terror post 9/11. For those who remember this period, the calls to go shopping as a form of patriotism may still echo. 'Get down to Disney World!' urged President Bush two weeks after the attacks in a (bizarre) consumerist defiance against terror.[74]

Branding proved to be highly adaptable to trends, to counter-cultural trends, even to anti-capitalist trends. For example, grunge and hip-hop, which were both counter-cultural politically relevant music movements highlighting issues of class and race inequality, became highly commercialised. Symptomatic of the absorption of counter-culture was that new brands emerging in the late 1990s and 2000s were those that tapped into desires for 'authenticity'. Testament to this new consumer trend was, according to brand consultant Michael Johnson, the 1999 launch of smoothie makers Innocent, with the tag-line 'Tastes Good, Does Good'.

---

[70] Ruth Buchanan, 'Perpetual Peace or Perpetual Process: Global Civil Society and Cosmopolitan Legality at the World Trade Organization' (2003) 16 *Leiden Journal of International Law* 673–699, at 675.

[71] Ibid.

[72] Quoted in Kristen Hopewell, *Breaking the WTO: How Emerging Powers Disrupted the Neoliberal Project* (Stanford 2016) 74 and in Quinn Slobodian, *Globalists: The End of Empire and the Birth of Neoliberalism* (Harvard University Press 2018) 276.

[73] Slobodian. 'Globalists' 276.

[74] 'At O'Hare, President Says "Get On Board"', Remarks by the President to Airline Employees, 27 September 2001, *The White House, President George W. Bush Archives*.

The ingredients were simple, the company was a humble start-up of three college friends, and they donated a significant amount of their sales to charity.[75] Branding was highly adaptable to its critics, with justice or cause branding turning into a multi-million business.[76]

3.4 International Law in the 1990s

Akin to the marketing industry, the 1990s was a decade of great optimism for the discipline of international law. On 17 November 1989, a mere eight days after the fall of the Berlin Wall, the UN General Assembly declared the period 1990–1999 as the 'United Nations Decade of International Law'. The main purpose of the new decade should be, *inter alia*:

(a) To promote acceptance of and respect for the principles of international law;
(b) To promote means and methods for the peaceful settlement of disputes between States, including resort to and full respect for the International Court of Justice;
(c) To encourage the progressive development of international law and its codification;
(d) To encourage the teaching, study, dissemination and wider appreciation of international law.[77]

Up until the late 1980s, the discipline of international law in the West had been considered as the exclusive remit of diplomats and government lawyers. Diplomatic and territorial disputes were up to this point viewed as the bread-and-butter part of the West's engagement.[78] The teaching of international law was regularly relegated into a marginal position in law schools, much to the dismay of those teaching the discipline, who

---

[75] Johnson, 'Branding' 281. By 2014, Coca-Cola owned 90 per cent of Innocent shares.

[76] 'Brand value' – the value of a having a recognisable brand name – is indeed a multi-trillion business. An industry-wide recognised ranking, the *Brandz™ Top 100 Most Valuable Global Brands*, found that the total brand value of the Top 100 brands was US$ 4.7 trillion in 2019; available at: https://brandz.com/admin/uploads/files/BZ_Global_2019_WPP.pdf.

[77] United Nations General Assembly Resolution 44/23, 'United Nations Decade of International Law', 60th plenary meeting at the 44th session (17 November 2019) UN Doc A/RES/44/23.

[78] This view is symptomatic of the sanitisation of the struggles for self-determination and the New International Economic Order by the Global South, which were played out under a specific international legal vocabulary and international legal institutions.

regularly repeated its relevance to global affairs.[79] The early 1990s, however, were to promise status and recognition for the international lawyer. International law, in the words of Philippe Sands, 'went public'. The discipline, until then largely operating 'in the corridors of foreign ministries', moved into 'the boardrooms of businesses, the lobbying newsletters of non-governmental organisations (NGOs), and the front pages of newspapers.'[80] Naturally, a general declaration of international law's importance could not itself make it so. The discipline could only garner attention and resources because certain conditions provided fertile ground for its resonance.

Just as the success of marketing and the rise of branding in the 1990s were described in the context of the incorporation and definition of new demands for individualism, technologies of visibility, global ordering, and the consolidation and concentration of power, these impulses are also relevant to the success of international law, and more specifically of ICL, in the 1990s.

The collapse of the Soviet Union not only provided new market opportunities for marketing, it also provided opportunities for international law. And as with marketing, international law not only expanded in the 1990s, it also partly reimagined itself. Most importantly for the purpose of understanding global justice projects is that a new accountability regime emerged, conceptualised and backed by an influential anti-impunity movement. This new regime included the setting up of two ad hoc criminal tribunals by the UN Security Council (the ICTY and the ICTR), the establishment of hybrid tribunals in the late 1990s/early 2000s, and the signing of the Rome Statute for the ICC in 1998. Such institutional flurry culminated in what has been described as the 'new tribunalism'.[81] One cannot help but take note of the adjective 'new' attributed to all these developments. The accountability regime and its institutions were, as with marketing at the time, based on the recognition of the currency of symbolism and lifestyle aspirations. Three notable shifts occurred in international law relevant to marketised global justice: a new interventionism legitimised through references to humanitarianism and development; the

---

[79] See for example Michael W. Reisman, 'The Teaching of International Law in the Eighties' (1986) 20 *The International Lawyer* 987–995, describing international law as a 'boutique course'.

[80] Philippe Sands, *Lawless World: Making and Breaking Global Rules* (Penguin 2006) 15.

[81] Thomas Skouteris, *The Notion of Progress in International Law Discourse* (T. M. C. Asser Press 2010) 164–179.

consolidation of an international economic order that de-politicised issues of redistribution; and the shift from human rights as a means for state accountability to individual criminal accountability as a means of state power.

3.4.1 New Interventionism

A distinct feature of international law in the 1990s was the legitimation of military interventionism under the labels of 'humanitarianism' and 'development', whereby interventionism was increasingly acceptable in internal conflict. Legally sanctioned interventionism took on many forms. The overcoming of the Cold War stalemate in the UN Security Council led to a burst of activity, with the number of resolutions doubling from 1989 to 1991 alone.[82] Increasingly, these resolutions authorised the use of force, invariably with operations led by the United States. In 1990, the UN Security Council authorised the use of force against Iraq, delegating power to a US-led coalition in support of Kuwait.[83] The military invasion was codenamed *Operation Desert Shield*. In 1992, the Security Council authorised the US-led multinational force United Nations Task Force UNITAF to use force in Somalia against anyone obstructing humanitarian aid.[84] The invasion of Somalia was named *Operation Restore Hope*. Following the coup that overthrew elected President Aristide in Haiti in 1991, the UN Security Council tested its new-found strength in multiple ways, deploying peacekeeping missions (no less than five during the 1990s), and imposing embargos. In 1994, the UN Security Council, for the first time, authorised the use of force to restore democracy in a Member State, stating its grave concern about 'the significant further deterioration of the humanitarian situation'.[85] A US-led coalition subsequently invaded Haiti under the operation name *Operation Uphold Democracy*. From a marketing perspective, these histrionic codenames cannot escape our attention. Moreover, we begin to see more clearly that the 'optimism' about

---

[82] *Resolutions adopted by the Security Council in 1989*, United Nations Security Council, available at: www.un.org/securitycouncil/content/resolutions-adopted-security-council-1989; *Resolutions adopted by the Security Council in 1991*, United Nations Security Council, available at: www.un.org/Docs/scres/1991/scres91.htm.

[83] United Nations Security Council Resolution (UNSC Res) 678 (29 November 1990).

[84] UNSC Res 794 (3 December 1992).

[85] UNSC Res 940 (31 July 1994).

international law in the 1990s was distinctly reserved for a small set of powerful states.

The UN Security Council expanded its powers for the 'responsibility for the maintenance of international peace and security', as set out in the UN Charter, to unprecedented forms when it decided to establish international criminal tribunals. Via UN Security Council Resolution 827, it breathed life into a tribunal dedicated to the prosecution of persons responsible for serious violations of international humanitarian law in the territory of the former Yugoslavia. The resolution also expressed the Security Council's conviction that the tribunal would put an end to the crimes and 'would contribute to the restoration and maintenance of peace'.[86] Rather than spelling the end to UN-authorised military intervention, this was to be an additional tool in the expanding tool-box of interventionism. The ad hoc tribunal model was repeated just one year later with the establishment of an ad hoc tribunal for Rwanda. In Resolution 955, the Security Council acknowledged the internal nature of the conflict by stating its conviction that the tribunal 'would contribute to the process of national reconciliation and to the restoration and maintenance of peace'.[87]

When Stephen John Stedman wrote in Foreign Affairs in 1992 that the '"new interventionism" ... combines an awareness that civil war is a legitimate issue of international security with a sentiment for crusading liberal internationalism',[88] he put his finger on an emerging trend. An intervention in the internal affairs of a state, hitherto running up against the constraint of the principle of sovereignty, was possible if legitimised on humanitarian grounds. UN Security Council Resolution 688 of 1991, which deemed that the Iraqi government's internal acts of aggression could be read as a threat to international order, was considered particularly significant. This reasoning was to be tested when humanitarian intervention was delinked from UN Security Council authorisation. In the late 1990s, when no resolution authorising the use of force could be obtained from the UN Security Council, NATO intervened anyway. Aerial bomb attacks were launched against the then-Federal Republic of Yugoslavia on behalf of Kosovo. International lawyers twisted and turned to nevertheless condone the intervention, with an ensuing

---

[86] UNSC Res 827 (25 May 1993).
[87] UNSC Res 955 (8 November 1994).
[88] Stephen John Stedman, 'The New Interventionists' (1992 1993) 71(1) Foreign Affairs 1–16.

awkward debate on its 'illegal but legitimate' nature.[89] Indicating the new
influence of (academic) international lawyers, this terminology was
carried forward in the principle of 'humanitarian interventionism'.
Although contested, humanitarian intervention nevertheless became the
widely acknowledged term for intervention without UN Security Council
approval. The literature on the Kosovo intervention began to locate
humanitarian values not within the UN system, but within the more
amorphous *international community*.[90] Despite the use of the term
'international', this was in fact a consolidation of the move from internationalism (as concerning action predominantly between states) to
globalism (as concerning action between a variety of actors). The moral
compass was increasingly placed within a space that transcended the
usual international sphere, which was viewed as too 'political'. Despite
the shifted site of legalised morality, the conviction about the need for
intervention, ultimately through military response, remained the same.[91]
This conviction became the orthodox view on humanitarianism, conveniently (and worryingly) evading the questions of violence and injustice effected in the name of internationalism. Humanitarianism
consequently became complicit in the marginalisation of peace projects
based on pacifism or diplomacy.

The 'new interventionism', prompted in part by the growing popular-
ity of the human rights discourse, spurred a rethinking of sovereignty.
Sovereignty was reconceptualised from a possible vehicle for economic
redistribution (as was suggested by states of the Global South in the
1960s and 1970s) and from a privilege (as suggested in the Western focus
on diplomatic relations) to a *responsibility*. It led to a new identity for
international lawyers. International lawyers were able to cast themselves
as belonging to the defenders and enforcers of a moral legality; they could
identify with a heroic mould.[92] Writing in the early 1990s, David

---

[89] Independent International Commission on Kosovo, *The Kosovo Report: Conflict,
International Response, Lessons Learned* (Oxford University Press 2000).

[90] Anne Orford, 'Muscular Humanitarianism: Reading the Narratives of the New
Interventionism' (1999) 10 *European Journal of International Law* 679–711, at 680.
One of the main proponents of the idea of an 'international community' was German
international law professor Christian Tomuschat. See for example, Christian Tomuschat
(ed.), *Kosovo and the International Community: A Legal Assessment* (Brill 2002). See also
Christian Tomuschat, 'The International Community' in *Collected Courses of the Hague
Academy of International Law* (Brill/Nijhoff, 1993).

[91] Orford, 'Muscular Humanitarianism'.

[92] Hilary Charlesworth, 'International Law: A Discipline of Crisis' (2002) 65(3) *Modern Law
Review* 377–392, at 387.

Kennedy described international law as 'an arena of desire and fantasy'.[93] Interventionism became the domain of action, of being committed to order. Those opposed to interventionism were cast as passive or committed to chaos. Anne Orford explains how this 'muscular humanitarianism' created a powerful sense of self as intervention narratives operate not only, 'in the realm of state systems, rationality and facts, but also in the realm of identification, imagination, subjectivity and emotion'.[94] Identification, imagination, subjectivity, and emotion are key objects of persuasion, as found in the marketing industry. But the parallels with marketing do not end there. The individual of action, who is decisive and takes risks, as the type of 'muscular humanitarian' described by Orford, has the character traits commonly associated with an entrepreneur. The individualism associated with the new interventionism was increasingly fusing with positive associations of market actors. This insight allows us to reconsider the opening sentence of this section, namely that the 1990s was a decade of optimism for the discipline of international law. We are reminded that this was a time of optimism only for some, for those at the centre of power. It was not a time of optimism for those who were subject to interventions, or for those who were in other ways not aligned with the US-centred policies of interventionism.

Notably, privatisation of interventionism made an entrance in a big way in the 1990s. As the necessity for conventional military budgets was questioned after the Cold War, these budgets were often restructured as multi-million dollar contracts. Activities that had previously been part of the state military were contracted out to private businesses, a model particularly favoured by the US government.[95] After several successful partnerships between state militaries and security corporations, private contracting (from security provisions to fully fledged warfare), grew exponentially in the 1990s. The US Department of Defense sets out that the ratio in the Iraq interventions was 1:1 in the relationship of military to contracted personnel. In Afghanistan interventions, the ratio of contracted personnel outstrips that of the

---

[93] David Kennedy, 'Autumn Weekends: An Essay on Law and Everyday Life' in Austin Sarat and Thomas R. Kearns (eds.) *Law in Everyday Life* (University of Michigan Press 1993), 191–235, at 231.

[94] Orford, 'Muscular Humanitarianism' 683.

[95] See, for example, P. W. Singer, *Corporate Warriors: The Rise of the Privatized Military Industry* (Cornell University Press 2011).

military 1.4:1. This is in comparison to a 1:7 ratio in World War II.[96] These private military corporations (PMCs) absorbed much of the ex-military labour floating around the market after the Cold War (and after decolonisation) downsizing of government armies. Meanwhile, technologies of warfare were changing at a rapid pace, decreasing the need for direct combat and increasing expertise in the operation of advanced technological weapons. PMCs signed huge contracts with governments; interventionism became an enormously profitable business.[97] In the new accountability regime of criminal law, the contracting of interventionism also (conveniently) shifted responsibility to individual contractors. If involved in what would conventionally have been called war crimes, the legal remedy would simply be the termination of the contract, mostly with the individual contractor. Or, if the crimes had become the object of public debate, as was the case with Blackwater's crimes in Iraq, the government could terminate the contract with the corporation itself.[98] States were able to distance themselves from the crimes committed by distancing themselves from the corporations in question. Indeed, the story of the terminated contract does not end there. Corporations, as opposed to state militaries, can 'rebrand' and, crucially *rename* themselves. Xe Services was the rebranded name of Blackwater, which returned to secure higher contracts than ever before.[99] For our purposes of understanding the marketisation of global justice, this illustrates not only that business logic progressively crept into the areas reserved for state action and democratic contestation, but that there is an explicit and real corporatisation at play.

---

[96] This information is available on the Defense Pricing and Contracting web pages of the Office of the Under Secretary of Defense for Acquisition and Sustainment at: www.acq .osd.mil/dpap/pacc/cc/history.html. Precise data on contracting is difficult to attain as private businesses are not required to provide data on request.

[97] Business research company Freedonia estimates that the global security market was at approximately US$ 152.5 billion in 2009. Freedonia, *World Security Services: Industry Study with Forecasts for 2014 & 2019* (The Freedonia Group 2011).

[98] The private security company Blackwater, founded in 1997, lost its contract with the US government following a scandal in which Blackwater employees shot at Iraqi citizens in Baghdad's Nisour Square.

[99] In 2011, the former Blackwater corporation was renamed again, this time to Academi. On the subsequent contracts secured, see: Kate Brannen, 'Blackwater's Descendants Are Doing Just Fine', *Foreign Policy*, 1 July 2014.

3.4.2   An International Economic Order

The above examples are indicative of the importance of the market for international law. In the 1990s, legal instruments and institutions were set up for the consolidation and protection of global trade. Globalisation, the new term *du jour* in this decade, was to become the rhetorical driver for this consolidation. Consolidation came in the form of new trade and investment treaties and organisations. Generally, these multilateral or bilateral treaties required a relaxation of state regulation and a simultaneous state obligation to protect the free flow of capital. The relationship between globalisation and international law became 'mutually reinforcing'.[100] Activities associated with globalisation increased the demand for international law, particularly international economic law, and in turn international economic law facilitated the international flow of goods, capital, people, and ideas.[101] Such mutual reinforcement implies a win-win situation for market liberalisation (and marketing). The state had a definitive role in this process, at once expected to construct walls around the market as well as expected to not interfere with these walls once they are erected. International law was to facilitate this process.

> [The state] must set up those military, defence, police and legal structures and functions required to secure private property rights and to guarantee, by force if need be, the proper functioning of markets. [. . .] State interventions in markets (once created) must be kept to a bare minimum [. . .].[102]

Quinn Slobodian argues that the 'turn to law' is key for understanding the formation of the neoliberal order. In Europe, the European Economic Community (the European common market system predating the European Union) and, on a global scale, the WTO were 'apparatuses of juridical power to encase the market beyond democratic accountability'.[103] This juridical power was bestowed upon the WTO when it was established as part of the reforms of the General Agreement on Tariffs and Trade (GATT). The GATT had only ever been intended as a provisional agreement on world trade; so with their envisioning of a global

---

[100] Jeffrey L. Dunoff and Joel P. Trachman (eds.), *Ruling the World? Constitutionalism, International Law, and Global Governance* (Cambridge University Press 2009) 5
[101] Ibid.
[102] David Harvey, *A Brief History of Neoliberalism* (Oxford University Press 2007) 2.
[103] Slobodian, 'Globalists' 266.

organisation for trade, the GATT reformers were more ambitious. They had in mind the template of the European model of governance. The European model was to be scaled up to the global, under the auspices of a proclaimed 'international rule of law'.[104] The WTO was, according to Slobodian, the culmination of a vision of neoliberalism advocated by German-speaking lawyers and economists, what he calls the 'Geneva School'. The defining role of the Geneva School (as opposed to its more *laissez faire* cousin the Chicago School), was the role of the state in ensuring a stable global economic order.[105] Historically, these lawyers and economists believed that democracy could be problematic for the free flow of capital. All efforts were therefore made to construct institutions that prevented the politicisation of the economy, following in particular the liberal model of a separation between the public and the private sphere. Regardless of whether the Geneva School really did possess the influence claimed by Slobodian, the enhancement of the judiciary and the legalisation of social relations was to become a crucial element in an international economic system. Ntina Tzouvala describes this as '"neoliberal legality" as a distinct kind of capitalist legality.'[106]

Once the WTO was in place, the juridical function was once again 'scaled up' to a debate on the constitutionalisation of the WTO. In the first issue of the first volume of the *Journal of International Economic Law* of 1998, Ernst-Ulrich Petersmann – a key advocate of an international economic constitution – elevates the political-economic project to a project of freedom:

> The worldwide guarantees of freedom, non-discrimination, intellectual property rights, and quasi-judicial dispute settlement procedures in WTO law illustrate that liberal international trade organizations can serve 'constitutional functions' for the protection of freedom, non-discrimination, private property rights and access to courts across frontiers.[107]

---

[104] Ernst-Ulrich Petersmann, *The GATT/WTO Dispute Settlement System: International Law, International Organizations and Dispute Settlement* (Kluwer 1997) 28–29.

[105] Slobodian, 'Globalists' 12.

[106] Ntina Tzouvala, 'Neoliberalism as Legalism: International Economic Law and the Rise of the Judiciary' in Ben Golder and Daniel McLoughlin (eds.), *The Politics of Legality in a Neoliberal Age* (Routledge 2017) 116–133.

[107] Ernst-Ulrich Petersmann, 'How to Promote the International Rule of Law? Contributions by the World Trade Organization Appellate Review System (1998) 1(1) *Journal of International Economic Law* 25–48, at 31.

But the dream of an integrated global economic order, kept in place through a corresponding constitution, was in danger of being the meta-phorical baby thrown out with the bathwater as the anti-globalisation protests in Seattle arose. Responding to the call of protesters who had mobilised against the 1999 Seattle WTO Ministerial Conference, a new 'humanised' idea of globalisation was introduced. This is the 'rebrand' mentioned above. Petersmann too adapted the narrative from inter-national rule of law to human rights law. He could not have been more explicit than the opening line of an article from 2000, which begins 'Human rights and liberal trade rules (including WTO rules) are based on the same values.'[108]

Meanwhile, another institution concerned with global economic policy, the International Monetary Fund (IMF), continued its policies of structural adjustment programmes, introduced in the 1970s, including the forced opening of markets as a further form of institutionalised economic interventionism. When countries experienced debt or currency crises, the IMF promised loans conditional on market-based reforms. Such reforms forced an opening up of the economy to global trade, foreign investment, and a borrower's economy. The IMF requires members 'to allow their currency to be exchanged for foreign currencies freely and without restriction'.[109] Loans were (and continue to be) attached to a particular type of 'conditionality', which regularly leads to domestic austerity politics, a diminution of public spending, and there-fore a squeeze on public healthcare, education, community projects, and other public services. In turn, conditions for businesses are eased to attract foreign investors and privatisation of public sector companies. In the 1990s, East Asian and Latin American states in particular received loans from the IMF tied to these conditions.[110] Interventionism by the IMF, justified under the term 'development', deepened the inequalities between the Global South and the Global North.

---

[108] Ernst-Ulrich Petersmann, 'The WTO Constitution and Human Rights' (2000) 3 *Journal of International Economic Law* 19–25, 19.

[109] David Driscoll, 'The IMF and the World Bank: How Do They Differ?', *International Monetary Fund*, 1 June 1995.

[110] The Latin American IMF programmes began in the 1980s as a purported remedy to its 'debt crisis'. For critical accounts of that time, see for example: Eric Touissant, *Your Money or Your Life: The Tyranny of Global Finance* (Haymarket Books 1999). More recently, see Ernst Wolff, *Pillaging the World: The History and Politics of the IMF* (Tectum Wissenschaftsverlag 2014). See also Naomi Klein, *The Shock Doctrine* (Penguin 2008).

It was in the 1990s, then, that the global economic order was sanctioned through international law and its institutions. Human rights law, previously seen and utilised as an expression of resistance against hegemonic power, particularly hegemonic state power, was – as we saw in Petersmann's descriptions of human rights – in the 1990s aligned ever closer with the state.[111] As the star of ICL rose, and began to merge with human rights law, international law was increasingly used as a means to protect capital. This not only aligned international law with the market, but also with marketing practices.

3.4.3   The Rise of Individual Criminal Accountability

The alignment of human rights with state power is described by Stephen Hopgood as a move from *human rights* to *Human Rights*, whereby the former is a bottom-up movement and the latter is a state-led institutionalisation.[112] The shift can also be described from a legal professional perspective as moving from Defence (defending against the power of the state) to Prosecution (prosecuting on behalf of the state). 'Today', wrote Karen Engle in 2015, 'to support human rights means to favour criminal accountability ...'.[113] This shift, from human rights to criminal law matters in the context of the new accountability regime in that human rights law predominantly concerns rights of individuals vis-à-vis the state, while ICL imposes responsibilities directly on individuals for the perpetration of the most serious crimes.

Prior to and up until the 1990s, human rights law as state accountability was the main contender for global justice – as Samuel Moyn famously put it, human rights was 'the last utopia'.[114] According to Moyn, the human rights movement did not, as is commonly assumed begin after World War II, but instead began in the 1970s. This occurred due to 'the collapse of prior universalistic schemes, and the construction of human rights as a persuasive alternative to them.'[115] We see some forerunners of the global justice sector in the 1970s. In Moyn's account of the recent

---

[111] For human rights as a mechanism against state power, see for example the anti-apartheid movement in South Africa. Saul Dubow, *South Africa's Struggle for Human Rights* (Ohio University Press 2012).

[112] Hopgood, 'Endtimes of Human Rights'.

[113] Karen Engle, 'Anti-impunity and the Turn to Criminal Law in Human Rights' (2015), 100 *Cornell Law Review* 1069–1128, at 1070.

[114] Samuel Moyn, *The Last Utopia: Human Rights in History* (Belknap Press Harvard 2012).

[115] Ibid 7.

history of human rights, Amnesty International (AI) played the 'vanguard role in the history of human rights advocacy'.[116] In the 1960s and 1970s, AI emerged as an NGO with a keen eye for practical innovations (writing letters to governments, a global membership scheme, and local chapters, for example) in combination with a profound understanding of the importance of symbolic gestures (lighting candles and using logos, for example).[117] And, perhaps most importantly, AI de-politicised its claims, stating instead that its causes transcended politics.[118] In the USA, this meant an explicit detachment of human rights advocates from the (political) civil rights movement. Human rights became the vessel for a moralistic-universal message. Engle picks up the AI story from the early 1990s when human rights advocacy moved from naming and shaming to finding ways to hold individuals criminally responsible.[119] She invites readers to consider how extraordinary this move was: AI's early campaigns of the 1960s were to a great extent directed towards *releasing* political prisoners; amnesty, not fighting impunity, was the primary objective.

The support for the anti-impunity movement in the 1990s came from a range of powerful civil society organisations, including AI, as well as an alliance of interested states with military and economic clout, and a highly emotive narrative, circulated by an eager media. It was the NGO Human Rights Watch that, in its report in 1992, called for the establishment of an international criminal tribunal to investigate war crimes in the former Yugoslavia.[120] A month later, the German Foreign Minister Klaus Kinkel, supported by French Foreign Minister Roland Dumas, called for the establishment of an international criminal court. Meanwhile, the United Nations Security Council was beginning to invoke obligations imposed upon individuals rather than states.[121]

---

[116] Ibid 131.
[117] Ibid 130.
[118] Ibid 132.
[119] Engle, 'Anti-Impunity' 1071.
[120] William Schabas, *The UN International Criminal Tribunals: The Former Yugoslavia, Rwanda and Sierra Leone* (Cambridge University Press 2012) 14, quoting Pierre Hazan, *La justice face à la guerre, De Nuremberg à la Haye* (Stock 2000) 37.
[121] James O'Brien, 'The International Tribunal for Violations of International Humanitarian Law in the Former Yugoslavia' (1993) 07 *American Journal of International Law* 639–659, at 640.

In 1993, UN Security Council Resolution 808 established the International Criminal Tribunal for the former Yugoslavia (ICTY).[122] It was not yet clear during the 1990s that human rights and ICL could be separate disciplines, or even competitors. The rise of the latter came first to be seen as part of the rise and affirmation of the former, complementing it, and only later as partly supplanting it.[123] The common understanding of the relationship between the two fields was that ICL's purpose was to *enforce* international human rights.[124] Speaking from the position of a long-standing career in international law, Anthony D'Amato remembers that when he was in law school in the 1960s 'the faculty, almost without exception, regarded the Nuremberg trials as a political aberration, as not "legal"'. Writing in 1990, D'Amato observes that the legal culture had changed. 'Nuremberg stands for the primacy, albeit in the limited areas of warfare and genocide, of individual rights over the state's. Human rights as a subject has an acknowledged place on the legal map.'[125] That which had made Nuremberg an 'aberration', namely individual criminal responsibility, had within thirty years already become part of the accepted legal and public discourse.

Moyn is correct in de-linking the human rights movement from the 1940s, but it was the anti-impunity movement of the 1990s that created the strongest visual and discursive links between its goals and values and the post-World War II world. It was in the 1990s that Nuremberg took on a near-mythical status, employed by an anti-impunity movement of NGOs, individual humanitarians, and certain states; it was a movement transitioning from human rights law to anti-impunity law. Nuremberg became the primordial moment for invoking state-backed intervention on the basis of global justice. In the 1990s, when persuasion became to be associated with market-oriented visual techniques and simple messages, the aesthetics of Nuremberg was foregrounded. This included the images, symbols, and objects of justice. In its aesthetics, much of the legitimation of the 1993 establishment of the ICTY, for example, was positioned with reference to the 1945–1946 Nuremberg trials. The circulation in the Western media of images of Bosnian Serb concentration camps put

---

[122] UNSC Res 808 (22 February 1993).

[123] Christine Schwöbel-Patel, 'The Comfort of International Criminal Law' (2013) 24(2) *Law & Critique* 169–191.

[124] For a strong enforcement emphasis see, for example, Antonio Cassese, 'Reflections on International Criminal Justice' (1998) 61(1) *Modern Law Review* 1–10.

[125] Anthony D'Amato, 'International Law in the Curriculum' (1990) 2 *Pace Yearbook of International Law*, 83–91, at 89.

ethnic cleansing and mass atrocity back on the agenda. What one might call the 'legitimation aesthetics' for the tribunal echoed memories of Nuremberg in numerous ways: the photographs of ethnic cleansing and mass graves were black and white (although colour photography had long been dominant), and the rhetoric was one that explicitly referred to Nuremberg.[126] Indeed, this rhetoric endures today. For example, the Nuremberg Academy, an academy set up to promote international criminal justice and human rights, held a workshop in 2017 titled: 'The revival of Nuremberg: ICTY – a milestone for the fight against impunity?'[127] The technologies of visibility, introduced during this time, also endure until today. Images of skulls and mass graves continue to constitute the dominant aesthetics of global injustice with a complementing idea of an aesthetics of court buildings as global justice.

As human rights in the guise of individual criminal accountability assumed a moral-historical link with the 1940s, the path was paved for 'a global structure of laws, courts, norms, and organisations that raise money, write reports, run international campaigns, open local offices, lobby governments, and claim to speak with singular authority in the name of humanity as a whole'.[128]. This also coincided with the deterioration of human rights as a rhetorically powerful mechanism to draw attention to issues of colonialism, apartheid, and self-determination. For Third World Approaches to International Law (TWAIL) scholars, there emerged a need to distinguish between human rights institutions and its discourse. As Balakrishnan Rajagopol has pointed out, the discourse of human rights 'provided a powerful weapon in the arsenal of the Third World ...'. And yet, 'the human rights discourse has also turned out to be a core part of hegemonic international law, reinforcing pre-existing imperial tendencies in world politics'.[129] Indeed, state officials

---

[126] On the website of the Mechanism for International Criminal Tribunals, the 'Establishment' of the ICTY is explicitly stated as being the first international war crimes tribunal 'since the Nuremberg and Tokyo trials', 'The Tribunal – Establishment', *United Nations International Criminal Tribunal for the former Yugoslavia*, available at: www.icty.org/en/about/tribunal/establishment

[127] 'The Revival of Nuremberg: ICTY – a Milestone for the Fight against Impunity?', *Nuremberg Academy, ICTY 2017*, available at: www.nurembergacademy.org/events/icty-2017/.

[128] Hopgood, 'Endtimes of Human Rights' viii–ix.

[129] Balakrishnan Rajagopal, 'Counter-Hegemonic International Law: Rethinking Human Rights and Development As Third World Strategy' in Richard Falk, Balakrishnan Rajagopal and Jacqueline Stevens (eds.) *International Law and the Third World: Reshaping Justice* (Routledge 2008) 767–783, at 768.

increasingly invoked human rights as the mechanism of choice to democratise (read: intervene in) states.

The establishment of the ICC marked the institutionalisation of the alignment of human rights with hegemonic state power. Following the establishment of the ICTY and ICTR, it became increasingly clear that tribunals would be financially unfeasible. This economic argument gave civil society institutions the influence they required to build on some political interest in the establishment of a permanent international criminal court. The NGO Coalition for the International Criminal Court (CICC) was established in 1995. Made up of AI, Human Rights Watch, and two dozen others, it was set up for one cause: to promote and lobby for an independent international criminal court. The CICC, which is still operative, had a key role to play in the transition of the rhetoric from international justice to global justice. Today, it urges on its website to 'join the fight for global justice'. Its Campaign for Global Justice has a simple formula:

> The problem: Uneven access to global justice for war crimes, crimes against humanity and genocide.
>
> The solution: Universal ICC membership, adoption of national laws to prosecute individuals for grave crimes and to cooperate with the ICC.
>
> The goal: 100% of humanity protected by the rule of law. Justice, deterrence of crime and peace.[130]

Even before its establishment in 1998, the court was already described as a global justice project. In particular the UN Secretary General at the time, Kofi Annan, did not miss an opportunity to promote the cause. In a speech in 1997, Annan introduced the idea of an international criminal court as one that he 'personally has great hopes for'.[131] He went on to say that there 'can be no global justice unless the worst of crimes – crimes against humanity – are subject to the law'.[132]

A key shift from 'international' to 'global' justice came with the proclaimed independence of the ICC from the UN. In the run-up to the conference in Rome in 1998, a 'like-minded group' was formed, with

---

[130] 'Campaign for Global Justice', *Coalition for the International Criminal Court*, available at: www.coalitionfortheicc.org/fight/global-justice-atrocities.

[131] 'International Criminal Court Promises Universal Justice, Secretary-General Tells International Bar Association' (Press Release) United Nations Secretary General/SM/6257 (12 June 1997).

[132] Ibid.

representatives from Germany, Canada, the Netherlands and other smaller European states, who pushed for an independent chief prosecutor, that is, independent of the UN Security Council. The Clinton administration delegates played a central role in the negotiations, attempting to push for greater power to be vested in the UN Security Council as regards a check on the prosecutor's powers.[133] A crucial point for the United States was that the Court should not be an institution of universal jurisdiction, meaning that the ICC should only have jurisdiction over nationals of its member states, and that US nationals should not be subjected to investigations by it. To make sure that there were no doubts as to how seriously the United States took the protection of its service men and women from foreign prosecution, it later passed the 2002 American Service-Members' Protection Act, otherwise known as 'The Hague Invasion Act'. The name says it all. The main breakthrough in negotiations at the Rome conference in 1998 came two days before the close of the conference, described by the disgruntled David Scheffer, Legal Advisor to the State Department, as a 'mysterious, closed-door and exclusionary process' run by a small number of delegates.[134] The final text was agreed on 17 July 1998, a day that was named 'World Day for International Justice', and has been commemorated at the ICC with a slew of (failed) social media campaigns ever since.[135] It was a notable moment in international relations when an international organisation was established without the membership of the United States. Despite not being a member state, the USA has continued to take a keen interest in the ICC.[136]

The alignment of human rights with state power through ICL shifted the audience of global justice to the centres of power. The simplified international criminal justice messages of 'evil warlords' and 'corrupt statesmen/rebel leaders' (from the Global South) appealed to those states holding economic power because it placed the emphasis clearly on physical violence rather than structural violence. It was a message that could easily be packaged for donor funding in the financial centres. With democratic pressures outside of the frame of ICL, it placed questions of

---

[133] For a summary of these negotiations see David Scheffer, 'The United States and the International Criminal Court' (1999) 93(1) *American Journal of International Law* 12–22.

[134] Ibid, 20.

[135] The ICC has been trying hard to make the 17 July celebration 'happen' on social media, trying out different hashtags and celebrity endorsements.

[136] Today, the ICC mainly receives kudos and a legitimacy boost when the United States displays its dismissal of the ICC.

redistribution to tackle inequality firmly outside of the global justice remit. ICL was, in short, a marketable idea.

3.4.4   Contradictions and Backlashes

In the preceding paragraphs, we have already gained a flavour of the contradictions of marketised global justice emerging in the 1990s: the anti-impunity movement shared roots with anti-globalisation and anti-state-power movements whilst also aligning with state power. ICL was both the first global institution to be established without the twentieth-century hegemon and a tool of hegemony too. Moyn observed something similar in the formation of the human rights movement thirty years earlier, namely, that it was both a part of the counter-cultural movement of 1968 as well as a beneficiary of its collapse.[137] ICL was both a part of the counter-hegemonic movement of the late 1990s as well as a benefi-ciary of its collapse. But this is not, as Moyn would have it, due to an 'accident' of history or due to competitors failing to live up to their promises.[138] Rather, the rise of ICL and demise of its competitors is due to ICL's unique ability to protect the power of certain states whilst upholding the global justice brand, shielding global justice from demands of redistribution whilst seeming to tackle the distributive inequalities, protecting the market from democratic contestation.

This raises the issue of a further seeming contradiction: as competition became the organising factor for global justice, the meaning of global justice did not become more diverse; it narrowed. In other words, with the centering of competition as determining the success of global justice projects, the choice of global justice projects decimated. During the 1990s, there were still strong alternatives to ICL as global justice. Contenders included truth and reconciliation projects (such as the South African Truth and Reconciliation Commission of 1994), transitional justice programmes, peace-building programmes, pacifist movements, and other alternative justice mechanisms. The focus on anti-impunity, however, narrowed the idea of global justice to exclude or invisibilise alternatives for a global audience. This contradiction of competition, as a seeming dynamic process of social justice that more often leads to monopolies or oligopolies, mirrors the contradiction of competition in capitalism. Contradicting capitalism's notion of freedom – and freedom of *choice* – is the fact that competition

---

[137] Moyn, 'The Last Utopia' 133.
[138] Ibid 7.

often results in monopoly or oligopoly, as stronger businesses drive out the weaker ones.[139] Neoliberalism creates the conditions for the power of super-brands, as the competition is either squeezed out of the market space or is swallowed in mergers and acquisitions processes.[140] Although this ultimately limits choice and, accordingly, the liberal adage of freedom, this contradiction is generally viewed as an aberration, which can be dealt with by competition law/anti-trust law.[141] Naturally, capitalists do not accept this form of monopoly when it is held by the state. David Harvey has explained that instead of being an aberration, however, monopoly power is *foundational* to the functioning of capital, existing in a contradictory unity with competition.[142] This chimes with the purpose of branding, which is not the creation of 'healthy' competition in a market but whose purpose is the elimination of the competition. Super-brands *want* monopoly power. Given the parallels with the way ICL works within the global justice sector, one could argue that those driving the project from an institutional perspective want to dominate the global justice market.

A further seeming contradiction, then, is that as international criminal justice was moving into a position of monopoly (and global legitimacy) within the global justice sector, the *criticism* of it grew louder. The consolidation of international power in a liberal legal humanitarianism in the 1990s somewhat oddly opened up a space for critique. Global solidarity and resistance movements were accompanied by a flourishing space of academic critique and activism. In the early 1990s, various strands of critical thought emerged. Feminist, post-colonial, Marxist, queer, and other critical or heterodox approaches were all added to the discipline of international law. But, we must acknowledge that the critique that finds the ear of practitioners of global justice is generally a 'liberal' critique, operating within the confines of liberal politics. Often, this critique is one of inclusion, pressing for the inclusion of more crimes to the core crimes catalogue, and suggesting the inclusion of more diverse voices in the debate on ICL. The widening of the ambit is at first blush not a bad thing, but, under marketisation this expansionism leads to the

---

[139] Harvey, 'Brief History of Neoliberalism' 67.

[140] Google, Amazon, and Apple are examples of well-known brands that became super-brands in the 1990s.

[141] Walter Frick, 'As More People Worry About Monopolies, An Economist Explains What Antitrust Can and Can't Do', *Harvard Business Review* (1 November 2017).

[142] David Harvey, *Seventeen Contradictions and the End of Capitalism* (Profile Books 2014) 134.

strengthening of the monopolistic position of ICL, as more ideas and people are subsumed under its remit.

3.5 Conclusion

Sarah Nouwen and Wouter Werner observed in 2016 that 'global justice' has been 'owned up' by ICL.[143] This chapter has positioned the roots of the 'owning up' of institutionalised global justice to lie in the 1990s. In that decade, marketing and global justice cross-fertilised to provide each other with meaning. Both fields incorporated and helped define new demands for individualism, technologies of visibility, global ordering, and the consolidation and concentration of power. The political-economic landscape of interventionism and financialisation prompted ICL to be the more competitive interpretation of global justice. At the most basic level, this tells us that global justice is not a neutral term, but one that has been aligned with a particular political project. This chapter honed in on branding as a marketing practice that transcends the product to co-opt social goods. The convergence between marketing and global justice has, despite its contradictions and despite backlashes, been astonishingly resilient (echoing the resilience of capitalism despite its contradictions). Although branding has moved on from the 1990s, particularly with the changed consumer landscape of social media, the use of values and social justice as marketing tools continues to this day. We saw this exemplified in the previous chapter with the Nike campaign featuring Colin Kaepernick. A further example is Pepsi's 'live bolder' 2017 campaign, which starred reality star Kendall Jenner taking part in a protest march. Jenner is seen skipping down the street with other pro-testers and at the end hands a police officer a Pepsi to de-escalate the rising tension. 'Live bolder' appears on the screen at the end of the ad. This form of marketised global justice appears both familiar as well as tedious to consumers. Within 24 hours, the ad was pulled following a huge backlash.[144] Cause-related marketing is generally thought to boost sales and brand loyalty, but, as with the Kendall Pepsi ad, brands can also over-do it. In extreme cases, this can lead to what is known in the

---

[143] Sarah Nouwen and Wouter Werner, 'Monopolizing Global Justice: International Criminal Law as Challenge to Human Diversity' (2015) 13 *Journal of International Criminal Justice* 157–176.

[144] Rebecca Nicholson, 'From Coke's Flower Power to Kendall Jenner's Pepsi Ad – How Ads Co-opt Protest', *The Guardian*, 5 April 2017.

industry as 'brandicide'. Unsurprisingly, both Kendall and Pepsi survived the backlash. Whether the global justice sector has caused the 'brandicide of genocide' is yet to be determined, and is discussed in more depth in the coming chapters.

A material historicisation of global justice teaches us that market-friendly iterations of global justice have been prioritised over alternatives. The periodisation of the marketisation of global justice has furthermore demonstrated the key role that international law played in the constitution and consolidation of the neoliberal order. What is hidden behind this dialectical relationship between marketing and global justice is a new understanding of value-creation. Although ideas such as revolution, democracy, and solidarity continue to carry political significance, arguably they have also been 'devalued' through their commodification. Chapter 4 deepens the analysis of value creation in marketised global justice, drawing on the history of marketisation from this chapter and the forms of persuasion and distraction discussed in the Chapter 2.

4

'A Picture Worth More Than a Thousand Words'

The Value of Global Justice

Business thrives on the ruins.[1]

4.1 Introduction

What is the value of global justice? This question must of course be answered in different ways depending on the meaning of 'value'. It can relate to *social* values – in particular, the moral compass of a group of people and its institutions – or it can relate to *market* values – in particular, the price at which an asset is tradable within a competitive setting. Anticipating at this early point in the chapter the climactic moment of the argument: the marketisation of global justice should be understood as the receding of social values in favour of market values. In (a historical materialist) economic theory of value, this can be mapped onto the receding of 'use-value' in favour of 'exchange value'. A critical component is that despite being present in the way in which values are perceived and legitimated, the market nevertheless remains hidden and de-politicised. This is the conjuncture between market and marketing.

International law is regularly considered as the legal 'expression' of global societal values.[2] This understanding may emerge by way of natural law ideas, namely that certain values exist prior to law. Or it may emerge from a positivist idea, namely that values are created through a practice of agreement. In any event, international law is regularly deemed to be a discipline that codifies, protects, and balances societal – and therefore *social* – values. Such values include human dignity, peace, accountability for wrongs, and environmental sustainability. The Rome Statute of the International Criminal Court (ICC) is frequently described as having

---

[1] Rosa Luxemburg, *Junius Broschüre, Die Krise der Sozialdemokratie [1916]* (Heptagon Verlag 2012) 2.

[2] Susan Marks, 'Value' (2016) 4(1) *London Review of International Law* 1–3, at 1.

enshrined universal values.[3] Social values as expressed through international law are generally thought of as separate to the everyday complex relationships of the market. Market values are believed 'to have an objective existence independent of, and analytically prior to, law'.[4] This means that market values tend to have a fairly narrow application in considerations about justice or law. The quantification of reparations calculations, or the quantification of damages for foreign investors are the few occasions when international lawyers explicitly deal with market value.[5] Consequently, market value merges with an understanding of 'fair market value' as a technical valuation technique in relation to assets. Social values as expressed in international law are therefore thought to exclude the market, and market values are largely thought to lie outside of the domain of international law. Marketisation, however, is the inflection, and ultimately colonisation, of social values with market values. Values that protect the market are given prominence but, crucially, these still come in the guise of social values – from human rights law, to global constitutionalism, to development.

This rather abstract hypothesis is supported here through a closer look at a medium of global justice that has taken on great importance in marketised global justice: the image. The use of imagery in international criminal law (ICL) is commonly justified through the need for publicity. Publicity is viewed as a necessary means of information. 'The publicity of hearings may extend beyond the courtroom', state the ICC's Regulations of the Court.[6] However, publicity is not (just) about information. Publicity, already definitionally, assumes an audience of consumers or donors and is therefore a communicative means of *exchange*.[7] The image

---

[3] 'International Criminal Court Marks Opening of Judicial Year 2019' (Press Release), ICC-CPI-20190118-PR1430 (18 January 2019).

[4] Marks, 'Value', 2.

[5] For example, Fuad Zarbiyev, 'From the Law of Valuation to the Valuation of Law? On the Interplay of International Law and Economics in Fair Market Valuation' in Theresa Carpenter, Marion Jansen, Joost Pauwelyn (eds.), *The Use of Economics in International Trade and Investment Disputes* (Cambridge University Press 2017).

[6] Regulation 21 refers to the broadcasting and publication of hearings before the ICC.

[7] The Oxford English Dictionary definition shows the development from the earlier and more general definition of the use as 'The quality of being public' to more recent definitions 'the publicizing or promotion of a product, person, concept, etc. ; the giving out of information for advertising or promotional purposes ' 'Publicity' in *Oxford English Dictionary* (3rd ed., Oxford University Press 2007).

that we follow on its publicity course is a photograph of Thomas Lubanga Dyilo of the Democratic Republic of the Congo (DRC) at the ICC.[8]

The image shows the defendant with this hands folded in front of his mouth, his elbows resting on the table in front of him. His gaze is lifted so that the lower whites of the eyes are visible. He is looking straight at the camera. Lubanga is wearing a shirt and a grey suit, of which only the top part of the lapels are visible. The expression is seemingly neutral, neither smiling nor frowning, but the slightly pursed lips indicate some form of strain. The photograph's circulation, I argue, illustrates the primacy of its exchange value as prioritised over its use-value. This particular photograph has travelled from the courtroom to news media, to non-governmental organisations (NGOs), to an artist's studio, and to an exhibition at the ICC's Assembly of State Parties. With each stop on its journey, the message of the image congealed further to one in which the ICC is the primary place for the fight against impunity and a legitimate 'dispenser' of global justice.[9] This was despite the trial of Lubanga being marred with all manner of problems and controversies. The image's journey demonstrates the move from use-value to exchange value on a scaled down version of marketised global justice. It therefore stands in for the marketisation of global justice writ large. After following the circulation of the photograph, the chapter closes with a stocktaking of marketised global justice so far, developing the critique of marketised global justice as mass distraction. Two points are highlighted in particular regarding the limits on what is *seen* as global justice: (a) the narrowing of visibility as impacting on a multiplicity of visions of global justice, and (b) the narrowing of visibility as rendering structural violence *in*visible.

While the previous chapters were made up of ingredients from marketing literature and international law scholarship (with a pinch of the attention economy and a sprinkling of intellectual property rights), this chapter goes deeper into literature on value, drawing on the work of theorists of political economy Karl Marx and Walter Benjamin as well as (more recently) Mariana Mazzucato. Literature exploring the political economy of visibility, by Jodi Dean and Susan Sontag in particular, completes the concoction.

---

[8] The photograph is distributed by ANP Foto. On request to reprint the photograph in this book, they asked for €4392.50 excl. vat for the licence rights.

[9] Adopting Tor Krever's terminology of 'dispensing' global justice. Tor Krever, 'Dispensing Global Justice' (2014) 85 *New Left Review* 67–97.

4.2 The Value of Global Justice

There has been a recent interest in theories of value by economists and lawyers alike.[10] Those studying neoliberalism tend to agree that it is essential to study 'value' in order to understand neoliberal techniques and technologies. The argument from the previous chapter is that something significant changed in the 1990s when the neoliberal project consolidated. In terms of economic theory, the processes of consolidation of neoliberalism cemented the idea of the subjectivity of (economic or market) value, building on an idea going back to the nineteenth century.[11] A very brief description of the subjectivity of value would be that value is determined by what the consumer considers to be of value. So value can be created by transferring ownership of a thing from one person to another without modification, simply because the other person values it more highly. In the hands of this person, the thing has attained greater value, which might also impact on its price.[12] Moving further back in history, and counterposed to the subjective theory is the objective theory. The objective (intrinsic) theory of value prevailed up until the nineteenth century, and still had its remnants in the way assets were calculated up until the 1990s. Here, value was determined by objective conditions, for example, the hours of labour required for production, the raw materials, and the quality of the labour. The labour theory of value is an example of an objective theory of value, which measures value through the labour required to produce a good or service.[13] This is based on the assumption that there must be a common social substance of all commodities outside of the commodity. This, according to Karl Marx, who built on economists Adam Smith and David Ricardo, is labour. Marx refined the labour theory of value to relate to 'socially necessary' labour time (the average labour time to produce a commodity).[14]

At the end of the nineteenth century, the swing from value determining price to price determining value coincided with the industrial

---

[10] In economics, see for example Mariana Mazzucato, *The Value of Everything: Making and Taking in the Global Economy* (Penguin 2018); in international law, see for example, Special issue on 'Value' (2016) 4(1) *London Review of International Law* 1–163.

[11] The subjective theory of value is attributed to the Austrian school of economics, beginning with the works of Carl Menger. For an overview, see George J. Stigler, 'The Economics of Carl Menger' 45(2) *Journal of Political Economy* (1937) 229–250.

[12] See Mazzucato, 'The Value of Everything' 6, 7.

[13] Adam Smith, *The Wealth of Nations* [1776] (Penguin 1982); David Ricardo, Ronald Max Hartwell (ed.) *Principles of Political Economy and Taxation* [1817] (Penguin 1971)

[14] Karl Marx, *Das Kapital* [1867] (Regnery Publishing 2009), chapter 12, 168.

revolution, workers demanding higher wages, and the industrial class in turn suppressing these demands.[15] The move away from the labour theory of value to the subjective theory of value displaces the labourer in the considerations of value, allowing the capitalist class of the nineteenth century to defend their appropriation of a larger share of output.

At the same time as workers were collectively organising and being repressed, there was an intellectual drive to make economics more technical and less political. The 'scientific' view of economics rather than the 'sociological' view prompted a new turn to statistics, indexes, and rankings. Economics and the market were increasingly described as having their own dynamics, only to be 'captured' by economists. By the 1920s, the prediction of markets was described as 'business barometers', already implying that 'the economy was like the weather, a sphere outside of direct human control.[16] As we recall from the introduction to Walter Lippmann (who coined the terms 'stereotype' and 'manufacturing consent'), a suspicion of the 'social' in economics paved the way for a separation of the market from democratic contestation, with the state placed in the position of protecting the market. Fast-forward to the 1970s when the United States allowed the dollar to 'float': the abandonment of a fixed currency (the post-War Bretton Woods arrangements of currencies measured against gold), gave way to the further consolidation of market demand dictating value. As already mentioned in the previous chapter, this marked a key point in the end of Keynesianism and the beginning of the consolidation of neoliberalism.[17] Many currencies across the globe followed the US example, further globalising subjective value and capital mobility.

Marketing, by its very nature, embraces the subjectivity of value, relying on it for value creation. Crudely put, if there were no marketing, all products could be sold at the cost of production. Marketing enables distortions of an equilibrium of supply and demand. According to Mazzucato, distortions should not all be viewed as 'value creation'. She proposes a clearer distinction between value extraction and value production based on the observation that value *extraction* is often confused

---

[15] Mazzucato, 'The Value of Everything' 7, 8.
[16] Quinn Slobodian, *Globalists: The End of Empire and the Birth of Neoliberalism* (Harvard University Press 2018) 61.
[17] Robert Leeson, *The Eclipse of Keynesianism: The Political Economy of the Chicago Counter-Revolution* (Palgrave New York 2000).

with value *creation*.[18] Marketing practices can increase the price of goods or services through making them more desirable but without needing to increase the quality of materials or labour, so without increasing their objective value – extracting value rather than creating value.

As the sports brand Nike is often the example used in marketing, let us briefly consider the production and marketing of running shoes. Two shoes are made with exactly the same materials and with the same time and skills spent on stitching, cutting, and gluing. One pair is adorned with a tick on the side (the Nike swoosh), the other pair with a lightning bolt. The Nike running shoes sell for four times the price of the lightning bolt shoes, which are sold in a budget supermarket. Marketing, and particularly branding, make this cleavage between objective value and price possible. The consumer is willing to pay the higher price as they believe that they are purchasing running shoes of higher value – even if they know that they are not necessarily of better quality.

In the global justice sector, we might conjure an image of two global justice actors that promise 'global justice'. Let us imagine that both actors are NGOs. One NGO directs resources into marketing: it creates a recognisable logo and a short and pithy slogan, which refers to a broad understanding of global justice that can appeal to a wide audience. It claims to be non-political, choosing to side with universal values rather than political struggles. This NGO uses and reuses the same photographs for all of its outlets, heart-wrenching images that at once attract and repel. The same message is repeated by all of its employees, volunteers, and donors until they finally also adopt the organisation's identity, making it their own. Supporters and donors of the organisation are invited to invest in 'awareness-raising campaigns'. All funds go into the dissemination of a message (accompanied by the logo and slogan). The other NGO, meanwhile, directs resources into the people working for it and into its projects. Its workers conduct research by speaking to individuals and organisations, looking at funding patterns and at exploitation, aiming to understand what is causing the injustice at root. This NGO takes a political stance in aligning with certain policies and critiquing others and has therefore aligned with labour movements and anti-imperial movements. With its supporters and detractors, this organisation has developed a means of struggle over understandings of global justice, organising and reorganising around it. This second organisation minimises the use of imagery,

---

[18] Mazzucato, 'The Value of Everything'.

slogans, and logos and rejects any business ideas that commodify the message. We know which of these two would generally be more successful at attracting resources in the neoliberal order.

4.2.1   Use-Value and Exchange Value

One way of explaining the success of the consumer-friendly global justice organisation is through distinguishing between means of communication, and in particular by distinguishing between the use-value and exchange value of these communicative means. The distinction relies on Marx's theorisation of value, according to which all commodities have a use-value and an exchange value. Use-value simply relates to the question: what is the commodity good for? Exchange value is a 'quantitative relation' and therefore relative.[19] The latter value is not the same as the price, but rather that which makes the commodity tradable – and therefore attain a price.[20] The exchange value of a commodity can be measured against other commodities (how much of one commodity can be exchanged for another commodity). Although originating in commodities, '[a]nalogous properties are found in other dimensions of the capital relation'.[21] Under capitalism, not only *things* are intended for exchange in the market. Bob Jessop explains that the worker is both a concrete individual with specific skills, knowledge, and creativity *as well as* an abstract unit of labour power substitutable by other such units or factors of production.[22] Money functions both as a 'national' currency circulating within a monetary bloc subject to state control *as well as* an international currency exchangeable against other monies in currency markets.[23] Land is 'a gift of nature' as well as 'a monopolistic claim on revenues'.[24] In each case, following Jessop, the latter is privileged over the former because neoliberalism 'privileges exchange-value over use-value'.[25] Applying this to global justice, one might say that global justice is both a means through which to address injustices in the world through

---

[19] Marx, 'Das Kapital' 2.

[20] The price is referred to as market value.

[21] Bob Jessop, 'The Heartlands of Neoliberalism and the Rise of the Austerity State' in Simon Springer, Kean Birch, Julie MacLeavy, *The Handbook of Neoliberalism* (Routledge 2016) 410–421.

[22] Ibid.

[23] Ibid.

[24] Ibid.

[25] Ibid.

political contestation *as well as* a tradable currency allowing the attraction of capital in a global market.

In the creation and primacy of exchange value is where the Marxist legal theorist Evgeny Pashukanis introduces the role of law. Law makes the exchange value possible on the basis of the abstraction inherent in the legal form. As a product attains value under capitalism, it also becomes ownable and inalienable. People acquire the capacity to be legal subjects and bearers of rights.[26] The relationship between the individual and objects manifests itself as the abstract will of the owner. This is based on the abstraction to legal subjectivity. For commodity exchange to take place, a formal abstract equality of the individuals involved must be recognised.[27] 'All concrete peculiarities which distinguish one representative of the *genus homo sapiens* from another dissolve into the abstraction of man in general, man as a legal subject.'[28] The legal-institutional aspect of neoliberalism, which extends the remit of exchange value, is therefore a key tool of transforming social values to market values. The market-friendly NGO in the above example is privileging the exchange value of global justice over its use-values. It is aligning itself with the immensely strong material (and therefore social and political) forces that demand commodification of social values.

4.2.2   Exchange Value and Visibility

Let us consider the structural link between capitalism and law in regard to exchange value and *visibility* a little further. 'In Marx's hands, value theory became a powerful tool for analysing society', states Mazzucato.[29] One particular aspect of this analysis relevant to our understanding of the marketisation of global justice refers to the commodity fetish. According to Marx, commodities take on a 'mystical character', an 'enigmatic character', something akin to 'the mist-enveloped regions of the religious world'.[30] This is not the hard economics that we might expect from political economy, but something that touches on affect. The social

---

[26] Evgeny B. Pashukanis, *Law & Marxism: A General Theory* [1929], trans. Barbara Einhorn (Pluto Press 1989) 112.

[27] 'Man becomes a legal subject by virtue of the same necessity which transforms the product of nature into a commodity complete with the enigmatic property of value', Pashukanis, 'Law & Marxism' 68.

[28] Pashukanis, 'Law & Marxism' 113.

[29] Mazzucato, 'Value of Everything' 57.

[30] Marx, 'Kapital' 38–39.

relationship, otherwise reserved for relationships with other people, is transferred to the relationship with the 'thing' – hence the use of the word 'fetish', as a reference to religious relationships between the human and God mediated through things. As already mentioned, spectacle shifts this alienation from the thing to the image; 'having' is no longer sufficient in the society of the spectacle, the visibility of having ('appearing') is key.[31] Walter Benjamin described this world of commodities and their visibility – in which use-value recedes into the background in favour of the glorification of exchange value that must be made visible – as a 'phantasmagoria'.[32] In the collection of essays compiled as *The Arcades Project*, Benjamin was particularly interested in the public exhibition of commodities in the nineteenth century. National and world exhibitions were huge events in nineteenth century Europe, attracting large visitor numbers to admire new manufactured products. 'World exhibitions are places of pilgrimage to the commodity fetish', wrote Benjamin.[33] Arguably foreseeing the attractions of surrender to the attention economy, Benjamin declared that the phantasmagoria is entered into *in order* to be distracted.[34]

Marx's law of value and an intuitive grasp of what Benjamin referred to as 'phantasmagoria' allows us to affirm again that marketised global justice is not about a casual adopting of the language of the market but rather that it signifies a shift in social values. Although market values become increasingly important, they do not become more available to political contestation but *less so*. Marketing is put to work to distract from political contestation, and images happen to be particularly potent tools for this distraction. Ultimately what remains is the empty shell of global justice in the form of 'devalued' notions of democracy, equality, and social justice. Marketing looks after this empty shell, making it nonetheless appear desirable.

4.3   A Global Justice Image

The image is not, therefore, just any old example of the political economy of global justice; it is a pivotal means by which exchange value is

---

[31] Guy Debord, *The Society of the Spectacle* (Black & Red 1984).
[32] Walter Benjamin, *The Arcades Project*, trans. Howard Eiland and Kevin McLaughlin (Harvard University Press 1999) 7.
[33] Ibid.
[34] Ibid.

prioritised over use-value. For global justice actors, images are a crucial form of communication with the public. There are numerous global justice exhibitions, documentaries, image-heavy websites, and cartoons. The enhanced use of imagery is not simply down to the truism that 'we live in a visual age',[35] nor is it simply due to new technologies of photography, mass communication, reproduction, and dissemination. Rather, the enhanced use of imagery is part of marketisation. A marketised form of global justice is also inextricably a visualised form of global justice.

Every object has multiple social use-values. An image's use-value mostly lies in its utility to visualise and to document. This means that it can be used as information and explanation. Typical tropes of global justice include the use of images to make the unimaginable imaginable, and the contention that an image can say 'more than a thousand words'. The photograph is typically the global justice actors' preferred medium of imagery. No doubt the preference for photography is due to a photograph's claim to truth. Indeed, photographs are often used in the courtroom as a form of evidence – an inanimate witness to the facts presented. 'A photograph', observed Susan Sontag in her famous book *On Photography*, 'seems to have a more innocent, and therefore more accurate, relation to visible reality than do other mimetic objects'.[36] Aside from photography, other common media in the global justice sector are film, paintings, drawings, and texts (images of written treaties, for example).

Global justice actors often justify the use of imagery by invoking its use for publicity. Publicity is even enshrined in the Regulations of the ICC as the reason to use photography in the courtroom.[37] But publicity is not simply about information; mostly its purpose is associated with *promotion* – it is a marketing practice.[38] Here we recall the marketing practices' common denominators, set out in Chapter 2 '*Ad*-Vocacy: What is Marketing Global Justice?': persuasion and distraction. Not only is this of interest in the context of what we know about competing actors in the attention economy, it also demonstrates that publicity is a tool utilised

---

[35] Roland Bleiker, 'Mapping Visual Global Politics', in Roland Bleiker (ed.), *Visual Global Politics* (Routledge 2018) 1.

[36] Susan Sontag, *On Photography* (Penguin 1979) 6.

[37] Regulation 21, Regulations of the Court, International Criminal Court, The Hague, 26 May 2004, ICC-BD/01-01-04.

[38] Oxford English Dictionary, 'Publicity'.

for acting in a competitive marketplace. According to Jodi Dean, publicity is a form of montisable communication which reconstitutes the public from political actors to consumers. The emphasis on making content 'public', according to Dean, 'provides a fetish screening the fact that there is no public that can act'.[39]

Before looking more closely at the circulation of the Lubanga photograph, let us briefly return to the phrase that an image is 'worth more than a thousand words' as a justification for an image's explanatory utility. As the term has taken on proverbial form, its history is difficult to trace. And yet, all histories of the phrase appear to lead to the advertising industry. The 'quotation sleuth' Burton Stevenson attributed the saying to Fred R. Barnard, national advertising manager of Street Railways Advertising.[40] Barnard had used variations of the phrase to create business for his advertising firm in the trade magazine Printer's Ink in 1921 and again in 1927 editions. He was, in a manner of speaking, advertising to advertise. The ad stated that advertisements for cakes would be much more effective if accompanied by 'an appetizing picture of the product'.[41] Linking imagery to the advertising industry allows us to place the proliferation of imagery in the context of a wider proliferation of communication through visuality. It also allows us to consider that a prioritisation of the exchange value of images is tied to an image's *circulation*.[42]

In the following, we will be tracking the journey, that is, circulation, of a photograph of Thomas Lubanga Dyilo, which was taken in July 2012 by Dutch photographer Jerry Lampen. Lampen had been hired by the media company ANP to take photographs at the ICC's sentencing decision of Lubanga. A few months earlier, Lubanga had been found guilty of war crimes.[43] Lubanga was founding member and president of a group who called themselves the Union des Patriotes Congolais (UPC), as well as

[39] Jodi Dean, *Publicity's Secret: How Technoculture Capitalizes on Democracy* (Cornell University Press 2002) 43.
[40] William Safire, 'On Language; Worth a Thousand Words', *New York Times*, 7 April 1996. Reference to Burton Stevenson, *MacMillan Book of Proverbs, Maxims and Famous Phrases* (Macmillan 1965).
[41] Ibid.
[42] See also Jodi Dean on content as contributions in Jodi Dean, *Democracy and Other Neoliberal Fantasies: Communicative Capitalism and Left Politics* (Duke University Press 2009).
[43] *The Prosecutor v. Thomas Lubanga Dyilo* (Judgment) ICC-01/04-01/06 (12 March 2012).

commander-in-chief of the Forces Patriotiques pour la Libération du Congo (FPLC), the military wing of the UPC. The group operated mainly in Ituri, one of the 26 provinces of the DRC. There had been continuous ethnic tensions in the Ituri and Kivu provinces since the 1990s, partly due to the refugee-overspill from the Rwandan genocide, and partly due to disputes about resources in the region, with Ituri being a gold- and mineral-mining region. Violence and political tensions caused the government of the DRC to self-refer its situation to the ICC in 2004.[44] From the outset, the prosecution's case was focused on crimes concerning the recruitment of child soldiers, whereby it could only investigate crimes committed since 2002, when the Rome Statute came into force. Lubanga was the first person arrested under a warrant issued by the ICC. The chief prosecutor at the time, Luis Moreno Ocampo, knew that the plight of children would create a compelling narrative. At a press conference in The Hague in 2006, marking the surrender to the court of Lubanga, Ocampo stated that 'Forcing children to be killers jeopardises the future of mankind.'[45] In case the gravity of the situation had not been made sufficiently clear with this statement, he also invoked the cases of World War II, the Balkans, Rwanda, and Sierra Leone, 'National states need help, that is why we need international justice. Congo is another example.'[46] As to Lubanga, the chief prosecutor relied upon the truth-telling powers of photography: 'We will show pictures of Thomas Lubanga Dyilo inspecting the camps where children were trained.'[47] Clearly exhilarated by his own words, Ocampo continued: 'For 100 years, a permanent international criminal court was a dream – This dream is becoming a reality.'[48] On 14 March 2012, Lubanga was found guilty of enlisting and conscripting children and using them to participate in hostilities.[49] Four months later, Lubanga was sentenced to fourteen years of imprisonment. It was on this day that the photograph of him was taken. Lubanga was transferred to a prison in the DRC in 2015.

---

[44] Ibid 63.
[45] Statement by Luis Moreno-Ocampo, chief prosecutor of the International Criminal Court, *Press Conference in relation with the surrender to the Court of Mr Thomas Lubanga Dyilo,* The Hague, 18 March 2006.
[46] Ibid.
[47] Ibid.
[48] Ibid.
[49] *Prosecutor v Lubanga,* Judgment.

4.3.1   Images in the Courtroom

Images can have different uses in the courtroom. As already noted, images can be used as evidence in the courtroom, or images in and of the *courtroom* itself can be used as evidence that justice is being done. The use-value of images in the courtroom (photographs, but also sketches, maps and so on) is primarily for information and verification. 'Photographs furnish evidence', stated Sontag.[50] That which may be doubted as an oral account can be proven with the image. Certainly, the images are still intended to persuade the judge or jury, or both, either in support of the prosecution's case or to support the defence's case. When it comes to images *of* the courtroom, the primacy of value of the images is different; here, the photographs are intended to be circulated.

The courtroom as the place from which images circulate was first tested with the Nuremberg trials after World War II. Here, both types of courtroom imagery coincided. Images shown as evidence were also circulated to a broader public. '[T]hese motion pictures speak for themselves in evidencing life and death in Nazi concentration camps', announced the assistant trial counsel for the prosecution before screening the documentary film *Nazi Concentration Camps* at the Nuremberg International Military Tribunal in 1945.[51] The photographs and film snippets that together make up the film, screened for the first time in the courtroom, are harrowing. Lawrence Douglas notes that it was not so much the images of atrocity that circulated in the journalism, diaries, and memoires; rather it was images from the courtroom: How the defendants reacted, how the judges reacted, and how the members of the public reacted, was a key part of the narrative of the emotive images.[52] From the perspective of posterity, where these images have been reproduced and circulated countless times, it is difficult to imagine the impact that the images will have had in explaining mass extermination of human life. After the fairly technical juridical meanderings of the first couple of trial days, these images showed the human loss of the war and the human degradation of the Jewish people. The use-value of these images was their ability to inform visually.

---

[50] Sontag, 'On Photography' 5.
[51] *Trial of the Major War Criminals before the International Military Tribunal, Nuremberg 14 November 1945–October 1946*, Official Text in the English Language, Volume II (Nuremberg Tribunal 1947) 433.
[52] Lawrence Douglas, *The Memory of Judgement: Marking Law and History in the Trials of the Holocaust* (Yale University Press 2001) 23–27.

Douglas stresses that Chief Counsel for the Prosecution Justice Jackson was emphatically opposed to introducing a 'human dimension' to the evidence, preferring to rely on documentation rather than eyewitnesses and survivor testimony. In view of spectacle as an analytic for ICL, it is notable that Jackson was worried about charges of hyperbole.[53] The *Nazi Concentration Camp* documentary was to be a middle-ground, with images doing the talking. 'Images, by not making their appeal to emotion explicit, provide a way to bring emotion to law despite law's expressed discomfort with emotions', states Rebecca Tushnet.[54] At the same time, we must not forget that the control over the dissemination of images is an important part of the communicative practice of victors' justice.

We return, then, to the ICC: The photograph of Lubanga in the courtroom appears to present some paradoxes. The gesture of Lubanga with his hands folded in front of his face as he gazes up might appear defiant. But his attire and posture are also calm and statesman-like. The 'monster' stereotype of defendants does not appear to be straight-forwardly served. As Sofia Stolk has argued, the defendant of ICL can paradoxically be cast as both an accountable agent, 'sophisticated', as well as inhuman, 'beastly'.[55] The sophisticated is emphasised in regard to forms of superior responsibility or command responsibility, fulfilling the stereotype of the 'criminal mastermind'. This portrayal in fact sits comfortably with the sentencing judgment, which repeatedly refers to Lubanga as an intelligent and well-educated individual and stresses his soundness of mind at the time of committing the crimes. The 'beastly' is perhaps invoked through the ever so slight smirk on Lubanga's face as well as the raised eyes. Did the photographer intend to capture this 'sophisticated beast' paradox? 'Even when photographers are most concerned with mirroring reality, they are still haunted by tacit imperatives of taste and conscience', observed Sontag.[56] Photographs are, just like paintings, also interpretations.[57] Other pictures of Lubanga in the courtroom exist: Lubanga wearing traditional dress in the courtroom, speaking

---

[53] Ibid 18.
[54] Rebecca Tushnet, 'Worth a Thousand Words: The Images of Copyright Law' (2012) 125 (3) *Harvard Law Review* 683–759, at 696.
[55] Sofia Stolk, 'A Sophisticated Beast? On the Construction of an 'Ideal' Perpetrator in the Opening Statements of International Criminal Trials (2018) 29(3) *European Journal of International Law* 677–701.
[56] Sontag, 'On Photography' 6.
[57] Ibid 7.

to his lawyers, smiling; but this particular image from his sentencing has undoubtedly gained the most currency through circulation.[58]

4.3.2   Publicity Outside of the Courtroom

The image of Lubanga is distributed through the Reuters news agency. We come across the same proverb again: 'Sometimes a picture really is worth a thousand words', the website states.[59] The image of Lubanga was used by several news sites to report on his sentencing. The US news outlet CBS News used the image in a story that described the sentencing of Lubanga as a 'watershed moment' for the ICC and a 'potential landmark in the struggle to protect children during wartime'.[60] The story also referred to Lubanga showing 'no emotion' as the decision was read out. The same story with the same image also ran in *The New York Times*, which referred to 'teething problems' of the court and described Lubanga as listening quietly while his sentence was read aloud.[61] Other news outlets of the Global North that used the photograph typically ran with a variation of the headline 'Congolese warlord jailed'.[62] The Coalition for the International Criminal Court (CICC), the NGO that was established for the purpose of supporting the ICC, used the image in a slightly different context. They used the Lubanga photograph to accompany a reposted story from the International Justice Monitor (a project of the George Soros funded Open Society Foundations), which reported on the reconsideration of Lubanga's sentence from 2015.[63] The original report on whether Lubanga's early release would be desirable weighs up the potential for fostering peace in Ituri, both from the perspective of

---

[58] See the ICC's Flickr account, which includes a great number of photographs from the courtroom: www.flickr.com/photos/icc-cpi/albums/72157654310290910.

[59] Reuters New Agency at https://agency.reuters.com/en/products-services/products/news-photos.html

[60] 'Thomas Lubanga sentenced to 14 years in prison for Congo war crimes, use of child soldiers', CBS News (10 July 2012), available at: www.cbsnews.com/news/thomas-lubanga-sentenced-to-14-years-in-prison-for-congo-war-crimes-use-of-child-soldiers/

[61] Marlise Simons, 'International Criminal Court Issues First Sentence', *New York Times*, 10 July 2012.

[62] For example, Michel Arseneault, 'Congolese Warlord Thomas Lubanga jailed', Radio France Internationale, 11 July 2012; 'Congolese Warlord Jailed for 14 Years over Child Soldiers', *The Telegraph*, 10 July 2012; 'Former Congo Warlord Sentenced to 14 Years over Child Soldiers', *Los Angeles Times*, 10 July 2012.

[63] 'Lubanga for early release? Views from Ituri', Coalition for the International Criminal Court, 10 September 2015. Availability at: http://www.coalitionfortheicc.org/news/20150910/lubanga-early-release-views-ituri.

Lubanga's early release and the perspective of him remaining in prison.[64] It is a relatively balanced report stressing that the reconsideration of his sentence is part of a *routine* procedure. Interestingly, the CICC chose the courtroom image of Lubanga to run the story whilst the original has no image. The CICC also chose a different headline. The original reads 'Reconsidering Lubanga's Sentence: Views from Ituri' and the reposted CICC version reads 'Lubanga for Early Release? Views from Ituri'. The CICC story is using the more emotive elements of the image and headline to reconstruct the report in a more sensationalist manner. Arguably, these slight adaptations intend to influence the reader to be predisposed to the belief that Lubanga should *not* be granted early release. The Lubanga image was circulated again a few years later, this time by the *Washington Post*, on the occasion of the twentieth anniversary of the signing of the Rome Statute.[65]

Patterns emerge in the selection of some images over others. One form of pattern, introduced in Chapter 2, is the stereotype. Representations of global justice actors coalesce around the repetition of traits. In this case, the circulated image creates or sustains preconceptions about black males as perpetrators, as 'warlords'. The typical image is of a single male, without family or friends, the camera lens zoomed into the face. Erased are any signs that the perpetrator may be a person who works, worries, loves, laughs, dances, cries. The perpetrator is reduced to a black man with 'no emotions'. For the ICC, this image reinforces the need to prosecute 'bad' people; its purpose as dispensing justice is fortified. The audience of the media image – the news readers and the supporters of NGOs – can seek comfort in this.[66] Justice has been done after a black man committed terrible crimes. The simplicity of this narrative creates, in the words of Immi Tallgren, 'consoling patterns of causality' against the background of social, political, and economic complexities.[67]

When Lippmann coined the term 'stereotype' in *Public Opinion*, he wanted to understand the images that people hold in their heads, and how these can be employed to achieve particular political ends.

---

[64] Olivia Bueno, 'Reconsidering Lubanga's Sentence: Views from Ituri', *International Justice Monitor*, 24 August 2015.

[65] Heidi Nichols Haddad, 'The International Criminal Court was Established Twenty Years Ago. Here's How', *The Washington Post*, 17 July 2018.

[66] Christine Schwöbel-Patel, 'The Comfort of International Criminal Law' (2013) 24(2) *Law & Critique* 169–191,

[67] Immi Tallgren, 'The Sensibility and Sense of International Criminal Law' (2002) 13(3) *European Journal of International* 561–595, at 593.

According to Lippmann, the most interesting portraiture 'is that which arises spontaneously in people's minds'.[68] This type of portraiture is spontaneous as it fits into already existing ideas of a person, their gender, race, and class. To illustrate this spontaneous ordering according to preconceptions, Lippmann describes the spontaneous affection for Queen Victoria as the girl-queen through the words of her biographer Lytton Stratchey. The affection for Queen Victoria was roused partly because of the contrast between the innocent, sweet girl and her mean and selfish uncles – 'nasty old men, debauched and selfish, pigheaded and ridiculous, with their perpetual burden of debts, confusions, and disreputabilities'.[69] Lippmann describes a similar phenomenon in respect of the hero worship of US generals and leaders of World War I. While everything 'good' was thought to come from the US leaders, 'everything evil originated in the Kaiser Wilhelm, Lenin and Trotsky'.[70] Moralistic good and evil dichotomies are particularly pitted against one another during conflict or other moments of social upheaval.

ICL by its very nature rejects ambiguity and nuance. ICL requires, according to international criminal lawyers, 'that the law be strictly construed and that ambiguity be resolved'.[71] In ICL, there are three main characters: the perpetrator, the victim, and the legal representative: the 'baddy', the victim, and the hero. As both media and activists can communicate this message about the law and its institutions without too much reliance on context, they instead rely on already existing narrative patterns of race, class, and gender. Specifically, as all defendants before the Court have been black, this fits into broader racialised and institutionalised stereotypes in Western countries of black offenders. For the media, such images have their own political economy, creating wider circulation through clicks, or more conventionally through print sales. The attention that stereotyped images attract, alongside sensationalist headlines, reveals the close alliance between corporate media actors and marketised global justice actors. For the ICC, the circulation of the image of a black, male perpetrator 'warlord' creates legitimacy for the Court, justification for its past and greater demand for the future. Publicity as a

---

[68] Walter Lippmann, *Public Opinion* [1922], (Greenbook Publications 2010) 8.
[69] Lytton Strachey, *Queen Victoria* [1901], (Chatto & Windus 1921) 72, cited in Lippmann, 'Public Opinion' 8.
[70] Lippmann, 'Public Opinion' 10.
[71] Robert Cryer et. al., *An Introduction to International Criminal Law and Procedure* (Cambridge University Press 2010) 14. Here referencing the principle of legality.

form of circulating images and narratives places the image's *exchange value* in the foreground.

Apart from the ICC more generally requiring legitimacy as a global justice actor, we might ask whether the Lubanga trial itself required publicity for its legitimacy. For those knowledgeable about ICL procedure, the question may appear farcical. It was a case mired with problems. One of the central issues was the process around evidence and witness testimony. There were repeated concerns over the Office of the Prosecutor withholding crucial (potentially exculpatory) evidence from the defence, resulting in the Trial Chamber twice imposing a stay of proceedings – an unusual measure ordering all proceedings to be halted.[72] During the trial, the Chamber moreover found several witnesses to be unreliable due to concerns about witness coaching. This was mainly due to the prosecution deciding not to work with witnesses themselves, instead relying on intermediaries to do the work for them. Intermediaries, mostly human rights activists, worked 'on the ground' to identify witnesses and to prepare them for the legal proceedings. Soon, worries arose that the preparation for trial included the preparation of testimony too, which would affect the search for truth.[73] In its judgment, Trial Chamber I found it likely that several intermediaries had persuaded, encouraged, or assisted witnesses to give false testimony.[74] The legal battles between Luis Moreno Ocampo and presiding Judge Fulford in the courtroom subsequently became the object of discussion, in the Court and in the media. As the courtroom drama shifted to centre stage, the situation in Ituri faded into the background. Moreover, the refusal to deal with sexual violence crimes and instead focus on child soldiers turned even the most ardent believer of the ICC into a critic. 'For most of the trial, the Chamber did what it could to hear as little as possible about how frequently young women were raped and enslaved', observes Jim

---

[72] See the ICC's 'Case Information Sheet, Situation in the Democratic Republic of the Congo, *The Prosecutor v. Thomas Lubanga Dyilo*, ICC-01/04-01/06 (October 2016). See also Christian M. De Vos, 'Case Note: Prosecutor v Lubanga, "Someone who comes between one Person and another": *Lubanga*, Local Cooperation and the Right to a Fair Trial' (2011) 12 (1) *Melbourne Journal of International Law* 217–236.

[73] *The Prosecutor v. Thomas Lubanga Dyilo*, (Decision Regarding the Practices Used to Prepare and Familiarise Witnesses for Giving Testimony at Trial) ICC-01/04-01/06, Trial Chamber I (30 November 2007).

[74] *The Prosecutor v. Thomas Lubanga Dyilo* (Judgment) ICC-01/04-01/06 (14 March 2012) p. 137, 158.

Freedman, who has published a book on the trial.[75] The Court had decided to focus on 'the children narrative', and therefore wanted no distractions from it. It was only at the sentencing stage that the prosecutor then referred to sexual violence crimes in order to argue for a more severe sentence. The trial took six years before a judgment was handed down, and an extra two years for the appeals procedure to complete, which under any domestic circumstances would be met with concerns over the defendant's fair trial rights. The trial was all in all a (tragi-)'comedy of errors'.[76] In the face of criticism, publicity was a necessary instrument to retain interest in the court and to create legitimacy for it. And, yet again, publicity was also a means of distraction – distraction from the legitimacy-deficits of the Court, distraction from alternative mechanisms of global justice, and distraction from the structural inequalities enshrined in ICL.

Whilst the corporate media plays an important role, publicity more broadly reaches beyond media platforms. Representative patterns through the circulation of some images over others reach far beyond the media and funding-generating NGOs. We are reminded of Naomi Klein's observation about the 1990s in which brands first began to travel.[77] Any space in which 'the brand' appears is a potential medium for communication, a potential 'site for building or consolidating relationships.'[78] For global justice actors, one of these visual spaces is the exhibition space.

4.3.3   Patronage Publicity

The discipline of ICL is awash with visualisation events. Alongside the plethora of documentaries on international criminal justice,[79] there are

---

[75] Jim Freedman, 'A Conviction in Question – Lessons from the International Criminal Court's Inaugural Trial', Justice in Conflict blog, 17 January 2018, available at: https://justiceinconflict.org/2018/01/17/a-conviction-in-question-lessons-from-the-the-international-criminal-courts-inaugural-trial/; Jim Freedman, *A Conviction in Question: The First Trial of the International Criminal Court* (University of Toronto Press 2017).

[76] Niamh Hayes, 'Sisyphus Wept: Prosecuting Sexual Violence at the International Criminal Court' in William A. Schabas, Yvonne McDermott, Niamh Hayes (eds.), *The Ashgate Research Companion to International Criminal Law: Critical Perspectives* (Ashgate 2013) 7–44.

[77] Naomi Klein, *No Logo* (10th anniversary edition, Fourth Estate, 2010).

[78] Liz Moor, *The Rise of Brands* (Bloomsbury 2007), 46.

[79] Some have already been mentioned in the preceding chapters. These include *Prosecuting Evil: The Extraordinary World of Ben Ferencz* directed by Barry Avrich, Melbar

many exhibitions. In this section, we direct attention to such exhibitions in order to analyse how far they too may be exercises in publicity. And, of course, the photograph of Lubanga will reappear once more. Global justice exhibitions often rely on photography and trial artefacts. When original artwork is included, it is mostly commissioned from those who promote ICL.

A prominent example of a global justice exhibition is the ICC's *Justice Matters* exhibition. It was launched on the occasion of the 10th anniversary of the coming into force of the Rome Statute. The exhibition was first installed at the World Forum in The Hague, and then moved to the Municipality of The Hague. It was sponsored by the city of The Hague and the government of Switzerland. Mostly, the exhibition was made up of large photographs with accompanying text. According to the ICC website, it sought to 'explore how justice matters to the individuals and communities affected by the crimes under the Court's jurisdiction'.[80] A slide-show of some of the images was made available for printing and exhibiting. The images alternate between black women and children and mainly white men. The black women and children are sparsely clothed, the primarily white men are wearing judicial attire, mostly gowns. The black women and children are photographed with prominent scars and mutilations. The mostly white men are photographed groomed and well-fed. The black women and children are outside, in parched land. The mostly white men are inside in a courtroom. One group are of course presumed to be the victims of conflict and crime. The other group are presumed to be legal professionals at the ICC.[81] The progress narrative from conflict to justice is visually displayed through the transition from sombre-looking victims with visual injuries at the beginning, to three dancing black women towards the end.[82] The online version of the exhibition was later renamed *Building a More Just World*.[83] It includes

Entertainment Group 2019; *The Court*, directed by Marcus Vetter and Michele Gentile, Filmperspektive GmbH 2012; *Prosecutor*, directed by Barry Stevens, White Pine Pictures 2010. See also Wouter Werner, 'Justice on Screen – A Study of Four Documentary Films on the International Criminal Court' (2016) 29(4) *Leiden Journal of International Law* 1043–1060.

[80] '"Justice Matters": Multimedia Exhibit opening in The Hague to commemorate the ICC's Tenth anniversary' (Press Release) ICC-CPI-20121115-PR853 (15 November 2012).

[81] Immi Tallgren, 'Come and See? The Power of Images and International Criminal Justice' (2017) 17(2) *International Criminal Law Review* 259–280.

[82] Justice Matters slideshow, available under the Resource Library of the ICC website: www .icc-cpi.int/iccdocs/PIDS/other/JusticeMattersSlideshow-ENG.pdf

[83] ICC, 'Building a more just world', available at: www.icc-cpi.int/morejustworld.

some additions to the original, with a notable difference being the publicising of the Court building – with reference to the city brand 'City of Peace and Justice'.[84] The themes are 'Justice Matters to Individuals', 'Justice Matters to Communities', 'Justice Matters to the World'. The 'communities' are portrayed as masses of black people (in camps, sitting on the ground, and in outdoor classrooms). 'The world' is portrayed through flags, photographs of government and ICC officials, and snaps of people taking part in the #JusticeMatters campaign.[85] The message circulated through this aesthetics of contrast is that violence and conflict occur only in the Global South – The Communities – and that the ICC, government officials, and social media users represent the concerned and giving Global North – The World. The act of seeing becomes mediated by the market.[86]

A further example is an online exhibition, launched in June 2019 by the International Residual Mechanism for Criminal Tribunals.[87] The title was 'Worth a Thousand Words'.[88] The exhibition was launched on the occasion of International Archives Day.[89] It is made up of a compendium of sketches and drawings created by witnesses before the two tribunals. Rather unusually for a global justice exhibition, it does not include photographs. Perhaps ironically given the title, the sketches decidedly require words for their explanation; text accompanies the images, alongside audio recordings from the courtroom. Evidence has been refashioned from a legal exhibit in the courtroom to an exhibit for the public. That which fulfilled a use-value in the courtroom as evidence is being repurposed for publicity.

Given that in these cases it was the courts themselves that curated the exhibitions, such publicity might be expected. But, what about artistic expressions of global justice?

---

[84] www.icc-cpi.int/morejustworld#3.

[85] www.icc-cpi.int/morejustworld#25.

[86] Walter Benjamin referred to this as 'art entering the service of the merchant', Benjamin, 'Arcades Project', 3.

[87] The Mechanism is the institution established to deal with remaining issues and cases of the International Criminal Tribunal for the former Yugoslavia (ICTY) and the International Criminal Tribunal for Rwanda.

[88] International Residual Mechanism for Criminal Tribunals (IRMCT), 'Worth a Thousand Words', available at: www.irmct.org/specials/1000words/index.html.

[89] 'Mechanism Releases "Worth a Thousand Words" Online Exhibition on International Archives Day' (Press Release) (07 June 2018).

Here, we return to the image of Lubanga. At a side event of the Assembly of States Parties (ASP) of the ICC in 2016, a preview of artist Bradley McCallum's exhibition *Weights and Measures: Portraits of Justice* was organised, including a life-like oil painting of the very Lubanga image whose circulation we have been following. The Brooklyn-based artist had recently completed a residency at the CICC, where he had been working on the exhibition pieces. The complete show comprised twenty large-scale oil portraits and photonegative inversions of major offenders from different tribunals and courts, as well as photographed portraits of leading legal practitioners. These works were exhibited in New York, Limerick, and Johannesburg, along with audio portraits, that is, sound testimonies from witnesses and victims.[90] At the ASP side-event in 2016, only a few portraits were exhibited, including that of Lubanga. We recall that 2016 was a rather fateful year for the ICC, with the announcement of the intention to withdraw from the Rome Statute coming from three states just a few weeks before the ASP began. The event was organised under the theme that bringing art and justice together demonstrated that perception matters; 'justice had to be seen to be done'.[91] According to McCallum, the portrait of Lubanga, copied from the photograph taken in the courtroom, was the first of the series. He painted it after attending the 2012 ASP meeting. The painting – oil on linen, 172.72 cm × 121.92 cm – is based on the photograph, but, according to McCallum, with a 'subtle manipulation'.[92] Simply put, the image is cropped, the skin is darkened and the whites of the eyes are brightened. The painting is titled 'Warlord'.

Asked in an interview whether the 'truth value' of photography factors into his work, McCallum states: '[I]t is incredibly important that the source photographs are taken within the courtroom and that the paintings memorialize the defendants' accountability and the end of their impunity.'[93] Despite going on to state that the paintings are not about

---

[90] For an account of attending the exhibition as a spectator, see Sarah-Jane Koulen, 'Blind Justice and the Portraits on the Wall' in Lianne J. M. Boer and Sofia Stolk (eds.), *Backstage Practices of Transnational Law* 91–107.

[91] Michael Benedict, 'Assembly of States Parties Side Event. Through the Looking Glass: Imagining the future of International Criminal Justice', Final Report, Wayamo Foundation, November 2016.

[92] 'Picturing Power: Alison K. Young in Conversation with Bradley McCallum', *Art Africa Magazine*, 14 August 2016. https://artafricamagazine.org/picturing-power-alison-k-young-in-conversation-with-bradley-mccallum/.

[93] Ibid.

guilt and innocence, he nevertheless carries the message forward of ending impunity. The uncompromising distinctions of artistic material – defendants at the ICC in oil paintings, legal representatives in photographs, and victims in audio installations – mirrors the legal categories of ICL. The adoption of the legal distinctions limits the artistic representations of fluidity between victims and defendants, or the social, economic, political, and cultural context, or the questioning of racial stereotypes typically adopted in the sector. His portrayal of the black male defendant titled 'warlord' is distinctly 'on brand'. Asked how he engages with local audiences, who may be affected by the actions of the portrayed defendants, McCallum states: 'In my practice, having the distance of being "other" can be an important asset, especially when looking at the legacy of traumatic situations'.[94] With this statement, McCallum is arguably co-opting the position of the 'other'. As a white Brooklyn-based artist with a residency in The Hague, faced with images of black victims and defendants, he has adopted for himself a label theorised in post-colonial studies to signify repression of those in the Global South for the benefit of the Global North. The use of the word 'asset', as well as the explicit use of metrics in the title of the exhibition 'Weights and Measures' are market-oriented concepts. The circulation of the image, then, not only serves the stereotypes that fuel marketised global justice, the artist also explicitly buys into its logic, therefore contributing to the distributive effects of marketised global justice. Financial support offered by powerful institutions is traditionally called patronage. Typically, the patrons of artwork are the elite classes. Typically, patrons are expected to gain a return on their investment: in exchange for their sponsorship they may expect an enhanced social status or a representation that portrays their power and influence. Exchange value is once more prominent.

4.4   Marketised Global Justice As Mass Distraction

Before investigating the political economy of representations of victims of conflict in Chapter 5 (moving from representations of defendants to victims), we pause here for a reflection on the critique of marketised global justice explored thus far. We recall the suggestion that marketised global justice is a form of mass distraction. This insight relies on the hypothesis that ICL is working *as it should*. Such a view is in contrast to

[94] Ibid.

most liberal critiques of ICL, which claim that ICL is *not* acting as it should and must therefore be reformed: Critics claim that ICL should be casting its investigative net wider; the ICC judges should stop their quarrels; ICL institutions should be spending their resources more wisely; there should be less grandstanding, more action.[95] What I have aimed to illustrate in the preceding chapters is that the ICC and other global justice actors who focus on the anti-impunity brand are acting exactly as they should within a marketised global justice sector. Already in 2002, the year in which the Rome Statute came into force, Immi Tallgren speculated that perhaps ICL's task is precisely

> to naturalize, to exclude from the political battle, certain phenomena which are in fact the preconditions for the maintenance of the existing governance; by the North, by wealthy states, by wealthy individuals, by strong states, by strong individuals, by men, especially white men, and so forth.[96]

Marketised global justice, particularly through its emphasis on the visual, seeks to protect existing privileges. This is what makes it both symptomatic and constitutive of neoliberalism as a political-legal project. Marketised global justice both seeks to protect the market from politicisation, privileging private capital, *and* to hide these privileges through persuasion and distraction.

We return here to a question posed at the end of Chapter 2: if marketisation is brought about through the employment of market practices in which the market is openly invoked, how can the market simultaneously remain hidden? A more specific way of asking this question in an ICL context might be to ask: How can it be that then-prosecutor of the ICTY Carla Del Ponte can speak so openly to Goldman Sachs of the 'dividends' of ICL, and the market at the same time be rendered invisible? Surely, the market cannot be more in the open than this fundraising speech? Through posing this last question rhetorically, we see how the market and market*ing* collude to create a de-politicised subject. The act of freedom, of choice, is perceived to lie in the market – the savvy, contemporary, smart (and seemingly only) *choice* is the market option. The way in which this choice is communicated, as visible and as public communication, creates the impression of a public space. We

---

[95] See, for example, on the ICC: Douglas Guilfoyle, Parts I, II, and III 'This is not fine: The International Criminal Court in Trouble', *EJIL Talk*, 21–25 March 2019, available at: www.ejiltalk.org/part-i-this-is-not-fine-the-international-criminal-court-in-trouble/.

[96] Tallgren, 'Sensibility and Sense', 595.

recall Dean's observation about illusions created through publicity: 'fas-
cinated by publicity in its normative, technological, and celebrity formats,
we disavow the fact that the public isn't there'.[97] Publicity stands in for an
absent public. The temptations of the market – its claims of efficiency as
well as its claims of being apolitical – are made irresistible through the
market's very own publicity tool: marketing. One of marketing's most
persuasive and distracting tools is the image. It is the foundational
element of the social relationships created as spectacle. The evaluation
of what is visible and what is rendered invisible is therefore central for
understanding marketised global justice as simultaneously preoccupied
by the market (and the primacy of market values) and at the same time
invisibilising the structural tools that uphold it.

4.4.1   Narrowed Visibility As an Impact on Multiplicity

Marketised global justice is narrowing what is *seen* as global justice.
Global justice actors that reproduce stereotypes are not simply reflecting
market practices with their use of imagery, but are themselves constituting them. The use of particular images is part of a liberal-legal undertaking to *order* experiences in a particular way. The images acquire a
separate status that is distinct from their use-value as explaining global
justice. Images become relational, not to their explanatory function, but
to their ability to provide a common sense for resource distribution.[98]
The selection of images and their circulation occurs according to
accepted distributional lines. The use of stereotypes that correspond with
widely held notions of the Global South as requiring development (the
more market-friendly term for 'civilisation'), is cementing notions of the
Global South as the place of global injustice. Consequently, the Global
South is seen as the place requiring global justice intervention, invariably
by the institutions of the Global North.

   Once again, there is something counter-intuitive about the narrowing
of the visual in the context of expanded and intensified communicativity.
Should more opportunities for sharing content online not increase
multiplicity? Dean has argued that instead of multiplicity, communicativity has led to the *concentration* of communication. Rather than 'enabling the emergence of a richer variety in modes of living and practices of

---

[97] Dean, 'Publicity's Secret', 43.
[98] Aesthetics as constituting 'common sense' is articulated in Jacques Rancière, *The Politics
of Aesthetics*, trans. Gabriel Rockhill (Bloomsbury 2004).

freedom, the deluge of screens and spectacles coincides with extreme corporatization, financialisation, and privatization across the globe'.[99] The Internet and particularly social media plays a major role in the dissemination of global justice projects, whether this is through individual humanitarians, NGOs or international organisations. While the positive effect on social justice crises, particularly of 'awareness-raising campaigns', is inconclusive (discussed in more depth in Chapter 6 '*Kony 2012*: Making an Accused *Famous*'), what is *certain* is that the social media corporations benefit from the adding of content on their sites. The networks to which the content is disseminated and its reception through 'Shares' and emoticons (likes, loves, LOLs) create data that is used for advertising purposes. Alice Marwick consequently describes the adding of content to social media as 'unpaid labour' for social media corporations.[100] Participating in social media through adding content creates value for these sites. User data accumulates, advertisements are viewed and can be tailored, and click-throughs are generated. What is seemingly a free platform for visibility is not free at all. The data collected by these giant corporations is transformed into other marketing projects. When global justice actors use these platforms, they are entering into a relationship of *exchange*. A visible platform in exchange for data. Victims of conflict or those accused of perpetrating international crimes are unknowingly also entering into the exchange: their images are employed to create narratives of legitimation, and often intervention.

The narrowing of what is *seen* as global justice and the emphasis on the *seeing* has wide-ranging effects beyond the Internet as marketplace. Mark Drumbl has observed that transplanting international law to the domestic level in areas of conflict leads to the 'squeezing out of local approaches that are extralegal in nature, as well as those that depart from the methods and modalities dominant internationally'.[101] Sarah Nouwen and Wouter Werner have built on this observation about the squeezing out of alternative approaches. They propose five alternative conceptions of justice that become marginalised through ICL's monopoly on global justice: restoration of relationships, ending ongoing violations, redistribution, accountability and punishment, and equality. The literature on

---

[99] Dean, 'Democracy and other Neoliberal Fantasies' 23.
[100] Alice E. Marwick, *Status Update: Celebrity, Publicity & Branding in the Social Media Age* (Yale University Press 2013) 194–195.
[101] Mark Drumbl, *Atrocity, Punishment, and International Law* (Cambridge University Press 2007) 122.

decolonisation takes this even further, highlighting the coloniality that determines which knowledge is considered as valid. Epistemologies, argues Boaventura de Sousa Santos, have been profoundly narrowed by capitalism, colonialism, and patriarchy;[102] so much so that epistemologies of the South can be described as having suffered an 'epistemicide'.[103] Inevitably Eurocentric visions are not regarded as 'local', but those of the Global South are. De Sousa Santos designates this division as an 'abyssal line'. The abyssal line marks a distinction between those included by modernity through legal protection and social emancipation versus those excluded in the colonies by appropriation and violence.[104] At the same time, decolonial thinking warns against a fetishised and commodified idea of 'the local'. Whether the Rwandan *Gacaca* courts, or the old Acholi reconciliatory tradition of *Mato Oput* in Uganda, many local judicial customs have received international attention because of their initial lack of attention. In the competitive market of social movements, the *Gacaca* courts and *Mato Oput* became international causes in their own right.[105] Film-makers from the West came to document the 'local' traditions, scholars, activists and organisations came to study the process.[106] The supporters of the process tend to encounter local customs not on their own terms but with the 'international community' in mind – not too far off from the visual distinctions set out in the ICC's *Building a More Just World* exhibition, which distinguishes between 'justice for communities' and 'justice for the world'. Although tempting – and correct – to cast an eye to 'the local' as a form of the critique of universalism, this particular view of the local often functions in the very parameters that create 'the global'.[107] Both the 'global' as well as the 'local' versions of marketised global justice embrace the local as an

---

[102] Boaventura de Sousa Santos, *The End of the Cognitive Empire: The Coming of Age of Epistemologies of the South* (Duke University Press 2018).

[103] Boaventura de Sousa Santos, *Epistemologies of the South: Justice against Epistemicide* (Routledge 2014).

[104] Boaventura de Sousa Santos, *Beyond Abyssal Thinking: From Global Lines to Ecologies of Knowledges*, 30(1) *Review* 46 (2007).

[105] See Bob Clifford, *The Marketing of Rebellion: Insurgents, Media, and International Activism* (Cambridge University Press 2005).

[106] Sarah Nouwen and Wouter Werner, 'Monopolizing Global Justice: International Criminal Law as Challenge to Human Diversity' (2015) 13 *Journal of International Criminal Justice* 157–176.

[107] See Jean and John Comaroff, *Ethnicity, Inc.* (Chicago University Press 2009).

'orientalised' object of study.[108] Meanwhile, radical visions of global justice that seek to problematise capitalism, colonialism, and patriarchy, are outside of what is *seen* as global justice.

4.4.2 Narrowed Visibility As Rendering Structural Violence Invisible

The *in*visible, yet often acutely *felt* by those on the wrong side of the 'abyssal line', is structural violence. Marketised global justice pays attention to the spectacularised side of violence and hides structures that create inequality, including inequality through competition, institutionalised racism and misogyny. Structural violence often manifests as discriminatory dispossessions at the intersections of gender, class, and race. Shifts in conceptions of violence invite observations about the social, economic, political, and cultural context: whilst marketised global justice speaks of ethnic tensions, no one is asking about the resource extraction that is creating these tensions, nor the colonial legacies that were instrumental in creating tensions. Whilst marketised global justice directs its view to African 'warlords', questions of corporate landgrabbing are outside of the frame. Whilst marketised global justice actors release press statements about Hollywood actor Angelina Jolie attending an ICC hearing, no one is asking about the military industrial complex that creates material incentives for war. Finally, whilst international law is placed at the centre of global justice, the contribution of international law in creating global injustice is ignored.

In the following chapters, we will investigate the de-politicising and de-historicising features of marketised global justice's mass distraction further. Here, let us turn briefly to the political and historical context that is omitted in the circulation of Lubanga's photograph taken in the ICC courtroom. It is of particular interest to the employment and construction of spectacle in the attention economy as it hides a profound paradox: much of the conflict over resources is not only down to the gold found in Ituri but also due to the conflict over coltan and cobalt. Coltan is a rock from which the element tantalum is extracted, a crucial element in the manufacture of mobile phones, computers, car electronics, and cameras. Cobalt is necessary for lithium-ion rechargeable batteries, and is therefore found in smartphones, tablets, laptops and electric vehicles.

---

[108] Edward Said, *Orientalism* [1978] (Penguin 2003)

The very medium through which the conflict in the DRC is simultaneously made visible and invisible is also the medium at the root cause of conflict.[109]
The DRC, Lubanga's home country, has 80 per cent of the world's supply of coltan. The Congo has a long history of resource appropriation and exploitation. Only some events can be sketched out here, but they should suffice to get a sense of what is missing when the ICC circulates the photograph of Lubanga as a form of publicity: The Congo's former colonial master, Belgium, operated a notoriously brutal regime, chiefly to enable the extraction of rubber and ivory. Under the personal rule of King Leopold II, famine, disease, mutilation, and death became widespread. The 1884–1885 Berlin Conference allocated the entire Congo Basin region to a private organisation run by King Leopold himself. The international treaty for the so-called Scramble for Africa placed the territory and all its affairs with Leopold II, who outsourced most of the activities to private entities. Because Leopold II was given this power, the affairs were secured and shielded through the international legal principle of sovereignty.[110] Formally, the Berlin Conference ended slavery, but there were economic reasons to end it in the Congo Basin area. Much of the European slave trade had depopulated central Africa and Leopold II needed labour to extract resources, particularly rubber. As the demand for rubber by industrialised states in the Global North rose in the late nineteenth century, forced labour became the norm in order to maximise profit. One form of slavery was replaced by another. In international law textbooks, the General Act tends to be remembered primarily as the treaty that ended slavery, not one that enabled privatised colonial structures of exploitation. One might venture to say that the treaty was a rather clever marketing stunt.

In 1908, following public outcry at the declining Congolese population due to disease, the territory was surrendered to the Belgian government. The borders that had brought together hundreds of ethnic groups into one territory remained the same, as they did more than fifty years later with decolonisation. The international legal principle of *uti possidetis* required stabilised borders of the post-colonial state.[111] In the 1960s, the

---

[109] For a discussion on screens as objects of international law, see Christine Schwöbel-Patel and Wouter Werner, 'Screen' in Jessie Hohmann and Daniel Joyce (eds.), *International Law's Objects* (Oxford University Press 2018) 419–430.

[110] Matthew Craven, 'Between law and history: The Berlin Conference of 1884–1885 and the logic of free trade' (2015) 3(1) *London Review of International Law* 31–59.

[111] For a critical analysis of *uti possidetis*, see Antony Anghie, *Imperialism, Sovereignty, and the Making of International Law* (Cambridge University Press 2005).

United States became interested in the Congo's cobalt, for its use in fighter jets armed for the Cold War. Today, cobalt remains one of the main resources extracted in parts of the DRC, with Chinese traders often acting as intermediaries. It is no secret that workers are exploited, creating huge profits for the corporations at the sunny end of the global value chain. Aside from the dismal labour conditions, mining for the minerals has polluted the water and earth. 'Business', observed Rosa Luxemburg aptly, 'thrives on the ruins'.[112] Structural violence points a clear finger towards corporate and financial power of the Global North. None of this is visible in the single image of a black man who has been branded a 'warlord'.

4.5 Conclusion

'Exchange value could arise only as an agent of use-value, but its victory by means of its own weapons created the conditions for its autonomous domination', comments Guy Debord about the relationship between use-value and exchange value.[113] In this quotation, Debord is employing the analogy of military battle to describe the ascendency of exchange value. Use-value has been reduced to the servitude of exchange value as its factual reality has become eroded.[114] Marketised global justice is the manifested emphasis on exchange value, not only of commodities, but of social justice. Social relationships and social values are exposed to the question of their market value. What market*ing* does – with its emphasis on the subjective – is to create the illusion that market values are in fact social values. The effects of this apparition are real, for this process has a distributive function, preventing *re*distribution and hiding structural inequalities.

This chapter has aimed to demonstrate the operation of the primacy of market values over social values in marketised global justice through following the circulation of a photograph taken at the ICC. Law and visibility are intimately entwined in the old adage that justice must be *seen to be done*. Similar to the marketing mantra *there is no such thing as bad publicity*, we have found that visibility is linked to legitimacy. The exchange that is occurring is not a metaphysical one; it is material. With legitimacy comes growth of the global justice sector: growth of tribunals,

---

[112] Luxemburg, 'Junius Broschüre'.
[113] Debord, 'Society of the Spectacle', para 46. Drawing on the conception by Marx that there is an internal conflict between use-value and exchange value
[114] Ibid, para 48.

growth of ICL courses taught at universities, growth of books published on ICL, growth of ICL documentaries, growth of non-fiction books dealing with anti-impunity themes, growth of tourist numbers attracted to the places of ICL, growth of the hospitality sector that provides for these tourists, and so on. Marketised global justice in its anti-impunity guise is a means through which the usual distributive channels are maintained (growth for those who are already privileged) *and* redistribution is prevented. Given the market-stimulating functions, it is not surprising then that the dominant aesthetics of ICL is skewed in favour of that which is most *marketable*, taking radical ideas outside of the sphere of public contestation. This has a profound impact on the victims of conflict. In a market economy of global justice, their faces are often the literal billboards of global justice. This is the object of study of the next chapter.

5

'Working It'

The Brand of the Ideal Victim

I felt free and very proud that I had done my work well.[1]

5.1 Introduction

In the cosmetics industry, it is highly profitable for models or actors to become the 'face' of a campaign. If a brand intends to use celebrity power to market their products, the use of the celebrity's 'face' and name comes with a hefty price tag. What about the faces of marketised global justice? Do they benefit from the use of their faces and stories being splashed on the billboards of global justice? From Chapter 4, we learned the centrality of visibility for marketised global justice as a means of gaining legitimacy. In this chapter, we focus on the most common 'faces' of global justice: victims of conflict. While the previous chapter employed economic theory to make sense of marketised global justice, this chapter continues with that theme but shifts the emphasis to a more personal approach of considering who is gaining, and especially who is losing, in marketised global justice. Contrary to the claims that global justice is for the benefit of victims of conflict, I propose that victims are exploited as the faces of global justice. The construction and reproduction (and normalising) of an 'ideal victim' will be discussed, which, in market terms is victim branding.[2] The commodification that ensues is, I argue, indicative of the emergence of a global victim industry – the main marketplace of marketised global justice.

As some victims seek relief through global justice organisations, they are, in a marketised manner of speaking, consumers of victim services. But, the victims who seek redress for their suffering as a consequence of

---

[1] Excerpt from a fictitious victim statement as part of a permanent exhibition at the ICC. The exhibition opened in November 2016.
[2] Earlier versions of this argument were published in Christine Schwöbel-Patel, 'The "Ideal" Victim of International Criminal Law' (2018) 29(3) *European Journal of International Law* 703–724 and Christine Schwöbel-Patel, 'Spectacle in International Criminal Law: The Fundraising Image of Victimhood' (2016) *London Review of International Law* 247–274.

conflict tend to have little purchasing power. Because there are third parties funding the use of victim services – in particular donors – victims are generally not the primary audience of global justice actors. Not only are they instrumentalised for an emerging victim industry, but more traditionally (and of course not entirely separately), they are used as a means to uphold existing normative and material frameworks. The focus of this chapter is on how the slippage of victims as users of services and victims as producers of services comes about in marketised global justice. In bids to secure resources for their vision of global justice, competing global justice actors invoke the marketable suffering of victims of global injustice.

Continuing with the prioritisation of exchange value over use-value set out in Chapter 4, the construction of 'ideal' victimhood is about hierarchies introduced on the basis of the most marketable attributes. From a market perspective, the value of the victim rises or falls depending on how many marketable attributes the victim fulfils. The use and re-use of such attributes to define victimhood deepens and institutionalises existing stereotypes of a feminised, infantilised, and racialised notion of victimhood. The decision as to who is a perpetrator and who is a victim is presented as reflecting political and economic power. This chimes with the critical approaches taken by the disciplines of criminology and victimology. In these disciplines, it is contested that crime is simply a legal category; instead, the emphasis is on its construction in and through society. In the aim to understand the preference for some victims over others in global justice projects, this chapter therefore draws primarily on the work of criminologists and victimologists.

I begin with a short historical overview in which I set out how the concern for victims as the 'forgotten subject' travelled from national (Western) jurisdictions to the international sphere, culminating in provisions at the international criminal tribunals and the International Criminal Court (ICC). Drawing on images, transcripts from the courtroom, and film, I then turn attention to the construction of the 'ideal victim'. The political economy analysis is foregrounded in a discussion on the commodification of victimhood and consequent alienation; in this section I focus again on the ICC.

5.2   The Victim: From Forgotten Subject to Brand

Global justice actors who emphasise the fight against impunity habitually place victims as the central driving force of their endeavours. Doing justice in a global context today means doing justice for the victims of crime.[3] Although this emphasis on victims may appear commonplace today, the turn to victims is a fairly recent development from a disciplinary and institutional perspective. In domestic Western criminal justice systems, attention to victim interests appeared in the 1950s and 1960s, prompting a host of state support schemes, including the expansion of victims' roles inside and outside of the courtroom.[4] Prior to this, the rationale of criminal justice was almost exclusively on upholding public order; victim justice was only incidental. Justice for victims was routinely thought to belong to the category of private wrongs and was therefore a matter for civil procedure.

International law (typically) lagged several decades behind. Although the suffering of people and peoples was rhetorically elevated after World War II, the traditional horizontal nature of international law continued to place the state at the forefront of international legal action and responsibility. The principle of sovereignty, understood as privilege, often obscured the view to the victims of conflict. We recall that the prime legal reasoning at Nuremberg rested on Germany's position of aggressor state, not its persecution and extermination of Jewish, Romani, LGBT, and disabled people. The first significant recognition of the protection of victims from the perspective of international law came with the 1985 United Nations (UN) Declaration of the Basic Principles of Justice for Victims of Crime and Abuse of Power.[5] The so-called Victims Declaration recognised the experience of people across the world who suffer harm as a result of crime and the abuse of power, and urged the adoption of national and international measures for their

---

[3] The representations of victims as the field's 'rationale' has been critically discussed in relation to international criminal law in Kamari Maxine Clarke, *Fictions of Justice. The International Criminal Court and the Challenge of Legal Pluralism in Sub-Saharan Africa* (Cambridge University Press 2009), and in Susan F. Hirsch, 'The Victim Deserving of Global Justice: Power, Caution, and Recovering Individuals' in Kamari Maxine Clarke and Mark Goodale (eds.) *Mirrors of Justice: Law and Power in the Post-Cold War Era* (Cambridge University Press 2009) 149–170.

[4] Victimology's roots lie in the discontent of some criminologists over the 'forgotten subject' of criminology. The term was first coined in Beniamin Mendelsohn,'The Origin of the Doctrine of Victimology' (1963) 3 *Excerpta Criminologica* 239–244. See also Sandra Walklate, 'Introduction and Overview' in Sandra Walklate (ed.), *Handbook of Victims and Victimology* (Routledge 2007) 1–10.

[5] United Nations Declaration of the Basic Principles of Justice for Victims of Crime and Abuse of Power (adopted 29 November 1985) A/CONF.121/22/Rev.1.

protection. As individual accountability in the international sphere took on increasing significance with the emergence of international criminal law (ICL), the role of victims also began to crystallise. The International Criminal Tribunal for the former Yugoslavia (ICTY) and the International Criminal Tribunal for Rwanda (ICTR) were modelled on the criminal law idea of concentrating criminal concerns between the prosecution and the defendant and therefore did not prioritise a participatory role for victims. In ICTY and ICTR proceedings, victims had the role only as witnesses.[6] Victims at the ICC, in contrast, can both participate in proceedings and claim reparations. Victim participation is permitted in the Rome Statute by Article 15(3) ('Victims may make representations to the Pre-Trial Chamber'), Article 19(3) ('[...] those who have referred the situation under article 13, as well as victims, may also submit observations to the Court'), and more generally by Article 68 (3) ('Where the personal interests of the victims are affected, the Court shall permit their views and concerns to be presented [...]').[7] However, the modalities of victim participation were not specified in any of the instruments. Instead, this was left for the judges to consider.[8] The practices of victim participation have therefore developed on a case by case basis. The ICC's manual for legal representatives, published by the Office of Public Counsel for Victims, summarises victims' aims as their desire to 'achieve their right to truth and justice', further explained as 'the right to contribute to the search for the truth, the right to be heard, and the right to reparations'.[9] Victim participation is of course mediated through legal representatives. At the ICC, three parties are heard: the prosecution, the defendant's representatives, and the victims' representatives. At the Extraordinary Chambers in the Courts of Cambodia (ECCC), the role of victims is further extended. Here, victims could

---

[6] United Nations Security Council Resolution 827 (25 May 1993) and United Nations Security Council Resolution 955 (8 November 1994).

[7] Rome Statute of the International Criminal Court (signed 17 July 1998, entered into force 1 July 2002) A/CONF.189/9.

[8] Rule 89(1) International Criminal Court Rules of Procedure and Evidence, ICC-PIDS-LT-02-002/13_Eng: '[...] the Chamber shall then specify the proceedings and manner in which participation is considered appropriate, which may include making opening and closing statements'.

[9] 'Foreword' in 'Representing Victims before the International Criminal Court: A Manual for Legal Representatives', The Office of Public Counsel for Victims (5th edn.) ICC-OPCV-MLR-005/19_ENG, 8.

apply to become civil parties to the case, providing them with additional participatory rights.[10]

The possibility of the representation and participation of victims in the courtroom has been accompanied by a proliferation of rhetoric around victimhood. Since Fatou Bensouda succeeded Luis Moreno Ocampo as chief prosecutor of the ICC in 2012, victim interests have increasingly been rhetorically mobilised as that which distinguishes ICL. We recall once more that at the ceremony at which Bensouda assumed her new role, she made her victim (and market) focus clear by stating: 'The return on our investment for what others may today consider to be a huge cost for justice is effective deterrence and saving millions of victims' lives.'[11] In the space of less than two decades, victims moved from the margins to the centre of ICL concerns, and by extension to the centre of global justice concerns.

But as the view on the victim came into focus, it simultaneously became obscured. The label 'victim' became a generic construction tied into debates about morality and crime more generally. Kieran McEvoy and Kirsten McConnachie describe this process as the instrumentalisation of victims in transitional justice contexts along with a 'morally corrosive language of a "hierarchy of victims"'.[12] Sara Kendall and Sarah Nouwen argue in relation to the ICC that the result of rhetorical, abstract representation is 'the creation of a deity-like and seemingly sovereign entity, "The Victim", which transcends all actual victims and corresponds to no individual victims in their particularity'.[13] This abstract idea of victimhood, I argue, has taken on a concrete form in the sense of a stereotype of what an 'ideal' victim is. As Kamari Maxine Clarke commented in regard to the work of the Special Court for Sierra Leone (SCSL):

> the figure of the victim exists as a necessary precondition for imagining the legitimacy of the international reach of the SCSL. The imagery with

---

[10] Extraordinary Chambers in the Courts of Cambodia Internal Rules (adopted 12 June 2007), Rules 12, 12 *bis*, 12 *ter*, and 23.

[11] Fatou Bensouda, 'Ceremony for the solemn undertaking of the Prosecutor of the International Criminal Court', 19 June 2012, available at: www.icc-cpi.int/NR/rdon lyres/561C232F-3C4F-47AC-91CB-8F78DCC6C3FD/0/15062012FBSolemnUndertaking .pdf.

[12] Kieran McEvoy and Sarah McConnachie, 'Victimology in Transitional Justice: Victimhood, Innocence and Hierarchy' (2012) 9(5) *European Journal of Criminology* 527–538.

[13] Sara Kendall and Sarah Nouwen, 'Representational Practices at the ICC: The Gap between Juridified and Abstract Victimhood' (2014) 76(3) *Law and Contemporary Problems* 235–262.

which this figure collaborates is that of the third-world sufferer – the indigent individual, the defenceless child soldier forced to bear arms, the raped or violated concubine, the (African, Christian, Muslim, Jewish) refugee, or the internally displaced.[14]

As the prime institution claiming to serve global justice, the ICC has the ability to *institutionalise* the stereotyping of victims and drive a victim economy. International criminal courts and tribunals reproduce a narrow idea of what an 'ideal' victim is, a brand of 'ideal' victimhood. This puts a rather more pessimistic spin on the 'cascading' potential of justice, coined by Kathryn Sikkink to describe a 'new world of greater accountability' emerging from human rights prosecutions.[15]

5.3   Constructing the 'Ideal Victim' of Global Injustice

The 'ideal victim' is a victimological concept made popular through the work of Norwegian criminologist Nils Christie. Writing in the context of 1980s Oslo, Christie explains that there is a category of individuals *'who – when hit by crime – most readily are given the complete and legitimate status of being a victim'*.[16] For Christie, the ideal victim is a little old lady who, on her way home from caring for her sick sister, is hit on the head by a big man who robs her for alcohol or drugs. He identifies five attributes, (1) the victim is weak (female, elderly), (2) the victim was carrying out a respectable project (caring for her sister), (3) she could not be blamed for where she was (she was in the street during the daytime), (4) the offender was big and bad, and (5) the offender was in no personal relationship to her.[17] Furthermore, the victim must be able to command just enough power to establish their identity as an ideal victim but *'be weak enough not to become a threat to other important interests'*.[18] The construction of the ideal victim is set out by Christie historically, with

---

[14] Kamari M. Clarke, 'The Rule of Law through Its Economies of Appearances: The Making of the African Warlord' (2011) 18 *Indiana Journal of Global Legal Studies* 7–40, at 13.

[15] Kathryn Sikkink, *The Justice Cascade: How Human Rights Prosecutions are Changing World Politics* (W. W. Norton & Company 2011) 252.

[16] Nils Christie, 'The Ideal Victim', in Ezzat A. Fattah (ed.), *From Crime Policy to Victim Policy: Reorienting the Justice System* (Palgrave Macmillan 1986) 17–30, 18. Emphasis in original.

[17] Ibid 19.

[18] Ibid 21.

reference to the European Medieval witch hunts.[19] Today, he explains, the collective guilt about witch hunts of the past expresses itself through directing attention, and action, to constructing elderly women as victims – whilst still insisting on the societal marginalisation of said 'little old ladies'. As Christie acknowledges, the construct is culturally specific, so one might ask: who is 'the little old lady' of global justice?[20] Drawing on visual and textual representations of victims by global justice actors (inside and outside the courtroom), I identify three attribute categories which seemingly make a victim of conflict 'ideal' in the global justice sector: vulnerability and weakness, dependency, and grotesqueness. These attributes are dealt with as a 'currency' by which the value of the victim can be measured. The 'ideal victim', and therefore the most valuable, is the victim who displays all three properties. The preceding chapters have already gestured towards the attributes named here: in the overview of racialised stereotypes and their distributive functions in Chapter 2, in the concern expressed over narratives employed to justify humanitarian intervention set out in Chapter 3, and in the normalising of the circulation of racialised images of victimhood critiqued in Chapter 4. The following aims to unpick the constitutive parts of this stereotype.

5.3.1   The Victim As 'Weak and Vulnerable'

Weakness as an ideal attribute applies to the victim in (Nils Christie's) Norway as well as the victim of global justice. Weakness as a physical attribute is mostly associated with children, but also (as we already know from the 'little old lady' stereotype) with women. As we recall from Chapter 4, then-Chief Prosecutor Luis Moreno Ocampo's prosecutorial strategy in the *Lubanga* case relied chiefly on an emphasis on the vulnerability of children. In his opening statement, the prosecutor claimed that the accused had 'committed some of the most serious crimes

---

[19] For a path-breaking historical analysis of the European witch hunts as part of the origins story of the entwinement between patriarchy and capitalism, see Silvia Federici, *Caliban and the Witch* (Autonomedia 2004).

[20] See also Joris van Wijk, 'Who Is the 'Little Old Lady' of International Crimes? Nils Christie's Concept of the Ideal Victim Reinterpreted' (2013) 19 *International Review of Victimology* 159–179. And Marian Duggan (ed.), *Revisiting the 'Ideal Victim': Developments in Critical Victimology* (Bristol University Press 2018).

of concern to the international community as a whole: crimes against children.'[21] In the documentary film *Prosecutor*, Moreno Ocampo is shown ending a meeting with his team before entering the courtroom, by urging them to 'Remember: children, children, children.'[22] Notably, the pushback that the prosecutor received from civil society organisations did not point out the potentially worrying stereotyping of racialised children, but focused most passionately on the regrettable exclusion of sexual violence crimes.[23]

'Vulnerability' as an attribute of victimhood is a reflection on the degree of susceptibility to harm. An 'ideal' victim would not deliberately put herself at risk. Vulnerability is therefore most obviously given when the environment poses the risk of harm without the victim's involvement.[24] The physical attributes of weakness enhance vulnerability since the victim is less likely to be able to defend themselves.[25] Criminologists historically place the (Western) origins of the essentialised and universalised image of the purity and vulnerability of women and children in the nineteenth century. As Tony Kearon and Barry Godfrey observe, the British Victorian period sketched out new moral and normative boundaries mediated through a growing cultural representation of moral transgression and moral resolution, the enthusiasm for moral enterprise by the growing print media, and the 'new journalism' of the era.[26] This moral enterprise involved the creation of symbolic and melodramatic 'ideal types of offender and victim whose publicly rehearsed travails reaffirmed normative frameworks in Victorian society'.[27] The new class

---

[21] *The Prosecutor v. Thomas Lubanga Dyilo*, (Opening Statement) ICC-01/04-01/06 (26 January 2009).

[22] *Prosecutor*. Directed by Barry Stevens, White Pine Pictures 2010.

[23] See 'Legal Filings Submitted by the Women's Initiatives for Gender Justice to the International Criminal Court', Women's Initiatives for Gender Justice, August 2012. See in particular *The Prosecutor v. Thomas Lubanga Dyilo*, (Pre-Trial Chamber I, Request Submitted Pursuant to Rule 103(1) of the Rules of Procedure and Evidence for Leave to Participate as Amicus Curiae in the Article 61 Confirmation Proceedings), ICC-01/04-01/06 (7 September 2006).

[24] For a critical take from the perspective of the political economy of vulnerability, see Simon Green, 'Crime, Victimization and Vulnerability' in Walklate, 'Handbook of Victims', 91–117.

[25] This is connected to a worry that male victims of sexual violence are often excluded from the narratives of vulnerability.

[26] Tony Kearon and Barry S. Godfrey, 'Setting the Scene: A Question of History' in Walklate, 'Handbook of Victims', 17–36, at 18. Documented also in Charles Dickens' novels.

[27] Kearon and Godfrey, 'Setting the Scene', 18.

consciousness of the nineteenth century tied these essentialised figures to ideas of productivity. Whilst the capitalist class (often the landed-gentry-turned-business-owners) was deemed productive, the workers were deemed unproductive, particularly those who were exploited in the colonies.[28] Providing workers in the colonies with a purpose (accumulating capital for the capitalists) was therefore rhetorically portrayed as a good deed, as a civilising deed; this was the so-called 'white man's burden'.[29]

There is a notable resemblance with today's construction of the ideal victim of global injustice. The simplified messages of 'good' and 'evil', the accentuation on the visual, and the iterative relationship between the media and the law as a means to disseminate and communicate societal boundaries, highlight the ideological forces that the law submits to and props up. Most striking is the parallel between the workers in the factories of the nineteenth-century industrial revolution and victims in twenty-first century neoliberalism. Victims are arguably 'put to work' in the courtroom, just as their images are put to work through their circulation. 'We are shown nameless starving, weeping, mourning strangers as part of a narrative in which we [in the First World] are spiritually enriched by the knowledge of our superiority and capacity to rescue and redeem these others', states Anne Orford.[30] At the same time, neither the witness accounts nor the images have a bearing on the redistribution of resources. The feelings of empathy that are evoked with weak and vulnerable victims are not redeeming, arguably often themselves being a form of colonisation. Empathy as 'the ability to imagine sympathetically the predicaments of another person',[31] can politically be a *proprietary* act that flows from the privileged to the exploited.

So, global justice actors are choosing the most lucrative means of attracting funds through tapping into well-known racialised stereotypes of black women and children in need: 'That look of starvation, helplessness, and victimisation is remarkably familiar to our imaginations', writes

---

[28] On labour aristocracy in the Global North at the expense of labourers in the Global South (complicating the class narrative of capitalists versus labourers), see Zac Cope, *The Wealth of (Some) Nations* (Pluto Press 2019).

[29] Famously inscribed as such by Rudyard Kipling in the poem 'The White Man's Burden'.

[30] Anne Orford, *Reading Humanitarian Intervention: Human Rights and the Use of Force in International Law* (Cambridge University Press 2003) 32–33.

[31] Martha Nussbaum, *Not for Profit: Why Democracy Needs the Humanities* (Princeton University Press 2010) 7.

Ratna Kapur of the Third World subject.[32] The female subject is, in this stereotype, victimised through sexual violence crimes. The reductionism of presenting narratives of violence as sex-based have, according to Chiseche Mibenge, led to the 'iconic image' of the brown woman as a raped woman.[33]

African children are plainly included in the transnational discourse of victimisation as part of a mission to 'save' and 'civilise' them. Just as the image of the 'brown raped woman' has become a common image of publicity for intergovernmental organisations, UN agencies, NGOs and other global civil society actors, so has the image of the 'innocent child victim'.[34] The focus of ICL on the Third World woman and child as the victim and on the African warlord as the perpetrator, arguably reinforces notions of the (post-)colonial subject as uncivilised and in need of 'saving'. Women and children in the Third World are portrayed as victims of their culture, privileging the culture of the West and reproducing the colonialist rationale for intervening in the lives of the native subject.[35] It has often, and correctly, been pointed out that the strategies of the prosecution at the ICC have solidified the stereotype of the black victim *and* black perpetrator.[36] This is all the more painful for many people in the Global South because the ICC harboured the promise of genuine egalitarianism and even anti-imperialism when it was established.

It is not only the ICC's prosecutorial strategy that further entrenches the racialised stereotypes of weak women and children. On a more general level, the law of individual criminal accountability for international crimes simplifies very real complex social structures through its moralistic ambition to distinguish between 'good' and 'evil'. The paradoxes incumbent in victimhood surface, for example, in the figure of the child soldier. The child soldier is both victim (often acting under duress) and perpetrator (acting of their own accord). In the ICC case of *Prosecutor v Dominic Ongwen*, the blurred lines between

---

[32] Ratna Kapur, *Erotic Justice: Law and the New Politics of Postcolonialism* (Glasshouse Press 2005) 95.

[33] Chiseche Salome Mibenge, *Sex and International Tribunals: The Erasure of Gender from the War Narrative* (University of Pennsylvania Press 2013).

[34] Mark Drumbl, *Reimagining Child Soldiers in International Law and Policy* (Oxford University Press 2012).

[35] Kapur, 'Erotic Justice'.

[36] John Reynolds and Sujith Xavier, '" The Dark Corners of the World": TWAIL and International Criminal Justice' (2016) *Journal of International Criminal Justice* 959–983.

victim and perpetrator became apparent as the perpetrator (and accused) was himself a child when recruited.[37] This presented a conundrum for the prosecution, particularly in light of their previous emphasis on the innocence of children. They therefore relied on legal and rhetorical tools to distinguish the child-victims from the child-perpetrators, whereby the latter category lost any child-like features in the narratives. As part of the confirmation of charges in *Prosecutor v Ongwen*, it was decided that there were substantial grounds to believe that Ongwen had not acted under duress because he had not fled, had risen in the ranks and had not taken efforts to reduce the harm to civilians.[38] These fairly ambiguous distinctions were used to mark the strict distinctions between 'good' and 'evil', differentiating Ongwen as a perpetrator rather than a victim. We see clearly here that the stereotype of the 'ideal' victim is very unlikely to match with many 'real' victims – as unlikely as the 'ideal' monstrous and calculating perpetrator.

5.3.2   The Victim As 'Dependent'

Criminologist Basia Spalek explains that the 'ideal victim' is typically also the 'deserving' victim, the sort of victim in whose name victim services are justified.[39] This brings us to the next attribute of ideal victimhood: dependence. The opening remarks of the Victims' Representatives in *Prosecutor v. Katanga and Ngudjolo* (the second case that went to trial at the ICC), typify this attribute:

> Your Honour – your Honours, believe me, this is a great moment, a great moment of hope for the victims who, for more than six years, have been waiting, waiting for justice to be served. They have waited for more than six years so that this Chamber can ensure that international justice will finally allow them to understand.[40]

The statement describes victims as condemned to *wait* without the action of their representatives. The victims of international crimes require the

---

[37] Mark Drumbl has stressed the rhetorical and legal techniques employed to construct the innocence of children and the monstrosity of the child soldier, for example, Mark A. Drumbl in 'Victims Who Victimise' (2016) 4(2) *London Review of International Law* 217–246.

[38] *The Prosecutor v. Dominic Ongwen* (Pre-Trial Chamber II, Decision on the confirmation of charges against Dominic Ongwen) ICC-02/-4-01/15 (23 March 2016) 68–69.

[39] Basia Spalek, *Crime Victims: Theory, Policy and Practice* (Palgrave Macmillan 2006).

[40] *The Prosecutor v. Germain Katanga and Mathieu Ngudjolo Chui* (Pre-Trial Chamber II, Opening of the Trial) ICC-01/04-01/07I (24 November 2009) 39.

Court to educate them so that they may *understand* their situation. Dependency is presented not only as one of legalistic formalities, but also one of education. The agents of the field – judges, prosecutors, victim representatives, legal officers at NGOs, and the media – claim for themselves the right to represent and to comprehend. Victims are not only deprived of a position of speaking for themselves, but also *understanding* for themselves. The very term 'victim', according to David Miers, inevitably promotes an image of passivity, where the victim has 'traditionally been viewed as the "sufferer" in a simple "doer-sufferer" model of criminal interaction'.[41] The ideal victim is constructed as a potential beneficiary of global justice who requires a subject – the agents of this field – to act for them.[42] The coaching of victims, mentioned in Chapter 4 as an issue arising in the ICC case of *Prosecutor v Thomas Dyilo Lubanga*, is symptomatic of a positioning of victims as dependent, as incapable of making sense of their own suffering.

Christie observed of the 'ideal victim' that they must be able to command just enough power to establish their identity as a victim and yet be too weak to become a threat to other interests.[43] In particular, victims become a threat when they seek to liberate themselves on their own terms.[44] The importance for 'ideal' victims to remain dependent can be exemplified through incidents in which victims *did* exercise agency and consequently lost certain privileges. Going to the heart of the question of representation, on occasion, victims have opted to choose their own legal representatives rather than the one provided by the Court. As a result, they were penalised for this exercise of agency. In May 2016, the ICC's Trial Chamber confirmed the Pre-Trial Chamber's ruling that legal aid to 1,434 victims participating in the *Ongwen* case should be denied on account of them choosing their own legal representative.[45] They wished to be represented by someone from their region or at least someone who

---

[41] David Miers, *Responses to Victimisation: A Comparative Study of Compensation for Criminal Violence in Great Britain and Ontario* (Professional Books 1978).

[42] Clarke, 'Fictions of Justice'.

[43] Christie, 'Ideal Victim', at 21 (emphasis in original).

[44] Martti Kosenniemi, 'The Lady Doth Protest Too Much: Kosovo, and the Turn to Ethics in International Law' 65(2) *Modern Law Review* (2002) 159–175, at 173–174.

[45] *The Prosecutor* v. *Dominic Ongwen* (Trial Chamber IX, Decision on the 'Request for a Determination Concerning Legal Aid' Submitted by the Legal Representatives of Victims) ICC-02/04-01/15 (26 May 2016).

spoke Acholi, their language.[46] In contrast, the remaining 592 victims *were* granted financial assistance; they had not chosen a legal representative themselves, accepting instead the assigned legal representative chosen by the Court. The judge informed the representatives chosen by two-thirds of the victims that they could notify their clients that legal aid could still be claimed if they changed their minds and chose the ICC's legal representative from the Office of Public Counsel for Victims instead. Whilst the negating of legal aid does not legally preclude representation, *de facto* it mostly does. The material coercion to submit to the Court's choice of representative sheds a light on the material precarity that comes with losing ideal victim status. In this case, the refusal was justified through neoliberal concerns about efficiency, with the court insisting that a choice of legal representative would result in 'an inevitably unwieldy system'.[47] Although common legal representation may be practical, 'it can also appear paternalistic, giving an impression that the courts know who can best represent victims' interests'.[48]

5.3.3 The Victim As 'Grotesque'

The web page of the ICC's Trust Fund for Victims includes images and video clips of victims who have visual scars of violence – burn marks, mutilations, and other injuries. Female victims bear scars and/or carry small children. Male victims, of which there are far fewer depictions, are badly maimed or 'feminised' by carrying children.[49] In her analysis of victimhood, Clarke further narrows down the stereotypes of 'ideal' victimhood by drawing attention to the kind of suffering

---

[46] *The Prosecutor v. Dominic Ongwen* (Pre-Trial Chamber II, Decision on Contested Victims' Application for Participation, Legal Representation of Victims and Their Procedural Rights), ICC-02/04-01/15 (27 November 2015).

[47] *The Prosecutor v. Dominic Ongwen* (Trial Chamber IX, Decision on Registry's Request for Clarification on the Issue of Legal Assistance Paid by the Court for the Legal Representatives of Victim) ICC-02/04-01/15-591 (14 November 2016). Similarly, in the case of *The Prosecutor v. William Samoei Ruto, Henry Kiprono Kosgey and Joshua Arap Sang*, the application of four victims to choose their own representative was rejected: (Pre-Trial Chamber II, Decision on the Motion from Victims a/0041/10, a/0045/10, a/0051/10 and a/0056/10 Requesting the Pre-Trial Chamber to Reconsider the Appointment of Common Legal Representative Sureta Chana for All Victims) ICC-01/09-01/11-330 (9 September 2011).

[48] Rachel Killean and Luke Moffett, 'Victim Legal Representation Before the ICC and ECCC' (2017) 15 *Journal of International Criminal Justice* (2017) 713–740, at 726.

[49] Trust Fund for Victims, available at: www.trustfundforvictims.org/en/victims-voices.

highlighted – a suffering that can be *seen*. Limbless amputees, raped girls with babies, and drug-addicted child soldiers are all part of the collective imagination of victims of global injustice.[50] 'The more spectacular the conjuring of the victim, the more urgent the call to support – morally, fiscally, legally, – the rule of law', according to Clarke.[51] In keeping with the emphasis on the visual, the ideal victim of global injustice displays external, often disturbing, impairments. The spectator is simultaneously repulsed and attracted by what they see, perhaps best captured through the term 'grotesque', the invocation of which maps onto the positive and negative attributes of spectacle. The grotesque is 'abnormal' and therefore unpleasant, but it is also weird and empathy-inducing. The grotesque is to be found in the exaggeration of certain features such as deep scars on a face with fine features, the bloated tummy on a small child's frame, the exposed lactating breasts of the thin and young mother, the boy who holds an enormous Kalashnikov.[52]

In the absence of actual imagery, legal representatives paint pictures of victims as grotesque through rhetoric. The former chief prosecutor of the Special Court for Sierra Leone uses 'the grotesque' to narrate encounters with victims of the Sierra Leonean civil war:

> During the course of the meeting a young woman, holding a child, stood up waiting to ask a question or make a comment. After answering the question at hand I turned to her to allow her to speak. This young Sierra Leonean woman was missing a large part of her face, her burn scars radiated down her shoulder, chest and arms. Blinded by her horrific injuries and through cracked lips she whispered 'the rebels have done this to me; do something about what they have done here'.[53]

'Grotesqueness' is conjured by reference to the deformed young mother; perhaps she was once beautiful. The deformation is unpleasant, but on account of her passive manner – waiting to speak, whispering through cracked lips – she nevertheless induces empathy. The fact that she is holding a child intensifies the imagery. This rhetorical embrace of

---

[50] Clarke, 'The Rule of Law through Its Economies of Appearances', at 11.

[51] Ibid.

[52] For an analysis, and ultimately endorsement, of the circulation of disturbing images of 'foreigners', see John Taylor, *Body Horror: Photojournalism, Catastrophe and War* (Manchester University Press 1998).

[53] Cited in David Crane, 'Dancing with the Devil: Prosecuting West Africa's Warlords – Current Lessons Learned and Challenges', in Edel Hughes, William Schabas, and Ramesh Thakur (eds.), *Atrocities and International Accountability: Beyond Transitional Justice* (United Nations University Press 2007) 133–141, at 133.

the grotesque to paint pictures is a common feature of opening statements in the courtroom.[54] The victim representative in the case against
Kenya's president, *Prosecutor v Uhuru Muigai Kenyatta*, for example, did
not hold back on the gory detail in his court presentation:

> When a machete lands on a human head, it can take many blows to kill.
> That became clear to victim 9309 one morning in Naivasha in January
> 2008. He had tried to escape his house, but Mungiki found him, hacked
> him repeatedly with a machete and then left him for dead. When I first
> met him five years after the attack on him, his head bore deep, deep scars,
> and part of his skull appeared to be hanging on by a miracle. On the
> evening of the attack, as he laid helplessly in hospital, he telephoned his
> wife, who told him that after he had been – after he had left, she had been
> gang-raped by a Mungiki, then doused in paraffin and set alight. Both of
> them were lucky to escape alive. Both of them want this trial to
> continue.[55]

The increased attention to (grotesque) victims is to be understood,
according to Sandra Walklate and other criminologists, in the context
of societal fascination with gory details and gothic horror.[56] Gothicism,
typified by gruesome injury, trauma, and shadowy figures, features
prominently in the way that suffering is stylised. 'The powers of horror
are an important feature of contemporary populism, and index the place
of emotion and fantasy in both institutional practices and political life,'
explains Claire Valier.[57] Images of grotesque victims are used in the
courtroom, in fundraising campaigns, in exhibitions, and in traditional
and social media. The maimed body of the victim encompasses the
popular (conservative) desire for retributive measures. Characteristic of
the narrations of the grotesque are the displacement from plot to gruesome spectacle, fuelling demand for penal severity and public protection.[58] The monstrosity of the villain is manifested in the grotesqueness
of the victim, the deflowering of beauty and potential.

---

[54] Opening statements often have a heightened degree of drama and pathos. See Sofia Stolk, 'A Solemn Tale of Horror: The Opening Statement of the Prosecution in International Criminal Trials' (doctoral thesis on file at Vrije Universiteit Amsterdam 2017).

[55] *The Prosecutor v. Uhuru Muigai Kenyatta* (Trial Chamber V, Status conference transcript) ICC-01/09-02/110 (5 February 2014) 17.

[56] Sandra Walklate, 'Perspectives on the Victim and Victimisation', in Walklate (ed.), *Handbook of Victims and Victimology* 12; Claire Valier, 'Punishment, Border Crossings and the Powers of Horror' (2002) 6(3) *Theoretical Criminology* 319–337.

[57] Ibid.

[58] Cynthia A. Freeland, 'Realist Horror' in Cynthia A. Freeland and Thomas E. Wartenberg (eds.), *Philosophy and Film* (Routledge 1995) 126–142.

5.4   Ideal Victim – Ideal Perpetrator – Ideal Representative Interrelationship

From the previous section, it has already become clear that it is impossible to isolate the construction of the victim from the perpetrator, or, for that matter, the legal representative. These roles co-constitute one-another.[59] The victim cannot appear weak and vulnerable unless the perpetrator is strong and the representative is rational. The more 'ideal' a victim is, the more 'ideal' the offender, making the legal representative also more 'ideal'. The ideal offender is typically portrayed as the antithesis of the victim: the offender is strong (male) and puts himself at risk; he is independent and politicised, and rather than carrying the empathy-inducing characteristics of the grotesque, the ideal offender is 'ugly' or 'aloof' – feeling no emotion. We recall from the previous chapter that the stereotype of the perpetrator can lead to a paradox, whereby the perpetrator is both an accountable agent, 'sophisticated', as well as inhuman, 'beastly'.[60] Switching from one stereotype to another depends on the relevant context. The beastly is highlighted in regard to victim suffering, often this will be an emphasis on the visceral. The sophisticated is emphasised in regard to forms of superior responsibility or command responsibility, fulfilling the stereotype of the 'criminal mastermind'.[61] The 'ideal' representative meanwhile is the reasonable voice in the emotive turmoil of the victim–perpetrator relationship. The legal representative might either be the distantly passionate prosecutorial team or the sombre defence team, or the compassionate victim representative.[62] Only on particular and rare occasions is the ideal representative 'passionate', such as the opening statements in the courtroom (and typically only if they are male). The legal representative generally speaks reason to chaos, makes reference to the neutrality and superiority of the law, and tempers the emotions through a language of expertise.

---

[59] As regards the co-construction of victim and perpetrator, see Christie, 'Ideal Victim', 25.

[60] Sofia Stolk, 'A Sophisticated Beast? On the Construction of an "Ideal" Perpetrator in the Opening Statements of International Criminal Trials' (2018) 29(3) *European Journal of International Law* 677–701.

[61] Ibid.

[62] This is reminiscent of Makau Mutua's three-dimensional compound metaphor of the savage, victim, and savior of human rights law. Mutua describes the relationship between the roles as 'uni-directional and predictable, a black-and-white construction that pits good against evil', Makau Mutua, 'Savages, Victims, and Saviors: The Metaphor of Human Rights' (2001) 42(1) *Harvard International Law Journal* 201–245.

The statement that global justice is for a 'higher cause' than remuneration is a common trope in regard to ideal representatives. It is worth mentioning that the real market value of victim representation goes beyond salaries. To be sure, the material value begins with the salaries and fees gained. This marketability continues with the administrative and professional services support and facilities required, with drivers, cleaning staff, catering, and childcare. Legal experts and administrators move from tribunal to tribunal, creating greater demand for their expertise, which they alone cannot meet. Accumulation continues with the new roles created to meet demand, the institutions founded and expanded to accommodate the experts, the expansion of the city structures in which the experts live, the restaurants that cater to them, the flights booked for work, pleasure and to see family and friends at home.[63] And so on. We are not just speaking of the social capital of being a global justice actor; this is capital in its economic meaning.

5.5   Commodification of Victimhood

Although the marketisation of global justice might imply a fairly straightforward reading of victims as consumers of services, this is not the case. Victims are far more prominently *used* in the industry than that they themselves make use of the industry. Anthropologist Bernard Hours employs the term 'victim industry' in order to capture the concern that '[v]ictims are anonymous and interchangeable, passive players in the emotive campaign leaflets of NGOs'.[64] In *The Marketing of Rebellion*, Bob Clifford discusses the fierce competition among victim representatives (whom he calls 'challengers') for transnational patrons: 'In this global morality market, challengers must publicize their [victim] plights, portray their conflicts as righteous struggles, and craft their messages to resonate abroad.'[65] Publicising plights, portraying struggles, and crafting messages are made possible with the use of a simplified narrative and spectacularised images of the suffering of victims – in the alliance between marketing and global justice. The morality market that

---

[63] The material gains for The Hague branding itself 'City of International Peace and Justice' are discussed in more detail in Chapter 8.

[64] Bernard Hours, 'NGOs and the Victim Industry', *Le Monde diplomatique* (November 2008).

[65] Bob Clifford, *The Marketing of Rebellion: Insurgents, Media, and International Activism* (Cambridge University Press 2007). 4.

Clifford refers to ties in with the observation that victims relay a moral purpose to projects, some that would otherwise be seen as merely vengeful or abusive.[66]

Metrics play an important role in the victim industry. According to Hours, states tend to manipulate victim numbers in order to either attract or detract aid agencies; Burma and China keep figures low, while countries in Latin America overestimate 'in order to make it into the global humanitarian agenda'.[67] This concern about the interchangeability and passivity of victims in the NGO sector – victims primarily as the objects of an industry – can be widened to the global justice sector. In a victim industry, the value of a victim is measured by how productive they can be to garner media attention, donor awareness, and public support for the respective global justice actor. Such utilisation of victims implies their *exploitation*, diametrically opposed to the promises of support and emancipation.

At the ICC, the victim industry is manifesting through the increasingly proceduralised selection programmes. One aspect, namely the choice of legal respresentation, has already been mentioned as the proceduralisation along the ideal victim parameters. More generally, it is noteworthy that the interchangability of victims most commonly flows from abstractions of individual suffering. In most legal societies, the harm is perceived as not only experienced by the individual victim but also by a polity, represented in criminal law through the prosecutor standing in for that polity. In the case of global justice, the harmed polity is globalised. Victims of 'crimes against humanity' in particular, are bundled together with the rest of *humanity*. These crimes are by definition crimes not only committed against the individual victim; all of humanity becomes a victim. This may have symbolic validity, but it also causes a significant distancing of the suffering from the subject.[68]

Proceduralised abstraction is mostly facilitated through a streamlining process that narrows victimhood from the level of humanity at large to a specified and exclusive group. Although victim participation continues to be determined on a case-by-case basis at the ICC, practices of

---

[66] McEvoy and McConnehie, 'Victimology in Transitional Justice', 530.

[67] Hours, 'NGOs and the Victim Industry'.

[68] Frédéric Mégret, 'In Whose Name?' in Christian De Vos, Sara Kendall, and Carsten Stahn (eds.) *Contested Justice: The Politics and Practice of International Criminal Court Interventions* (Cambridge University Press 2015) 23–45, at 27 with reference to Daniel Levy and Natan Sznaider, 'The Institutionalization of Cosmopolitan Morality: The Holocaust and Human Rights' (2004) 3 *Journal of Human Rights*' 143–157, at 144.

streamlining are nevertheless prominent. At the most basic level, stream-lining occurs at a definitional level. The ICC's Rules of Procedure and Evidence define 'victims' widely as any natural persons who have suffered harm as a result of the commission of a crime that is in the jurisdiction of the Court. Victims may even include organisations or institutions.[69] In keeping with the cleavage between rhetoric and process (image and content), victims are defined widely, but Court procedure significantly narrows the category. Fundamentally, victimhood is necessarily dependent on the charges brought by the prosecution. Due to the narrow prosecutorial focus, a large number of 'de facto victims' are excluded.

A further simultaneous abstraction of the category 'victim' and narrowing to 'ideal victim' occurs through the victims' participation process. Collective representations hide individual stories of suffering, instead creating generic (and often spectacularised) stories. This is done through the organisation of victims into groups with common interests and similar geographical location as well as through the collectivisation of applications.[70] As a result of the economies of scale in representing mass violence, widely divergent victims' groups are treated as a single homogenous group with uniform preferences and needs.[71] Generally, this is justified for reasons of efficiency. However, such reasoning can mask the filtering process of victims that are 'non-ideal' from those that are 'ideal'. Meanwhile, despite its purported focus on victims, the Rome Statute does not allocate funds to victim reparations; rather, a separate body, the Trust Fund for Victims (TFV) was set up for this purpose. The TFV largely relies on donor money.[72] Donors are more likely to respond to the fundraising image of 'ideal' victimhood than a complicating narrative of structural inadequacies. The under-emphasis of victims' interests in the ICC's procedure, then, lies in stark contrast to the over-emphasis in the ICC's rhetoric. These particular practices of narrowing

---

[69] Rule 85, International Criminal Court Rules of Procedure and Evidence.

[70] For example, see *The Prosecutor* v. *Bosco Ntaganda*, (Pre-Trial Chamber II, Decision on Common Legal Representation of Victims) ICC-01/04-02/06-160 (2 December 2013).

[71] Luke Moffett, 'Elaborating Justice for Victims at the International Criminal Court: Beyond Rhetoric and the Hague' (2015) 13(2) *Journal of International Criminal Justice* 281–311.

[72] On the sources of funding, see 'Establishment of a Fund for the Benefit of Victims of Crimes Within the Jurisdiction of the Court, and of the Families of such Victims' ICC-ASP/1/Res 6 (9 September 2002). Carla Ferstman, 'The International Criminal Court's Trust Fund for Victims: Challenges and Opportunities' (2009) 6 *Yearbook of International Humanitarian Law* 424–434.

and 'juridifying' are specific to the ICC,[73] but at the same time are exemplary of the selection practices of the global justice sector as a whole. What is significant about the ICC's streamlining is that it shapes an institutionalised notion of the ideal victim for all its member states and beyond. The selection of victims highlights the material value ascribed to juridified victims, inviting an extension of the term 'juridified victimhood' to 'commodified victimhood'.

5.6   Alienation from Suffering

Being the 'face' of global justice is not only about the outward marketisation of victims as a victim 'brand'; it is also about the altering of victim identity to suit the brand. In branding, this process is referred to as internal branding, what we learned from discussions in Chapter 2 on Advocacy as the idea of 'living the brand'. In the context of victim identity, we might also call this a process of alienation. As we already know, victims must 'live up to' the brand of the ideal victim, or they risk either missing out on privileges or losing them. In *Ethnicity, Inc.*, John and Jean Comaroff call the relevant market the 'identity economy', where 'the corporeal meets the corporate, where essence becomes enterprise'.[74] 'Ethnic incorporation' for the Comaroffs, as with marketised global justice here, 'rides on a process of homogenization and abstraction'.[75] Victims of conflict, despite all their diverse ways of living and suffering, become one. This process is 'all the better to conceive, communicate, and consume' for those driving marketisation but it also becomes a matter of self-construction.[76] In their analysis of 'ethnopreneurialism' in South Africa, Vanuatu, Argentina, Peru, Kenya, and the United States, the Comaroffs do not only expose ethnicity to a market critique, but stress a dialectical relationship. The market may be shaping various ethnic groups, but this is only one part of the story; the other part is the 'mode of reflection' and 'self-construction'.[77] Stereotypes such as the feminised, infantilised, and racialised 'ideal' victim are not only produced in marketised gobal justice, they are inhabited and co-produced.

---

[73] Kendall and Nouwen, 'Representational Practices at the ICC'.
[74] Jean and John Comaroff, *Ethnicity, Inc.* (University of Chicago Press 2009) 9.
[75] Ibid 12.
[76] Ibid.
[77] Ibid 9.

Figure 5.1 ICC Visitor Centre
(photograph taken by the author)

The dialectical relationship between imposed identities and identity self-construction of victims is particularly explicit in the ICC's Visitor Centre. The exhibition is situated just to the left of the reception desk of the main building, which one enters after clearing the security and identity checks. It includes a series of exhibits portraying the work of the ICC through images, texts, and sound.

Strolling through the 'victim' section of the exhibition with a smartphone-type device, one can listen to a statement titled: 'What was it like being represented or testifying in the courtroom'. A heavily accented female voice states:

> Testifying felt like letting go of something I had been holding on to. I felt free and very proud that I had done my work well. We would be forgotten without the Court. The Court is there so our voice is heard.

These words were never uttered by a real victim. The words represent not only the construction of victimhood by the ICC, but also the projection of an idea of self-construction. Most interesting is that the victim's suffering is constructed as labour: *I felt like I had done my work well.* The victim's court testament is arguably transformed into labour expended on the production of goods and services for the global justice sector.

According to revolutionary and post-colonial thinker Frantz Fanon, colonialism consists of two moments: the first is economic and material inferiority as a result of colonial subjugation; the second is when this inferiority is internalised.[78] Kapur's work provides further empirical evidence of the internalisation and reproduction of this form of repression. In her work, she has demonstrated that the image of the brown raped woman is reproduced and inhabited by the international women's rights movement in the post-colonial context.[79] To be sure, the inhabiting of the stereotype reveals something of the perceived necessity to argue within the existing power parameters to achieve recognition, but it also shows a lack of alternative identities and a narrowing of the possibility of alternatives. The emerging neoliberal victim industry is one in which victims *themselves* understand their suffering to be in competition with the suffering of other victims.

Criminologist Simon Green draws a compelling parallel between a worker's exploitation and alienation under capitalism and a victim's exploitation and alienation in the market place.[80] On account of the striving for the accumulation of wealth through wage labour, workers must consider both the fruits of their labour and their labour itself as another man's property.[81] The labour becomes alien to the worker; it is a powerful object independent of them. Meanwhile, as the capitalist strives for the greatest amount of surplus value, '[t]he worker becomes all the poorer the more wealth he produces'.[82] The worker is dependent on the capitalist, as wages constitute livelihood. The workers have become enslaved to their work, at the same time as becoming alienated from it and from their fellow human beings. As to victims: the chains of representation (pun intended) inside and outside of the courtroom – being passed from lawyer to bureaucrats to NGO workers who shape the experience of victimhood in accordance with market demand – appropriate the

---

[78] Frantz Fanon, (Charles Lam Markmann, trans), *Black Skin, White Masks* [1952] (Pluto Books 2008).

[79] Green, 'Crime, Victimization, and Vulnerability'.

[80] Ibid. Drawing on Karl Marx's conceptualisation of alienation, which is hinged on stratified social classes in which capitalists own the means of production. Alienation is explained in Karl Marx, *Economic and Philosophic Manuscripts of 1844*.

[81] Karl Marx, 'Economic and Philosophic Manuscripts of 1844', [1932] in *Early Writings* (Penguin 2000).

[82] Ibid.

lived experience of suffering. The victim is labouring (testifying, being photographed, being filmed) for the creation of surplus value in the global justice sector. Marketised global justice consequently 'steals [a victim's] experience, and puts in its place a cheap and ghastly imitation'.[83] Guy Debord articulated the process of representation in the society of the spectacle as a process by which 'the tangible world is replaced by a selection of images which exist above it, and simultaneously impose themselves as the tangible *par excellence*'.[84] The real experience of suffering is replaced by a stereotype of suffering. This suffering exists beyond the lived experience, and simultaneously imposes itself as the experience itself. Neoliberalism's ability to reimagine political subjects as entrepreneurs and consumers sharpens this concern: victims find themselves on the global victim market-place where they offer their suffering for sale. The victim status becomes riddled with precarity: if victims find a 'buyer' for their suffering, they can retain their status, but it is dependent on demonstrating and maintaining features of the 'ideal' victim. If demand for victims on the market is low, say because the attention economy is demanding attention elsewhere, the victims' suffering becomes obsolete. As with the demand for the labour of the worker, a victim's hopes for representation 'depends on the whim of the rich and the capitalists'.[85] Similarly to the worker, the victim is treated like any other commodity. And it is a bit of luck for them if they can find a buyer.

5.7 Conclusion

When it comes to victims, the 'popular presumption today is that to utter the words "victims want justice" is to assume that "victims want adjudication".[86] In Chapter 1, I asked who benefits from the narrative of victims wanting adjudication. Victims? Or their representatives in the global justice sector? Put bluntly, the victim industry organised around anti-impunity as global justice does not serve the interests of victims of conflict, but rather exploits victims' suffering for the purposes of capital growth. This market thinking around definitions of victimhood privileges

---

[83] Susan Marks and Andrew Clapham, 'Victims' in *International Human Rights Lexicon* (Oxford University Press 2005) 399–410.

[84] Guy Debord, *Society of the Spectacle* [1967] (Black & Red 1984) para. 36.

[85] Marx, 'Economic and Philosophic Manuscripts'.

[86] Kamari Maxine Clarke, '"We Ask for Justice, You Give Us Law": The Rule of Law, Economic Markets and the Reconfiguration of Victimhood', in De Vos, Kendall and Stahn, 'Contested Justice' 272–301, at 274.

some victims over others, creating a hierarchy whereby victims who demonstrate certain marketable features are prioritised over others. The dominance of this stereotype means that victims themselves begin to submit to the brand. In branding, this is the idea that the brand experience must become the 'authentic' experience; from a Marxist perspective, this is a process of alienation.

Picking up on a point made in Chapter 4, the victim industry is not, however, marketised global justice 'gone wrong'. The structure of marketised global justice was never intended to lead to a redistribution of resources. We can apply the conclusions from Chapter 4 to this chapter too: channelling victim demands towards a particular set of products and services hides alternative mechanisms for global justice as well as renders structural violence invisible. As Michel Foucault argued in his analysis of institutionalised power, expert institutions strategically deploy discourses not as a means to neutrally channel information about social harms to the public but also to reinforce dominant values that lessen potential opposition to the *status quo*.[87]

From the preceding chapters, we note that marketised global justice takes shape in the interconnection between: (a) branding, (b) the attention economy, (c) spectacle, (d) ICL, (e) neoliberalism, and (f) neocolonialism. The case studies of Chapters 6, 7, and 8 highlight different aspects of these six themes in how they have aligned, and how they operate. In the coming analysis, I distinguish between particular actors of the global justice sector. I have selected the NGO Invisible Children as representing marketised global justice from the perspective of the non-governmental world; the ICC as illustrative of marketised global justice from the perspective of an international organisation; and the place branding practices of The Hague, South Africa, and Cambodia as illustrative of marketised global justice from a place/nation state perspective. The case studies will first illustrate the modalities of marketised global justice, picking up on ideas from Chapter 4. They then turn to an analysis of the backlashes and resistance against marketised global justice, which will create the foundations to the question, dealt with in Chapter 9, of whether there is a way of resisting marketised global justice.

---

[87] Michel Foucault, *Discipline and Punish: The Birth of the Prison* (trans. Alan Sheridan) (Pantheon 1977) 304.

6

Kony 2012

Making an Accused *Famous*

> In order for the people to care, they have to know. And they will only know if Kony's name is everywhere.[1]

6.1 Introduction

On 5 March 2012, the US-based non-governmental organisation (NGO) Invisible Children launched *Kony 2012*, a 29-minute documentary-style advocacy clip on the Internet. The video begins with the words: 'Nothing is more powerful than an idea whose time has come. Nothing is more powerful than an idea whose time is now.'[2] At the centre of the clip are the entwined lives of four people: The San Diego-based film-maker Jason Russell at the helm of the campaign, his young son Gavin, a former Ugandan child soldier named Jacob Acaye, and Ugandan militia leader Joseph Kony. The aim of the film was to make Kony *famous* in order to bring him to justice before the International Criminal Court (ICC). The ICC's Pre-Trial Chamber had issued an arrest warrant against Joseph Kony for war crimes and crimes against humanity seven years earlier.[3] The situation that the clip aimed to draw attention to was the forced recruitment of child soldiers by Kony's army.[4] The video is an emotive mix of personal stories, celebrity endorsements, government promises, grand narratives, and slick editing. Within hours, the video went viral and became the most widely distributed video of all time. Invisible Children raised over US$ 26 million in the financial year of 2012.[5]

---

[1] Jason Russell in the 'Kony 2012' campaign video, available at https://invisiblechildren .com/kony-2012.

[2] Ibid.

[3] *Situation in Uganda* (Pre-Trial Chamber II, Warrant of Arrest for Joseph Kony Issued on 8 July 2015 as Amended on 27 September 2005) ICC-02/04-01/05 (27 September 2005).

[4] Conscripting or enlisting children under the age of fifteen years is a war crime according to Articles 8(2)(b)(xxvi), 8(e)(vii) of the Rome Statute.

[5] This is twice the amount they raised the year before. Invisible Children Inc, 'Financial Statements' (30 June 2012), available at: https://invisiblechildren.com/financials.

A week after the video launch, the US Congress supported a resolution 'Expressing support for robust efforts by the United States to see Joseph Kony [. . .] brought to justice and the group's atrocities permanently ended'.[6] Kony did become famous. Despite these successes, there were also significant defeats for the NGO. Kony was not arrested, neither by the specially deployed troops, nor by his fellow countrymen. And although the video was shared millions of times, the campaign was unable to garner the necessary support for its so-called 'Cover the Night' mission, which encouraged supporters to hang up Kony posters on 20th April 2012. 'We will blanket every street of every city', says Russell in the video clip. The mission did not achieve the desired results.[7] Just over six weeks after the video went viral, the momentum was already lost.

Kony 2012 is the first of three case studies of marketised global justice. The hypothesis that the case studies seek to test is that global justice actors are giving primacy to market values over social values by consti- tuting a global market in which they compete for resources. Indicative as well as constitutive of such a market is the employment of marketing practices such as branding that emphasise a spectacularised idea of anti- impunity specifically and global justice more generally. Six key terms emerged from the previous chapters as making up the central building blocks for the operation of marketised global justice: (a) branding, (b) the attention economy, (c) spectacle, (d) international criminal law, (e) neoliberalism, and (f) neo-colonialism. The three case study chapters illustrate how marketised global justice operates in different parts of the global justice sector through the intersection of these themes. This will illustrate how broad the global justice sector is, and yet how narrow its aims are. Each chapter draws out slightly different emphases of the key themes of marketised global justice.

That NGOs seek to attract funding and operate in a competitive environment is fairly undisputed. However, the argument is that here

---

[6] House of Representatives (Expressing support for robust efforts by the United States to see Joseph Kony, the leader of the Lord's Resistance Army, and its top commanders brought to justice and the group's atrocities permanently ended') H.Res.583, 112th Congress (13 March 2012). The USA had deployed military personnel a year earlier in the form of 100 military advisers – something that is wildly celebrated in the Kony 2012 video.

[7] Rory Carroll, 'Kony 2012 Cover the Night Fails to Move from the Internet to the Streets', The Guardian, 21 April 2012; Patricia Daley, 'Rescuing African Bodies: Celebrities, Consumerism and Neoliberal Humanitarianism' (2013) 40 Review of African Political Economy 375–393, at 386.

too spectacle has an ordering function for global justice. Marketing practices are facilitating the distribution of attention and capital to a narrow set of issues while simultaneously impoverishing the meaning of global justice. The NGO sector is of course extremely broad, and different practices are engaged, some closer to the market, some further from it. With *Kony 2012*, I have chosen a perhaps extreme example of marketised global justice. Although extreme, it was also at its time the mainstream.

Beyond the description of the operation of marketised global justice in the NGO sector, the present chapter aims to highlight three things in particular: the close alliance between the anti-impunity movement and military intervention, the global justice sector's alliance with racial capitalism, and the more general de-politicisation of global justice that is linked to viewing donors as consumers. This last consequence of marketised global justice becomes particularly apparent not only in the analysis of the success of the *Kony 2012* campaign, but in the analysis of the *backlash* against it. While *Kony 2012* was symptomatic and constitutive of marketised global justice, I argue that its backlash was too.

Before we direct attention to the marketing practices employed by Invisible Children, let us first consider some context. Although Russell in *Kony 2012* highlights the urgency of the *now,* the conflict in northern Uganda had been ongoing for many years. The Lord's Resistance Army (LRA) was one of several rebel movements founded in 1987 in proclaimed opposition to President Yoweri Museveni and his government policies, many of which were cast in ethnic terms against the Acholi people in northern Uganda. The northern Ugandan region had become destabilised under Idi Amin's rule, but the situation worsened when Museveni took power and implemented *Operation North.*[8] A civil war began, which claimed the lives of tens of thousands of civilians. From the mid-1990s, Museveni enacted policies of forced displacement, ostensibly to protect the population, which by the early 2000s drove an estimated 1.8 million people, and almost 90 per cent of the northern Ugandan population, into internally displaced camps.[9] Most of the violence,

---

[8] *Operation North* included arming small groups with bows and arrows as a defence mechanism against the LRA. As the LRA operated with modern weapons, the Acholi people were easily defeated. Kony felt betrayed by the people and intensifed the violence by the LRA. Adam Branch, 'Exploring the Roots of LRA Violence: Political Crisis and Ethnic Politics in Acholiland' in Tim Allen and Koen Vlassenroot (eds.) *The Lord's Resistance Army: Myth and Reality* (Zed Books 2010) 25–44, at 26.

[9] United Nations Office for the Coordination of Humanitarian Affairs, 'Consolidated Appeal for Uganda 2006', 30 November 2005.

including murder, rape, torture, abductions, and looting occurred in the regions of Acholi, Lango, and Teso.[10] The LRA's leader Joseph Kony, who declared himself a prophet and claimed that spirits spoke to him, won support among the persecuted Acholi people. But he also lost supporters due to the violence he used as a military tactic.[11] It was Museveni who referred 'the situation concerning the Lord's Resistance Army' to the ICC in December 2003,[12] thereby giving the prosecutor cause to begin investigations and to identify potential perpetrators of international crimes. As the ICC only has jurisdiction for crimes committed since 2002 (when the Court began to operate), only a year of Kony's operations could be taken into account in the arrest warrant. It was around the time of the referral of the situation in Uganda to the ICC that Jason Russell first visited the country. He witnessed a chilling phenomenon, which began in the early 2000s, where thousands of children would walk for miles from the internally displaced camps in the night to find a safe place to sleep, typically bus terminals, hospital corridors, and verandas of private and commercial properties in nearby towns. The children 'commuted' out of concern that they would otherwise be abducted in their sleep. The so-called 'night commuter' phenomenon was what prompted Jason Russell and his friends to set up Invisible Children. Russell was determined to draw attention to the events in Uganda. He was of course quite right to recognise that the mass movement of children would have caused worldwide outrage had these been American children.[13]

6.2   Marketing Joseph Kony

Kony 2012 was one of the greatest brand awareness campaigns ever – 100 million hits on social media in just six days. Big brands can only dream of such circulation figures of their content. How did a relatively small NGO attract this kind of attention? A great deal of the work of

---

[10] Phil Clark, *Distant Justice: The Impact of the International Criminal Court on African Politics* (Cambridge University Press 2019) 13, 14.

[11] Branch, 'Exploring the Roots of LRA Violence'.

[12] 'President of Uganda Refers Situation Concerning the Lord's Resistance Army (LRA) to the ICC' (Press Release) ICC-20040129-44-En (29 January 2004).

[13] The racial dimension is notable, as the United States holds hundreds of children in cages, separating them from their parents and forbidding any human contact. David Remnick, 'Trump's Cruelty and the Crying Children at the Border', *The New Yorker*, 19 June 2018.

NGOs involves awareness-raising for the organisation, its causes, and its projects. NGOs have neither the backing of the state apparatus to raise awareness for their work, nor (usually) the budget of corporations.[14] So they must find ways of attracting attention through other means. Attention, they hope, translates into donations. Needless to say, NGOs are reliant on voluntary contributions. Contributions can be made through membership fees, through purchasing merchandise or donated goods, or through one-off donations. In order to raise awareness, NGOs typically look to the kinds of marketing practices used by corporate actors. Today, it is common for NGOs to cultivate a brand, to refer to a 'consumer' base, and to devise mass communications strategies. Branding has become so common in the sector that it is not unusual to hear about *re*-brands as a process of renewal for growth. 'In the charity and NGO sector, to maintain or increase market share, many charities are now seeing re-branding as a strategic tool to drive awareness and to propel their commercial activities and fundraising'.[15]

Human rights NGOs, in particular, have a clearly defined idea of their donors as a 'consumer base': they target, almost exclusively, donors in the Global North.[16] In the NGO world, the appeal to a particular donor's needs and desires is sometimes referred to as a 'donor-centric engagement strategy'. The narrative and aesthetics that emerges from such a specific identification of market potential is one that often exaggerates already existing rifts between North and South. The donors in the North are presented as the saviours, and those in whose name campaigns are launched, the beneficiaries, are often cast as the innocent victims in the 'ideal' victim construction set out in Chapter 5.

Today, social media plays a central role in marketing strategies, particularly for NGOs working on global causes. Indeed, most NGOs have substantially expanded their communications teams in the age of social media and the chase after a viral campaign.[17] Driven by the idea that communications media is bridging the gap between causes at home and

---

[14] Although the large NGOs do manage million dollar budgets, including Amnesty International, Human Rights Watch, and Invisible Children. See on the emergence of this phenomenon, James Petras, 'NGOs: In the Service of Imperialism' (1999) 29 *Journal of Contemporary Asia* 429–440.

[15] Michael Johnson, *Branding in Five and a Half Steps* (Thames & Hudson 2016) 18.

[16] Bob Clifford, *The Marketing of Rebellion: Insurgents, Media, and International Activism* (Cambridge University Press 2005).

[17] '2018 Global NGO Technology Report', Nonproht Tech for Good, February 2018 The report uses data from 5352 NGOs from 164 countries, available at: http://techreport.ngo/.

far away, NGOs are decreasing their operations 'on the ground'. NGOs instead tend to focus on awareness-raising, with photographs and video footage of the relevant distant place standing in for the whole conflict. The move to awareness-raising initially included the dissemination of shaky camera footage – the realist aesthetic of humanitarianism.[18] The realist aesthetic, however, was already in decline at the time of *Kony 2012*, 'eclipsed by the full integration of corporate brand culture and humanitarianism.'[19] Such integration focuses more on storytelling, recognisable characters, and a cleaner editing. This, according to Melissa Brough, is prompted by the idea of the 'humanitarian *donor as consumer.*'[20] The following pages analyse Invisible Children's awareness-raising marketing techniques, asking first when the focus on awareness raising became prominent, then why the shift to anti-impunity occurred in the NGO sector, and finally why *fame* was so central to the *Kony 2012* campaign.

6.2.1   Save Darfur *As Precedent*

One of the first campaigns to focus on awareness-raising of a fairly unknown conflict far away from the donor base was the *Save Darfur* campaign led by the Save Darfur Coalition. The similarities between *Save Darfur* and *Kony 2012* are notable. The Coalition was founded in New York in 2004, and was headquartered in Washington DC. The *Save Darfur* campaign was brought to (mainly American) households through the work of US activist John Prendergast and Hollywood actor Don Cheadle, the actor who played the hero hotel manager in the movie *Hotel Rwanda.*[21] The campaign aimed to raise awareness about the genocide in Darfur, focusing on 'people making noise' to pressurise their governments to intervene. It became the world's largest Facebook campaign at the time.[22] Mahmod Mamdani, an outspoken and diligent

---

[18] Melissa M. Brough, '"Fair Vanity": The Visual Culture of Humanitarianism in the Age of Commodity Activism' in Roopali Mukherjee and Sarah Banet-Weiser (eds.), *Commodity Activism: Cultural Resistance in Neoliberal Times* (New York University Press 2012) 174–198 at 178.

[19] Ibid 178.

[20] Ibid 176. Emphasis in original.

[21] Don Cheadle and John Prendergast, *Not on Our Watch: The Mission to End Genocide in Darfur and Beyond* (Hachette Books 2007). *Hotel Rwanda.* Directed by Terry George, United Artists 2004.

[22] Bhakti Shringarpure, 'The Rise of the Digital Saviour: Can Facebook Likes Change the World?' *The Guardian*, 18 June 2015.

critic of the campaign, critiqued, among other things, the fact that the campaign was organised by a full-time ad agency. '[A]dvocacy had turned into a series of advertisements'.[23] Apart from its celebrity engagement and use of social media, the campaign laid the groundwork for some by now familiar tropes. The cover of the co-authored book *Not on Our Watch: The Mission to End Genocide in Darfur and Beyond* features a black African child staring into the camera.[24] The music compilation by Amnesty International has the title *Instant Karma*, an orientalised tagline that suggests that donating will create good karma.[25] Bono, the lead vocalist of U2, who recorded 'Instant Karma' for the album famously said: 'Africa is sexy and people need to know that'.[26] Indeed, this was part of an effort to 'rebrand' Africa.[27] Given the attention that *Save Darfur* received (by the Western media), it was named 'the largest international social movement since anti-apartheid'.[28] Finally, on the basis of the pressure laid on it by the likes of the ICC prosecutor himself, the Western media, and other NGOs, the UN Security Council referred the situation to the ICC. The UN Security Council referral led to the arrest warrant of Sudan's President. On 4 March 2009, the first warrant of arrest for Omar Al Bashir was issued by the ICC's Pre-Trial Chamber.[29] As with *Kony 2012*, the *Save Darfur* campaign experienced a severe backlash.

Invisible Children was founded in 2004, the same year as the Save Darfur Coalition, and was very much inspired by it. Indeed, the three friends Jason Russell, Laren Poole, and Bobby Bailey initially set off to Sudan to document the 'hidden holocaust' of Darfur. This journey is documented in their film *Rough Cut*.[30] Beginning in 2003 in Kenya, the

---

[23] Mahmood Mamdani, *Saviors and Survivors: Darfur, Politics and the War on Terror* (Verso 2009) 51.

[24] Cheadle and Prendergast, 'Not on Our Watch'.

[25] *Instant Karma: The Amnesty International Campaign to Save Darfur*. Warner Music México 2007. 'Instant Karma' is U2's cover of the 1970 John Lennon song on the compilation.

[26] David Carr, 'Citizen Bono Brings Africa to Idle Rich', *The New York Times*, 5 March 2007.

[27] Ibid.

[28] David Lanz, 'Save Darfur: A Movement and its Discontents' (2009) 108 *African Affairs* 669–677.

[29] *The Prosecutor v. Omar Hassan Ahmad Al Bashir* (Pre-Trial Chamber I, Warrant of Arrest for Omar Hassan Ahmad Al Bashir) ICC-02/05-01/09-1 (04 March 2009).

[30] *Invisible Children: Rough Cut*. Directed by Laren Poole and Jason Russell, Invisible Children and People Like You Productions 2006.

three friends start their journey through documenting their experience of an orphanage they happen across. Here, the children were often only fed once a day, they explain, but 'when they danced, they danced'. The footage moves from dancing children to black and white footage of arid land and broken buildings.

> We left Kenya and headed to the country we had set out to explore and conquer: Sudan. We came to this country as brave travelers but we were determined to face the danger head-on and leave as *warriors*.[31]

During the narrative, the music reaches a triumphant climax as the shadow of each traveller emerges from a pile of rubble. Despite their best efforts at storytelling through editing, the three friends expressed their disappointment at the lack of dramatic footage. They decided to leave Sudan and travel to neighbouring northern Uganda instead, where many Sudanese refugees had fled. In the refugee camps, and camps for the internally displaced, they got the dramatic footage they had hoped for. Forced to stay in Gulu, northern Uganda, over night, the three friends witnessed thousands of children 'commuting' to the city at night. 'Needless to say, we found our story', says Russell in *Rough Cut*.[32]

6.2.2   Global Justice NGOs

The purpose of making Kony *famous* was to have him arrested and brought to The Hague. On their website, Invisible Children describe their involvement in Uganda as 'demanding justice'.[33] NGOs have embraced the idea of fighting for anti-impunity as global justice with gusto. A number of NGOs frame their causes expressly as 'global justice' causes. Global Justice Now and Global Justice conceptualise campaigns around broad global issues of inequality concerning trade, health, and education. Human rights tend to play a central role for mobilising support: 'fight for the right to health' or 'fight for the right of others to be free from sexual slavery'. Human rights law can also play a role procedurally as a means of enforcing international laws, including advocacy at various United Nations bodies; the Global Justice Centre focuses on this type of work, for example. The most favoured enforcement mechanism, however, is individual criminal accountability through an international criminal

---

[31] Ibid.
[32] Ibid.
[33] https://invisiblechildren.com/kony-2012/.

court or tribunal. The NGO Coalition for the International Criminal Court (CICC), which centres its campaigns around global justice terminology, has already been introduced. 'We are 2,500 civil society organizations, small and big, in 150 countries, fighting for global justice for war crimes, crimes against humanity and genocide,' claims the homepage.[34] Other notable organisations who support the ICC and use the narrative and imagery of anti-impunity are Amnesty International and Human Rights Watch. For example, to draw attention to its annual report *State of the World's Human Rights,* Amnesty International USA claims on its website: 'Global Justice Gap Condemns Millions to Abuse'.[35] The global justice gap ostensibly concerns the efforts of powerful governments to block 'advances in international justice'. Amnesty International proclaims it is 'calling on governments to ensure accountability for their own actions, fully sign up to the International Criminal Court and ensure that crimes under international law can be prosecuted anywhere in the world'.[36] One of the Amnesty International merchandise slogans, emblazoned on T-Shirts to notebooks, is: 'Fighting Bad Guys Since 1961'.[37] The enthusiasm for the ICC has slightly been tempered in the past years. Human Rights Watch (HRW) still has a *Global Justice: The Expanding Reach of Accountability* guide on its website.[38] The guide includes an interactive map, and a time-line beginning with the 'Pinochet precedent'. However, although still active on the website, the guide was compiled in 2010, arguably around the peak of the 'ICC for global justice' trend. Today, HRW is more cautious, noting in its 'International Justice' section on the website that the ICC will need to 'rise to the challenge'.[39] Although the enthusiasm for the ICC may not be as exuberant as it once was, the commitment to anti-impunity as justice remains strong. The International Justice Program of HRW, for example, still foregrounds criminal accountability. 'Though limited in number and scope, these

---

[34] www.coalitionfortheicc.org.
[35] 'Global Justice Gap Condemns Millions to Abuse', Amnesty International USA, available at: www.amnestyusa.org/global-justice-gap-condemns-millions-to-abuse/.
[36] Ibid.
[37] See www.amnestyshop.org.uk.
[38] 'Global Justice: The Expanding Reach of Accountability', Human Rights Watch, 26 May 2010, available at: www.hrw.org/video-photos/interactive/2010/05/26/global-justice-expanding-reach-accountability.
[39] 'International Criminal Court', Human Rights Watch, available at: www.hrw.org/topic/justicia-internacional/international-criminal-court.

[criminal accountability] cases are a beacon of hope for victims', says Balkees Jarrah of HRW in a stirring video.[40]

Despite the trends of global justice, and the fluctuations in support for international criminal courts and tribunals, the timing of the commitment of NGOs to international criminal justice and anti-impunity is noteworthy. Notably, the turn to anti-impunity coincided with a sustained turn of the sector to the market. The embrace of international criminal justice came at a time when humanitarians, in the words of Stephen Hopgood, 'increasingly had to show *value for money*'.[41] As demands for the accountability and transparency of NGOs themselves became louder, an international court and tribunal system that claimed to go after 'bad guys' through de-politicised legal processes, proved a strong ally. NGOs now had a specific regime of accountability to rely on as well as a place, 'The Hague', to reference. The ease with which this regime of accountability could be condensed down to slogans and logos was not incidental; it was key for using this particular accountability regime over others. The employment of marketing practices such as branding is once again more than simply a cosmetic exercise, but indicative of deeper marketisation. It is now entirely normal that NGOs are routinely run like businesses. Particularly popular (although not without its critics) is the work of individuals who can run a non-profit like a start-up, also referred to as 'philanthropreneurs'.[42] Indeed, what used to be distinct about NGOs – their less professional demeanour and ways of conducting campaigns, their community-focused work, and their dedicated volunteers – has, in many cases, given way to professionalisation and entrepreneurialism, as well as greater volatility. Many NGOs dealing with human rights, humanitarianism, and development are trendy, open to taking risks, competitive and growth-oriented. The growth of such entrepreneurial NGOs can be traced alongside the popularisation of the view that the public sector does not create value, instead situating value creation as exclusive to the private sector.[43] As was discussed in the

---

[40] 'War Crimes Prosecutions in Europe: Video Q&A Highlight Cases Spurred by Syrian, Iraqi Refugees', Human Rights Watch, 20 October 2016, available at: www.hrw.org/news/2016/10/20/war-crimes-prosecutions-europe.

[41] Stephen Hopgood, *The Endtimes of Human Rights* (Cornell University Press 2013) 104. Emphasis in original.

[42] Amr Al-Dabbagh, 'How to Run Your Non-profit Like a Startup', *Fortune*, 2 February 2015.

[43] As set out in Mariana Mazzucato, *The Value of Everything: Making and Taking in the Global Economy* (Puffin 2018).

previous chapters, this shifting idea about value creation notably consoli-dated in the 1990s. The philanthropreneur and the entrepreneurial NGO are ultimately viewed as providing high returns on investments. Market orientation of NGOs has also altered the way in which campaigning is conducted as value for money. A simple message of action is valuable in the attention economy because its market value can, to a certain extent at least, be measured. This might be the prosecution of a war criminal. But, it might also be more tenuous empirics about visibility. Since 'making a difference' is difficult to prove empirically, particularly in the short-term, the attention economy rewards visibility of campaigns as measured through signatures, shares, and likes. The de facto impact of more visible versus less visible campaigns remains opaque. But, that is largely beside the point in an economy that rewards visibility for its own sake. Unsurprisingly, advertising agencies and consultants for NGOs are a common feature of the visibility economy. *Save Darfur*, for example, hired the advertising agency M + R Services, based in Washington DC, to take care of its publicity. Indeed, just how important marketing was for the Save Darfur Coalition, as pointed out by Mamdani, is illustrated by the fact that Bill Wasserman, the president of M + R Services, served as the Coalition's interim executive director from 2007–2008.[44]

NGOs typically commit to marketised global justice on a substantive level by framing their causes in terms of international crimes, most notably the 'atrocity crimes' enshrined in the ICC's Rome Statute: geno-cide, war crimes, and crimes against humanity.[45] The narrative of inter-national crimes tends to be accompanied by familiar atrocity images: black-and-white memory-jolting photographs of mass graves and evil leaders. Hitler frequently makes an appearance. The language is mostly around human rights, indicating the prevailing rhetorical purchase of human rights, despite procedurally being more straightforwardly inter-national criminal law (ICL), that is, about individual criminal account-ability. Legally universalised notions of good versus evil, violence, and individualised guilt, are communicated through aesthetic signifiers. The fight against impunity, as concerning individual 'evil perpetrators', 'inno-cent victims', and 'rational legal representatives', is regularly embedded in a racialised and gendered stereotype. As was discussed in Chapter 4 on 'The Value of Global Justice', there is a certain visual economy of such

---

[44] Mamdani, 'Saviours and Survivors' 23.
[45] The fourth 'core crime' is the crime of aggression over which the ICC gained jurisdiction in 2017.

stereotyped images, which operates on the basis of deep-seated notions of neo-colonialism. The colonial discourse, particularly of the nineteenth century, was buttressed by the visual construction of narratives of civil-isation on the one hand and primitivism on the other hand. These visual constructions reified the Western 'self' as 'civilised', while the non-Western 'Other' was presented in contrast as 'primitive' and in need of civilising.[46] It was a visual signifier for Western progress. Despite branding being about distinctiveness, the NGOs promoting global justice, humanitarianism, human rights, or development all strikingly follow the same 'business model' for raising awareness for suffering in distant places.[47] In an ethnography of northern Uganda, Ayesha Anne Nibbe explains: 'The good, pure, blameless children caught in the midst of "evil-Africa" is a fundamental marketing tool to sell a humanitarian cause to the international community.'[48] The Global South is compressed to backwardness, conflict, dependence. The victim stereotype – feminised, infantilised, and racialised – stands in for the countries affected by conflict, or even for the whole of the Global South. As regards Africa, there is a particular affinity of the Western upper-middle classes to the narrative of the 'scourge of Africa'. Nibbe explained the context as:

> a constant barrage of images of African children infantilizes the continent in the consciousness of the international community; Africa remains a place of need, of dependency, and junior status.[49]

Nuance and context are the casualties of communication in the attention economy. While other causes may appear oblique or ambitious, inter-national criminal justice promises the authoritative language of the law, international institutions, simple messages, and celebrity backing.

Kony 2012 was released around the time of the pinnacle of the 'international criminal law as global justice' moment. As the ICC's brand-manager of global justice, Ocampo fully embraced the attention. Ocampo features several times in the clip. Towards the end of the video, he says 'It's not bad for the youth, it's bad for the *world* if we fail. It's not just important for Ugandan people, it's important for *everyone*'.

---

[46] Brough, 'Fair Vanity' 177.
[47] Hopgood, 'The Endtimes of Human Rights' 105.
[48] Ayesha Anne Nibbe, 'The Effects of a Narrative: Humanitarian Aid and Action in the Northern Uganda Conflict', unpublished PhD thesis, Department of Anthropology, University of California Davis (2011), 275.
[49] Ibid 276.

6.2.3 The Dissemination Strategy and the Donor As Consumer

In terms of dissemination, Invisible Children had a two-part strategy: screening videos about Kony and his forced recruitment of child soldiers to US school children and college students, and circulation of content through social media. The strategy placed awareness-raising at the centre of the campaign. The school and college talks began as early as 2005, with teams of volunteers going into schools across the United States in search of supporters for their cause and purchasers of their 'merchandise'. Russell recognised that the most effective way to grab attention involves a captive audience.

> There are only a few spaces in the world where there is a captive audience. That is the prison system, 'cause they're forced to be there, and schools, 'cause you have to be there by law, so we decided to go to schools'.[50]

Awareness can only be raised if attention is arrested. Incidentally, Tim Wu's *Attention Merchants* begins with an episode from a school in central California that was suffering under government cuts to education and was presented with a tantalising funding opportunity: all they needed to do was to make advertising space available to their students for big corporations, mostly on screens in schools. By the very nature of compulsory education, students' attention can be transformed into an 'asset' for brands such as Coca-Cola and McDonald's.[51] Invisible Children also began capitalising on their captive audience, recruiting young supporters and donors. And 'recruiting' is exactly what they did: 'All of this was funded by an army of young people', Russell states in *Kony 2012*. 'We will fight war!', the young people chant. 'Join our army for peace' urges the video. The moral ambiguity of recruiting an 'army of children' to campaign against child soldiers is quite extraordinary on one level, and entirely ordinary on another level. After all, these US children had grown up in the 1990s under the 'new interventionism' narrative. Mostly, the recruits were teenage girls, white, from upper-middle-class backgrounds, and Christian. In an interview, Russell describes this audience as their 'core'.[52] This form of dissemination – school and college talks – had

---

[50] 'Kony 2019', *Undiscovered* (podcast), Science Friday and WNYC studios, 2 April 2019, at 12.35.

[51] Tim Wu, *Attention Merchants: The Epic Scramble to Get Inside Our Heads* (Vintage Books 2016) 3, 4.

[52] Amy C. Finnegan, 'Beneath Kony 2012: Americans Aligning with Arms and Aiding Others' (2013) 59(3) *Africa Today*, 136–162, at 146.

already led Invisible Children to lobby the US government for military intervention. In 2011, Barack Obama deployed Special Operations forces to the region. Between 2011 and 2017 (when the mission was ended), the United States spent US$ 800 million on efforts to capture Joseph Kony.[53]

The second, connected, part of Invisible Children's dissemination strategy was the social media campaign. The aim was to attract the attention of a wider public that would make Kony famous on a greater scale and lead supporters to purchase the 'Action Kit'. The kit included a Kony T-shirt, a Kony bracelet, Kony stickers and a Kony poster. The poster is titled 'The Worst', portraying Kony, Osama bin Laden and Hitler. The poster has a strikingly similar aesthetics to the Barack Obama pop art poster from his 2008 presidential election campaign, which was captioned 'hope', 'change', or 'progress'.

Figure 6.1   *Kony 2012* campaign poster, Invisible Children

---

[53] Helene Cooper, 'A Mission to Capture or Kill Joseph Kony Ends, Without Capturing or Killing', *The New York Times*, 15 May 2017.

Despite their presentation as a small start-up NGO, Invisible Children had already gained substantial support prior to 2012, particularly in the United States.[54] But it was the *Kony 2012* video going viral on social media that catapulted them into the awareness of the general public and an international audience. 'Right now, there are more people on Facebook, than there were on the planet 200 years ago', begins Russell's gentle drawl at the opening of the *Kony 2012* video. The video is addressed to a young generation of connected internet users who 'see each other' and 'hear each other'. To construct and distinguish the young tech-savvy audience, Russell refers to the concern of 'older generations' about the potential of the connectedness of the young. The perceived short attention span of this young generation is addressed by Russell urging watchers: 'You have to pay attention.' Further urgency is provided through a seemingly arbitrary 'expiration date' of 31 December 2012. Russell's cute son Gavin acts as the proxy through which the audience learns about Kony. In the clip, Russell sits his son down to explain to him what they are about to do. According to Russell, all his son knows up until then is that 'I work in Africa'. He slides a picture in front of his son of a black male: 'This is the bad guy Joseph Kony.' He then explains that the bad guy takes children away from their parents, gives them guns, and forces them to do bad things. The other picture that Russell slides in front of his son is that of former child soldier Jacob. Jacob, 'our friend in Africa', represents the 'invisible children'.[55] The video moves to footage of a host of African children, many with mutilated faces. The narrative then switches to ICC Chief Prosecutor Luis Moreno Ocampo who is in his office in The Hague. Ocampo ensures the viewer that all peace talks were thwarted by Kony and that therefore his arrest is the only and best option. In reality, this version of events is strongly contested.[56] The storytelling takes a further manipulative turn when Russell suggests that Kony's was the first arrest warrant because he was the 'worst' criminal. In

---

[54] On the steady increase of supporters prior to 2012, see Finnegan, 'Beneath Kony 2012' 137–139.

[55] It goes without saying really, but these children were of course not 'invisible' to their families, friends, to the rebels, to other organisations working in the internally displaced people (IDP) camps, or to the government in Uganda. They were only 'invisible' to the distant donor base that Invisible Children was aiming to appeal to.

[56] The peace agreements that various government representatives had facilitated since the late 1980s were largely seen as thwarted through Kony's arrest warrant. Betty Bigome's decades of work on negotiating a peace agreement with the LRA are documented in *Peace versus Justice*. Directed by Klaartje Quirijns, Submarine Channel 2012.

the film, Gavin, Ocampo, and Russell agree 'we should stop Kony'. 'And then', Ocampo says 'solve other problems'.

When *Kony 2012* was launched, Invisible Children was already seen as a 'leader in innovative uses of Web 2.0 platforms for nonprofit campaigning'.[57] This attention to 'new media' is also reflected in how their donations are allocated. Roughly half of Invisible Children's funds are directed towards media and event production. What Invisible Children had (quite literally) banked on was the idea of awareness raising as being about entertainment.[58] The *Kony 2012* clip did not only use celebrities to raise awareness; it placed celebrity at the very centre of its concept. Making Kony *famous* was the primary objective. In the clip, Hollywood actor George Clooney states: 'I'd like indicted war criminals to enjoy the same level of celebrity as me.' Clooney's talking head is replaced by two *Time* magazine covers: one of Clooney on the left (real) next to one of Kony on the right (fictional). 'That seems fair', Clooney says. 'That's our objective, is to just shine a light on it.' In his historical study of fame *The Frenzy of Renown*, Leo Brady writes that when we call someone 'famous', what we are fundamentally saying is 'pay attention to this'.[59] Building on Brady, James Williams concludes about the attention economy:

> It's entirely to be expected that in an age of information abundance and attention scarcity we would see an increased reliance on fame as a heuristic for determining what and who matters (i.e. merits our attention), as well as an increased desire for achieving fame in one's own lifetime.[60]

Marketing students learn that awareness precedes action, and grabbing the attention is key, *almost* at any cost. Invisible Children adopted this approach by using celebrities, clichés, and stereotypes. They knew that grabbing the attention for a conflict happening in Africa requires such tactics. 'As a rule, African tragedies happen in isolation and in silence', observes Mamdani, so '[w]hen corporate media does focus on Africa, it seeks the dramatic, which is why media silence on Africa is often punctuated by high drama'.[61] But what *Kony 2012* pioneered through

---

[57] Brough, 'Fair Vanity' 181.
[58] Ibid 176.
[59] Leo Brady, *The Frenzy of Renown: Fame and its History* (Vintage 1997).
[60] James Williams, *Stand Out of Our Light: Freedom and Resistance in the Attention Economy* (Cambridge University Press 2018) 47.
[61] Mamdani, 'Saviors and Survivors' 19.

spectacle was the emphasis on consumption, the primacy of the *appearing* as conceptualised by Guy Debord.[62] The donor as consumer is unapologetically open to marketisation. The close collaboration between celebrity, NGOs and the ICC reached a crowning moment with a Hollywood dinner party dedicated to Moreno Ocampo a few weeks after *Kony 2012* was launched. A Reuters article reporting on the dinner (hosted at the home of 'Independence Day' director Roland Emmerich) noted that attendees included *Law and Order* actor Sam Waterston, *Star Trek* actor Zachary Quinto and *Battlestar Galactica* director Bryan Singer.[63] Entertainment and humanitarianism at this dinner-party were inseparable. But, not only ICC prosecutors and Hollywood directors could be donors as consumers; anyone who was willing to submit to the brand could be a part of it. The T-shirts and other merchandise allowed the kind of tribal attachment to a logo, colour scheme, and symbols associated with big brands.

6.2.4   Backlashes Against Kony 2012

Almost as soon as the video was released, there was an enormous backlash against the campaign, against Invisible Children, and against Jason Russell, who within days of the clip going viral suffered from a highly publicised breakdown. The backlash against *Kony 2012* began when former supporters began expressing doubts, and when journalists began probing into the reasons for the video resonating with so many people. Backlashes included worries about where the money was going, concerns that the campaign was a case of slacktivism/clicktivism, charges that the focus on the Ugandan conflict was unjustly excluding the accountability of other individuals, and the suspicion that Invisible Children was employing a patronising 'white man's burden' narrative. I outline these briefly:

6.2.4.1   Concerns About Donation Transparency

A great deal of the backlash in the media concerned the (mis)use of funds by Invisible Children. Within days of the video launch, corporate and social media were awash with demands for transparency, despite the

---

[62] Guy Debord, *Society of the Spectacle* [1967] (Black & Red 1984), para. 17

[63] Mary Slosson, 'ICC Prosecutor courts Hollywood with Invisible Children', Reuters, 2 April 2012, available at: https://af.reuters.com/article/commoditiesNews/idAFL2E8F203020120402.

accounts of Invisible Children being public.[64] The most contentious aspect was that only about 30 per cent of the funds went towards programmes in northern Uganda and surroundings. The rest was spent in the United States on employee salaries, film-making, film production, office rent in San Diego, and (US) travel expenses. Much of the reasoning for the critique was that Invisible Children should spend more on their programmes 'on the ground'. Whilst this criticism is well-founded, it is also problematic. Transparency of donations criticisms arguably normalise the rationale of managerial efficiency. The articulation of concerns over incorrect allocation of funds imply that there is a 'correct' allocation of funds that would remedy legitimacy shortfalls. This also more generally omits the troubling of the assumption about the validity of the transfer of funds from the Global North to the Global South through 'donations'. One might raise the issue of the continuation of dependency through this model as well as the erasure of political obligations arising from value appropriation due to colonialism.[65] A more apt modus of transfer of funds might, for example, be reparations facilitated through the state apparatus rather than NGOs. Suffice to say that the concern about the allocation of funds and calls for them to be used in a more transparent and efficient way are accepting of donations to NGOs as a means for solving global injustices.

6.2.4.2   Concerns About Slacktivism/Clicktivism

The charge of slacktivism/clicktivism centres on the ease with which individuals can pledge support to campaigns, without needing to sacrifice a great deal.[66] One click on social media is all it takes. It is an arms-length form of engagement. Slacktivists tend to be placed in contrast with 'real' or 'engaged' activists. One science communications consultant wrote about the slacktivism of *Kony 2012* : 'Normally, without the influx of

---

[64] https://invisiblechildren.com/financials/

[65] Sundhya Pahuja, *Decolonising International Law: Development, Economic Growth and the Politics of Universality* (Cambridge University Press 2011).

[66] Christopher Boulton, 'In Defense of "Slacktivism": How KONY 2012 Got the Whole World to Watch' in Danielle Sarver Coombs and Simon Collister (eds.), *Debates for the Digital Age: The Good, the Bad, and the Ugly of our Online World* (Vol. 1 ABC Clio 2016) 321–332.

slacktivists, a group or campaign would have high quality investors (meaning more highly involved or dedicated), that would keep watchful eyes on the actions of the group and utilization of donor funds'.[67] The 'slacktivists' are portrayed as personally lacking, and not sufficiently *invested*. This is indicative of a market approach to activism in which returns can only be expected if a serious investment is made. The individualised slacktivism charge also ignores the instrumentalisation of the supporters, many of them teenagers, and highly suggestive. More generally, the slacktivism charge precludes a critique of the instrumentalisation of NGOs themselves. Adam Branch, who worked in Uganda for many years, notably described Invisible Children piercingly as 'useful idiots'.[68] According to Branch, those in the US government who sought to expand military presence in central Africa used Invisible Children as an excuse for increasing weapons and military aid to the region. This view takes heed of the history of cooperation between President Museveni's government and military power of the United States. In his work on the ICC and its impact on African politics, Phil Clark explains how Washington had viewed Museveni's government as a key regional ally against the Sudanese government and the 'terrorist' threat of the LRA ever since the 1990s.[69] The position of regional ally became ever more relevant with the rise of the anti-Western terrorist group Al-Shabaab in Somalia. Incidentally, Al-Shabaab pledged allegiance with Al-Qaeda in the same year as the launch of the Kony campaign, 2012. The manipulation of marketing practices and the ease of engagement through social media can easily entice supporters unaware of the broader role that they or the organisation plays in complex political, economic, social, and cultural conditions. The charge of slacktivism/clicktivism mostly misses this, instead focusing on the failure of those doing the clicking.

6.2.4.3   Concerns About One-Sidedness

When news provider Al Jazeera reported on the phenomenon of *Kony 2012* in its programme 'Inside Story', it criticised the campaign for

---

[67] Kevin Zelno, 'On Slacktivism: Lessons from #Kony 2012', *Scientific American*, 14 March 2012, available at: https://blogs.scientificamerican.com/evo-eco-lab/on-slacktavism-lessons-from-kony2012/.

[68] Adam Branch, 'Kony 2012 from Kampala', Critical Investigations into Humanitarianism in Afiica, 11 March 2012 available at: www.cihablog.com/whats-wrong-with-the-kony-2012-campaign/.

[69] Clark, 'Distant Justice' 90.

making 'a villain out of one man in a conflict full of bad people'.[70] Critical observers, scholars and civil society organisations, also responded to *Kony 2012* by stating that focus should *also* have been on Ugandan government atrocities.[71] The one-sidedness, even hypocrisy, became a point of contention with the general public, when a photo was circulated showing the NGO founders posing with weapons alongside personnel of the Sudan People's Liberation Army (who were supported by the US military). These critics are correct about needing to cast the net wider in order to understand the context in which crimes are committed. So as to avoid a 'victors' justice' accusation or a suspicion of bias, caution needs to be exercised to prevent the excessive focus on certain individuals. But, the demand for *also* considering government crimes betrays a naturalising of the frame of global justice as an anti-impunity fight. These 'whatabout' calls are ultimately accepting of the premise that individual criminal accountability constitutes the most appropriate path to justice. Particularly in the context of northern Uganda, this is problematic. Here, anti-impunity is a fairly recent addition to various modes of addressing injustices, including peace talks and amnesties.[72] A recent example is the Ugandan government's Juba peace talks, which took place from 2006–2008. During this period, northern Ugandans often expressed concerns over the undermining of peace talks through ICC investigations. Clark points out that in turn the ICC repeatedly 'expressed immense skepticism toward peace negotiations'.[73] The ICC's skepticism has to be understood against the background that peace negotiations simply would have put the ICC out of business. Peace negotiations often mean amnesties, and amnesties mean no prosecutions. With the Ugandan situation being its first, the ICC had great expectations to live up to. No less the expectation that the prosecution of LRA leaders would provide 'a litmus test for the much celebrated promise of global justice'.[74]

---

[70] 'Inside Story – "Kony 2012": The future of activism', *Al Jazeera English*, 11 March 2012, available at: www.aljazeera.com/programmes/insidestory/2012/03/201231111225766134 .html

[71] 'Efforts to arrest Joseph Kony must respect human rights', Amnesty International UK Press Releases, 8 March 2012, available at: www.amnesty.org/en/latest/news/2012/03/ efforts-arrest-joseph-kony-must-respect-human-rights/

[72] Clark, 'Distant Justice' 188.

[73] Ibid 91.

[74] Payam Akhavan, 'The Lord's Resistance Army Case: Uganda's Submission of the First State Referral to the International Criminal Court' (2005) 99(2) *American Journal of International Law* 403–421, at 404.

Eventually, the peace talks collapsed, with many in Uganda blaming the arrest warrant for Joseph Kony as impeding incentives for the LRA. Clark observes that ongoing armed conflict was more useful for the ICC's purposes.[75] Whilst 'whatabout' positions are useful from an expressivist position of highlighting the narrow scope of global justice actors, they also often themselves submit to this narrow scope.

6.2.4.4   Concerns About the White Man's Burden

'Sometimes good intentions aren't enough' ends an article on the 'soft bigotry of *Kony 2012*'.[76] The concern that idealistic Westerners are portraying themselves as white saviours was a further key element of the backlash following the release of the video. The argument about bigotry is clearly justified. Throughout the video, racial stereotypes make for some uncomfortable viewing. This includes narratives of the black 'bad guy', the black 'good and innocent' victim dependent on the white saviour.[77] However, despite the criticism being justified, it arguably misses the mark in terms of structural inequality. Essentially, the criticism is directed towards an American audience that understandably wants to do something 'rewarding and ennobling' but is misguided in these efforts. The perspective of the 'clumsy humanitarian' often nevertheless takes the saviour lens for granted; it simply demands the saviour be more sensitive and savvy. 'How much money has Invisible Children soaked up that could have gone to actually effective campaigns or more experienced NGOs?', asks the author on bigotry. Other commentators have highlighted the stereotyping, demanding the amplification of 'local voices' through 'audience-oriented' storytelling.[78] The demand for 'local' storytelling is tempting, but can fall into the same trap of paternalism through the distinction of 'the world' and 'communities' (a distinction made by the ICC, we recall from Chapter 4), which is mapped onto the distinction between 'global' voices and 'local' voices.

In (improbable) defence of Invisible Children, it is notable that Russell and his team had not envisaged the global reach of the video. *Kony 2012* was always intended to be for a young US audience. Invisible Children's Jedidiah Jenkins, with the peculiar job title of Director of Ideology, stated

---

[75] Clark, 'Distant Justice' 91.

[76] Max Fisher, 'The Soft Bigotry of *Kony 2012*' *The Atlantic*, 8 March 2012.

[77] Teju Cole, 'The White Savior Industrial Complex', *The Atlantic*, 12 March 2012.

[78] Sam Gregory, 'Kony 2012 Through a Prism of Video Advocacy Practices and Trends' (2012) 4(3) *Journal of Human Rights Practice* 463–468.

in an interview with US news provider CBS that one of their key goals was: 'to change the mind-set of Western young people to see themselves as global citizens'.[79] The 'invisible children' of Kony 2012 were branded to meet the attributes of victimhood imagined in the United States. That the video resonated far beyond the US audience says more about global racial stereotypes than necessarily about Invisible Children. What is missing from the 'white saviour' critique is arguably the fact that donors are *beneficiaries of racism* in the form of racial capitalism. Against the background of structures of latent white supremacy in neoliberal societies, the call for donors to be more sensitive simply imagines a more ethical white saviour rather than the undoing of white supremacy.

The backlashes against Kony 2012 were, in sum, framed simply as bad investments. The main object of the backlash was to highlight that Invisible Children did not provide the promised return, financially or morally. The backlash itself was market-oriented. A market-driven backlash has arguably something to do with causes failing to connect with more traditional political movements, say the labour movement traditionally supported by Trade Unions, or black liberation struggles. Where historical and class-based solidarity is missing, there can only ever be momentary, fleeting moments of action. Attention on a global justice cause is particularly fickle in the attention economy. As soon as the brief hold on the attention is broken, the support for a cause is in danger of dissipating. The constant diversion of attention is a particular feature of a consumer society, where consumption opportunities continually change, and the desirable thing becomes the 'new' thing. Marketing is central in creating and facilitating market-relevant processes of renewal, hence the need of brands to re-brand. Fast and disposable political action as in the case of Kony 2012 can therefore just as quickly become yesterday's news. Mamdani writes about the imagery of the Save Darfur Coalition as 'pornography of violence': rapes, burnings, killings. None of the imagery reveals context, the causes of political violence, or possible consequences of a military intervention.[80] Mamdani insists on the de-politicising properties of pornography of violence: 'The pornography is meant to drive a wedge between your political and moral senses, to numb the former and appeal to the latter [...].[81]

---

[79] CBS This Morning archive (9 March 2012 7:00am–9:00am EST).
[80] Mamdani, 'Saviors and Survivors' 56.
[81] Ibid 57.

There was one element in which the NGO was successful: lobbying for military action. Paradoxically, awareness-raising that prompts lobbying addresses one of the more seasoned criticisms of NGOs, namely that NGOs divert attention and resources away from state action. Traditionally, NGOs have filled gaps where states have failed to act. As resources flow from individuals to unelected NGOs for societal problems such as poverty, the state feels absconded from dealing with these issues through public resources. The issues dealt with are consequently individualised according to what NGOs and their supporters prioritise. Awareness-raising, in contrast, is often about lobbying *governments* into action, pressurising the state to direct resources to the problem made visible by an NGO. *Kony 2012* prompted the US government to act. The aforementioned problems are not alleviated in this case, merely shifted. The state is pressurised into acting only in the case of the spectacularised issues at the expense of structural issues, and state intervention is often militarised instead of focused on redistribution. This tells us something critical about humanitarianism in the attention economy: The cause is framed as spectacle, which means that the response must be spectacular too – violence is the response to violence. Indeed, Invisible Children was subsequently described as a group of private military actors working ultimately for the US military.[82] The description does not seem far-fetched in light of Invisible Children's efforts to set up Early Warning Systems to track the movements of the LRA and their distribution of leaflets seeking defectors. The militarisation narrative was interestingly not part of the backlash against *Kony 2012*, an indication of its normalisation.

The backlash against *Kony 2012*, moreover, omitted any critique of international law. The majority of the criticisms stress that Kony *should* be arrested. There was no problematising of international law's role in creating conditions that lead to violence and sustain inequality. The violence is, together with Uganda's poverty, considered as an aberration, generally resulting from a few 'rotten apples', *not* as inherently linked to structural inequalities.[83] The backlash therefore left intact the issues of legal morality imposed by the ICC's involvement and the attendant de-politicisation of global justice; it did not question interventionism in the

---

[82] Adam Taylor, 'Was #Kony2012 a failure?', *Washington Post*, 16 December 2014.
[83] Tor Krever, 'International Criminal Law: An Ideology Critique' (2013) 26(3) *Leiden Journal of International Law* (2013) 701–723, at 721.

form of military aid, and it did not question the racial capitalism running through the episode.

6.2.5   Resistance Against Kony 2012

In contrast to backlash, there was also resistance from those people and communities affected, as well as those who aimed to act in solidarity with them. Resistance, in contrast to backlash, I argue, implies the recognition of a longer history of exploitation. To be sure, resistance can also be immediate, but in contrast to backlash, it ties into struggles against economic, political, social, and cultural oppression. The struggle can be violent or non-violent, rash or considered. Here, resistance concerns the contextualisation of Kony 2012 within a history of intervention. In the case of Kony 2012, resistance was articulated less around Kony or Invisible Children as objects of critique, but more around the structural issues of racial capitalism and militarisation of conflict of which Kony 2012 was symptomatic.

Resistance against racial capitalism is illustrated in the reactions of Ugandans who watched Kony 2012. Due to patchy internet access, the clip was largely unavailable in northern Uganda. An African-based NGO, the African Youth Initiative Network (AYINET), decided therefore to organise screenings in Lira and Gulu. The Lira screening caused such an outcry in the audience, including the hurling of objects at the screen, that AYINET halted further screenings in the region.[84] In interviews conducted immediately after the screening, it is notable that marketisation was a particular point of contention.[85] The premise of 'making Kony famous' and the distribution of 'merchandise' (posters, bags, T-Shirts) featuring the pop art version of Kony's face, were considered insensitive. As an Al Jazeera reporter noted: 'One woman I spoke to made the comparison of selling Osama Bin Laden paraphernalia post 9/11 – likely to be highly offensive to many Americans, however well intentioned the campaign behind it'.[86] Certainly, the selected interviews only paint part of the picture, with all the selection bias that goes into reporting 'from Africa'. However, it is worth distinguishing between the reactions of Ugandans in contrast to the reactions of donors. The dissatisfaction

---

[84] Rosebell Kagumire and David Smith, 'Kony 2012 Video Screening Met with Anger in Northern Uganda, The Guardian, 14 March 2012.
[85] Malcolm Webb, 'Ugandans React with Anger to Kony Video', Al Jazeera, 14 March 2012.
[86] Ibid.

expressed by the Ugandans interviewed is not directed against a false investment, as in the backlash explained above. Rather, it sits within a longer history of value appropriation through racial capitalism.

Racial capitalism is defined by Nancy Leong as 'the process of deriving social and economic value from the racial identity of another person'.[87] Leong uses the term 'racial capitalism' in order to draw attention to the tokenistic use of non-white people to meet 'diversity' goals for value extraction, especially to boost a brand. Commodification of racial identity reduces race to a feature that can be bought and sold. In the case of *Kony 2012*, victims of the conflict are reduced to victims of Joseph Kony; they are prevented from articulating their own experiences. More specifically, they are forced to align with the 'ideal' victim brand. The dismissal of Ugandans as those who can 'know' their own victimhood is symptomatic of the epistemological inequality expressed in coloniality. The usefulness of the term 'racial capitalism' in understanding the structural processes at the heart of *Kony 2012* (beyond identity), derives from the recognition of race as a social form that places a 'determining role in structuring imperialist social formations'.[88] This method does not depart from historical materialism but challenges the assumption, articulated in Karl Marx's writings, that capital accumulation would diffuse evenly outside of the capitalist core.[89] Even diffusion cannot account for the de facto uneven distribution of wealth between the Global South and the Global North, or the scramble for colonial territory.[90] As Robert Knox argues, most key moments of capitalist expansion 'were also steeped in racism', whether colonialism, the slave trade, nineteenth-century 'civilisation' projects, or early experiments in limited self-determination such as the League of Nations Mandates of the UN Trust territories.[91] All of these were based on notions of European superiority. Race, then, is a key factor in capital accumulation. Capital can only accumulate by producing and moving through relations of severe inequality: those with property, and those without; those with the means of production, and those without. These lines are divided through a process of racialisation. As

---

[87] Nancy Leong, 'Racial Capitalism' (2013) 126(8) *Harvard Law Review* 2151–2226.

[88] Robert Knox, 'Valuing race? Stretched Marxism and the Logic of Imperialism' (2016) 4(1) *London Review of International Law* 81–126, at 104.

[89] James Morris Blaut, *The Colonizer's Model of the World: Geographical Diffusionism and Eurocentric History* (Guilford Press 1993) 8–26. Referenced and explained in Knox, 'Valuing Race?'.

[90] Knox, 'Valuing Race?' 86.

[91] Ibid 99.

Jodi Melamed observes: 'Most obviously, [capitalism] does this by displacing the uneven life chances that are inescapably part of capitalist
social relations onto fictions of differing human capacities, historically
race.'[92] That is not to say, however, that the view on race, or the
identification of racial capitalism, precludes the equally important inter-
sectional issues of gender and – perhaps more obviously – class.[93]

(Racial) capitalism has typically gone hand in hand with militarism,
often to force value extraction where there has been resistance.[94] While
violence in the colonies was traditionally cast as 'barbarism', military
intervention is traditionally cast as 'bringing order'. International law has
historically played a key role in this co-existence of value extraction from
the Global South (institutionalised in international organisations such as
the IMF or WTO) and military interventionism (often labelled as
humanitarianism). Indeed, activism of *Kony 2012* sits comfortably within
this historical narrative in its reinforcing of the US militarisation of
Africa.[95] *Kony 2012* is an occasion of militarism and international law
collaborating, ultimately for the purposes of capital accumulation. The
law of the use of force (also known as international humanitarian law),
which regulates military interventions, has historically cast certain people
as legitimate targets for military intervention. Previously, this narrative
operated under the terms of 'savage' or 'uncivilised';[96] today, it operates
under the organising properties of atrocity crimes, drawing upon established racialised tropes. The link between individual accountability and
military intervention is important for the anti-impunity movement's
claim of 'justice then peace'. 'Justice then peace', or its variation of 'No
peace without justice', is built on the tacit assumption of justice as
supported by military intervention. The anti-impunity movement often
glosses over this aspect, but fighting against impunity enjoys a close

---

[92] Jodi Melamed, 'Racial Capitalism' (2015) 1(1) *Critical Ethnic Studies* 76–85.

[93] Here, it serves the purpose of highlighting one aspect of capitalism, which is particularly
relevant to the analysis and might, if remaining unnamed explicitly as 'racial', be missed.
On intersectionality as overlapping discrimination, see famously Kimberlé Crenshaw,
'Demarginalizing the Intersection of Race and Sex: A Black Feminist Critique of
Antidiscrimination Doctrine, Feminist Theory, and Antiracist Politics' (1989) 1
University of Chicago Legal Forum 139–167.

[94] Conceptualised in Rosa Luxemburg's notion of imperialism in Rosa Luxemburg, *The
Accumulation of Capital* [1913] (Routledge 2013).

[95] Finnegan, 'Beneath Kony 2012' 139.

[96] Antony Anghie, *Imperialism, Sovereignty, and the Making of International Law*
(Cambridge University Press 2005); Makau Mutua, 'Savages, Victims, and Saviors: The
Metaphor of Human Rights' (2001) 42(1) *Harvard International Law Journal* 201–245.

relationship with military intervention–whether this is Uganda (albeit on a relatively small scale) or Libya (on a full-blown military scale), or Rwanda (as the too-late but better than never scale). The USA often leads these military operations, but they can also be led by other states of the Global North. For example, the 2013 military intervention in Mali was led by France (its former coloniser), which was followed by the *Al Mahdi* case at the ICC two years later.[97] While the geopolitical interests at stake in military interventions are commonly the object of debate and controversy, this is less so with the anti-impunity movement – as evidenced with the framing of the backlash against *Kony 2012*.

From the perspective of value extraction it appears particularly relevant that at the time in which Invisible Children was formed and gained traction, commercially viable oil was discovered in Uganda. Oil is of course one of the main movers of geopolitical strategies and interventionism. Extraction in Uganda is due to begin in 2021.[98] The extraction of resources from the Global South is part of a long history of value extraction that is reproduced from the cash crops forced on farmers to the forced labour of natural resource extraction. The primitive accumulation of capital (accruing of capital through explicitly violent means) that has marked capitalism's racialised expansion is perhaps best demonstrated through land grabbing – an issue, which Branch points out, is a major contemporary concern in Uganda.

> Land speculators and so-called investors, many foreign, in collaboration with the Ugandan government and military, are grabbing the land of the Acholi people in northern Uganda, land that they were forced off of a decade ago when the government herded them into internment camps.[99]

Driven by a growing consumer demand for agricultural products in the Global North, farm land is plundered from formerly displaced returning

---

[97] *The Prosecutor v. Ahmad Al Faqi Al Mahdi* (Judgment and Sentence) ICC-01/12-01/15 (Trial Chamber VIII, 27 September 2016).

[98] 'Uganda Announces Oil Discovery', *IOL News*, 9 October 2006, available at: www.iol.co .za/news/africa/uganda-announces-oil-discovery-296822; Ed Stoddard, 'Uganda Expects First Oil Production in 2021, Refinery by 2023, *Reuters* (8 November 2018), available at: https://uk.reuters.com/article/africa-oil-uganda/uganda-expects-first-oil-production-in-2021-refinery-by-2023-idUKL8N1XJ3VR.

[99] Branch, '*Kony 2012* from Kampala'. On primitive accumulation, see Karl Marx, *Das Kapital* [1867] (Regnery Publishing 2009) Part VIII.

farmers for the purposes of foreign investment. In Uganda, the land is used for maize, wheat, rice, and cereal productions, as well as for poultry and cattle.[100] Land grabbing is often enforced by the military. This tends to happen under the mantle of 'development'.[101] *Kony 2012* foreclosed donors' access to this kind of awareness of global production-consumption relations. Instead, the donors remained consumers engaged in 'low-cost heroism'.[102] At worst, the image-over-substance approach of marketised global justice *displaces* and eventually *replaces* solidarity activism.

6.3   Conclusion

Today, the LRA are decimated, but continue to operate, seemingly still under the leadership of Kony, in the region. Several of the bases are located in South Sudan, Sudan, and Garamba National Park in north-eastern Democratic Republic of the Congo, where they continue to trade in illicit diamonds, elephant poaching, and ivory trafficking.[103] Jason Russell, meanwhile, is now a consultant, a 'creative entrepreneur', who helps organisations to re-brand. He has recently co-published a children's book titled *A Little Radical* with his wife. The website states in a blue bubble font: 'It's cool to care!'.[104] When Dominic Ongwen was apprehended in 2015 in enforcement of the ICC arrest warrant, the prosecutorial energy for the Ugandan situation before the ICC shifted from Kony to Ongwen. The prosecution expanded the charges from seven under the initial arrest warrant of 2005 to *seventy* in 2015.[105]

---

[100] In 2010, the main investors were Egyptian and Chinese, Samuel B. Mabikke, 'Escalating Land Grabbing in Post Conflict Regions of Northern Uganda: A Need for Strengthening Good Land Governance in Acholi Region', conference paper presented at the International Conference on Global Land Grabbing (2011) *Land Deal Politics Initiative*. Data extracted from *The Global Land Project International Project Office* , 1 GLP Report (2010).

[101] Ariane Goetz, *Land Grabbing as Development?: Chinese and British Land Acquisitions in Comparative Perspective* (Transcript Verlag 2019).

[102] Lisa Ann Richey and Stefano Ponte, *Brand Aid: Shopping Well to Save the World* (University of Minnesota Press 2011) xiv.

[103] Cooper, 'A Mission to Capture or Kill Kony Ends'.

[104] https://alittleradical.com/

[105] Subsequently confirmed in: *The Prosecutor v. Dominic Ongwen* (Decision on the confirmation of charges against Dominic Ongwen) ICC -02/04-01/15 (Pre-Trial Chamber II 23 March 2016).

In the NGO world, *Kony 2012* is regarded as a 'cautionary tale'.[106] It was successful in its awareness-raising for the brand, but ultimately the brand suffered. Opinions appear to be divided on whether capturing Kony contributes to the lack of success, or whether the deployment of troops was in fact the success story. In the marketing world, unsurprisingly, the campaign was admired for its ability to reach so many people. An article in *Marketing Week* marvels: 'Who would have imagined in this age of global clutter and nano-second attention spans that we'd all be talking about an old-fashioned 30 minute film – and one that examines social justice and global equality at that'.[107] In the critical literature, *Kony 2012* signifies a new form of consumer culture within humanitarian work. What has become a normalised feature of contemporary humanitarianism is effectively made strange by Lisa Ann Richey's and Stefano Ponte's simple question: why has humanitarianism become a reason to *shop*?[108] The issue of consumer culture connects to two broader issues. Do NGOs that claim to be addressing global injustices ever have a redistributive effect? And can campaigns spur real political action? As regards the redistributive effect, this merits further research but we may get an indication from the Global Trends in Giving Report. The report found that the two countries which *received* the highest donations of 119 countries were the USA (17 per cent of all donations) and Israel (8 per cent of all donations).[109]

Kony 2012 is arguably the attention economy working at its most effective: channelling both cause *and* backlash into individualised narratives of what it *really* means to care about global justice while narrowing the political remit to individual action. Such distraction has the effect of removing individuals from structural thinking and preventing rather

---

[106] Shannon K. Vaughan and Shelly Arsneault, '*Kony 2012*, A Cautionary Tale about Social Media' in, *Managing Nonprofit Organizations in a Policy World* (Sage Publishing 2013) 169–186.

[107] Mark Ritson, 'Mark Ritson: The Lessons We Can Learn from *Kony 2012*', *Marketing Week*, 15 March 2012.

[108] Richey and Ponte, 'Brand Aid', xi. Richey and Ponte question in particular the RED product lines, from American Express cards to iPods, which claim to 'make you feel great about spending' because you are also raising awareness for the HIV/AIDs pandemic in Africa.

[109] Survey results of 6,057 donors worldwide. The survey was published in Arabic, English, French, Portuguese, and Spanish. 'Children and youth' were with 15 per cent the most common causes, followed by 'health and wellness' at 10.8 per cent. Peace and nonviolence received a mere 0.8 per cent of donations. '2018 Global Trends in Giving Report', Nonprofit Tech for Good, 15 September 2018, available at: https://givingreport.ngo/.

than creating actions of solidarity. The ultimate casualty of marketised global justice in the NGO sector, then, may be solidarity. The attraction for donors, who donate to causes in the Global South, is that it appears as though they *need* not feel responsible, but instead *choose* to.[110] Any form of causality between the donors' wealth and the receivers' lack of wealth is erased. The anti-impunity movement does not require of its supporters that they experience suffering, or even take any substantial risks. No sacrifice, except for a minor sacrifice of attention and money, is required. The mass publicity of covering spaces with posters is a 'form of protest, unlike conventional methods such as street marches, [which] is silent, anonymous and non-confrontational.'[111] Writing about the 'triumph of marketing' in global human rights, Hopgood observes that none of the activities

> has the kind of direct implications possessed by civil rights demonstra-
> tions in the American South or gay rights activism in San Francisco or
> reclaim the night marches through New York City. In each of these cases
> your own identity or neighbourhood was at issue and your own security
> was often wagered.[112]

On the whole, awareness-raising campaigns, through aiming to 'sell' global justice, tend to construct a *consumer* of global injustice rather than a *political actor* of global justice. The foregrounding of market values in *Kony 2012* demonstrates that the global justice sector is not a self-contained market, but fundamentally constitutes neoliberalism as a legal-institutional project. The links between militarism, racial capitalism, and de-politicisation illustrate the violent structures at the heart of this project. After gaining a sense of the role of NGOs within this process, Chapter 7 examines the role of the most significant inter-governmental organisation in marketised global justice: the ICC.

---

[110] Mamdani, 'Saviors and Survivors' 62.
[111] Daley, 'Rescuing African Bodies' 385.
[112] Hopgood, 'The Endtimes of Human Rights' 104.

7

Special Effects

The International Criminal Court in the Global Market

The African bias is a cover up argument like the denial of the Holocaust.[1]

7.1 Introduction

If typing 'ICC' into a search engine, one is likely to be directed to the website of the International Cricket Council or to the International Chamber of Commerce. With this error discovered, a researcher of anti-impunity quickly refines the search and no further thought is given to the 'other' ICCs. In this chapter on the International Criminal Court, two ICCs enter into a more meaningful relationship (and, lamentably for some, cricket does not feature). The International Chamber of Commerce was established in Paris in 1920 and took up a key role in the modern development of global capitalism, becoming, in the words of Quinn Slobodian, 'an important institutional partner for the Austrian neoliberals' who later were instrumental in the establishment of the World Trade Organization (WTO).[2] In this chapter, we will see how another ICC, the International Criminal Court, has similarly become an important institutional partner for European neoliberals in the twenty-first century. The argument builds on and extends the argument made by Slobodian about neoliberalism as a legal-institutional order that enables and encases the market by highlighting the legal and aesthetic role of marketised global justice to protect the status quo.[3]

In the previous chapter, I began with marketing practices in order to show that 'selling' global justice is not simply a metaphor, but is a material reality. This further underlined the predominant use of global

---

[1] Luis Moreno Ocampo, 'From Brexit to African ICC Exit: A Dangerous Trend', Just Security blog, 31 October 2016, available at: www.justsecurity.org/33972/brexit-african-icc-exit-dangerous-trend/.
[2] Quinn Slobodian, *Globalists: The End of Empire and the Birth of Neoliberalism* (Harvard University Press 2018) 34
[3] Ibid.

justice as a means for capital growth. In the for-profit sector, the potential for global justice as a means for capital growth prompted the rise of 'brand activism'; in the competitive not-for-profit global justice sector meanwhile marketing practices are used in order to attract donors from the Global North. This chapter begins not with market*ing* but with the market. We return to market*ing* later on in the chapter. We recall from Chapter 6 that the global justice sector is not a self-contained sector, but rather a crucial part of a mechanism of the neoliberal order. In other words, the global justice sector giving primacy to market values over social values is not only reflective of neoliberalism but co-constitutes the neoliberal order. On a rather grand scale, this presumes a configuration of 'justice' as integrated with a global market. On a smaller scale, this chapter analyses a mechanism that facilitates this integration: the focus at the beginning of the chapter is on the Cotonou Partnership Agreement (CPA), first signed in 2000, between the European Union (EU) and the African Caribbean and Pacific group (ACP). It is a treaty intended to support cooperation in development, politics, and trade. Intriguingly, a provision about the ICC was introduced in its 2005 amendment.[4]

After setting out some of the mechanics of the integration between a global market and global criminal law regime, the next section shifts focus to the widely discussed 'crisis' of the ICC, which reached a momentary apex in 2016. In this 'crisis year', three African states announced their withdrawal from the ICC. Mostly, this is described as 'backlash', but I seek to show how this in fact constituted 'resistance' against the integration of the global market and global criminal law regime, thereby creating a link between the forces behind the CPA and the forces behind withdrawal from the ICC. I argue that 2016 culminated in a moment of laying down tools, a collective refusal to continue to labour for the marketised global justice sector. Unsurprisingly, the ICC's response was to seek answers in the market. Indeed, the response in 2016 displays all the features of what in the marketing world is described as a re-brand, which is where we return to market*ing*.[5] Re-branding

---

[4] The Cotonou Partnership Agreement (signed on 23 June 2000, revised on 25 June 2005, revised on 22 June 2010).

[5] Christine Schwöbel-Patel, 'The Re-branding of the International Criminal Court (and Why African States Are Not Falling for It)', Opinio Juris blog, 28 October 2016, available at: http://opiniojuris.org/2016/10/28/the-re-branding-of-the-international-criminal-court-and-why-african-states-are-not-falling-for-it/.

provides the *illusion* of change (through special effects), whilst in reality moving the institution even closer towards the market.

7.2 Neoliberalism and the ICC

At first glance, there appear to be very few commonalities between the ICC and the 'usual suspects' of neoliberalism's institutions and principles. Free trade, privatisation, financialisation, and capital mobility all appear rather remote for an institution dealing in international crimes. And yet, as we have seen in previous chapters, international criminal law (ICL) and its institutions narrow the scope of what is understood as global justice, excluding the economy and redistributive mechanisms from the remit of global justice. In addition, the narrowing of the view on what global justice is invisibilises structural inequality. So far, the book has focused mostly on the *distractions* through marketised global justice, although Chapter 6 aimed to show the *focus* on militarism, racial capitalism, and de-politicisation too. The impression, however, which might be created is that neoliberalism is occurring in one space and ICL as global justice is happening in another space. This chapter begins with an effort to counter the impression that global justice actors are creating distractions far off from the main event; instead, I illustrate that global justice actors are *constituting* the neoliberal order. It would be wrong to assume therefore that marketised global justice forces the gaze away while neoliberalism has taken hold; in fact, whilst observing marketised global justice, we have been looking straight at neoliberalism. Anti-impunity as global justice is right at the centre of the main event; it has just been using 'special effects' to create the illusion that its primary focus is to fight hegemony.

Neoliberalism as legal-institutional project *enables* the market – by putting legal mechanisms in place that allow for capital flows – and *encases* the market – by putting legal mechanisms in place that protect the market from democratic contestation.[6] Neoliberalism as legal-institutional project that enables and encases the market is generally centred on multilateral, and occasionally important bilateral, agreements

---

[6] Encasing the market is discussed in Slobodian, 'Globalists'. Also analysed in Sundhya Pahuja, *Decolonising International Law: Development, Economic Growth and the Politics of Universality* (Cambridge University Press 2011); Claire Cutler, *Private Power and Global Authority: Transnational Merchant Law in the Global Political Economy* (Cambridge University Press 2003).

on trade and financialisation. In Slobodian's book *Globalists,* the intellectual history of neoliberalism as legal-institutional project constituting a neoliberal order begins with the International Chamber of Commerce (the 'other' ICC), and ends with the establishment of the WTO. Slobodian identifies linkages between different generations of economists and lawyers, who pushed for their vision of a global economy that enables and encases the market. The Austrian representative of this earlier ICC was, from 1925 onwards, Ludwig von Mises. Von Mises's tireless work on removing trade barriers and giving primacy to business interests would significantly influence the establishment of the WTO in Geneva seventy years later. Although von Mises was suspicious of the nation state as a mechanism to regulate the market, he nevertheless believed that nations should remain embedded in an international institutional order that protected capital and allowed for capital flows across borders.[7] The Mises Institute continues this tradition, although in a more laissez-faire register, and today largely condemns the WTO.[8] Significantly, it was the International Chamber of Commerce that first proposed 'the recasting of trading rights, market rights and capital rights as *individual* rights'.[9] Today, the International Chamber of Commerce describes itself as 'the voice of world business championing the global economy as a force for economic growth, job creation and prosperity'.[10] The WTO, meanwhile, is largely paralysed at present, with the so-called 'US-China trade wars' in particular leading to political impasses.[11] But this does not mean that it is not functioning as it should; its radiating effect on regional trade and investment treaties remains. And the idea that institutions should protect the right to trade and move capital, reimagined as *human rights,* remains strong. Meanwhile, as Slobodian has shown, those international economic lawyers pressing for the right to trade and the right to move capital are often opposed to individual rights when these are employed by actors from the Global South.[12]

---

[7] Slobodian, 'Globalists' 9.
[8] Carmen Elena Dorobat, 'The WTO: Useless for Trade, Useful for the State', Mises Institute, 12 September 2017, available at: https://mises.org/wire/wto-useless-trade-useful-state.
[9] Slobodian, 'Globalists' 277.
[10] International Chamber of Commerce website at: https://iccwbo.org/.
[11] Joost Pauwelyn, 'WTO Dispute Settlement Post 2019: What to Expect?' (2019) *Journal of International Economic Law* 1–25.
[12] Slobodian focuses in particular on the long career of Ernst-Ulrich Petersmann as indicative of the selective move to individual rights, in 'Globalists', 278.

One of the distinct features of marketised global justice emerging in the previous chapters is the prevalence of legal-institutional mechanisms that are racialised and at the same time hide racial capitalism through avowals of humanitarianism, human rights, and development. Racialised economic domination is particularly evident in trade and investment agreements between capital exporting states of the Global North and capital importing states of the Global South. Capital is exported and imported through investments (foreign direct investments) and loans. The provisions for WTO-compliant free trade agreements 'pit some of the world's most advanced industrial economies against some of the poorest nations on earth'.[13] One such agreement that frames the political-economic relationship between the North and the South is the CPA. The fact that this is an EU agreement is significant for an analysis of an emerging integrated international market and criminalisation system: it was after all the EU countries, Germany in particular, which commanded much of the political power at the Rome Conference negotiations for the establishment of the ICC in 1998.

Let us take a brief detour to the negotiations for the 1998 ICC before returning to the mechanisms of the CPA: Germany's Foreign Minister, Klaus Kinkel, played a leading role in facilitating the role of the ICC as a political stalwart against the United Nations (UN) Security Council. He had previously appointed Hans-Peter Kaul as head of the German Foreign Ministry's International Law Department and made sure that the German delegation had a significant presence at the Preparatory Committee meetings in the run up to the Rome Conference.[14] Kaul was instrumental in organising the so-called 'Like-Minded Group' at Rome. The group was made up of 'other non-UNSC states with global ambitions, like Canada, and European Community minions, like the Netherlands'.[15] They collectively fought for an independent ICC (independent of the powers of the UN Security Council Permanent Five); they also insisted on a court that would only step in when the domestic judicial system was 'unwilling or unable' to do so.[16] With the

---

[13] Oxfam Briefing Note, 'Unequal Partners: How EU-ACP Economic Partnership Agreements (EPAs) could harm the development prospects of many of the world's poorest countries' (September 2006) 2.

[14] For more details see Ronan Steinke, *The Politics of International Criminal Justice: German Perspectives from Nuremberg to The Hague* (Hart 2012) 101.

[15] Tor Krever, 'Dispensing Global Justice' (2014) 85 *New Left Review* 67–97, at 74.

[16] Independence of the Prosecutor is enshrined in the *proprio motu* powers in the Rome Statute (art. 13 (c), 15, 53(1)) and the 'unwilling and unable' doctrine is enshrined in the

United States at a distance, China positioning itself against the ICC, the enthusiasm of the United Kingdom, France, and Russia muted, this was the political opportunity for EU countries to make their mark. Kaul was later rewarded for his efforts by being appointed a judge at the ICC. While Germany was exercising political power in Rome, Germany's economic position within Europe was looking rather more precarious. In 1999, when the euro was introduced, Germany was described by *The Economist* as the 'sick man of the euro' . . . 'Thus the biggest economic problem for Europe today is how to revive the German economy'.[17] The new Chancellor Gerhard Schröder of the social-democrat party (SPD) announced major reforms of the welfare system, moving from social democrat to neoliberal policies. Market integration into a legal-institutional framework has been the recurring pattern of the neoliberal order. And so it transpired with the CPA of 2000. Notably, negotiations between the EU and the ACP began in 1998, the same year as the Rome conference.

7.3   Enabling the Market

'It is surely no coincidence', muses international lawyer Martti Koskenniemi, 'that only three years separated the establishment of the World Trade Organization (WTO 1995) and the International Criminal Court (ICC 1998). But just how those projects relate together may be hard to decipher [. . .]'.[18] Here I argue that the relation between these two projects lies in their enabling and encasing of a global market. In previous chapters, we already encountered a variety of ways in which the market has been enabled through marketised global justice, from commodifying victims of conflict to placing the exchange value of images at the centre of a legitimacy programme of anti-impunity. The CPA represents the intersection of the market and global justice actors at treaty level. The CPA stands out on the one hand as it encourages WTO-compliant economic partnership agreements, so it is an umbrella agreement for widening the ambit of trade liberalisation under a WTO system; on the

---

complementarity provisions (art. 17). The provisions on complementarity were important to Germany, in particular, as its fighter jets were about to be sent to war in the wake of the Kosovo crisis.

[17] 'The Sick Man of the Euro', *The Economist*, 3 June 1999, available at: www.economist .com/special/1999/06/03/the-sick-man-of-the-euro

[18] Martti Koskenniemi, 'Foreword' in Immi Tallgren and Thomas Skouteris (eds.) *The New Histories of International Criminal Law: Retrials* (Oxford University Press 2019) v–vi.

other hand, it stands out because it rather unusually includes an explicit provision about the ICC – a black-letter-law intersection between market provisions and international crime.

The CPA is the successor agreement of the Lomé Conventions, which were treaties negotiated between the EU and former colonies of 79 African, Caribbean and Pacific countries. The 1975 Lomé Conventions were remnants of the post-decolonisation bargaining power of states in the Global South.[19] They included non-reciprocal trade preferences such as ACP states being able to levy taxes on imported commodities to deter EU states from dumping their product on the market. The preferences were to be undone with the CPA, underpinned by the requirements to comply with the core principles of the WTO.

The CPA, which includes forty-eight countries from Sub-Saharan Africa, came into force in 2000 in the period between the signing of the Rome Statute and its coming into force. The CPA has as its objective 'poverty eradication, sustainable development and the gradual integration of the ACP countries into the world economy'.[20] It is based on three pillars: development cooperation (particularly distribution of aid through the European Development Fund), economic and trade cooperation (regulated through individually negotiated regional economic partnership agreements), and a political dimension.[21] Under the first pillar, aid is controlled through an application system, with the EU retaining tight control over the suitability of projects, its partners, and funds. The second pillar of the CPA describes the framework provision for economic partnership agreements, which are intended to remove barriers to trade. According to Article 36 of the CPA, the Parties 'agree to take all the necessary measures to ensure the conclusion of new WTO-compatible Economic Partnership Agreements'. Due to their commitment to market liberalisation as a purported means to development, these provisions have been described as symptomatic of 'the hegemonic dominance of neoliberalism within political elites'.[22] The Rome Statute provisions fall

---

[19] For a periodicisation see Adom Getachew, *Worldmaking after Empire: The Rise and Fall of Self-Determination* (Princeton University Press 2019).

[20] Preamble, The Cotonou Partnership Agreement (signed 23 June 2000, revised 25 June 2005) European Commission, Directorate-General for Development and Relations with African, Caribbean and Pacific States.

[21] Ibid.

[22] Stephen R. Hurt, 'Co-operation and Coercion? The Cotonou Agreement between the European Union and ACP States and the End of the Lomé Convention' (2003) 24(1) *Third World Quarterly* 161–176, 161.

under the third pillar, the political dimension. They were included in a revision from 2005 and were slightly amended again in the 2010 revisions. They can be found under Article 11, titled 'Peace building policies, conflict prevention and resolution, response to situations of fragility'. The Article stresses the need for political stability in order to achieve economic prosperity. This is very much in line with the reasoning behind the quote guiding much of the analysis in this book made by former ICTY and ICTR Prosecutor Carla Del Ponte at Goldman Sachs on the dividends of justice.[23] Article 11(7) ACP states:

> In promoting the strengthening of peace and international justice, the Parties reaffirm their determination to:
> — share experience in the adoption of legal adjustments required to allow for the ratification and implementation of the Rome Statute of the International Criminal Court; and
> — fight against international crime in accordance with international law, giving due regard to the Rome Statute.
> The Parties shall seek to take steps towards ratifying and implementing the Rome Statute and related instruments

In order to understand the purpose of including a provision on the Rome Statute in the agreement, we need to consider the interests represented through this provision. Ruby Evadne Coye, Head of the Mission of Jamaica to the European Community (EC), refers in her report from 2005 to the difficulties in the negotiations. According to her, the provisions regarding the ICC (as well as the provisions regarding the non-proliferation of weapons of mass destruction) 'caused the greatest difficulty for the ACP during the negotiations'. Interestingly, she goes on to note that 'consensus was reached some might say, as a result of the EC's status as dominant partner in the negotiations'.[24] The explicit mention of the unequal positions of the parties corresponds with the description of the CPA as a 'diktat rather than a true partnership'.[25] The chosen wording implies the forcefulness with which the EU delegates must have argued. In fact, it very much sounds like the benefits running from the ACP – such as financial assistance for smaller states – were being made conditional upon states signing up

---

[23] Carla Del Ponte, 'The Dividends of International Criminal Justice', Goldman Sachs, London, 6 October 2005.

[24] 'Cotonou Partnership Agreement' 8.

[25] Adrian Flint, 'The End of a "Special Relationship"? The New EU–ACP Economic Partnership Agreement (2009) 36 *Review of African Political Economy* 79–92, at 79.

to the Rome Statute.[26] Similar ICC clauses have become standard in European Policy Action Plans and Cooperation Agreements with third countries.[27]

7.3.1   EU Interests in an Integrated Trade Law and Criminal Law Regime

What did the EU have to gain from the inclusion of the ICC clause that it bargained for it so hard? For the EU, there were arguably three main motivators: first, the making of African, Caribbean and Pacific states safe for investment; second, an integrated protection system for private property; and third, the disruption of South–South solidarity.

On the motivation to make ACP group states safe for investment: the assurance of states having signed up to the Rome Statute provides a means by which foreign direct investment can be attracted. This is, at this point in the analysis of marketised global justice, a familiar argument. There is a distinct marketing aspect to this too in that an exploitative trade deal looks less like exploitation if all member states have signed up to a human rights-related treaty. The reciprocal benefits for ACP states will no doubt have been laid out in negotiations although, as we shall see, the ACP states have not been entirely convinced by such arguments. The second benefit for the EU is that the integration of trade and criminal-isation provides an elevation of property rights. Where the trade agree-ments ensure the flow of capital across borders, the international crimes framework provides the potential criminalisation of its prevention. This has arguably become more relevant since the Office of the Prosecutor's (OTP's) re-brand in 2016, when it communicated its intentions to focus on property crimes.[28] The re-brand will be discussed further below, but it is worth mentioning here that the much-celebrated transition from physical violence crimes to property crimes sustains and continues what Sundhya Pahuja has referred to as 'propertisation' in the post-colonial landscape. When the OTP refers to crimes regarding the illegal exploit-ation of natural resources or the illegal dispossession of land, it is

---

[26] Mia Swart, 'Layers of Coloniality: How to Navigate the Political Nature of the International Criminal Court', (draft paper on file with the author).

[27] Salla Huikuri, *The Institutionalization of the International Criminal Court* (Palgrave Macmillan 2019) 150.

[28] 'Policy paper on case selection and prioritisation', The Office of the Prosecutor, ICC, 15 September 2016 (hereinafter 'OTP Policy Paper 2016').

engaging in the 'conceptual inclusion within the regime of property of the thing in question and the creation of associated property rights with respect to it'.[29] Natural resources are conceptually interpreted as '"raw materials" to be "exploited"'.[30] In the developmental progress narrative, explains Pahuja, propertisation is part of the capitalist story, which regards '*private* property as the marker of civilisation'.[31] Far from targeting the corporate power that lies behind land-grabbing and environmental destruction, the ICC's new policy to go after the 'middle ranking' perpetrators further embeds the notion of perpetrators of international crime as those from the Global South.[32]

A further, third, incentive for the EU to include the Rome Statute provision in the trade agreement is that it is a tool for disrupting South-South solidarity. If one were to pinpoint the beginning of the disillusionment of African states with the ICC, it would most likely be 2005, which also happens to be the year in which the ICC amendment to the CPA was included. It was in 2005 that the UN Security Council referred the situation in Darfur to the ICC's prosecutor, with Sudan being a non-member state.[33] This brought back the reality of the powerful hegemon (in the form of the UN Security Council) pulling strings despite repeated reassurances of the independence of the fledgling court. It also reinforced fears of Western intervention on the basis of American public opinion. (We learned about the public pressure exerted by the Save Darfur Coalition in Chapter 6.) In addition, and most alarmingly, it became a real possibility that a sitting head of state, and member of the African Union (AU), could be subject to an ICC arrest warrant. Even if the violence in Darfur was causing concern across the continent, and Al Bashir was not necessarily popular, the peace negotiations were still considered as concerning, first and foremost, Africa.[34] Although increasingly a distant memory, African states knew that it was South-South solidarity that had provided the newly independent states of the 1960s

---

[29] Pahuja, 'Decolonising International Law', 125.

[30] Ibid.

[31] Ibid, 126.

[32] What Gerry Simpson has referred to as 'outlaw states' in Gerry Simpson, *Great Powers and Outlaw States: Unequal Sovereigns in the International Legal Order* (Cambridge University Press 2009).

[33] 'Security Council Refers Situation in Darfur, Sudan, to Prosecutor of International Criminal Court' (Press Release) SC/8351 (31 March 2005).

[34] Muammar Gaddafi, whom the court would later charge with war crimes in Libya, was at the time the AU's chairman, and oversaw peace negotiations.

and 1970s significant bargaining power in multilateral agreements.[35] This allowed for a range of economic benefits set out in the New International Economic Order, with the UN General Assembly as the chosen global political forum. Notably, the President of the ACP group Alhaji Muhammad Mumuni explained that states from the South were resisting the negotiations of the EPAs proposed by the EU because: 'states are encouraged to trade with the European Union but not amongst themselves'.[36] Traditionally, South–South solidarity was less focused on private property rights and more focused on collectivisation. Signing up to the Rome Statute, and the CPA, was a further division of this solidarity. The Rome Statute imposed obligations to arrest those issued with ICC arrest warrants, essentially heads of states of neighbouring countries. This obligation was one of the main issues leading to resistance against the ICC in 2016.

7.3.2 ICC Interests in an Integrated Trade Law and Criminal Law Regime

What interests are served for the ICC by the integration of trade treaties and criminal law? On a basic level, the provision in the CPA potentially increases membership of the ICC, leading it to its ultimate goal of universal jurisdiction. Although neither the arguably most powerful states (the United States, China, and Russia) nor the most populous states (China again, and India) are signatories, it nevertheless boasts a sizable number of currently 122 member states. The significance of the African bloc for the success of the Rome Statute cannot be underestimated. It was this bloc that enabled the Like-Minded Group's success through their endorsement at the Rome Conference, even breaking ranks with their usual southern partners such as India.[37] African states make up the largest number of state parties to the Rome Statute from any region. Among other incentives, they had been attracted to the idea of an

---

[35] During the period of decolonisation, in the 1960s and 1970s, developing countries used the General Agreement on Tariffs and Trade (GATT) for market access demands. Developing countries were able to lobby for important exemptions within the treaty, enabling their access to the global market.

[36] 'EU Pressures Seven African Countries to Complete Trade Agreements', Euractiv online (23 April 2013), available at: www.euractiv.com/section/development-policy/news/eu-pressures-seven-african-countries-to-complete-trade-agreements/

[37] Sivuyile Maqugo, 'The African Contribution Towards the Establishment of an International Criminal Court' (2000) 8(1) African Yearbook on International Law 333–350.

anti-hegemonic institution. The positioning of the ICC as anti-hegemonic was a major pull for multiple states of the Global South. Indeed, despite its poor record in anti-hegemonic prosecutions, this continues to be the message purveyed by the Office of the Prosecutor. 'Law provides power for all regardless of their social, economic, or political status; it is the ultimate weapon that the weak have against the strong', declared Fatou Bensouda as freshly minted prosecutor at a lecture in 2012.[38] Indeed, hopes for the ICC were not dissimilar to hopes for the WTO: an international forum that would allow for a power realignment, or at the very least allow for a forum to highlight the hypocrisy of Western states. The ICC meanwhile relied heavily on African states from a business perspective: for setting up shop in the first place (African states were among the first to ratify the Rome Statute and helped it achieve the required 66 ratifications); for identifying victims and perpetrators to suit a Western donor audience; and for creating a global justice narrative to ensure expansion.

So whilst the ordo-liberals in Europe were dreaming up a neoliberal constitution in Geneva, creating the illusion of development for the Global South, their cousins in Rome were dreaming up a way of creating (the illusion of) a power shift away from the hegemonic states. All the while, both power bases were creating the primacy of property rights: one as a means for ensuring surplus value extraction in the Global South, and the other as a punitive system against the violation of property rights. Overall, there were various carrot and stick mechanisms put into place in order to ensure the integration between the global trade regime on the one hand and the global criminalisation regime on the other. For some, this was the carrot of aid and the stick of the Rome Statute (smaller states signing up to the CPA); for others it was the carrot of the Rome Statute and the stick of market integration (larger states signing up to the CPA). But, the next twenty years were to demonstrate that both regimes were 'sticks' for the states of the Global South. African states signed off on exploitation of their resources *and* signed off on their criminalisation. At the same time, ICC interests were so vehemently protected that anyone daring to question them was in danger of being branded a supporter of brutal dictators. Luis Moreno Ocampo arguably took it the furthest in his attempts to discipline solidarity emerging from claims of the ICC's anti-African bias. In October 2016, Ocampo published a piece in the widely

---

[38] Lecture published in: Fatou Bensouda, 'Reflections from the International Criminal Court Prosecutor' (2012) 45(4) *Vanderbilt Journal of Transnational Law* 955–961.

read 'Just Security' blog with the click-bait title of 'From Brexit to African ICC Exit: A Dangerous Trend'. In this he argued: 'The African bias is a cover up argument like the denial of the Holocaust. It should not be considered as an argument but rather as an alibi to ignore crimes and it should be exposed as such.'[39] This type of polemics is not only intended to discipline African states into alignment with the ICC; it is also intended to align its critics with fascism.

7.4 Encasing the Market

Spectacularised rhetoric is a means to shut down democratic contestation; evoking the history of the Holocaust is arguably the strongest means to dismiss an argument. The German word for the dismissal of dissent through cliché is rather fittingly *Todschlagargument* (literally 'manslaughter argument'). It is an effective, and affective, tool for encasing the market. A related, although more benign, means by which proponents of the ICC have shut down contestation is through tried and tested mechanisms of insisting that the work of the court is law and not politics. Sarah Nouwen and Wouter Werner quote the first president of the ICC as stating '[t]here's not a shred of evidence after three-and-a-half years that the court has done anything political. The court is operating purely judicially.'[40] ICC Prosecutor Fatou Bensouda has been quoted many times giving assurances that the officials of the Court have 'nothing to do with politics', even if she recognises that 'we operate in a political atmosphere'.[41] The continued insistence of the non-political operation of the ICC begs the question of whether 'the lady doth protest too much'. The separation of politics from law creates an idea that law must reign in politics but not vice versa. It assigns significant powers to lawyers. ICL is habitually distinguished not only from the sphere of the political, but also from the sphere of the economic – the market. This follows the liberal tenet of the separation between public and private authority. The most prolific proponents of the separation of law and the

---

[39] Moreno Ocampo, 'From Brexit to African ICC Exit'.

[40] Steve Herman, 'Japan's Expected to Support International Criminal Court', *Voice of America*, 6 December 2006, quoted in Sarah Nouwen and Wouter Werner, 'Doing Justice to the Political: The International Criminal Court in Uganda and Sudan' (2010) 21(4) *European Journal of International Law* 941–965, 942.

[41] Fatou Bensouda, as quoted in Pascal Airault and Brandice Walker, 'Fatou Bensouda: The Victims Are African', *Africa Report*, 22 December 2011, available at: www.theafricareport .com/7894/fatou-bensouda-the-victims-are-african/

political in ICL are the prosecutors. Indeed, they expend so much energy on promoting a particular vision of ICL as global justice, and as distinct from the political, that their role can be defined as brand managers of global justice. The irony of the corporate (private) practice of brand management in order to protect the legal (public) practice of global justice is, I am sure, not lost on the attentive reader. One marketing agency explains brand management on its website in the following way:

> Persuasive brand messages are always brief and convey critical aspects of a firm's brand. And they often intentionally oversimplify concepts that, in reality, may be complex and nuanced. This *oversimplification is a good thing*, however, because the goal of a brand is to be noticed, remembered and desired.[42]

The ICC does not exclusively cast itself as a global justice brand, but chooses from a variety of legal slogans to describe itself. It invokes 'humanity', 'international justice', 'taking action against atrocious crimes', and the like. The oversimplification employed on simple good–evil distinctions has already been explored in the previous chapters. The prosecutor regularly employs stereotypes in order to achieve the highest impact. The role of aesthetics in the visual recognisability of the brand is utilised in a similar fashion. In the early days of the Court, the first prosecutor made sure that the ICC was never far from the public eye, even if there were no trials occupying the new courtrooms. Moreno Ocampo's salesmanship included press conferences, institutional videos, guest talks, courting celebrities, and appearances in documentaries. The idea of the prosecutor without borders appeared to be the perfect brand-manager role for a universal criminal justice system. The promises of the Court became loftier and loftier. One investigator who had worked with the prosecutor believed that Moreno Ocampo had in fact mistaken the purpose of the ICC to be about 'naming and shaming'.[43]

Slowly but surely, Moreno Ocampo was changing from media darling to an embarrassment, an easy target for ICC sceptics. Moreno Ocampo's outspokenness prompted one legal commentator to warn that 'ICC

---

[42] Lee Frederiksen, 'Elements of a Successful Brand 8: Messaging' Hinge Marketing online, 14 May 2018. emphases added, available at: https://hingemarketing.com/blog/story/elem ents-of-a-successful-brand-8-messaging

[43] James Verini, 'The Prosecutor and the President', *New York Times Magazine*, 22 June 2016.

prosecutors should not be grandstanding their own cases'.[44] The same commentator described the prosecutor in 2011 as 'the best asset for those opposed to the international criminal court'.[45] Despite these early warning signs, Moreno Ocampo pressed on in his brand management role, although increasingly becoming a liability for the brand. Just as the concern about anti-African bias was becoming more widely spread, Moreno Ocampo tailored the global justice message *more* not less for those with buying power. The 'international community' addressed was the community that would be the audience of press statements and promotional videos, live streams of the court, and op-eds in newspapers. The message was overtly designed to speak to organisations and individuals who find the simplified, feminised, infantilised, and racialised narrative of victimhood appealing. The linkage between the donor 'core' of the *Kony 2012* campaign discussed in Chapter 6, and the donor 'core' of the ICC is unmistakable.

This connection between spectacularised criminality and the quelling of forms of dissent against the market was already insinuated by Karl Marx in the nineteenth century:

> The [figure of the] criminal breaks the monotony and everyday security of bourgeois life. In this way he keeps it from stagnation, and gives rise to that uneasy tension and agility without which even the spur of competition would get blunted. Thus he gives a stimulus to the productive forces.[46]

Breaking the monotony and everyday security of bourgeois life through the consumption of spectacle is an escape into representation and a de-politicised world, a nineteenth-century reflection on the attention economy. Today, the focus on the evil warlord, the innocent victim, and the hero lawyer, are productive of an economy of global justice but blind to the real social injustices behind those roles. However, the states of the Global South have not simply allowed this commodification and distraction to happen; they have both actively facilitated as well as resisted it.

---

[44] Joshua Rozenberg, 'ICC prosecutors Should Not Be Grandstanding Their Own Cases', *The Guardian*, 18 August 2010.

[45] Joshua Rozenberg, 'Prosecutor Luis Moreno-Ocampo Is the Best Asset of Those Opposed to the International Criminal Court', *The Guardian*, 21 April 2011.

[46] Jon Elster (ed.) 'Theories of Surplus Value' in *Karl Marx. A Reader* (Cambridge University Press 1986) 321.

7.5   Crisis at the ICC

In late 2016, South Africa, Burundi, and The Gambia announced their withdrawal from the ICC. Although there were multiple motivations for this, the common ground shared between these states was that the ICC was protecting Western interests and powers at the expense of Africans. Perhaps the most incendiary of them was the Gambian information minister's declaration that 'the ICC, despite being called International Criminal Court is in fact an International Caucasian Court for the persecution and humiliation of people of colour, especially Africans'.[47] Further African states announced their potential withdrawal, and yet others reaffirmed their support. A suggestion for a 'mass-withdrawal' was tabled at the AU summit the following year, which led to the conceptualisation of a withdrawals strategy.[48] Withdrawal from the Rome Statute became a new political currency. Or rather, *announcing* withdrawal from the Rome Statute became the new political currency (in the end, only Burundi actually withdrew). The states from the Global South decided to use their power of sovereignty collectively – arguably the most effective power they have in multilateralism – to stir things up at the ICC.

The crisis did not come from nowhere. Both inside and outside of the African continent, critique of the ICC, and the broader discipline of ICL, had become commonplace. As Frédéric Mégret observed in 2013, to a certain degree everyone assessing ICL is in some way critical of it and few, if any, of its defenders engage in full-blooded apologias for it.[49] Observations that the 'honeymoon is over'[50] and that international criminal justice had entered into its 'post-romantic' phase were not unusual.[51] Few were under the illusion that the ICC would magically bring about global justice. But that it would fail so spectacularly was still unexpected. In 2008, the Rwandan president Paul Kagame claimed that

---

[47] Siobhán O'Grady, 'Gambia: The ICC Should be Called the International Caucasian Court', *Foreign Policy*, 26 October 2016.

[48] 'Withdrawal Strategy Document' African Union, Leaked document available at: www.hrw .org/sites/default/files/supporting_resources/icc_withdrawal_strategy_jan._2017.pdf.

[49] Frédéric Mégret, 'International Criminal Justice: A Critical Research Agenda' in Christine Schwöbel (ed.) *Critical Approaches to International Criminal Law* (Routledge 2014) 17–53, at 17–18.

[50] David Luban, 'After the Honeymoon: Reflections on the Current State of International Criminal Justice' (2013) 11 *Journal of International Criminal Justice* 505–515.

[51] Payam Akhavan, 'The Rise and Fall, and Rise, of International Criminal Justice' (2013) 11 *Journal of International Criminal Justice* (2013), 527–536, at 527.

the ICC was operating within the tradition of 'colonialism, slavery, and imperialism'.[52] At the UN, African states' concerns about the ICC were recognised as early as 2009. Then Secretary-General Kofi Annan stated in a *New York Times* reflection on 'Africa and the International Court' that the ICC is viewed by some African leaders as 'an imposition, if not a plot, by the industrialised West'.[53] In 2013, an AU 'Extraordinary Summit on the ICC' was held.[54] On this occasion, it was Kenya that was lobbying its fellow AU members to exit the statute.[55] Simultaneously, there was a concern about universal jurisdiction cases of European states that were targeting African leaders.[56] Despite the writing being on the wall, the 2016 announcements and threats of withdrawal still came as a surprise to many. In the media, political commentary, and civil society commentary, the crisis was flattened to one of 'autocratic leaders are refusing account-ability'.[57] While headlines such as 'major loss for victims' prevailed, the charge of neo-colonialism was largely ignored.[58]

In Chapter 6, the distinction was made between backlash and resist-ance in order to differentiate between the kind of response that is market-driven and responses that are sensitive to histories of exploitation and oppression. The critique of neo-colonialism refers to the making present

---

[52] 'Rwandan President Says ICC Targeting African Countries', *Sudan Tribune*, 31 July 2008, available at: www.sudantribune.com/spip.php?article28103. In that year, Kagame's chief of protocol, Rose Kabuye, was arrested in Germany pursuant to a French arrest warrant in connection with the shooting down of the former Rwandan president's plane, which triggered the 1994 genocide. He was fighting against universal jurisdiction exercised by European states as well as against the jurisdiction of the ICC.

[53] Kofi Annan, 'Africa and the International Court', *The New York Times*, 29 June 2009.

[54] 'Extraordinary Session of the Assembly of the African Union', African Union, Ext/Assembly/AU/Dec.1-2 (12 October 2013).

[55] In September of that year, Deputy-President of Kenya William Ruto had voluntarily come to The Hague following an arrest warrant charging him with crimes against humanity for his alleged role in orchestrating post-election violence of 2007.

[56] Belgium issued an arrest warrant for the DRC's then-minister of foreign affairs, Abdoulaye Yerodia Ndombasi, in 2000, which was brought before the International Court of Justice in *Case Concerning Arrest Warrant of 11 April 2000* (*Democratic Republic of the Congo* v. *Belgium*) Judgment [2002] ICJ Rep 3. Domestic universal jurisdiction cases have notably also included US officials (particularly for crimes com-mitted in Iraq), although none have been arrested or convicted.

[57] 'The International Criminal Court and Accountability in Africa', LSE blog, 31 January 2018, available at: https://blogs.lse.ac.uk/africaatlse/2018/01/31/the-international-crim inal-court-and-accountability-in-africa/.

[58] 'Burundi: ICC Withdrawal Major Loss to Victims', Human Rights Watch, 27 October 2016, available at: www.hrw.org/news/2016/10/27/burundi-icc-withdrawal-major-loss-victims

of these histories as continuations. Backlashes against marketised global justice overwhelmingly occur within the market values parameters of global justice rather than the social values parameters of global justice. This creates a distinction between de-historicised and de-politicised backlash on the one hand and historically sensitive and politically radical resistance on the other hand. Admittedly, the distinction does not translate quite as neatly into reality, but it serves the purpose of distinguishing between different types of responses, particularly serving to distinguish between those on the receiving end of global justice interventions and those on the intervening end.

Backlashes against the ICC are common and are generally couched in terms of the efficiency of funds. The backlash against the ICC was (and continues to be) similar to the backlash against *Kony 2012*: voiced mainly by those in the Global North who are concerned about the ICC being a 'bad investment'. Resistance, meanwhile, has come in different forms from the Global South and those acting in solidarity with it. Much in the way that some forms of resistance to neo-colonialism have operated *within* the WTO mechanism and therefore within the confines of neoliberalism, so have some of the responses to coloniality operated *within* the boundaries of the ICC system. Resistance has not always been clearly marked as either operating outside of international law as a clear-cut division of revolution (outside international law) or reform (inside international law). We will return to this in the final chapter. For now, it is instructive to understand the withdrawals, and threats thereof, as a radical form of resistance to the global justice sector.

7.5.1   Backlash Against the ICC

Before turning to resistance, let us briefly consider the typical backlash market-responses. Backlash is mostly articulated around the budget of the ICC in a value for money register: €1.5 billion have been spent, so, this argument goes, there should be more than only three core crimes convictions.[59] From a 'value for money' perspective, the record is indeed dire. The court had almost made it to the twenty-year mark since the signing of the Rome Statute with four core crimes convictions, until shortly beforehand the ICC Appeals Chamber overturned the conviction of Jean-Pierre Bemba, former vice president of the Democratic Republic

---

[59] See, for example, Andrew Murdoch 'UK Statement to the Assembly of States Parties 17th session', Assembly of States Parties 17th Session, 5 December 2018.

of the Congo (DRC).[60] Bemba subsequently filed for compensation of
€68.8 million from the ICC for his ten-year detention as well as the
alleged mismanagement of his assets.[61] After twenty years only the cases
of *Katanga, Lubanga,* and *Al Mahdi* are completed, and these by no
means stand out as case studies for the effectiveness of international
criminal justice. Germain Katanga was sentenced to twelve years after
eight in custody. He had therefore already served almost two-thirds of his
sentence when he was found guilty. Katanga's sentence was reduced by
the ICC Appeals Chamber one year later, meaning that his total period of
incarceration from sentence to release was 21 months. The problems
with the Thomas Dyilo Lubanga trial were set out in Chapter 4 'A Picture
Worth More than a Thousand Words' in detail. Suffice to say here that
Lubanga was sentenced to twelve years after six years in ICC detention.
Ahmad Al Faqi Al Mahdi, a mid-level militia fighter, pleaded guilty and
was sentenced to nine years. This is generally considered as the only
'successful' case to date. Investigations into the post-election violence in
Kenya were dropped, including an arrest warrant against its President
Kenyatta.[62] And in 2019, two defendants Laurent Gbabgo and Charles
Blé Goudé, the former president and youth minister of Côte d'Ivoire
respectively, were acquitted of all charges because the prosecution had
failed to provide any evidence to support even the most basic of legal
requirements.[63] In 2019, the ICC then stated that it would not pursue
further investigations into the situation in Afghanistan, which could
have seen Western leaders implicated in international crimes for the first
time.[64] This statement came quick on the heels of the United States
cancelling visas for the office of the prosecutor to pursue investigations.[65]

---

[60] *The Prosecutor* v. *Jean-Pierre Bemba Gombo* (Judgment on the Appeal of Mr Jean-Pierre
Bemba Gombo against Trial Chamber III's "Judgment Pursuant to Article 74 of the
Statute'), ICC-01/05/08 A (8 June 2018).

[61] *The Prosecutor* v. *Jean-Pierre Bemba Gombo* (Order on the Conduct of the Proceedings
Related to "Mr Bemba's Claim for Compensation and Damages") ICC-01/05-01/08 (14
March 2019).

[62] *The Prosecutor* v. *Uhuru Muigai Kenyatta* (Decision on the Withdrawal of Charges
Against Mr Kenyatta) ICC-01/09-02/11 (13 March 2015).

[63] *The Prosecutor* v. *Laurent Gbagbo and Charles Blé Goudé* (Transcript, Trial Chamber I)
ICC-02/11-01/15-T-232-ENG (15 January 2019).

[64] *Situation in the Islamic Republic of Afghanistan* (Decision Pursuant to Article 15 of the
Rome Statute on the Authorisation of an Investigation into the Situation in the Islamic
Republic of Afghanistan) ICC-02/17 (12 April 2019).

[65] Jennifer Hansler, 'US denying visas to International Criminal Court staff', CNN,
15 March 2019, available at: https://edition.cnn.com/2019/03/15/politics/pompeo-icc-
visa-restrictions/index.html

Inexplicably, there was surprise expressed about this entirely foreseeable move by the ICC.

The 'value for money' argument is given further support because the ICC is spending an inordinate amount of money on *internal* litigation. Again, the investors are not wrong to be frustrated. As Kevin Jon Heller summarised, the employment litigation of ICC former employees at the International Labour Organisation added up to roughly €2 million in the space of just two years.[66] In addition, there has been a general shaking of heads at the ICC judges pursuing litigation because they believe that their annual tax free €200,000 salary (combined with several other perks) is insufficient. A glance at the fairly sparse case docket of the ICC indeed further stokes the value for money fire of discontent. As Douglas Guilfoyle notes, there is a possibility that the Administrative Tribunal of the International Labour Organization 'could be deciding more cases about the ICC than the ICC resolves cases of its own'.[67] Suggestions to overcome these issues are also couched in economic terms, with state representatives calling for 'multi-stakeholder engagement with the court'.[68] In 2019, four former presidents of the ICC's Assembly of States Parties co-authored a comment in which they proposed a 'small group of international experts' to 'fix' the ICC. According to them, this would provide a common reference point for Court officials and 'all stakeholders' going forward.[69]

In the 'crisis year', 2016, the budget was €139.5 million and the entire court had just moved to a brand new €200 million building.[70] Notably, the somewhat reputation-rescuing *Al Mahdi* case had just taken place,

---

[66] Kevin Jon Heller, 'ICC Labor Woes Part II: What's Two Million Euros Between Friends', Opinio Juris blog, 30 July 2018, available at: http://opiniojuris.org/2018/06/30/the-iccs-labor-woes-part-ii/.

[67] Douglas Guilfoyle, 'Part I – This is Not Fine: The International Criminal Court in Trouble', EJILtalk, (21 March 2019), available at: www.ejiltalk.org/part-i-this-is-not-fine-the-international-criminal-court-in-trouble/.

[68] The Danish representative to the General Assembly quoted in 'Facing Political Attacks, Limited Budget, International Criminal Court Needs Strong Backing to Ensure Justice for Atrocity Crimes, President Tells General Assembly', General Assembly Plenary 73rd Session, GA/12084 (29 October 2018).

[69] Prince Zeid Ra'ad al Hussein, Bruno Stagno Ugarte, Christian Wenaweser, and Tiina Intelman, 'The International Criminal Court Needs Fixing', Atlantic Council, 24 April 2019, available at: www.atlanticcouncil.org/blogs/new-atlanticist/the-international-criminal-court-needs-fixing/.

[70] Al-Bashir's travels to South Africa, which is a state party to the Rome Statute, were discussed in the media. For example, Stephanie van den Berg, 'ICC Declines to Refer South Africa to U.N. for Not Arresting Sudan's Bashir', Reuters, 6 July 2017, available at:

and the ICC had opened its first investigations in a non-African situation.[71] At the heart of the ICC, reassurances were made: 'I do think the global demand for justice will outweigh the suspicion and resistance that some stakeholders show towards the ICC', said then-ICC President Sang-Hyun Song.[72] With both problem and solution framed in market terms, global justice was reduced to a cost-benefit argument. The benefit had to be something very specific: convictions for core crimes, preferably for perpetrators from the Global South, whose population were to express gratitude for the intervention.

7.5.2 Resistance to the ICC

The states from the Global South, however, were by 2016 no longer willing to play along with this narrative. By 2016, the 'global justice as international criminal justice' idea had proven to be an illusion for African states. It was clear to many African states that the ICC had not served as the counter-hegemonic institution they had hoped it might be. So it was in this crisis year that three states acted in the only form of resistance open to them in the global justice sector: to announce the withdrawal of labour from it. It was a 'putting down tools' moment in which African states were no longer willing to contribute to the machinery. The states in the Global South had very much understood how this industry was panning out. Its focus on Africa, and its lack of seeing through investigations that could implicate strong Western powers, was repeatedly described as 'neo-colonial'. Certainly, the charge is the loudest when made by political leaders; it is predictable when made by defence counsel. But, overall, it is an important lens onto a longer history of international law and institutions subjugating the states in the Global South. In this longer history, the ICC is one of the latest in a long line of mechanisms through which international law aims to 'civilise' the Global South. To add insult to injury, the ICC promised emancipation but did not deliver on this promise, instead falling short of highlighting the

---

https://uk.reuters.com/article/uk-warcrimes-sudan-safrica/icc-declines-to-refer-south-africa-to-u-n-for-not-arresting-sudans-bashir-idUKKBN19R1UE.

[71] *Situation in Georgia*, (Decision on the Prosecutor's Request for Authorization of an Investigation) ICC-01/15 (27 January 2016).

[72] 'Former ICC President: Continue to Seek Global Justice and Change' *The University of Melbourne News*, 29 February 2016, available at: http://law.unimelb.edu.au/news/MLS/former-icc-president-continue-to-seek-global-justice-and-change.

legacies of colonialism that continue to mark conflict in the Global South, and Africa in particular.

The year 2016, therefore, proved to be a critical year as regards the AU states manoeuvring themselves into a collective bargaining position. In January 2016, the AU decided to mandate its Open-Ended Committee on the ICC to develop a 'comprehensive strategy' that included withdrawal from the ICC. The committee met on 11 April, and identified three conditions to avoid the AU calling for a mass withdrawal from the ICC: a demand for the recognition of the immunity of sitting heads of state, as recognised in customary international law; intervention by the ICC only after the cases were submitted to an AU body; and a reduction in the powers of the ICC prosecutor.[73] In May 2016, Ugandan President Museveni felt confident enough about anti-ICC support that at his inauguration ceremony he called the people working at the Court 'a bunch of useless people'.[74] Not only did this sting because Uganda was the first state to refer its own situation to the ICC, it was also an act of defiance to the Western diplomatic corps present. Sudanese President Omar Al Bashir, who had been issued with an arrest warrant by this point, was also defiantly in attendance.

Particularly troubling for the ICC was the decision of South Africa to withdraw from the Rome Statute. South Africa was one of the most ardent supporters of the Court during the Rome Conference, and as the regional hegemon it also has substantial influence over its neighbouring states. At issue for South Africa was both the neo-colonial focus on Africa as victims and perpetrators as well as the diplomatic immunity of heads of states. As regards the latter (and implicitly the former), the government stressed that diplomatic immunity was crucial 'in order to effectively promote dialogue and the peaceful resolution of conflicts wherever they may occur, particularly on the African continent'.[75] It is worth noting that the concern over ongoing peace processes is a reasonable argument against the background that the ICC had failed to produce peaceful relations in *any* of the situations it had intervened in. But the announcement of withdrawal was covered in the media and civil society

---

[73] 'UN/African Union: Reject ICC Withdrawal', Human Rights Watch, 22 September 2016, available at: www.hrw.org/news/2016/09/22/un/african-union-reject-icc-withdrawal.

[74] 'Western Officials Walk out of Museveni Inauguration', *Al Jazeera*, 13 May 2016, available at: www.aljazeera.com/news/2016/05/western-officials-walk-museveni-inauguration-160513093336340.html.

[75] 'SA Formally Withdrawing from ICC', *SA News*, 21 October 2016, available at: www.sanews.gov.za/south-africa/sa-formally-withdrawing-icc.

in such a dramatic tone that the withdrawals appeared not only unreasonable, but irresponsible. Human Rights Watch declared a 'continent wide outcry' and a 'slap in the face for victims'.[76] Amnesty International responded by stating that South Africa is 'betraying millions of victims of the gravest human rights violations'.[77] During this period, there were also many statements of support issued by NGOs working in sub-Saharan Africa, who were no less dramatic in their coverage.[78]

7.6 Responses to Resistance

The response to the neo-colonialism charge, if engaged with, is typically dismissed by *supporters* of marketised justice in one of four ways: first, through a 'tyrants want impunity' response; second, through a 'self-referrals' response; third, through a 'diversity at the ICC' response; and fourth, through a 'victims are African' response. Each of these deserves a book of its own, so only a cursory discussion and initial unsettling of the dismissals is possible here.[79] The 'tyrants want impunity' dismissal appears persuasive against the background that Burundi's President Pierre Nkurunziza was being investigated by the prosecution at the time of Burundi's notification of intention to withdraw from the ICC. Post-colonial leaders have often exacerbated violence and corruption. But the continued interference – and denial of it – by Western states aiming to control resources is critical for understanding Africa's relationship with

---

[76] 'South Africa: Continent Wide Outcry at ICC Withdrawal', Human Rights Watch, 22 October 2016, available at: www.hrw.org/news/2016/10/22/south-africa-continent-wide-outcry-icc-withdrawal.

[77] 'South Africa: Decision to Leave International Criminal Court a "deep betrayal of millions of victims worldwide"', Amnesty International Press Release, 21 October 2016, available at: www.amnesty.org.uk/press-releases/south-africa-decision-leave-international-criminal-court-deep-betrayal-millions.

[78] For an account of civil society responses to withdrawal, see Christopher R. Rossi, 'Hauntings, Hegemony, and the Threatened African Exodus from the International Criminal Court' (2018) 40(2) *Human Rights Quarterly* 369–405. Noting the importance of NGOs and government agencies in effectively implementing the work of the ICC in Africa, see Benson Chinedu Olugbuo, 'Implementing the International Criminal Court Treaty in Africa: The Role of Nongovernmental Organizations and Government Agencies in Constitutional Reform' in Kamari Maxine Clarke & Mark Goodale (eds.), Mirrors of Justice: Law and Power in the Post-Cold War Era (Cambridge University Press 2010) 106–130.

[79] Compare with Phil Clark, *Distant Justice: The Impact of the International Criminal Court on African Politics* (Cambridge University Press 2019) 53–65 for a discussion of what he identifies as three responses to the neo-colonialism charge.

international organisations. An engagement with the neo-colonial argument allows for a more extensive view on causal connections between conflict, individual perpetrators, and colonialism. And yet, with criminal accountability stopping short of an analysis of structural violence, the scapegoats remain African leaders.

According to the Rome Statute, state parties may refer a situation to the prosecutor for investigation.[80] Self-referral occurs when a state notifies the prosecutor of alleged crimes committed in their own state. The majority of cases that have progressed to trial stage were self-referrals. States that self-referred include the Democratic Republic of the Congo, Uganda, the Central African Republic (twice), Mali, and Gabon. It has become common to dismiss the charge of neo-colonialism on the basis of these self-referrals. However, the dismissal ignores the way in which the OTP was actively seeking opportunities for self-referral. As Phil Clark notes, the OTP was in fact 'chasing' the first self-referral cases, initiating negotiations with the Ugandan and Congolese governments well before the referrals took place.[81] It is also worth noting that self-referrals do not automatically result in the opening of an investigation, as sometimes insinuated by the one-sidedness of the self-referral argument. According to Article 53 Rome Statute, the OTP must decide whether there is a 'reasonable basis' to begin an investigation of a situation or case. These cases are therefore much more prosecution-led than the established terminology of 'self-referral' would have one believe.

The 'diversity of the ICC' dismissal of neo-colonialism is mostly based on the fact that Chief Prosecutor Fatou Bensouda is herself a black woman. However, Bensouda's position does little to alleviate the racial capitalism underlying the Court; nor does the leadership position of one black woman undo structural racism. On an equally flat level, one might retort that The Gambia was the third state to claim its intention to withdraw from the Rome Statute, the very state in which Bensouda had been justice minister prior to her appointment at the ICC. The same myopia applies to the 'victims happen to be in the Global South' dismissal: this argument hides the structural inequality underlying North-South relations in which inequality is ia function of the North gaining wealth on the basis of the South's exploitation. Supporters of the Court have even undertaken metrics projects to claim that victims are African. One group of academics devised a 'seriousness index' of 'worst countries'

---

[80] Article 14 Rome Statute.
[81] Clark, 'Distant Justice', 55.

to 'empirically' prove that the anti-African bias argument is 'exaggerated'.[82] Another supporter, from South Africa no less, claimed that the colonialism argument is a 'myth' that is not 'substantiated by true facts.'[83] Much in the vein of the Holocaust argument made by Moreno Ocampo, this commentator dismisses Mahmood Mamdani's concerns over the ICC being a 'Western court to try African crimes against humanity',[84] by stating: 'The danger with each of these arguments is that they will find traction – not surprisingly – with dictators and their henchmen who seek reasons to delay or resist being held responsible under universally applicable standards of justice'.[85] Typically, resistance arguments are therefore dismissed as either inconsequential *or* potentially dangerous. Given the marketing practices used to create this contradiction, it appears particularly ironic that Fatou Bensouda spoke of the 'propaganda' of individuals who describe the ICC as anti-African.[86]

Despite the currency of universality and the dismissal of the neocolonial charge, it is in fact difficult to deny that ICL has followed Western ideas of criminal justice. The crimes, procedure, prioritisation of consequentialist and punitive means of criminal justice, and standards and procedure of courts and detention facilities, are modelled on Western criminal justice paradigms. Pertinently, in Western states, criminal law is an area of law in which nation states enjoy the powers of moral surveillance and regulation. The principle of complementarity in the Rome Statute, even as it purports to decentralise international criminal justice to domestic judiciaries if they are 'willing and able' to prosecute, has proved to be a vehicle for a hegemonic centralisation of international criminal justice.[87]

---

[82] Alette Smeulers, Maartje Weerdesteijn, and Barbora Hola, 'The Selection of Situations by the ICC: An Empirically Based Evaluation of the OTP's Performance' (2015) 15(1) *International Criminal Law Review* 1–39, at 38.

[83] Max du Plessis, 'The International Criminal Court and Its Work in Africa: Confronting the Myths' (2008) Institute for Security Studies, paper 173, 2.

[84] Mahmood Mamdani, 'Responsibility to Protect or Right to Punish?' (2010) 4(1) *Journal of Intervention and Statebuilding* 53–67, at 61.

[85] Du Plessis, 'The International Criminal Court and its Work in Africa', 2.

[86] David Smith, 'New Chief Prosecutor Defends International Criminal Court', *The Guardian*, 23 May 2012.

[87] Christine Schwöbel, 'The Market and Marketing Culture of International Criminal Law' in Christine Schwöbel (ed.), *Critical Approaches to International Criminal Law – An Introduction* (Routledge 2014) 264–279, at 269–270. See also Krever, 'Dispensing Global Justice', 94–95.

The recognition of the pervading neo-colonialism of international legal institutions by no means supports a one-dimensional understanding of dependency of the Global South.[88] Rather, the neoliberal order as the integration of a global trade and criminalisation regime has been both supported *and* resisted from the Global South. Just as 'developing countries were advocates of both protection and liberalization at the same time,'[89] AU states were advocates of nationalist and regional criminalisation *and* universal criminalisation at the same time.

7.7   Re-branding the ICC

The ICC's predictable response to market-focused backlash is to seek solutions in the market. In large part because market-oriented criticisms are taken seriously (in contrast to charges of neo-colonialism), the ICC's response tends to be expressed in affirmations of 'efficiency gains and cost savings'.[90] The OTP's Strategic Plan 2019–2021 expresses a 'powerful work ethic' as one of its values.[91] It also stresses somewhat sourly that '[s]takeholders expect the Office to deliver more and better results, preferably within a shorter time and for some, within existing or even fewer resources'.[92] In the 'crisis year' of 2016, the OTP responded by undergoing what in the marketing world would be described as a 're-brand'. Implementation of the re-brand has been slow, but noticeable. Its aim has been twofold: to move away

---

[88] According to dependency theory, the Global North could only achieve its prosperity at the expense of the Global South. The fledgling industrialisation was wiped out in order to make space for raw materials. Through unequal exchanges, including various tariff arrangements, the states of the Global South were prevented from developing or manufacturing the raw materials. Exceptions to the rule are the countries with close ties to the United States, including Japan, Taiwan, and South Korea. This arrangement meant that the Global North could keep its monopoly on industry and could use the Global South for its agrarian needs. The term is attributed to Andre Gunder Frank, *Capitalism and Underdevelopment in Latin America: Historical Studies of Chile and Brazil* (*Monthly Review Press* 1967). Dependency theory has been criticised for its Western-centric view in that it leaves no space for contestation and agency from the Global South. It suffocates the potential for resistance. The stringent distinction between neoliberalism imposed from the North and protectionism from the South has been debunked in favour of a more nuanced approach.

[89] Slobodian, 'Globalists', 202.

[90] 'Strategic Plan 2019–2021', Office of the Prosecutor, 17 July 2019.

[91] Ibid 8.

[92] Ibid 12.

from (protracted and politically sensitive) trials of heads of state and rebel leaders and instead go after mid-ranking officials, and to focus on property crimes instead of physical crimes.

In September 2016, a month before the notifications of withdrawal from three member states, Bensouda's office published a policy paper, which stated its new priorities for case selection, namely a 'particular consideration to prosecuting Rome Statute crimes that are committed by means of, or that result in, *inter alia*, the destruction of the environment, the illegal exploitation of natural resources or the illegal dispossession of land'.[93] Part of the motivation for this re-brand was the perceived successful trial of Al Mahdi. The trial, opening on 22 August 2016 with an admission of guilt by the defendant and delivering its judgment on 27 September 2016, was the first seen by the ICC concerning the intentional destruction of cultural, religious, and historic monuments. Al-Mahdi, a mid-level militiaman, pleaded guilty to the destruction of mausoleums in Timbuktu, Mali.[94] It is notable that the OTP decided to charge Al-Mahdi with the crime of the destruction of cultural heritage instead of the possible alternative case of murder and rape committed during The Northern Mali Conflict.

The shift to property crimes was received positively.[95] The international NGO Global Witness reported enthusiastically: 'Company executives could now be tried for land-grabs and environmental destruction.'[96] However, although the re-brand *appears* to target corporate power, it is in fact arguably facilitative of a deepening of the integration of the global market and criminal justice regimes. First, the prohibition of the destruction of monuments is pretty straightforwardly a prohibition of not smashing up property. Despite the understandable motivations behind the protection of cultural property, it is also politically a

---

[93] OTP Policy Paper 2016, 14.

[94] *The Prosecutor* v. *Ahmad Al Faqi Al Mahdi* (Judgment and Sentence) ICC-01/12-01/15 (Trial Chamber VIII, 27 September 2016).

[95] For example, Marina Aksenova, 'The Al Mahdi Judment and Sentence at the ICC: A Source of Cautious Optimism for International Criminal Justice', EJIL:Talk!, 13 October 2016, available at: www.ejiltalk.org/the-al-mahdi-judgment-and-sentence-at-the-icc-a-source-of-cautious-optimism-for-international-criminal-justice/.

[96] 'Company Executives could now be tried for Land Grabs and Environmental Destruction', Global Witness, Press Release, 15 September 2016, available at: www.globalwitness.org/en/press-releases/company-executives-could-now-be-tried-land-grabbing-and-environmental-destruction-historic-move-international-criminal-court-prosecutor/.

conservative desire.[97] Indeed, resistance and protest movements are often exactly about the smashing up of property that symbolises a colonial past; we need only consider the decolonisation debates around the fall of the statute of Cecil Rhodes at the University of Cape Town.

As regards land-grabbing cases, at the ICC they are unlikely to target corporate power. Under the Rome Statute regime corporations cannot be held criminally liable, and so far no corporate executives have been held to account.[98] Even if a land-grabbing situation were to arise, it is unlikely that this would lead to the issuance of arrest warrant for a Western CEO. Given the lack of transparency of relationships between contractors and sub-contractors, the cooperation of the relevant corporations to identify responsibility at the parent company would be highly unlikely. Ultimately, it is much more likely that a land-grabbing case would instead criminalise the national government officials allocating land to businesses. Alternatively, a dispute over land grabbing could result in an investment arbitration case with the state carrying liability. The account-ability of governmental action would again place the focus on criminality in the Global South, which is most seriously affected by land-grabbing. In the end, the message continues to be that international crimes are committed in the Global South and are prosecuted in the Global North, but with the added inflection of the need to protect private property for achieving global justice.

7.8   Conclusion

As a reminder, the six key organising terms of marketised global justice identified are: (a) branding, (b) the attention economy, (c) spectacle, (d) ICL, (e) neoliberalism, and (f) neo-colonialism. This chapter has focused mainly on one important feature of these configurations of marketised global justice, namely, the enabling and encasing of the global market through an integrated international trade and ICL regime.

---

[97] See Mark A Drumbl, 'From Timbuktu to The Hague and Beyond: The War Crime of Intentionally Attacking Cultural Property' (2019) 17(1) *Journal of International Criminal Justice* 77–99.

[98] Interestingly, this is in contrast to what could have been a historical precedent of the industrialists in the 'subsequent trials' in Nuremberg, including Gustav Krupp as 'the main organiser of German industry'. See instructively, Grietje Baars, 'Capitalism's Victor's Justice? The Hidden Stories Behind the Prosecution of Industrialists Post-WWII' in Kevin Heller and Gerry Simpson (eds.), *The Hidden Histories of War Crimes Trials* (Oxford University Press 2013) 163–192.

Since its establishment, the ICC has won global justice shares over competing global justice ideas. Despite the backlash, the ICC has generally been more successful in attracting public and media attention and funding than its global justice competitors. The present chapter has sought to illustrate that the ICC's success in attracting resources is in large part due to its choice to serve as an institution that enables and encases the market. Remarkably, in this endeavour it follows in the institutional footsteps of a different ICC, the International Chamber of Commerce. The modalities of the enabling of the market from a multilateral perspective were illustrated through an analysis of the entanglement between the ICC and contemporary trade regimes. Despite some critique of the ICC, the entanglement between trade and criminal law have largely remained without critical investigation. Backlash against the ICC, which has remained within the confines of marketised global justice, was incapable of accessing the underlying structural inequalities as an object of critique. And yet, the 2016 announcement and threats of withdrawal from the Rome Statute displayed a form of resistance in which those who had been commodified under the global justice sector reasserted themselves as political agents. Through a position of collective bargaining, these states were, for a short time at least, able to disrupt business in the global justice sector. Some of the states cast as victim and perpetrator states were no longer willing to submit to an image that denies them their agency. To be sure, these did not always have the higher moral ground from a perspective of recent events, but they forced a politicisation of the global justice debate forgrounding neo-colonialism. However, the neoliberal system proved again resilient, and marketing was engaged for its powerful function of renewal. The ICC used the special effects of branding to appear as though it were responding to backlashes and resistance. But ultimately, this use of 'special effects' was to enable and hide further propertisation.

The trends illustrated continue to consolidate. In 2011, the Council of the European Union published an 'Action Plan' as regards the ICC.[99] The objective is to achieve universal participation of the Rome Statute and 'to maximise political will' for the 'ratification, accession and implementation

---

[99] 'Action Plan to follow-up on the Decision on the International Criminal Court' and Annex (Council of the European Union) 12080/11 (12 July 2011). See also Ionel Zamfir, 'International Criminal Court: Achievements and challenges twenty years after the adoption of the Rome Statute', *Briefing of the European Parliament*, (European Parliament Research Service July 2018).

of the Rome Statute'. The Action Plan encourages ICC clauses to be included in other agreements between the EU and non-EU countries. The ambitious project is to increase support for the ICC in political and human rights dialogues, as well as at summits and other 'high-level meetings'. Moreover, the action plan encourages references to ICC universality in diplomatic engagements between the EU and other member states.

After the crisis year of 2016, the ICC experienced a further set-back just under a year later. Thousands of documents were leaked, shedding light on hitherto publicly unknown dealings of Luis Moreno Ocampo during and after his time in office. The French investigative website Mediapart gained access to a whole host of internal papers, contracts, bank documents, and emails, which were analysed by the research network European Investigative Collaborations (EIC) with participating news outlets, including the German news magazine Der Spiegel.[100] The documents obtained by Mediapart reveal, among other things, that during his term in office, Moreno Ocampo maintained personal offshore accounts in Panama, the British Virgin Islands, and Belize – all well-known tax havens. When challenged, he responded with the bumper-sticker logic reminiscent of the US gun lobby: 'Offshore companies are not illegal. You can make illegal activity with them. But they are not illegal.'[101] One would expect a person of 'high moral character' to understand the social justice issues of distribution that underpin taxation systems.[102] Profiteering from the system arguably betrays a deep knowledge of the integration of the trade and criminalisation systems. To make matters worse, Moreno Ocampo complained to EIC investigators that the (tax free) €200,00 per annum salary he was earning at the ICC was 'not enough'.[103]

---

[100] For an English version of the article in Der Spiegel, see Sven Becker, Marian Blasberg, Dietmar Pieper, 'The Ocampo Affair: A Former ICC Chief's Dubious Links' Spiegel Online, 5 October 2017, available at: www.spiegel.de/international/world/ocampo-affair-the-former-icc-chief-s-dubious-libyan-ties-a-1171195.html; 'Court Secrets', European Investigative Collaborations and Mediapart. Publications available at: https://eic.network/projects/court-secrets.

[101] Quoted in 'Secrets of the International Criminal Court Revealed', The Black Sea, 29 September 2019, available at: https://theblacksea.eu/stories/secrets-of-the-international-criminal-court-revealed/.

[102] Art. 42(3) Rome Statute: 'The Prosecutor and the Deputy Prosecutors shall be persons of high moral character.'

[103] Mediapart, 'Mon salaire n'était pas suffisant', available at: www.youtube.com/watch?v=-vGlaG_h0kI.

In tune with the understanding of the profits to be gained from the global justice sector, after his term at the ICC had ended, Moreno Ocampo made a US$ 3 million deal to consult the Libyan oil magnate Hassan Tatanaki.[104] Tatanaki is a former supporter of the Gaddafi administration, a regime that Moreno Ocampo's office investigated and against which he himself had issued arrest warrants. The leaked documents appear to reveal that the former chief prosecutor used the knowledge from the case to advise his client on how to evade investigation by the ICC.[105] Not only that, he also evidently used his contacts within the OTP for updates on potential investigations against his client.[106] Moreno Ocampo responded to the revelations by claiming that they should not have been leaked as they did not constitute 'public interest' and were part of a 'campaign of character assassination aiming to infect the entire Court and its officers'.[107] Moreno Ocampo states his 'sadness' for 'victims who trusted us, like a woman in Kenya who lost everything and had hopes in our interventions'.[108] Spectacularised victimhood serves the purpose of distraction once again. He closes his statement by mentioning a different campaign: 'a year-long campaign to strengthen global support for the court and justice to celebrate the upcoming 20th anniversary' [of the Rome Statute].[109] The 'campaign versus campaign' narrative is instructive.

Quite separately from the leaked documents, Moreno Ocampo has established expertise in what could be described as profiteering from global (in)justice in his private practice. He is founder and main share-holder of 'a unique strategic alliance combining the best experience on global justice with a top whistleblower firm'. Moreno Ocampo represents the global justice side of the firm. The firm is called 'Transparent Markets', using (ironically) whistleblower reward legislation on tax fraud to make money.[110] All of this happens confidentially, the website states, 'without exposing the company'.[111] The government rewards the whistleblower and the company is fined. Moreno Ocampo's CV describes the

---

[104] Becker, Blasberg, Pieper, 'The Ocampo Affair'.
[105] Ibid.
[106] Ibid.
[107] 'Ocampo Speaks out on Leaked Emails', Journalists for Justice, 4 December 2017, available at: https://jfjustice.net/ocampo-speaks-out-on-leaked-emails/.
[108] Ibid.
[109] Ibid.
[110] 'US Laws Reward Whistleblowers Globally' www.transparentmarkets.com/.
[111] www.transparentmarkets.com/why#why-companies.

firm as 'an international company who use market forces to increase transparency and efficiency in public procurement'.[112]

In its marketised form, global justice is an effective means for capital growth. The employment of global justice for capital growth is not only practised by NGOs (such as Invisible Children), international organisations (such as the ICC) and its employees and entrepreneurs (such as the former ICC chief prosecutor); it is also practised by nation states, as will be seen in the next and final case study.

---

[112] 'Curriculum Vitae Dr. Luis Moreno Ocampo', available at: www.europarl.europa.eu/meetdocs/2009_2014/documents/afet/dv/201/201003/20100323ocampo_en.pdf.

8

Branding the Global (In)Justice Place

Withdrawing from the International Criminal Court may hurt SA as investment destination.[1]

8.1 Introduction

The statement about withdrawing from the International Criminal Court (ICC), published on a South African business and finance news website, first and foremost urges the government to consider potential investment implications.[2] A direct link is drawn between South Africa as a state that is part of the international legal community subscribing to anti-impunity for international crimes on the one hand, and South Africa as attracting foreign investments on the other hand. From a business perspective, this may seem like an odd statement, considering that the ICC is not a profit-generating organisation. International law, or rather its sub-disciplines, also have trouble making sense of this connection: whilst international criminal law (ICL) is concerned with accountability of individuals, international investment law is concerned with regulating conduct between the investors of one country who invest in the enterprise of another country. There is no obvious connection.

The discipline and practice of place branding, meanwhile, concerns the material value to a nation state, region or city, of immaterial values and associations. Place branding begins from the premise that places stand in competition over scarce resources, and to attract resources (in the form

---

[1] Carien du Plessis, 'Withdrawing from International Criminal Court May Hurt SA as Investment Destination', Fin24, 30 August 2018, available at: www.fin24.com/Economy/World/withdrawing-from-international-criminal-court-may-hurt-sa-as-investment-destination-20180830.

[2] The article attributes this question to Richard Calland, Associate Professor of Constitutional Law at the University of Cape Town. Calland speaks as an analyst interacting with investors.

of investment, tourists, and trade), states, regions, and cities must create certain associations. From the perspective of place branding, the positioning of South Africa vis-à-vis the ICC is not necessarily a question of 'fighting impunity' or of 'accountability for serious crimes'; it is rather of prime importance for attracting investment, tourists, and trade because of its associations with global justice. South Africa has invested heavily in the establishment of Brand South Africa, a nation brand intended to create associations of successfully overcoming injustice. Having explored how non-governmental organisations (NGOs), international organisations, and individuals mobilise global justice for capital growth in the previous chapters, this chapter turns to cities, regions, and most prominently states.

Just as automobiles, fashion, and landscapes add to the make up of a nation's brand, so can its place within the international legal community as a global justice – or even global *in*justice – nation, city, or region. 'Even the more abstract aims of place branding have material benefits', stated a *Guardian* columnist about the 'booming business of nation branding' in 2017.[3] In regard to the conduct of states vis-à-vis other states, abstract aims of place branding often include the characteristic of being peaceful or being peacemakers.[4] From the perspective of nation branding, the statement from the South African business website therefore makes sense: Brand South Africa, which includes an association with global justice (the immaterial value), could be harmed if it is seen to be acting in contravention of its global justice credentials. Global justice is – once more – reconfigured from an immaterial value of social justice to a resource for capital growth, which is marketable and monetisable. This chapter shows how ICL's simplified images and rhetoric of 'good' versus 'evil' prove to be a particularly market-friendly interpretation for a nation's global (in)justice brand.

As with the previous case studies, this chapter is intended to shed light on a particular condition of marketised global justice. By focusing on the practice of place branding, I aim to draw attention to the mechanics of external and internal branding as a decidedly de-politicising feature of marketised global justice. The *external* brand is the story, or promise, about the dominant features of the product or service to the outside

---

[3] Samanth Subramanian, 'How to Sell a Country: The Booming Business of Nation Branding' (2017), *The Guardian*, 7 November 2017.

[4] Melissa Aronczyk, *Branding the Nation: The Global Business of National Identity* (Oxford University Press 2013) 76.

world; the *internal* brand is the configuration of identity from within. For corporations, internal branding is directed at employees. They are encouraged to 'live the brand', to allow it to shape who they are outside of their work place. For nation states, the audience and constituents of nation branding are citizens. Place branding highlights the commercially lucrative values of identity thereby co-producing market-oriented local, regional, or national identities. This implies that individuals are not only constructed as consumers of global justice – and therefore de-politicised – by NGOs; individuals are also constructed as predominantly market actors by the nation state itself.[5] Set apart from political processes of contestation, the formation of national identity through the market has a profoundly de-politicising effect. As with previous chapters, the analysis of marketised global justice is intended to bring a critique of neo-colonialism to the fore. Distinctions between place branding as global justice-dispensing and global justice-receiving places is marked by a racialised dividing line, which is further complicated by class divides.

Three 'mini' case studies will illustrate the dynamics of marketised global justice and place. The use of global justice as a resource for place branding from the perspective of a justice-*dispensing* place will be demonstrated through an analysis of The Hague's city branding. One of the key elements of 'Brand The Hague', is, according to the Bureau City Branding, its position as 'International City of Peace and Justice'. South Africa, the second example, is employing global justice credentials in order to demonstrate its successful transition from injustice to justice. South Africa – as a state eager to show its completed transition from apartheid to a 'key investment location'[6] – considers it crucial to maintain an image and narrative of multilateralism and commitment to global legal values. In these two studies, the global justice brand is one that demonstrates market-friendliness. Alongside the branding of justice and peace, there are also other ways of using global justice to generate revenue. In some cases, global injustice is employed as a brand attribute. The demand for visiting sites of injustice – skulls, graves, torture cells – is met with so-called 'dark tourism'. This brand attribute is not generally constructed for the purpose of attracting corporate investment, but instead for the purpose of generating tourism returns. Cambodia is employed as an example of a nation that uses global *in*justice as brand

---

[5] Naturally, brand activism in the for-profit sector seeks a similar outcome.
[6] Brand South Africa website, available at: www.brandsouthafrica.com/investments-immigration.

attribute, viewed from the Global North as a justice-*receiving* nation. However, this is complicated by other actors within Cambodia who are using global *justice* to compete against other justice receiving states for the attribute of 'transition'. Employing Cambodia as a 'mini' case study alongside The Hague and South Africa illustrates that in the absence of a top-down nation branding enterprise, the use of justice or injustice is split down class lines. The elites may invoke the potentially richer picking of 'justice', while the rest can only invoke global 'injustice', which has far smaller returns.

8.2   Place Branding As a Practice and a Field

Place branding is the application of the profit-based marketing technique of branding to cities, regions, and nations. For the purposes of a global justice analysis, *nation* branding tends to be the most relevant. How nations position themselves vis-à-vis global justice is often framed in relation to their membership of (or rejection of) international institutions and multilateral treaties. Despite this focus, the following also analyses the city of The Hague. The Hague as self-made 'City of International Peace and Justice' occupies an important space in place branding and global justice and therefore forms one of the key 'mini' case studies here. Cities are important actors in the international legal landscape. Some are, of course, nation states themselves (sovereign city states such as Singapore) and some *act* like nation states (an example might be London amid the United Kingdom's exiting from the EU insisting 'London is open for business'). The central space of cities as actors in the international sphere has prompted a wealth of research.[7] Despite this significant position of cities within the international legal landscape, The Hague remains an exception to the rule, albeit an important one. This is also reflected in the literature on place branding, which gives greater significance to nation branding.

Place branding emerged in the 1990s – the decade that, as we recall from Chapter 3, incorporated and helped define new demands for

---

[7] Saskia Sassen, *The Global City: New York, London, Tokyo* (Princeton University Press 2001); Janne Elisabeth Nijman, 'Renaissance of the City as Global Actor. The Role of Foreign Policy and International Law Practices in the Construction of Cities as Global Actors' in Andreas Fahrmeir, Gunther Hellmann and Miloš Vec (eds.), *The Transformation of Foreign Policy: Drawing and Managing Boundaries from Antiquity to the Present* (Oxford University Press 2016) 209–239.

individualism, technologies of visibility, global ordering, and the consolidation and concentration of structures of power. Nation branding came about through the convergence of fairly disparate bodies of work concerned with the nation, national identity, and place branding. Antecedents of nation branding can be found in state propaganda – for example, for the purposes of constructing a national identity for citizens in order to enlist soldiers in war – and in public diplomacy.

The influential voices of the nation branding field, beginning in the late 1990s and early 2000s, tend to be at the intersection between the academy and consultancies. Two British men, Simon Anholt and Wally Olins, are described as nation branding's 'gurus'.[8] They have an unmistakable market agenda for promoting the discipline. The hybrid academic-business literature is, unsurprisingly, replete with the urgent need for states to engage in branding. On the occasion of the publication of the second edition of their book on place branding, Eugene Jaffe and Isreal Nebenzahl state: 'We believed, and still believe, that proper management of a nation's image can give its business institutions a competitive advantage in world markets.'[9] In this orientation, the academic-consultants were harbingers of what would later be termed 'the neoliberal university'. By forging close links with industry, and arguing that the task of the public realm, including the state, is to guarantee optimal conditions for economic activity and individual prosperity, the field merged with the practice.[10] This approach indicates great optimism about the market: the market is the realm of freedom and equality and any symptoms of inequality are generally to be blamed on the failings of individuals. It begs the question of 'value' once more.

Melissa Aronczyk, who authored an important critique of nation branding, places its rise in the context of a transformation of valuation techniques in the 1990s.[11] As financial indicators – annual reports, employee bonuses, share options – came to be seen as less reliable as sources of market value, alternative methodologies were conceptualised to assess value. Value was increasingly 'based in the perception of its

---

[8] György Szondi, 'Public Diplomacy and Nation Branding: Conceptual Similarities and Differences' (2008) *Discussion Papers in Diplomacy*, Netherlands Institute of International Relations 'Clingendael' 1.

[9] Eugene D. Jaffe and Israel D. Nebenzahl, *National Image & Competitive Advantage: The Theory and Practice of Place Branding* (2nd ed. Copenhagen Business School Press 2006) 10

[10] What a successful 'impact case study' these individuals would be able to produce today!

[11] Aronczyk, 'Branding the Nation', 25.

various appellants: consumers, investors, shareholders, and the general public'.[12] As discussed in Chapter 4 on 'The Value of Global Justice', value creation was overtly opened up to subjective elements, prompting a significant shift in the notion of 'stakeholder', and to a whole new area of expertise. Apart from its better-known occurrence in the corporate sphere, the shift to subjective perception for measuring value also occurred in the sphere of the construction of national image. Rather than the shift to the subjective having a diversifying effect, this has had a streamlining effect. Aronczyk highlights how legacies of political difference, sources of cultural diversity, and divergent ethical commitments are only ever incorporated into the construction of national image insofar as these are productive for capital.[13]

Nation branding as a *practice* appeared when more and more states around the world began to commit resources to the development of their nation brand.[14] The market integration that came with globalisation brought with it, according to Dinnie, greater challenges for nations to distinguish themselves from their competitors.[15] Distinguishing one nation from another in the international sphere begins with the more 'cosmetic' features of branding, including logos and slogans, and then moves to the deeper questions of identity. The consultancy Wolff Olins were among the first to work on place branding. Co-founder Olins worked on branding projects for cities such as London, and countries such as Mauritius, Poland, Portugal, and Lithuania. Bloom Consulting is a further large consultancy specialising in nation and place branding. Its clients are tourism boards (Germany, the Algarve, Sweden, Finland), ministries (the Polish Ministry of Economy) and governments (Paraguay and Portugal). The Institute for Identity is another London-based place consultancy, which has specialised in branding Eastern European cities and regions.[16] It is worth emphasising, given our interest in epistemologies spreading through material circumstances, that the offices of these marketing agencies are all based in the Global North, particularly in London. Nation and city branding can be commissioned by private companies and by public bodies anywhere in the world, but the knowledge production of place branding emerges

---

[12] Ibid 25.
[13] Ibid 170.
[14] Keith Dinnie, *Nation Branding: Concepts, Issues, Practice* (2nd ed. Routledge 2016) 4.
[15] Ibid 5.
[16] http://instid.org/.

in the Global North. Perhaps it is unsurprising then that the market-isation of an identity that is *distinct yet 'normal'* is according to place branders the most likely to succeed in attracting investment, tourists, and trade.[17]

What does nation branding look like in practice? If passing through New York City's subway in 2006, one was likely to encounter huge billboards depicting German model Claudia Schiffer, seductively lying on her side wrapped in a German flag. 'Come on over to my place', 'See you in Germany', 'Follow your instincts. Invest in Germany', 'Want to get down to business?' were some of the slogans on the posters. This was part of a branding campaign supported by the German Federal Ministry of Economics and Technology portraying Germany as 'Land der Ideen' [land of ideas]. The campaign sought to build on the goodwill that had been created through Germany hosting the World Cup in 2005. Germany's ministry decided it was time to show the innovative and fun side of Germany. Let us say goodwill is required for understanding the slogans as either 'innovative' or 'fun'.

The desire to shed the image of technology, punctuality, and thor-oughness, to a more creative and dynamic image had in fact been articulated a few years earlier. According to early nation branding spe-cialists Jaffe and Nebenzahl, the German television network ZDF approached identity consultants Wolff Olins in 1999 to create a national brand for Germany that would show the country as 'exciting and sur-prising'.[18] In the early 2000s, Jaffe and Nebenzahl declared this project a failure. Constructing a positive nation brand of Germany was impossible due to the deep-set negative images stemming from World War II.[19] Fast-forward to 2018 and Germany topped the annual rankings list of Anholt-GfK Nation Brands Index. Out of fifty countries, Germany was first. The index measured perceptions of the country based on tourism, exports, people, culture, governance, immigration, and investment.[20] Whether it was Claudia Schiffer, the World Cup, a generational shift in *Vergangenheitsbewältigung*, or skewed indexing, nation branders are clearly seeing a significant shift in Brand Germany.

---

[17] Aronczyk, 'Branding the Nation' 76.
[18] Jaffe and Nebenzahl, 'National Image & Competitive Advantage' 151.
[19] Ibid 154.
[20] Germany was followed by Japan, the United Kingdom, France, and Canada. 'Ipsos Public Affairs. Anholt Ipsos Nation Brands Index (NBI)', Ipsos 2018. 'Germany Retains Top "Nation Brand" Ranking, U.S. Out of Top Five Again', Ipsos.com, 25 October 2018.

Regardless of the empirical evidence of reputation and indexing, what is interesting is the increased purchase and 'success narratives' of place branding. Indeed, the place branding literature is brimming with success stories, from New Zealand to South Korea (where a 'Brand Academy' to train around 500 branding specialists annually was established[21]) to Spain. And yet, despite the success narratives emerging from those engaged in marketing, there are – apart from The Hague – only a few case studies that empirically support a successful brand. We are here reminded of the 'success stories' of international criminal courts and tribunals. A further similarity is that the absence of empirically measurable successes is often put down to place branding being a 'young discipline'. Notwithstanding a lack of empirical evidence, more and more cities, regions, and nations are dedicating resources to branding.[22]

8.3   Nation Branding and International Law

Given the object of study – the nation and its behaviour – it is rather surprising that the relevance of nation branding has so far been ignored by international lawyers.[23] While international law acknowledges, through realist contributors in particular, the political relevance of acting in the international sphere, the political-economic implications of the role of nations within a neoliberal setting is still under-researched. In international law, the image of a state, the perception of it, or its reputation is generally considered as relevant to soft law and/or 'soft power' (only).[24] In international human rights law, the reputational value of 'naming and shaming' has been considered as significant, but generally

---

[21] Dinnie, 'Nation Branding' 15.

[22] Melissa Aronczyk estimates 'at least forty countries have sought the expert counsel of international consultants and strategists to help them brand their jurisdiction', Aronczyk, 'Branding the Nation' 3.

[23] Scholars from diverse disciplines have engaged with nation branding, including from cultural sociology (Patricia Cormack, '"True Stories" of Canada: Tim Hortons and the Branding of National Identity' (2008) 2(3) *Cultural Sociology* 369–384); public relations (Rasmus Kjærgaard Rasmussen & Henrik Merkelsen, 'The New PR of States: How Nation Branding Practices Affect the Security Function of Public Diplomacy' (2012) 38(5) *Public Relations Review*, 810–818); and geopolitics (see Special issue: 'Nation Branding and Competitive Identity in World Politics' (2017) 22(3) *Geopolitics* 481–664).

[24] On reputational capital and treaty compliance see Roda Mushkat, 'State Reputation and Compliance with International Law: Looking through a Chinese Lens' (2011) 10(4) *Chinese Journal of International Law* 703–737.

only in regard to treaty compliance.[25] International investment law meanwhile mostly concerns regulation *after* a decision on investment has already been made. Certainly, there are attempts at understanding the privatisation phenomenon through studies in transnational law, and private international law, but the role of the nation in what is deemed as a competitive market, remains underexplored. What these sub-disciplines of international law largely miss are the mechanisms employed by state organs or privately outsourced businesses to attract investment to a country, and how this shapes the state's identity as well as citizens' identity.

The field of nation branding is explicit about the material benefits of acting in the international sphere. Jaffe and Nebenzahl proudly present their work on the 'monetary value' of the nation's image and a how-to guide on monetising country image.[26] 'The need to estimate the economic value, or to *monetize* country image, is of utmost importance for managerial sourcing decisions as well as national image policies.'[27] They draw parallels between brand image, brand equity, and brand value on the one hand and country image, country equity, and country value on the other hand.[28] It is worth stressing that pointing out the neglect of international lawyers to consider nation branding does not mean that international lawyers should support the turn to marketisation; it means that they should be more aware of the ways in which the object of their study and the field that they are constituting demonstrates its affinities with, and constitutive modalities of, neoliberalism.

While for the purposes of demonstrating marketised global justice, the norms, institutions, and practices of ICL are pertinent, nation branding is relevant to other sub-fields of international law too. As already mentioned, this includes international investment law as the law that regulates and protects foreign investment. The country that hopes to attract foreign investment must 'sell' itself on the global market as having the resources, infrastructure, governance, and labour in place to make it an attractive investment location. Nation branding is also relevant to the laws of war, as a cursory look at the case of the 2011 intervention in Libya and its entanglement with nation branding demonstrates. In 2006,

---

[25] Emilie M. Hafner-Burton, 'Sticks and Stones: Naming and Shaming the Human Rights Enforcement Problem' (2008) 64(4) *International Organization* 689–716.

[26] Jaffe and Nebenzahl, 'National Image & Competitive Advantage' 10, 11 and 59f.

[27] Ibid 59. Emphasis in original.

[28] Ibid 60–63.

Libya's leader Colonel Muammar Gaddafi hired the consultancy Monitor Group to improve his and Libya's image, at US$ 250,000 a month.[29] This seemed to bear fruits. In 2009, Gaddafi was invited to address the UN General Assembly, an event he incidentally used to demand US$ 7.7trillion in compensation for the ravages of colonialism in Africa; by 2010, he was selected as chair of the African Union (AU). On his travels, he was described by the Western media as 'eccentric'.[30] The tone of the media changed amid the turmoil of the so-called Arab Spring with protesters taking to the streets of the Libyan city of Benghazi in early 2011. Gaddafi was instead labelled as a 'mad dog' and 'foaming at the mouth' by the press.[31] Interestingly, the disrepute of Libya's leader and that of Monitor Group coincided shortly before the military intervention. Just seven days before the military intervention in 2011, *The Guardian* ran a piece titled 'US Firm Monitor Group Admits Mistakes over $3m Gaddafi Deal'.[32] The discrediting of the positive image that Libya may have attained through exposing the consultancy behind it seems a convenient pretext to garnering further public support for military intervention. Notably, intervention not only marked the end of Gaddafi's rule, it also marked the end of the nation branding consultancy. Eight months after intervention, Monitor Group filed for bankruptcy.[33] The military intervention in Libya illustrates how the delegitimising of a nation's brand can contribute to delegitimising a nation's leadership and at the same time legitimise military intervention.

If international lawyers are still not convinced about the relevance of nation branding to their discipline, then how about when nation branders establish a new country? Stating that there are 760 million people who see themselves as citizens of the world first, and then citizens of their own country, nation brander Simon Anholt co-founded the country called a 'Good Country'. The paradox of founding a nation state

[29] Ed Pilkington, 'US Firm Monitor Group Admits Mistakes over $3m Gaddafi Deal', *The Guardian*, 4 March 2011.

[30] Ed Pilkington, 'UN General Assembly: 100 Minutes in the Life of Muammar Gaddafi', *The Guardian*, 23 September 2009.

[31] Chris Hughes, 'Libya: Brits Blitz Mad Dog Gaddafi', *The Mirror*, 22 March 2011; Jon Henley, 'Gaddafi's Wild Words Show He Hasn't Learned Anything', *The Guardian*, 22 February 2011.

[32] Pilkington, 'US Firm Monitor Group Admits Mistakes over $3m Gaddafi Deal'.

[33] Euny Hong, 'Consultant, Consult Thyself: Why Gaddafi's Former Spin Doctor, the Monitor Group, Filed for Bankruptcy' Quartz, 11 November 2012, available at: https:// qz.com/26285/once-prestigious-monitor-group-files-for-bankruptcy/.

for *cosmopolitans* seems to escape Anholt. In any event, he identifies 10 per cent of the world's population as sharing the same hopes and fears as himself: 'If it were a country, it would be the third largest country on the planet.' The Good Country exists only online because 'territory is a nuisance because then you need an army to defend it'.[34] On the website, one is invited to cross the virtual border. Using a website, social media, and TED talks as means to promote it, new citizens were invited to 'subscribe' in 2018. There is a fee to subscribe, described by Anholt as a 'tax'. On the technicalities of state formation, he seems confident:

> Who says you can't do that? Who says you can't start a new country if you feel like it? Nobody. Nobody has ever shown me a law or a regulation in the international community that says if you've got 760 million friends and you want to start a country together you're not allowed to. So we're doing it.[35]

Quite extraordinarily, nation branding 'guru' Anholt is seeking to profit from the *undoing* of the competitive environment that he had a key part in facilitating. The text beside Anholt's image on the Good Country's website asks 'What's gone wrong with the world?'.[36] According to the statement, instead of working together to address global problems of climate change, terrorism, pandemics, migration, and economic chaos, states are competing: 'nations spend all their energy and resources competing against each other. This has to change if we want the world to work.'[37] Twenty-first-century cosmopolitanism is not afraid of contradictions.

8.4   Place Branding and Global (In)Justice

When Carla Del Ponte (then-prosecutor of the International Criminal Tribunal for the former Yugoslavia) spoke at investment bank Goldman Sachs about the 'dividends' of international criminal justice, in particular stating that the 'profits' of ICL lie in its ability to stabilise war-torn countries so that private actors may then invest in the state, she was

---

[34] Simon Anholt 'We've Just Started a New Country. Want to Join?', TEDx at Progressvideo, November 2018. Video available at: http://progressvideo.tv/videos/we-ve-just-started-a-new-country-want-to-join-simon-anholt-tedxprimorskipark.

[35] Ibid.

[36] www.goodcountry.org/

[37] Ibid.

presenting global justice as value added.[38] ICL's profit (a dividend is the amount paid annually to shareholders from profits or reserves) is stability; this profit can be financially utilised in the form of foreign direct investment in the conflict or post-conflict state. This commodified vision of global justice presents justice as a resource to attract investment. Aronczyk explains that the branding of *peace* as a national structure is, alongside 'normalcy', a common trope.[39] One brand consultant interviewed by Aronczyk explained the branding strategy for Macedonia in preparation of its pitch to join the EU. Macedonia wanted to construct a nation brand around being the peacemaker for the region:

> And we will be the peacemaker of the Balkans. And we will think about setting up an international peace study center and we will train diplomats; we'll do all the other economic development things as well, but this is the thing we'll be known for. We'll basically have this as a core component of our identity and now for the brand of Macedonia, in the international world where people come to think of it, they'll think, oh, that's the place that makes peace. For the Balkans.[40]

The Economist refers to the early 1990s adage of 'peace dividend', promoted by UK Prime Minister Margaret Thatcher and US President George H.W. Bush following the end of the Cold War. According to *The Economist,* the peace dividend for states transitioning from conflict is 'economic growth and a boom in foreign investment'.[41] Both 'normal' governance conditions as well as peace are particularly attractive for investment.

Nation and place branding consultancies have long been aware of the branding value of global justice. For example, Madrid-based company Bloom Consulting has developed a place brand strategy based on the challenge of 'Branding the impossible'.[42] The Abraham Path Initiative, an NGO established through a World Bank fund, promotes its 'Abraham Path Experience' along the path that the religious father-figure Abraham

[38] Carla Del Ponte, 'The Dividends of International Criminal Justice', Goldman Sachs, London, 6 October 2005.
[39] Aronczyk, 'Branding the Nation' 76.
[40] Anonymous interview with a London-based nation branding consultancy, quoted in Aronczyk, 'Branding the Nation' 76.
[41] 'To Hell and Back. How Nations Torn Apart by Atrocity or Civil War Can Stitch Themselves Together Again', *The Economist,* 5 April 2014, available at: www.economist .com/international/2014/04/05/to-hell-and-back.
[42] www.bloom-consulting.com/en/city-branding-case-studies.

took over 4,000 years ago.[43] The path passes through areas of conflict, including Israel, the West Bank, Jordan, Syria and Iraq. According to Bloom Consulting, the initiative is 'to attract tourists to the new trail to walk in unison and peacefully protest to change people's perceptions about the Middle East'.[44] That which is branded is notably the justice movement, not the trail: 'Bloom Consulting recommended the Abraham Path not to brand the trail itself, but to brand the movement as a protest for peace.'[45]

In place branding practices, we encounter the exigencies of the perceived attention economy once more. From a perspective of places competing on the global market for trade, tourism, and investment, simple messages that encapsulate the distinctiveness of a nation, region, or city are considered to be the most competitive. Stereotypes of 'good' versus 'evil' constitute the type of simplified messages that have appeal in an information-overloaded society, replete with concerns about conflict, the rise of populism, and environmental disaster.

8.5   Justice Investment: The Hague and The Netherlands

Today, most international organisations that are open to the public will include a gift shop. 'Justice merchandise', including trinkets, postcards, and stationary embossed with the organisation's logo, can be acquired at the centres of justice tourism, including in The Hague.[46] The Hague has capitalised on justice in more ways than gift shops though. It has an entire city branding strategy of *International City of Peace and Justice*, which makes up an important part of 'Brand The Hague'. The Bureau City Branding is an administrative body dedicated to branding the city. According to the Bureau City Branding, the goal of the marketing policy of the two elements of 'City by the Sea' and 'International City of Peace and Justice' is

> to make the city more attractive and to make people, businesses and organisations choose The Hague as a travel destination or as a business or residential location. This helps to stimulate the local economy as well as job creation.[47]

---

[43] http://abrahampath.org/.
[44] www.bloom-consulting.com/en/city-branding-case-studies.
[45] Ibid.
[46] See, for example, Sophie Rigney, 'Postcard from the ICTY' in Jessie Hohmann and Daniel Joyce (eds.) *International Law's Objects* (Oxford University Press 2018) 366–376.
[47] Bureau City Branding at www.denhaag.nl/en/in-the-city/business/bureau-city-branding .htm.

A particular focus of Brand The Hague is on attracting more international organisations to the city. The Hague has a long history of hosting international organisations, and before that, international conferences. In 1893, T. M. C. Asser initiated, and hosted, the first Hague Conference on Private International Law. The Hague Conferences of 1899 and 1907 were early international conferences. The resultant Hague Conventions concerned the regulation of warfare. From 1901 to 1913 the Permanent Court of Arbitration was housed at Prinsegracht 71, The Hague. The Peace Palace, a building that has become iconic for the city, was completed in 1913 to house the Permanent Court of Arbitration. From 1922 to 1946, the Peace Palace was also home to the Permanent Court of International Justice (PCIJ). In 1945, the PCIJ was renamed as the International Court of Justice. In 1988, the Dutch government launched a campaign to attract international organisations. After becoming host city for the International Criminial Tribunal for the former Yugoslavia (ICTY) from 1993 onwards, the biggest prize was the ICC. The Dutch diplomats 'played a version of "total football" the likes which had not been seen since Johan Cruyff captained the Dutch soccer squad in the 1970s', observes Janet Anderson about the Dutch pitch for being the ICC's host city.[48] Playing hardball clearly paid off as The Hague was selected as the new centre for dispensing global justice with no competition.

From 2005 onwards, The Hague began a focused branding strategy around 'International City of Peace and Justice'. A video in the 'brand book', which is viewable on the Brand The Hague website, boasts of 26 inter-governmental organisations, 135 non-governmental organisations, and 20,000 experts. A student walking to The Hague campus of the University of Leiden marvels in the video, 'when I walk to university I feel I am in a very powerful city. The Hague *really is* the international city of peace and justice.'[49] The brand extends beyond The Hague, with the Netherlands also wanting to capitalise on the positive branding – wanting a piece of the peace and justice pie. A Ministry of Foreign Affairs document on 'International Organisations in the Netherlands: An

---

[48] Janet Anderson, 'The Hague, the ICC, and the Economic Benefits for Being a Centre for Justice', *The Guardian*, 25 September 2012.

[49] City of Peace and Justice: Footage City of Peace and Justice' at www.brandthehague.nl/footage-city-peace-and-justice.

Overview' shifts the view from city to nation.[50] The Minister of Foreign Affairs states that 'The Netherlands wants to encourage new organisations to establish a base in our country.'[51] In 2005, the Cabinet decided to develop a coherent, government-wide policy to improve the Netherlands' performance as a host country, which included the appointment of a special ambassador for international organisations. Although the realisation of the global justice branding potential for The Hague may have come fairly late in the day, by 2012 the Dutch were described as 'full of ways to cash in on their identity as justice capital of the world'.[52] A recent addition to the brand is that of 'security'. The Hague brand book emphasises international law, justice, and *security* as the features of The Hague. This mirrors the global move towards securitisation, which finds an ally in ICL's emphasis on retributive justice. The addition of security to respond to a global demand for securitisation, particularly in the Global North, is part of the renewal of branding: As soon as one approach appears to be stale or waver – the tempering of the euphoria for the ICC, for example – another approach is launched.[53]

The visual, as we have learned from the preceding chapters, plays a key role in the construction of marketised global justice. The visual representations of Brand The Hague as a global justice brand focuses largely on buildings and flags. The icons of global justice used in the place branding strategies, and reproduced in the branding of the respective international organisations themselves, are predominantly the buildings that house international organisations. The Peace Palace in particular is the recurring image of global justice as part of Brand The Hague. Buildings represent permanence and locality, a space for the sometimes nebulous idea of global justice to live and for it to be grounded. This visual representation of buildings stands in contrast to the visual representation of victims discussed in earlier chapters as the 'faces' of global justice. From a *place branding* perspective, victims are – in The Hague at least – visually rendered invisible. Instead, emphasis is placed on the declared neutrality of The Hague, which is visually presented in buildings. For example, on the occasion of the Dutch government announcing

---

[50] 'International Organisations in the Netherlands: An Overview', Ministry of Foreign Affairs, The Netherlands, May 2014.

[51] Frans Timmermans, Ibid, 4.

[52] Anderson, 'The Hague, the ICC, and the Economic Benefits of Being a Centre for Justice'.

[53] As described in Tim Wu, *Attention Merchants: The Epic Scramble to Get Inside Our Heads* (Vintage Books 2016) 53.

The Hague as host city for the new Kosovo court (the Kosovo Relocated Specialist Judicial Institution), a statement was made on the Dutch government website that the conflict 'is a sensitive issue in Kosovo. Possible suspects may be seen by sections of Kosovan society as freedom fighters, and witnesses may feel threatened in Kosovo'.[54] Hence, The Hague was selected. The Hague is framed as a place in which the uncertainties of distinguishing between war criminal or freedom fighter based on political partisanship does not exist. It is presented as a neutral place. Former mayor Jozias van Aartsen parroted in relation to the new tribunal: 'As long as there is no justice, there can be no truly lasting peace... That's why it's of the utmost importance that this court can do its work here in our city.'[55] The mayor who is speaking on behalf of the city is, importantly, also speaking on behalf of its citizens. His representation matters as regards identity-formation.

In order to get a sense of identity formation through marketisation, 'living the brand', we must briefly venture outside of The Hague. We take a detour to the town Celebration in Florida, United States. The town Celebration, situated just outside of Disney World, is in fact the *company* of Celebration, founded by the Walt Disney Company. Here, residents can live in one of six property types, enjoy the restaurants and shops and green spaces, leisure facilities and schools – all designed by the architects and designers of Walt Disney. It is, in the words of Naomi Klein, 'the world's first branded town'.[56] The idea of community is central to the town. The website states: 'There's a reason Celebration is not a town, but a community in every sense of the word.'[57] In a promotional video, one resident says: 'It's like a completely different world ... It's like the old days and everything, where people would just talk to you and smile.'[58] Place branders would celebrate. According to Anholt, a feature of a successful nation brand is when 'the public, not just civil servants and figureheads – gets behind the strategy and lives it out in their everyday

---

[54] 'Kosovo Court to Be Established in The Hague', Government of the Netherlands, News item, 15 January 2016, available at: www.government.nl/latest/news/2016/01/15/kosovo-court-to-be-established-in-the-hague.

[55] Ibid.

[56] *No Logo: Brands, Globalization and Resistance*. Directed by Sut Jhally, Media Education Foundation, 2003. Transcript available at: www.mediaed.org/transcripts/No-Logo-Transcript.pdf 8.

[57] https://celebration.fl.us/celebration-about/.

[58] Celebration, Florida www.youtube.com/watch?v=KvZrycQsH1Y.

dealings with the outside world'.[59] Klein notes that it is interesting 'that there are no brands there'. No franchises or billboards can be found; this is not only because of the 'Disney look', enforced through strict design regulations, but also because these might be unwanted competing messages, spoiling 'this perfect synergized, cross-promoted marketing moment'. Klein concludes: 'That's why what we're really talking about is monopoly.'[60]

Associated with de-politicisation is also a process of de-historicisation. by basing identity creation on positive attributes, The Hague as the 'city of peace and justice' continues and perpetuates the silence on Dutch imperial history. The brand book for The Hague refers to the height of the empire, as is typical in The Netherlands, as 'the Golden Age'.[61] As is both well-known and also well-forgotten, at least in light of associations of the Dutch as 'liberal', the Dutch were an imperial power with colonies across the world, and particularly in East Asia.[62] Acquired by force and legitimised through international law, the overseas territories and trading posts, administered by the Dutch East India company, were anything but symbols of peace and justice. The enduring positive associations are in no small part due to international lawyers. Celebrated widely as the Father of International Law, Hugo Grotius's treatise *mare liberum*, published in 1609, facilitated and legitimised Dutch seafaring.[63] By arguing that the sea is 'free', Grotius found a legal means to disrupt Portuguese East Indian trade monopolies. Prior to this, Grotius had equated the ethical standards of individuals with that of states, arguing that self-preservation was a law of nature. In turn, as explained by Richard Tuck, this legitim-ised private trading companies to stand in for states to wage war.[64] The Dutch were able to assume a competitive position vis-à-vis the Spanish, Portuguese, and growing power of the English. Eventually, the Dutch dominated over the Portuguese. Far from being associated with the legal tools to secure imperialism, Grotius is mostly remembered and revered as the Dutch patriarch of the discipline of international law, incidentally the very same discipline that has most recently once more brought capital

---

[59] Simon Anholt, *Brand New Justice: The Upside of Global Branding* (Oxford Butterworth-Heinemann 2003) 123

[60] Klein, 'No Logo', transcript, 6.

[61] 'The Shortest History of The Hague', www.brandthehague.nl/shortest-history-hague.

[62] Richard Tuck, *The Rights of War and Peace: Political Thought and the International Order from Grotius to Kant* (Clarendon Press 1999).

[63] Hugo Grotius, *The Free Sea* [1609], (David Armitage (ed.), Richard Hakluyt (trans.) (Liberty Fund 2004).

[64] Tuck, 'The Rights of War and Peace'.

into the country.[65] Not only does the story of the 'Golden Age' erase historical awareness of the violence of empire; it also erases histories of resistance.[66] This top-down rewriting of history is of course distinctly in tune with the progressive narratives of international criminal justice.

Given what we already know about marketing and global justice, it is perhaps unsurprising that, in 2017, the Netherlands came out on top of the list of 'good countries' collated by Simon Anholt and widely publicised across the media.[67] For The Good Country Index, as opposed to the Nation Brands Index mentioned above, Anholt collated data from the UN, the World Bank and the World Health Organisation. According to the website, Anholt looked at categories that indicated the good that countries are doing for the global community, using the index to determine which country 'contributes to the greater good of humanity'.[68]

8.6   Transition Tourism and Investment: South Africa

In 2002, the South African government launched a major initiative: Brand South Africa. The logo is made up of the colours of the South African flag and its current slogan is 'Inspiring new ways'. According to Thebe Kalafen, founder and chairman of 'Brand Africa', the African nation branding agencies (Kenya, Botswana, Ghana, and Nigeria also have nation branding agencies) have been charged with the responsibility to 'proactively establish a compelling, coordinated and harmonised nation brand that catalyses investment, tourism, trade and export, and national identity'.[69] Justice plays a prominent cultural role in South Africa, given its history of overcoming apartheid, and appears as an *asset* in the nation branding field. 'Transitional countries [...] may turn to nation branding to distance their countries from the old economic and political system which existed before transition', observes Györgi Szondi,

---

[65] The sanitised image around Grotius as the 'father of international law' or a 'founder of international law' is reproduced in many international law syllabi and textbooks across the world.

[66] A recent book outlines the 'formidable competitors who frequently outmaneuvered or outfought' the Dutch and English East India companies. Tristan Mostert and Adam Clulow (eds.) *The Dutch and English East India Companies: Diplomacy, Trade and Violence in Early Modern Asia* (Amsterdam University Press 2018).

[67] www.goodcountryindex.org/results.

[68] www.goodcountryindex.org/.

[69] Thebe Kalafeng, 'Branding New Africa – An Emerging Global Challenger' quoted in Dinnie, 'Nation Branding' 20.

a leading voice in the field of nation branding.[70] The iconic figure of Nelson Mandela is described by nation brander Dinnie as an 'innate asset', as 'powerful and authentic means of differentiation for the nation brand'.[71] Mandela appears a second time in the same book on nation branding, this time as a 'sonic manifestation of national identity'.[72] Voices, too, can be commodified. The Brand South Africa's website announces proudly in 2019: 'Here's to 25 Years of Democracy.'[73] Unsurprisingly, the South African image conveyed is of newness, a clear break with the apartheid era. At the same time, the market professionals are eager to show that transition is not *too* new. South Africa aims to demonstrate its successful transition to a global justice state, rather than the process of transitioning. So although South Africa is commonly associated with transitional justice mechanisms of truth and reconciliation, these associations are not pronounced on its brand page. In 2012, Brand South Africa decided to change its slogan from 'Alive with Possibility' to 'Inspiring New Ways' to mark that the country was no longer one of possibility but had already delivered on some of its promises. The successful hosting of football's FIFA World Cup was considered a milestone in this delivery. The CEO of Brand South Africa stated: 'South Africa has moved beyond possibility to delivery. Our delivery has necessitated a change in the brand positioning, to keep up with and lead the way that we are perceived by the world.'[74] This government-approved slogan, and the government's embrace of nation branding more generally, appears to support what commentators described as the post-apartheid governments' neoliberal turn in the 1990s.[75]

But the external image was not enough; the government needed South Africans to buy into the branding in order for it to work. A campaign to sell the brand (their own brand) to South Africans was launched.[76] Former

---

[70] Györgi Szondi 'The Role and Challenges of Country Branding in Transition Countries: The Central European and Eastern European Experience' 3(1) *Place Branding and Diplomacy* 8–20.

[71] Dinnie, 'Nation Branding' 68.

[72] Dinnie, 'Nation Branding' 115.

[73] www.brandsouthafrica.com/.

[74] 'Inspiring New Ways: SA's New Slogan', Brand South Africa, 8 March 2012, available at: www.brandsouthafrica.com/south-africa-fast-facts/news-facts/08-mar-12-4603

[75] See for example, Zine Magubane, 'The Revolution Betrayed? Globalization, Neoliberalism and the Post-Apartheid State', 103 (4) *The South Atlantic Quarterly* 657–671.

[76] Yasuko Murai describes three campaigns in the form of TV ads, launched 'as a kick-start to the building of partriotism and good feeling among the population'. Yasuko Murai, '"Alive with Possibility": Brand South Africa and the Discursive Construction of South

CEO of the International Marketing Council, a government-funded agency, which helped establish Brand South Africa in its early days, declared the intention 'to sell South Africa to South Africans'.[77] The Brand South Africa website has a specific section, endorsed and supported by the South African government, dedicated to this participatory form of nation branding, under the title 'Play Your Part'. Its objective is to 'lift the spirit of our nation'.[78] This corporatisation of national identity requires of citizens that they adhere to a certain narrative, in the case of South Africa that they buy into the success of the country's political transformation. Branding moves again from the 'cosmetic' and seemingly benign associations with certain colour pallet combinations, fonts, and icons to a (distinctly political) de-politicising force. Constructing a market-friendly identity for the relatively small city of The Hague – where many of its citizens are already in some way or another bound up with the success or failure of the international organisation they work for – is one thing. For South Africa, a deeply divided country along ethnic, racial, and class lines, of over 58 million people, it is another. South Africa's brand of global justice differs from that of The Hague in that it does not claim to dispense justice, but it claims to have overcome injustice successfully. Whilst The Hague brand erases certain aspects of Dutch history that do not fit with its contemporary image, the South African brand erases contestation and resistance, as well as internal differentiation. Branding's work, argues Aronczyk, 'is to erase the prominence of those attributes which might compromise the legitimacy of the nation-state in a market democracy'.[79] Despite the unofficial slogan of post-apartheid South Africa as a 'rainbow nation' – a phrase coined by Archbishop Desmond Tutu – it remains a deeply unequal nation with wealth and opportunities continuing to be distributed along racial(ised) lines. A process of historical revisionism by market-oriented entities can also be described as a form of state-supported corporate hegemony. The description of nation branding in diplomatic circles as 'soft power' therefore diminishes the hard power that privileges one form of history over another.[80] It is worth re-emphasising the role of the state in

---

African National Identity', Dissertation, LSE Department of Media and Communications, 2011, Media@LSE Electronic MSc Dissertation Series 17.

[77] Yvonne Johnston, 'Country Case Insight: South Africa', in Dinnie, 'Nation Branding' 3.

[78] www.brandsouthafrica.com/play-your-part.

[79] Aronczyk, 'Branding the Nation', 78.

[80] Ibid, 81.

distributing resources for nation branding. The homogenising of identity is attached to the allocation of funds as well as the shaping of policies. We see again that the nation has not disappeared in a post-Westphalian haze of globalisation; rather the state is mobilised for the purposes of protecting capital flows and protecting the market from political contestation.

8.7   Dark Tourism and the Patron–Client Relationship of Global Justice: Cambodia

Although Cambodia is, like South Africa, deemed to be a state transitioning from conflict to justice, it has not fully embraced the transitional justice route of committing to the rule of law in a Western liberal model. Instead of the top-down communication of a national brand such as in The Hague or South Africa, we find a fragmented approach to global justice and injustice – albeit also one that uses global (in) justice as a source for capital growth. On the one hand, there is a prominent 'dark tourism' industry, which appears less interested in the idea of transitioning, instead capitalising on the aesthetics of death and suffering of the Khmer Rouge era, which was at its peak roughly from 1975 to 1979. On the other hand, influential institutions, such as the Extraordinary Chambers in the Courts of Cambodia (ECCC) and the Documentation-Centre of Cambodia (DC-Cam), follow the Western liberal model of retributive justice and a progress narrative. Arguably, this division of how to use global justice is split down class lines, with the elites commanding the Western model and the ordinary people capitalising on associations of 'dark tourism'. These lines are not clear-cut, but they demonstrate that the neoliberal legal-institutional model is different in the so-called least developed countries. Although it has an effect on everyone in the country who is dealing in the currency of global justice, the power to claim to be a global justice actor is unequal. This includes the inequality of global justice aesthetics, and the question of who can 'own' the aesthetics of being on the right side of moral history.

As with all conflicts, the Cambodian Khmer Rouge era and the civil war that followed must be understood against the background of a wider geopolitical history. It is impossible here to do justice to this vast history, so whilst I touch on a fairly narrow set of issues concerning nation branding and global justice, the exclusions of my narrative are not intended to reaffirm the simplistic historical narratives often circulated about Cambodia, or circulated *within* Cambodia.[81] Cambodia is one of the prime spots of 'dark tourism'. Whether out of 'morbid curiosity' or for 'feeding trauma fetishes', visiting sites of suffering is a growth area in the tourism industry.[82] Also described as 'thanatourism', Cambodia has certainly carved out a market for travellers based on its history of atrocity.[83] Places of 'dark tourism' have all developed means of commercial activity. However, '[t]here is possibly no place that has benefited from dark tourism as much as Cambodia', writes one travel writer.[84] Destination branding is an aspect of nation branding focusing mostly on tourism, with marketers insisting on a need for an integrated approach.[85] With dark tourism, Cambodians are embracing the marketisation of injustices, particularly for a Western audience. Cambodian entrepreneurs capitalise on the coloniality at work in the global justice sector. Concerns about dark tourism highlight rather than diminish assumptions of inequality. On the 'overwhelming sense to give back', one travel writer for Forbes recommends: 'By taking a locally guided tour, you are already providing a form of aid.'[86] The assumption is of course that the visitors to dark tourism sites are those who dispense aid, while the tourist destination is the place that receives aid.

Two of the most famous tourist destinations in Cambodia are the Tuol Sleng Genocide Museum, set in the building of the former S-21 prison in the centre of Phnom Penh, and the infamous Killing Fields (Choeung Ek), the site of mass executions of dissidents during the Khmer Rouge regime. On a dark tourism website, Tuol Sleng and Cheung Ek rank at

---

[81] David Chandler has set out how successive Cambodian governments first demonised the Khmer Rouge, and then 'enforced a policy of collective amnesia'. David Chandler, *A History of Cambodia* (2nd ed. Silkworm Books 1993).

[82] Described as 'morbid curiosity' by Lavanya Sunkara, 'From Auschwitz To Chernobyl: Tips on Respectfully Visiting Dark Tourism Sites', Forbes, 1 August 2019; and as 'feeding trauma fetishes' by Tara Tadlock, 'Dark Tourism in Cambodia: Exploitation and Cultural Insensitivity', World Foot Prints, 17 February 2019, available at: https://worldfootprints .com/dark-tourism-in-cambodia-exploitation-and-cultural-insensitivity/.

[83] A. V. Seaton, 'Guided by the Dark: From Thanatopsis to Thanatourism' (2007) *International Journal of Heritage Studies* 234–244.

[84] Tadlock 'Dark Tourism in Cambodia: Exploitation and Cultural Insensitivity'.

[85] Antonios A. Giannopoulos, Lamprini P. Piha, and George J. Avlonitis, '"Desti-Nation Branding": What for? From the Notion of Tourism and Nation Branding to an Integrated Approach' (April 2011) Cultural Diplomacy, paper presented at the 2011 Berlin International Economics Congress, Berlin, Germany (March 15).

[86] Sunkara, 'From Auschwitz To Chernobyl'.

number five in the top ten of dark tourism sites, ordered by 'degree of darkness/significance'.[87] Perhaps unsurprisingly, the Nazi Auschwitz-Birkenau concentration camp in today's Poland ranks as number one. Rather than emphasising Cambodia's transition to peace and stability, the website of Tourism of Cambodia emphasises the parallels with the genocide of the Nazis: 'Like the Nazis, the Khmer Rouge was meticulous in keeping records of their barbarism', the website states about the S21 prison. The text is accompanied by an image of white tourists with backpacks standing outside the prison building.[88] Tourism Cambodia does not shy away from the spectacle of death or from more complicated victim narratives: 'As the Khmer "revolution" reached ever-greater heights of insanity, it began devouring its own children.' The children referenced are torturers and executioners who were themselves made victims of the regime. The website goes on in more gory detail:

> When Phnom Penh was liberated by the Vietnamese army in early 1979, they found only seven prisoners alive at S-21. Fourteen others had been tortured to death as Vietnamese forces were closing in on the city. Photographs of their decomposing corpses were found. Their graves are nearby in the courtyard.[89]

As if to challenge the visitors, the account of the tourist destination ends: 'Tuol Sleng is not for the squeamish.'[90] We are reminded again of the marketability of the visceral. The horrors of torture and violent death command the attention, but also narrow the understanding of global justice and injustice. Against the background of the disproportionate attention to spectacular forms of violence, scholars have aimed to draw attention to other forms of harm experienced during the Khmer Rouge era – less spectacular ones such as poverty and starvation. Randle DeFalco has described the inattention to famine as an international crime as a 'prosecutorial gap'.[91] DeFalco points out that (spectacularly), Cambodia's severe famine in the years between 1975 and 1979 was the

---

[87] 'Top 10 Dark Tourism Sites by Degree of Darkness/Significance', www.dark-tourism .com/index.php/18-main-menus/mainmenussubpages/618-list-of-top-10-dark-touristz-sites-by-degree-of-darkness.

[88] www.tourismcambodia.com/attractions/phnompenh/toul-sleng-museum.htm.

[89] Ibid.

[90] Ibid.

[91] Randle DeFalco, 'Accounting for Famine at the Extraordinary Chambers in the Courts of Cambodia: The Crimes against Humanity of Extermination, Inhumane Acts and Persecution' (2011) 5(1) *International Journal of Transitional Justice* 142–158, at 142.

'worst in recent history'.[92] After conducting fieldwork in Cambodia, Cheryl Lawther, Rachel Killean, and Lauren Dempster describe the dark tourism sites as having created 'a hierarchy of harm' in which the prioritisation of violent death came at the expense of other harms.[93] Skulls and bones make up a large part of the aesthetics of global injustice. In photographs, the white of the bones is set against the brown of the dirt or the green of the fields. At the sites themselves, glass cabinets of skulls have been set up, ordered by sex and age. In case the visitor is not sure what they are seeing, the language does away with subtlety: 'Killing tree against which executioners beat children', one sign reads in Khmer and English. The website of Tourism of Cambodia under the category of 'Things to See and Do – Phonm Penh, Cambodia' displays first the image of skulls, then the text.[94] In the S21 prison, hundreds of black-and-white photographs of those executed are hung up in large frames. The most iconic picture is that of the 'skull map', a map of Cambodia made up of skulls and bones.[95] This former installation at the Tuol Sleng museum was viewed by thousands of tourists despite great concern expressed by Cambodia's Buddhist population.[96]

While South Africa as a nation fully embraced the transitional justice idea of overcoming past atrocities in favour of a brighter future of foreign investment, Cambodia has only partly sought to please potential investors in global justice. Rather than being a national programme, global justice has tended to be a programme supported by particular individuals and patrons. For example, the documentation centre that has documented much of the mass atrocities of the Khmer Rouge era, was set up through a United States Congress act. The Cambodian Genocide Justice Act provided for the funding of a new documentation centre, which was to become the Documentation Centre of Cambodia. In 1994, US$ 400,000 were authorised from the Department of State budget for

---

[92] Ibid. citing Cormac Ó Gráda, *Famine: A Short History* (Princeton, NJ: Princeton University Press, 2009).

[93] Cheryl Lawther, Rachel Killean, and Lauren Dempster, 'Transitional Justice at Sites of "Dark Tourism": The Case of Genocide Memorials in Cambodia', Justice in Conflict blog, 28 January 2019, available at: https://justiceinconflict.org/2019/01/28/transitional-justice-at-sites-of-dark-tourism-the-case-of-genocide-memorials-in-cambodia/.

[94] www.tourismcambodia.com/travelguides/provinces/phnom-penh/what-to-see/5_cheung-ek-killing-field.htm.

[95] James Palmer, '"Skull Map" of Killing Fields is Laid to Rest', *The Independent*, 11 March 2002.

[96] According to Buddhist belief, cremation of the remains is preferred as this releases the soul from the physical form, readying it for reincarnation.

each of the fiscal years 1994 and 1995 for what was to become DC-Cam.[97] Congress urged the president to encourage the establishment of a national or international criminal tribunal in order to prosecute those accused of genocide. Notably, it was at the same meeting of Congress that the Senate put forward its findings on the establishment of a permanent international criminal court, stating that 'the time is propitious for the United States to lend its support to this effort'.[98] The US government was in the midst of a transitional justice hype. This also happened to be the day on which President Bill Clinton spoke about America's role in the 'miracle of South Africa's rebirth' in a Presidential Radio Address. South Africa had just held its first post-apartheid general elections and Clinton was making a case for similar 'vigorous American engagement and leadership ... around the globe'.[99] The State Department grant for documenting international crimes in Cambodia was managed by Yale University's Cambodian Genocide Programme, which formally established DC-Cam 'as its Phnom Penh field office'. The Act of Congress put in place various reporting and accountability mechanisms. Two more State Department funds followed in 1997 and 1998.[100] The Executive Director of DC-Cam, Youk Chhang, himself a survivor of the Khmer Rouge regime, is the organisation's figure-head. The US Ambassador-at-large for War Crimes David Scheffer played a vital role in facilitating the negotiations for the establishment of the hybrid tribunal of the ECCC.[101] Although every justice project has certain key figures, the DC-Cam and ECCC projects particularly stand out as personal projects. As regards Cambodia, this fits within the analysis of Cambodian neoliberalism reinforcing patron-client relations. What makes Cambodian neoliberalism 'distinctly Cambodian', according to Simon Springer, is the co-option of neoliberal reforms.[102] The situation 'has served to consolidate the wealth and privilege of the elite while simultaneously placing even more pressure on the limited

[97] 'Foreign Relations Authorization Act, Fiscal Years 1994 and 1995', United States Congress, PL 103–236, (30 April 1994), 108 Stat 486; 22 USC 2656, Sec. 571–574.

[98] Ibid Sec. 517.

[99] US Presidential Radio Address, 30 April 1994.

[100] 'DC-Cam, 1995–2005', Genocide Studies Program, Yale University, available at: https://gsp.yale.edu/dc-cam-1995-2005.

[101] David Scheffer, All the Missing Souls: A Personal History of the War Crimes Tribunals (Princeton University Press 2013).

[102] Simon Springer, Cambodia's Neoliberal Order: Violence, Authoritarianism, and the Contestation of Public Space (Routledge 2010) 4.

economic means of the poor'. This latter observation is certainly not distinctly Cambodian, but the patron-client relations seem like a good fit within the division of how global justice is managed on the one hand and how global injustice is managed on the other. In regard to the former, this is a project of the country's elite working side by side with international organisations.[103] The ECCC has itself preferred a reductive history of mass crimes, precluding the possibility of taking the period prior to the Khmer Rouge into account. As stated in the first trial against Duch, the historical background concerns events 'between October 1975 and 6 January 1979 at S-21, a security centre in Phnom Penh, Cambodia'.[104] Given the source of the funding, this may not be so surprising. The United States, after all, dropped a higher tonnage of bombs onto Cambodia than the total of all allied bombs used in World War II.[105] However, that is not to say that the Cambodian elites have consistently cooperated with Western elites. Kirsten Ainley, for example, has described the corruption in the hiring process at the ECCC, stating that the international staff presume that their Cambodian counterparts were appointed on the basis of their connections to government.[106] As the Court became a thorn in the eye of Prime Minister Hun Sen, these staff members seemingly played their part in obstructing proceedings by objecting to further investigations, even recommending ongoing cases to be closed.[107] Divisions between the international and the national became evident. But, instead of deferring to international elites for views on global justice, Prime Minister Hun Sen engaged in a competition over the meaning of justice. Invoking the peace versus justice debate, Hun Sen claimed

---

[103] The biggest donor contributions came from Japan (30 per cent), the US (11 per cent) and Australia (11 per cent), whereby the United States only contributes to the international component of the budget, not the national one. 'ECCC Financial Outlook as at 30 September 2017', available at: www.eccc.gov.kh/sites/default/files/ECCC%20Financial%20Data%20as%20at%2030%20September%202017.pdf.

[104] *Prosecutor v Kaing Guek Eav alias Duch* (Appeal Judgment) 001/18-07-2007-ECCC/SC (3 February 2012) 5.

[105] Christopher Hitchens, *The Trial of Henry Kissinger* (Verso 2001).

[106] Kirsten Ainley, 'Transitional Justice in Cambodia: The Coincidence of Power and Principle' in Renee Jeffrey (ed.), *Transitional Justice in the Asia-Pacific* (Cambridge University Press 2014) 125–156.

[107] Ibid.

that additional prosecutions would threaten peace in Cambodia.[108] Memories are short when it comes to global justice, for it was only twenty years earlier that Hun Sen had himself started calls to prosecute Khmer Rouge leaders as part of a peace process; the United States, in turn, resisted any form of inquiry.[109] Ainley summarises this period as one in which '[p]eace was unequivocally prioritised above justice by international actors'.[110] Both international actors and Hun Sen did a 180-degree turn on their interpretation of global justice. This use of global justice as currency rather than principle is undoubtedly allowing the elites of nation states of the Global South to view themselves as competitors for the global justice stakes. Those with no monetary bargaining power, meanwhile, are left with the far poorer returns of dark tourism. Jean and John Comaroff rather fittingly state that 'culture' is one of the few things that those who have nothing or very little can sell: 'Recourse to the cargo of cultural tourism, which has a long history, has become a universal panacea, an autonomic reflex almost, for those with no work and little to sell.'[111]

8.8 Backlashes and Resistance

Given that the three 'mini' case studies of national branding and global justice differ greatly, it is difficult to analyse backlashes and resistance as a global phenomenon. However, a connection pertinent here is the link between nation branding and the global rise of populism. In its top-down corporate approach to commodifying national identity as a product that can be utilised for profit on a global market, nation branding is fundamentally de-politicising.[112] But this de-politicisation, prompted by corporatisation, financialisation, and marketisation, is also causing a re-politicisation. In light of the growing appetite of governments to hire experts to help with national

---

[108] Ian MacKinnon, 'Prosecutor Wants to Indict Five More Khmer Rouge', *Financial Times*, 7 September 2009.
[109] Helen Jarvis and Tom Fawthrop, *Getting Away with Genocide? Elusive Justice and the Khmer Rouge Tribunal* (UNSW Press 2005) 98.
[110] Ainley, 'Transitional Justice in Cambodia' 145.
[111] Jean and John Comaroff, *Ethnicity, Inc.* (Chicago University Press 2009) 9. They reference as a comparison George Pierre Castile, 'The Commodification of Indian Identity' (1996) 98(4) *American Anthropologist* 743–749.
[112] Sue Curry Jansen, 'Designer Nations: Neo-liberal Nation Branding – Brand Estonia' (2008) 14(1) *Journal for the Study of Race, Nation and Culture* 121–142, 121.

identity branding, people are articulating their own visions in protest. Whether this is nationalist right-wing populism, which insists on sovereignty and exclusions, or left-wing populism, which takes on austerity politics, populism, one might say, is the fight for national identity. Nation branding and populism are not always diametrically opposed of course. Many contemporary forms of populism exist *within* neoliberalism, having willingly adopted its marketised ideas of popular politics.[113]

Wendy Brown has explained how analogies of the nation as a home, particularly by right-wing populists, is indicative of the privatisation of the nation, and related to a limited politicisation within neoliberalism.[114] 'We need to remember that part of the entire moral project of neoliberalism is to privatize everything including the nation', stated Wendy Brown in an interview in early 2019.[115] If the nation is reimagined as a house that is owned by its inhabitants, then there is a greater justification, morally and legally, to keep those who were not its initial occupants out. The privatised nation then may act like a *corporation* when attracting resources and like a *home* when keeping unwanted people out. Nation branding is the bridge between the two ideas of the nation as corporation and nation as home: the marketisation of public goods such as global justice is viewed as a means to attract resources for the benefit of the occupants of the home, not for the benefit of wider social values.

8.9   Conclusion

The international sphere in the twenty-first century is mostly considered as a marketplace. In this marketplace, nation states are regarded as being in competition over resources. As in the commercial sphere, nation states, and also cities and regions, are adopting logos and slogans in order to set themselves apart. As certain natural resources, goods, landscapes, and character traits are reimagined as brand attributes, global justice and global injustice have emerged as resources that may attract investments, tourists, and trade. Such branding, we have learned, is not only for the purpose of creating an external brand, but also for the

---

[113] Quinn Slobodian, 'Neoliberalism's Populist Bastards: A New Political Divide between National Economies', Public Seminar, 15 February 2018, available at: https://publicseminar.org/2018/02/neoliberalisms-populist-bastards/.

[114] Atossa Abraxia Abrahamian, 'Beyond the Wall: A Q&A With Wendy Brown', *The Nation*, 9 January 2019.

[115] Ibid.

purpose of creating an internal brand of national identity. The perhaps best example for the success of global justice place branding is The Hague. The nation branding of South Africa exemplifies the attractions of marketised global justice as a resource for capital growth in order to please the investors of the justice-dispensing conglomerate. The example of Cambodia further complicates this dynamic by demonstrating the unavailability of the global justice rich pickings for the poor. Whilst elites may enter the competition over global justice, the rest must attempt to capitalise on donors' voyeurism. This explains why victims of conflict are invisibilised in the place branding of The Hague.

Of particular concern in this chapter has again been the neo-colonialism at work in the distinction between states branded as just-ice-*dispensing* and those branded as justice-*receiving*, a distinction that can be mapped onto the capital-exporting and capital-importing binary. This binary becomes particularly apparent through representational practices of victims of conflict, namely, in the hyper-visibility of victims in the Global South and the invisibility of victims in the Global North. In dark tourism, victims' suffering of mass atrocity is 'the main attraction'. In justice tourism, meanwhile, victims are generally hidden. The visibility or invisibility of victims depends on the funders: when attracting invest-ment and businesses, victims tend to be rendered invisible; when attracting atrocity tourism, victims tend to be made visible. This division reminds us of the racialised notions of who is deemed as *seeing* and who is deemed as *seen*.[116] Marketised global justice fixes these distinctions by presuming that justice-dispensing states and elites deal in global justice and justice-receiving states and 'the rest' deal in global injustice.

The relationship between place branding and global justice as the third and final case study is a further indication of the deeply embedded idea of marketised global justice. Places are not only using global justice to shape their brand, highlighting the manipulability for commercial purposes of global justice, these places (and their brand consultants) are themselves shaping global justice. Global justice has been moulded for the purpose of attracting capital. This dialectical relationship has multiple effects: not only does it frame global justice in a simplified manner, it also closes down avenues for contestation. However, we have also seen different modes of resistance against marketised global justice. This resistance is the focus of the next, and final, chapter.

---

[116] Susan Sontag, *Regarding the Pain of Others* (Penguin 2004) 65.

9

'Occupying' Global Justice

Is this reform or revolution? If it extends, it's revolution. It changes the institutional structure of society.[1]

9.1 Introduction

Given the deeply entrenched marketisation of global justice projects, is there a possibility for 'non-marketised', or perhaps better 'anti-marketised', forms of global justice? Can this even be envisaged in a world dominated by the neoliberal order? Could an anti-marketised form of global justice advance the interests of the oppressed and exploited? And can international (criminal) law assume a place in anti-marketised global justice? In this chapter, I consider these questions from the vantage point of ideas and practices of 'occupying' global justice. 'Occupying' global justice draws on the theory and praxis of social and political movements such as 'Occupy Wall Street' and Black Lives Matter (BLM). The defining idea of occupied global justice is the use of tactics that view the unsettling of structural inequality as necessary, and as struggle. Occupying global justice has an overtly destabilising element to it: it aims to destabilise epistemological certainties, it aims to destabilise the reproduction of hegemony, and it aims to destabilise the normalisation of market-thinking in non-market spaces. Occupying global justice takes seriously the need for a radical departure from the given system, in this way connecting to the post-financial crash Occupy movements and more recently the BLM movement.[2] At the same time, it acknowledges utility in the 'global justice' debate more generally as a grounds for political struggle for

---

[1] Noam Chomsky, *Occupy* (Penguin 2012) 62.
[2] Occupy Wall Street began as a protest movement in 2011. The Canadian anti-consumerist collective Adbusters first called for the 'occupation' of Wall Street.

equality, redistribution, and anti-imperialism. In particular, it resurfaces the undermined anti-imperial origins of global justice movements.[3]

In the previous chapters, I have aimed to set out the mechanisms by which global justice has become de-politicised and de-historicised. This was illustrated, for example, in the insistence of International Criminal Court (ICC) representatives on the separation of politics and justice. De-politicisation and de-historicisation were also, for example, illustrated as a consequence of place branding for the purposes of attracting investment, tourists, and trade. Global justice has increasingly been removed from popular contestation. A system of expertise, institutions, and removed elites has shifted justice to a confined space that is not open to political contestation; this was perhaps most apparent through the nation branding indexes, reports, and benchmarks noted in Chapter 8. When in 2011 activists called upon 'the 99%' to 'Occupy Wall Street', it was a call for the re-politicisation of debates around inequality and redistribution that had been narrowed to the expert parlance practiced by the financial sector and a small elite group gathering annually for the World Economic Forum in Davos.

A similar approach to re-politicisation is proposed here. As expressed through the choice of 'occupying' terminology, I do not propose a universal idea for a New Global Justice; rather, I propose four tactics of occupying global justice. The four tactics are neither alternatives nor elements of a whole and include overlaps, contradictions, and limitations: first, *unplugged global justice*, which concerns the abandonment of marketised visual and linguistic habits; second, *de-spectacularised global justice*, which emphasises the slow and quiet, therefore finding the time and means to focus on context; third, *unmasked global justice*, which reveals and unsettles stereotypes by means of irony and satire and has a theatrical element to it; and fourth, *resistance global justice*, which foregrounds agency and insists on an internationalism of solidarity.

Occupied global justice does not stop at disciplinary boundaries, but takes a broad view on resistance through inter-disciplinarity, through structural thinking, learning from history, and through an opening of sense experience. In this broad approach, it takes seriously 'non-rational'

---

[3] Adom Getachew, *Worldmaking after Empire: The Rise and Fall of Self-Determination* (Princeton University Press 2019) 175.

forms of intervention.[4] 'Occupying' global justice means to create ruptures in the dominant norms, institutions, representations, and ways of
thinking and being; and to consider alternatives, not of argument, but of
being shaped by common themes of struggle and resistance. These are big
debates and I can only seek to suggest very small impulses. In order to
maintain a focus on marketised global justice, I mainly discuss the
creation of ruptures between the six key themes of marketised global
justice. These are tactics of disconnection between the congealed themes
of (a) branding, (b) the attention economy, (c) spectacle, (d) international criminal law (ICL), (e) neoliberalism, and (f) neo-colonialism.
The hope is that such ruptures will create a space for the renewed
flourishing of social values.

Before turning attention to the four tactics, I devote some pages to the
well-trodden path of asking about 'reform or revolution?' Is there a
potential for reform of given structures, or must resistance be concerned
primarily with revolution? In other words, is any attempt at reform a
revisionist attempt at working within – and therefore ultimately
strengthening – the current limitations? In yet other words, can tactical
moments of resistance really achieve anything in the long-term, or is this
merely a 'cop-out' and ultimately strengthens the status quo? In order to
gain a grasp over these questions, I rely on the work of political theorist
and dedicated socialist internationalist Rosa Luxemburg. Luxemburg was
immersed in the 'reform or revolution' debate within the Social
Democratic Party of Germany (SPD) at the beginning of the twentieth
century. Luxemburg did not see reform and revolution as necessarily in
opposition to one another. Her thoughts are illuminating for considering
what kind of tactics can be employed for an anti-marketised
global justice.

9.2   Reform or Revolution?

The question of 'reform or revolution?' precedes further investigation as
to 'what next?' for a project that seeks to create ruptures in the existing
system. Reformism is often rejected as revisionist, and as ultimately
undermining long-term strategic goals. Revolution is often rejected both

---

[4] James Brassett refers to irony and narration as non-rational forms of intervention. In
James Brassett, 'British Irony, Global Justice: A Pragmatic Reading of Chris Brown, Banksy
and Ricky Gervais' (2009) 35 *Review of International Studies* 219–245, 219.

as negatively loaded through bad historical precedents and as being too ambitious.

At the beginning of the twentieth century, Luxemburg was at the centre of a fierce debate on the reformism of the SPD. Her published views were mostly directed against Eduard Bernstein, who represented the views of the reformist faction of the SPD. Luxemburg spear-headed the revolutionary faction. Her work on 'Reform or Revolution' was informed by an interest in the situation in Russia at the time, particularly the events precipitating the Russian Revolution. Luxemburg believed that reformism as proposed by Bernstein ultimately undermined the goals of socialism. The deep rifts in the party between revolutionaries and reformists were apparent in party debates over the mass strike (which Luxemburg observed in Russia with enthusiasm),[5] the role of the trade unions, whether to appeal to the middle class and cooperate with Liberals, and questions of militarism and imperialism which ultimately split the party in 1914.[6]

In 1900, Luxemburg begins her thoughts on reform or revolution by dismissing the dichotomy: 'Can the Social-Democracy be against reforms? Can we counterpose the social revolution, the transformation of the existing order, our final goal, to social reforms? Certainly not.'[7] Bernstein, in contrast, had made clear that the final goal meant little to him: 'the movement is everything'.[8] Bernstein formed this opinion because he had seen the adaptability of capitalism in the face of crises and challenges: the intensification of trade, the development of the credit system, and the consolidation of the middle classes. Because of this, and perhaps understandably for an observer of the time, he had expressed his doubt that capitalist development would lead to a general economic collapse.[9] Luxemburg saw this as the negation of the necessity for socialism.[10] Indeed, she saw an important contradiction in Bernstein's claim that that which was used to suppress the contradiction of capitalism (cartels and the credit system, for example) could not at the same

---

[5] Rosa Luxemburg, 'The Mass Strike, The Political Party and the Trade Unions' [1906] in Helen Scott (ed.), *The Essential Rosa Luxemburg: Reform or Revolution and the Mass Strike* (Haymarket Books 2008).
[6] Ibid 39.
[7] Ibid 41.
[8] Quoted in ibid 41.
[9] Quoted in ibid 46 under Bernstein, 18 *Neue Zeit* (1897–1898).
[10] Ibid 46.

time be suitable tactics for socialism.[11] In sum, for Luxemburg, then, reforms are not incompatible with revolution, but the reforms must be directed towards the ultimate aim of anti-imperialism and socialism. For her, this cannot include reformism that emanates from capitalism itself. Such reforms ultimately strengthen capitalism rather than undermine it.

Let us pause at this critical juncture and return to our question about reforming global justice or revolutionising global justice. If we apply Luxemburg's thoughts to global justice projects, then the condition of marketised global justice cannot be cured through the symptoms of marketised global justice. A 're-brand' of global justice is out of the question. But, reform and revolution can complement one-another. So long as the reforms work towards an ultimate aim of overturning the dominant material conditions structuring social relationships.

9.2.1   Strategy and Tactics

We might develop this further for the question of global justice through reference to Robert Knox's discussion of strategy and tactics.[12] Asking how critical international lawyers should intervene in political debates, Knox sets out the difference between strategy (the long-term structural aim) and tactics (the short-term practices). This distinction mirrors the revolution or reform differentiation. Finding a problematic move towards exclusively tactical interventions, which are mislabelled as strategic, Knox asks: 'Is it really the case that we should always engage in debates purely on the terms that we find them? In so doing, do we not run risk winning the particular argument, whilst at the same time legitimating those broader structures we wish to undermine?'[13] Knox warns against liberal legalist interventions that may foreclose strategic interventions. Winning the argument in the short-term, according to Knox, may be a capitulation to liberal legalism rather than a mere utilisation of it.[14] But, although some tactical interventions as day-to-day struggles may be mere palliatives, they may nevertheless be framed by the ultimate strategic goal. Knox references here Karl Marx's views on the workers' struggles for the eight-hour working day. Whilst this

---

[11] Ibid.
[12] Robert Knox, 'Strategy and Tactics' (2010) 21 *Finnish Yearbook of International Law* 193–229.
[13] Ibid 194.
[14] Ibid 208, 209.

struggle assumes workers in the capitalist system, it is also constituting workers as a political class to ultimately overturn the social conditions that exploit them.[15] Adopting this argument to the contestation over 'occupying' global justice, liberal legalist interventions that, even if temporarily, paint the law as operating in a neutral sphere, ultimately collapse into 'plain old liberal legalism'.[16] Meanwhile, tactical interventions that create a political collectivity are not only in keeping with strategic aims, they are essential. In practice much of the contestation plays out around what legitimate tactics are.[17]

9.2.2 Decoloniality

A tactic underlying all four tactics of occupying global justice, and therefore worth noting first, is that of decoloniality. The rich decolonising traditions and struggles can hardly be broken down into a few paragraphs. Indeed, there is a danger that the struggles appear just as glib as the branded global justice projects mentioned in this book. The best place to begin is with the links between decoloniality and epistemology: decoloniality includes an understanding of coloniality as the continued subjugation and exploitation of actors in and from the Global South for the benefit of the Global North, expressed in dominant epistemologies, in ways of *knowing the world*. But decoloniality is not only about ideas; decoloniality aims to grasp and expose the material benefits of epistemic dominance in order to undo them. It concerns a consciousness of the social relationships that constitute our lives while contesting 'the totalising claims and political-epistemic violence of modernity'.[18] Decoloniality, as ways of thinking, knowing, being, has a history as long as, and preceding, colonial enterprises and invasions.[19] There have long been movements from the Global South to decolonise received knowledges. And yet, as we have learned in the previous chapters, the

---

[15] Ibid 218 with reference to Karl Marx, *Capital* (Oxford World Classics 1999) 181–182.

[16] Ibid 211.

[17] Ayça Çubukçu, *For the Love of Humanity: The World Tribunal on Iraq* (University of Pennsylvania Press 2018).

[18] Catherine E. Walsh and Walter D. Mignolo, 'Introduction' in Walter D. Mignolo and Catherine E. Walsh, *On Decoloniality: Concepts, Analytics, Praxis* (Duke University Press 2018) 1.

[19] Catherine E. Walsh, 'The Decolonial For: Resurgences, Shifts, and Movements' in Walter D. Mignolo and Catherine E. Walsh, *On Decoloniality: Concepts, Analytics, Praxis* (Duke University Press 2018) 17.

dominant sites of global justice continue to be shaped by coloniality. This is particularly evident in the manifestations of the imaginings of the main characters of ICL: the victim, perpetrator, and legal defendant. As was shown, these characters continue to be expressed and institutional-ised along what Boaventura de Sousa Santos has described as 'the abyssal line',[20] or what W.E.B. Du Bois called the 'global color line'.[21] Decolonising these sites of privileged knowledge production must there-fore be a key aim of occupying global justice. When conceptualising and putting into practice any form of epistemological break, voices from the Global South, as well as other marginalised voices on the basis of gender, race, sexual orientation, and disability, need to be included, elevated, and memorialised. And yet, decolonisation is so much more then 'adding and stirring'. Indeed, the diversification approach of 'adding and stirring' is often revisionist in that it displaces the movement in favour of a privil-eging of the individual. Paul Gilroy has shown how 'diversification' sits comfortably with an idea of the individual as the primary social unit in its view to 'economic betterment through thrift, hard work and individual discipline'.[22] The becoming-comfortable of institutions with multi-culturalism as a question of individual identity has, according to Gilroy, led to political inertia and the loss of the *movement*.[23] The call to anti-racism of institutions, where race is situated in essential differ-ences only, and is therefore de-historicised and de-theorised, 'trivialises the struggle against racism and isolates it from other political antagon-isms'.[24] Decolonising, in contrast to institutional anti-racism, is about nothing less than 'unlearning'.

Decolonising unsettles most clearly marketised global justice's key theme of neo-colonialism, but the element of decolonising that aims to 'unthink' and 'unlearn' seeks to destabilise all other features of marke-tised global justice too. Decolonisation means to take those in the Global South into the realm of 'the knowing' and 'the seeing' as active

---

[20] The abyssal line marks a distinction between those included by modernity through regulation and social emancipation versus those excluded in the colonies by appropri-ation and violence. Boaventura de Sousa Santos, *Beyond Abyssal Thinking: From Global Lines to Ecologies of Knowledges* (2007) 30(1) *Review* 45–89, 46.

[21] W.E.B. Du Bois, *The Souls of Black Folk* [1903] (Penguin 1996).

[22] Paul Gilroy, 'The End of Anti-racism' 17(1) *Journal of Ethnic and Migration Studies* (1990) 71–83.

[23] Ibid 72.

[24] Paul Gilroy, 'The End of Anti-Racism' in Wendy Ball and John Solomons (eds.), *Race and Local Politics* (Macmillan 1990) 191–209, at 193.

participants in the global justice project. At the same time, it is necessary to think about how labour is distributed. Surely, it cannot be the case that agency and self-representation of actors in and from the Global South absolves the Global North of its labour or responsibilities.

9.3   Tactics

Mark Fisher famously termed the current condition 'capitalist realism', articulating that capitalism is so embedded as the only political and economic system that 'it is now impossible to even *imagine* a coherent alternative to it'.[25] Imagining structural change begins with seeing the weaknesses in the current system. Indeed, the crude forms of marketing indicate the *weakness* of neoliberal capitalism, as it attempts to gain traction through distraction. Its weakness comes from its self-perception of standing in competition with other forms of imaging the global political economic order. It is precisely this that can be tactically exploited for strategic aims. As neoliberalism is *not* all-encompassing and omnipotent, and is in fact failing, there is a space for thinking about different forms of global justice.

And yet, the route to 'occupying' global justice for the purposes of resistance to marketisation, and ultimately imperialism and structural inequality, is likely to be imperfect, compromised, and contradictory. Even though the distinction between strategy and tactics should operate as a compass, there are no guarantees for 'pure' tactics. Historical examples of attempts of this 'purity' were generally not effective. Indeed, this is what arguably affected the cause of the *Situationist International* (SI). The SI was a group of (neo-)Marxist thinkers, writers, and artists, who wished to transcend genre to transcend capitalism. The objective was to construct a new revolutionary praxis of life.[26] One of the key figureheads of the SI, Guy Debord, has appeared throughout this book as a leading thinker and un-thinker of spectacle. At the formation of the alliance of artists and political theorists, who came from Algeria, Belgium, Denmark, France, UK, Italy, and Czechosolovakia, there was a distinct call for 'new values of life'.[27] Politically, the SI aligned with revolutionary political struggles of the time (Poland and Hungary),

---

[25] Mark Fisher, *Capitalist Realism: Is There No Alternative?* (Zero Books 2009) 2.

[26] Frances Stracey, *Constructed Situations: A New History of the Situationist International* (Pluto Press 2011) 1.

[27] Ibid 2.

major workers' strikes in Spain, and anti-colonial struggles in Indochina, Korea, Algiers, and Congo.[28] The Situationists sought authentic 'situations' in which the spectacle could be uncovered and dismantled. The motto of the Situationists was 'Never Work'. Active from the late 1950s to the early 1970s, they critiqued their contemporaries' attitude towards 1960s pop culture and consumerism as deeply compromised. Although seeking collaborators, the SI became famous for its expulsions.[29] The SI were influential in the 1968 student movements, but at the same time condemned it as co-opted. Generally, the *Situationists* fiercely attacked others for 'not doing it right' in what they termed 'recuperation' – the cultural normalisation or 'mainstreaming' of radical politics. There is much to learn from the SI and their prescient critique of spectacle. In terms of organisation, there is also much to learn: namely, that purist critique tends to spur inward-looking small collectives rather than broad solidarity movements. Taking this seriously then means addressing the limitations of the proposed tactics head-on.

9.3.1   Unplugged Global Justice

Marketised global justice taps into our desire for spectacle. With limited attention in a world of information-overload, we are drawn towards the visceral, the dramatic, the sensational. Global *injustice* is aestheticised in the images of mass atrocity, with evil perpetrators and 'grotesque' victims. Global *justice*, meanwhile, is represented in architecturally imposing buildings, cool-headed legal representatives, and the language of expertise. As we have found in past chapters, the spectacle of marketised justice is best understood when placed in conversation with the attention economy that views attention as a limited resource. Only that which grabs the attention is rewarded. This relies not only on a commodified idea of attention but also on an idea of audience that allocates attention according to the drama it promises.

Generally speaking, resistance to spectacle is minimal. We may shake our heads at ourselves to find we have fallen into the trap of an affective story of victimhood which legitimises military intervention, ironically tell ourselves that the click-bait story about the movie star advocating for peace is 'using their platform', or worry briefly about whether viewing victim images is voyeuristic; but overall our resistance to spectacle is

---

[28]   Ibid 2.
[29]   Ibid 3.

dulled. Resistance is dulled by the paradoxical phenomenon of the normalisation of spectacle. Resistance is also, relatedly, dulled by the decades of distraction through marketing, through the normalisation of consumer-oriented and de-politicised figures such as 'celebrities' or 'influencers', and the illusion that among all the glitz and glamour there is still a well-intentioned core at the centre of marketised global justice.

One option to activate resistance is to *unplug*, to look away, to not feed the spectacle's desire for attention and content. Unplugging global justice means both to *look away* from spectacular images of atrocity, as well as to *not be seen*. It furthermore has a non-visual dimension in the *silencing* of business-inflected speech patterns of talking about global justice. Tim Wu suggests that to 'ignore, tune out, and unplug' may be the appropriate response to attention merchants. Wu exemplifies the work of attention merchants through a by now familiar story of corporate power in (formerly) public spaces. Schools in the USA, struggling through dried up public funds, agree to cash injections by corporations in return for advertising space.[30] Identifying the problem of commodification of attention, not just in schools but also in particular on the Internet, Wu notes that there are precedents of pushing back. Indeed, 'if popular grievance is great enough, [the push-back] can sometimes turn into a full-fledged "revolt"'.[31] According to Wu, unplugging can be demonstrated through the backlash to Parisian poster art in the nineteenth century. Given the poster art already mentioned in the book (from the ICC documentary, to Obama, to Kony), this merits a brief explanation. From the late 1860s onwards, enormous and vibrant posters started adorning the walls of Paris. The new posters, which due to the latest printing technologies could be easily reproduced, were largely the work of artist and graphic designer Jules Chéret, who was commissioned by companies, cabarets, music halls, and theatres of Paris, including the famous Moulin Rouge.

From Parisian entertainment, to cigarette papers, to motor oil, the posters typically depicted beautiful women. The posters were celebrated, as was their artist.[32] But, as imitators flooded the market and the walls, there was a backlash by the Parisians who believed the 'poster craze' had gone too far. Far from being a radical form of resistance to marketisation, this resistance came largely from a bourgeois notion of aesthetics and 'the

---

[30] Tim Wu, *Attention Merchants: The Epic Scramble to Get Inside Our Heads* (Vintage Books 2016) 3–5.
[31] Ibid 7.
[32] Ibid 21–22.

beauty of France'. Parliamentarians in France attempted to curb advertising on several occasions, and were finally successful with prohibiting advertising posters on designated landmarks in 1910. A Senate report from that year identified posters and billboards as almost always aesthetically displeasing, a phenomenon 'deplored by all men of taste'.[33] Wu, however, takes heart from this example and similar examples of disenchantment with the way in which our attention is exploited. The idea is that if a corporation overstretches that which is acceptable in marketing, by being untruthful or deceitful, for example, one simply does not buy their product. He also suggests means and methods of ad-blocking. This method places the onus on the individual to amend a supply and demand relationship. However, Wu believes that there is a potential for a movement or "revolt", notably in scare quotes.[34] Overall, Wu's is less structural critique, and more critique of marketing methods, which not only relies on agency but assumes agency. As Naomi Klein observed about branding, mostly the 'point is that you don't have the choice whether or not to turn it off ... The point is to take choice out of the equation.'[35] However, a collective consciousness of visual stereotypes can arguably nevertheless lead to 'unplugging' through refusal to participate in the visual economy of global justice. This might be a refusal to share content that displays the symptoms of marketised global justice. For example, this could encompass objections to images of sad African children that are used to grab the attention of a Western donor community. Thinking about Wu's consumer-oriented form of backlash already gives us a sense that tactics for global justice depend very much on who the actor is.

Unplugging global justice means, more generally, a tackling of the heavy reliance on visuality in global justice projects. To paraphrase Debord, not all that appears is good.[36] Unplugging may include the reclaiming of the visual sense or it might be a decentring of it altogether. This tactic draws attention to the fact that the visual element has moved from a supplementary to a primary factor in iterations of global justice projects: justice must be *seen* to be done first. Unplugging global justice means to question and to limit the emphasis on the visual, particularly

---

[33] Elizabeth Karlsgodt, *Defending National Treasures: French Art and Heritage Under Vichy* (Stanford University Press 2011) 114.

[34] Wu, 'Attention Merchants' 22.

[35] Naomi Klein in *No Logo: Brands, Globalization and Resistance*. Directed by Sut Jhally, Media Education Foundation, 2003. Transcript available at: www.mediaed.org/tran scripts/No-Logo-Transcript.pdf 7.

[36] Guy Debord, *The Society of the Spectacle* [1967](Black & Red 1984) para 12.

when the aesthetics appear as a means to grab the attention. For example, Judith Butler reflects on the role of the media by asking in which way:

> those of us who watch the wars our governments conduct at a distance are visually solicited and recruited into the war by embedded reporting and publicly approved media reports, under what conditions can we refuse that recruitment effort? What restructuring of the senses does that require and enable?[37]

Do we refuse the recruitment effort by 'looking away'? Susan Sontag reminds us that the power to look away is autonomy.[38] We might refuse our own complicity with the depicted suffering, but this does not leave us less complicit. Indeed, we might be tempted otherwise to think that 'we' as the consumers of images of conflict have been exploited. Certainly, consumers, predominantly in the Global North, have been taken advantage of in the attention economy – but they (we) have not been exploited. Unplugged global justice in this form appears as a tactic for the privileged. For those who are exploited, not in seeing, but in *being seen*, unplugging global justice may appear in the form of what Édouard Glissant termed the right to opacity.[39] The right to not be seen is a response to the presumption of reductiveness behind being seen, and therefore being understood. Opacity for Glissant, a poet and philosopher from Martinique, is 'unknowability'. Against the background of the metrics of visibility and therefore knowability, as well as the assumptions of political power through visibility, Glissant's suggestion for unquantifiability offers a radical departure.

Apart from the visual dimension noted, unplugging global justice as a tactic also has a rhetorical dimension. As we learned from previous chapters, the language that global justice actors have adopted is one that reflects and constitutes its business culture. The language of 'stakeholders', 'dividends', 'returns on investment', and 'selling' is both reflective and productive of marketisation.[40] Although these terms seem innocent or normal, they are not. This condition is similar across the fields of education, health, the arts, and communication more generally. Despite

---

[37] Judith Butler, *Frames of War: When is Life Grievable?* (Verso 2009) xii.
[38] Susan Sontag, *Regarding the Pain of Others* (Penguin 2004).
[39] Édouard Glissant, *Poetics of Relation* (Betsy Wing, trans., University of Michigan Press 1997).
[40] John Patrick Leary, *Keywords: The New Language of Capitalism* (Haymarket Books 2018) 162. Interestingly, according to Leary's ethymology of the term 'stakeholder', It was a term first developed by a Harvard *law* professor, E. Merrick Dodd.

appearing neutral, the ethymologies of the language reveal their newness, often as specifically historically situated within neoliberalism.[41]

If we take this language-orientation seriously as part of the way in which we narrate the world, then a place to begin is to question the deep-seated linguistic habits of marketised global justice. This not only means a questioning of the words we use but also requires us to talk about what global justice is *for*. As Stefan Collini notes, 'our actions are only identifiable as this action rather than that action in terms of the language in which we describe them'.[42] The terms on which speaking about global justice is done matters. This could be a *refusal* to speak of victims of conflict as 'stakeholders' and a refusal to engage in action that derives from an understanding of the 'dividends' of global justice. The attention to language once again emphasises that ideas matter. We imagine the world through the language available to us. This means of course that language is also struggle, the struggle for meaning. Unplugging might therefore begin to dislodge the interlinkages between branding and global justice as marketised imagery and language is questioned; it might dislodge the links between the attention economy and global justice as the commodification of attention is questioned, and it might begin to dislodge some of the neo-colonialism at work in global justice through challenging the reproduction of stereotyped images.

9.3.2   De-spectacularised Global Justice

Debord stated: 'A critique seeking to go beyond the spectacle must know how to wait'.[43] Another way of approaching an anti-marketised global justice is to prioritise the slow over the visceral, and the quiet over the din of attention-grabbing. While unplugged global justice is the tactic of silencing, de-spectacularised global justice is the tactic of the quiet. As will be explained, this is an active quietness rather than a passive quietness. De-spectacularised global justice pays attention to that which is slow for a richer understanding of the world, insisting on complexity instead of simplification, and context instead of the de-contextualised. This might require a broader understanding of global *in*justice. Rob Nixon invites his readers to think of 'slow violence' as a form of de-spectacularised violence. Slow violence is 'violence that occurs gradually

---

[41] Ibid 4.
[42] Stefan Collini, *Speaking of Universities* (Verso 2017) 3.
[43] Debord, 'Society of the Spectacle', para. 119.

and out of sight, a violence of delayed destruction that is dispersed across time and space, and attritional violence that is typically not viewed as violence at all.'[44] The shifting of the view to slow violence means to expand ideas of global *in*justice. As global justice has been narrowed to individual criminal accountability as responses to mass atrocity committed by evil individual perpetrators, other forms of violence have been hidden from view. Environmental catastrophes, for example, often unfold incrementally and accretively, rather than spectacularly or instantaneously. Nixon notes how the main casualties of the focus on spectacular violence are 'the poor'. Whether as victims of waste dumping or climate change refugees, the environmentalism of the poor is compounded by the invisibility of the slow violence.[45] Nixon explains the rise of the attention economy in the context of 'turbo-capitalism, wherein the present feels more abbreviated than it used to'.[46] De-spectacularising has several functions here: The de-centring of spectacle allows a view to the long term, inviting a wider understanding of violence, and introducing complexity. Complicating accepted assumptions about violence is only possible through broadening the ambit of what we consider to be unjust and as requiring action. Furthermore, de-spectacularising potentially shapes thinking about action. Just as the conceptualisation of slow violence invites a more considered view to what constitutes violence, the responses too can be more considered. Slowness allows time and collectivisation for structural thinking rather than short-term band aid approaches, which risk the capitulation to the existing imperial frame. Kevin Quashie, for example, introduces the notion of the 'sovereignty of quiet' as a means to think 'beyond resistance'. Quashie asks what 'quiet' can mean for black culture in particular, which has typically been described as 'expressive, dramatic, or loud'.[47] He explores attentive attitudes such as non-passive waiting and patience as quiet modes.[48] Nixon's suggestion is to create alternative narrations. He attributes a major role to the environmentally concerned writer-activist for such alternative narrations. In his view, 'imaginative writing can help make the unapparent appear, making it accessible and tangible by humanizing

---

[44] Rob Nixon, *Slow Violence and the Environmentalism of the Poor* (Harvard University Press 2011) 2.
[45] Ibid 4.
[46] Ibid 8.
[47] Kevin Quashie, *The Sovereignty of Quiet: Beyond Resistance in Black Culture* (Routledge 2012).
[48] Ibid.

drawn-out threats inaccessible to the immediate senses'.[49] When it comes to the 'environmentalism of the poor', the great advantage is that the writer-activist may make victims visible, what Nixon calls 'a different kind of witnessing: of sights unseen'.[50]

The limitations of the tactics of de-spectacularised global justice lie once more in the assumption on who is 'seeing' and who is 'being seen'. The representational challenges and imaginative dilemmas that Nixon addresses are challenges of the privileged, extending the already problematic category of 'the seen' to 'the poor'. Both the writer-activist as well as the audience are likely to be privileged in regard to their position of 'seeing'. And yet, there may be utility in the tactics of this form of de-spectacularised global justice in presenting alternative experiences of injustice, thereby slowly but surely altering the stereotypes of victimhood that are so securely lodged in 'our' minds' eye. As we have seen, conflict and violence offer opportunities for political (or corporate) power to shift towards simplified narratives and personalities, pitting 'good' against 'evil'. The pull to accept simplification is great. Walter Lippmann, who we recall coined the term 'stereotype', observed that such 'symbols of public opinion' tend to be 'subject to check and comparison and argument' during times of moderate security, but contestation tends to disappear in times of conflict.[51] This is particularly pertinent against the background of the so-called forever war. The global conflict that began as a response to 9/11, has cast certain states as 'outlaw states', and has constructed deeply held stereotypes about victims and perpetrators.[52] As Lippmann suggests, stereotypes, made up of a mix of reality, fiction, and symbols, have an ordering function in societies.[53] It is difficult to imagine a million victims, so one victim stands in for the million. Indeed, as Lippmann observes, this is not simply about human nature, it is about socialisation. He himself was enticed by the idea of experts who reveal the facts that construct the stereotypes, reveal that which informs the imagination and images. He saw the media as unsuitable for this function.[54] Perhaps he would even have been comfortable

---

[49] Nixon, 'Slow Violence' 15.
[50] Ibid.
[51] Walter Lippmann, *Public Opinion* [1922] (Greenbook Publications 2010) 5.
[52] On the 'forever war' see Mark Danner, *Trapped in the Forever War* (Simon & Schuster 2016); On 'outlaw states' see Gerry Simpson, *Great Powers and Outlaw States: Unequal Sovereigns in the International Legal Order* (Cambridge University Press 2004).
[53] Lippmann, 'Public Opinion' 5.
[54] Ibid 13.

with Nixon's idea of writer-activists. However, there is also need for caution about such experts or writer-activists. The enticement with an organisation of experts is likely to be one of the elements that the organisers of the Walter Lippmann Colloquium experience in their object of study. When the term 'neoliberalism' was coined at the Colloquium in Paris in 1938, the gathered participants concluded that it was necessary to 'renovate' liberalism.[55] Critically, and again learning from Lippmann's cultural and social astuteness, neoliberalism came to be defined beyond statistics and business cycle research as instead concerning orders.[56] As individuals were seen as manipulatable, the market was separated as far as possible from democratic contestation. Such de-politicised expertise is a warning for de-spectacularised global justice, which emphasises context and care – often the domain of 'the expert'.

In contrast to Nixon's conceptualisation, the SI developed de-spectacular tactics that were experiential rather than representational. They called one of these tactics '*détournement*', translated as hijacking or diversion. 'It does this by damaging and polluting given spectacles so as to trigger or re-mediate a different social imagery based on non-alienated relationships'.[57] The idea is to make strange the mediated world of images. *Détournement* as a technique is playful, momentary, and a patchwork of materials and methods.[58] For example, the SI created 'detourned' films, including a film adaption of Debord's *The Society of the Spectacle* resulting in a delirious collage of image and film snippets.[59] A particular aspect of *détournement* as critique of consumerism finds echoes in 'culture-jamming', an artistic practice of the subversion of icons of capitalism. This use of subverted symbols – such as the bar-code art on the cover of this book – is a means of questioning the predominance of market symbols in social life. A further experiential technique devised by the SI was *dérive*, the practice of 'drifting'. The SI drifted through urban

[55] It was decided that an International Study Center for the Renovation of Liberalism should be established. Jurgen Reinhoudt and Serge Audier, *The Walter Lippmann Colloquium: The Birth of Neo-Liberalism* (Palgrave MacMillan 2018); Arnaud Breenetot, 'The Geographical and Ethical Origins of Neoliberalism: The Walter Lippmann Colloquium and the Foundations of a New Geopolitical Order' (2015) 49 *Political Geography* 30–39.

[56] Quinn Slobodian, *The Globalists: End of Empire and the Birth of Neoliberalism* (Harvard University Press 2018) 58.

[57] Frances Stracey, 'Constructed Situations' 7.

[58] McKenzie Wark, *Fifty Years of Recuperation of the Situationist International* (Princeton Architectural Press 2008) 11.

[59] *La société du spectacle*. Directed by Guy Debord, 1973.

spaces, avoiding commercial centres, in order to experience urban life differently. But the drifting was not directionless, the Situationists looked 'for consistencies of ambience, making connective threads through the street grid.'[60]

Whilst *détournement* and *dérive* may have been effective for Parisian bohemians in the 1960s and 1970s, they may appear less suitable to occupying global justice. But, despite the eccentricity (or maybe because of it), there are elements of these practices that may serve ideas and practices of an 'occupied' global justice. First, to complement Nixon's writer-activist, de-spectacularised global justice is not quietness as passivity, but rather a form of activity that forces individuals to consider themselves as political agents, not merely as consumers.[61] Whilst the experiential may be alien and discomforting, it could in turn be generative of the kind of thinking that has been suppressed by Fisher's notion of capitalist realism. Second, in a more concrete way, the making unfamiliar of spectacularised global justice may be useful in representations of victimhood. One might imagine *détourned* representations of victims of conflict in an 'unfamiliar' setting or engaged in an 'unfamiliar' task. Rather than being depicted as weak and dependent, victims of conflict might be depicted as resilient and as taking their lives into their own hands. De-spectacularised global justice, by inviting a consideration of agency in the form of a quiet every-day agency, challenges the deep-seated connection between global justice and the spectacular.

9.3.3   Unmasked Global Justice

In 2017, popstar Ed Sheeran, together with Comic Relief, won an award. The achievement for getting the Rusty Radiator award: using the greatest number of stereotypes about poverty in one campaign. The jury's comments were: 'This is a video about Ed Sheeran. It's literally poverty tourism.'[62] The Norwegian Students' and Academics' International Association Fund (SAIH) had made these annual awards an important part of their research on stereotypes and poverty. Not only did they

---

[60] Wark, 'Fifty Years of Recuperation of the Situationist International' 18.

[61] For examples of art projects that seek to represent this, see Joshua Lubin-Levy and Aliza Shvarts, 'Living Labor: Marxism and Performance Studies' (2017) 26(2–3) *Women & Performance: A Journal of Feminist Theory* 115–121.

[62] www.radiaid.com/radi-aid-awards-2017.

Figure 9.1 Radi-Aid. SAIH: Norwegian Students' and Academics' International Assistance Fund

evaluate charity videos, they also made them. One notable video 'Africa for Norway' is a charity single in which a group of African singers get together 'in this time of need for Norway', to help them to warm up with radiators.[63] The singers wear T-shirts emblazoned with a radiator logo. One of the rappers solemnly says 'it's kind of just as bad as poverty if you ask me ... Frostbite kills too'.[64] The dreamy clips of the singers in the recording studio are interspersed with images of white people battling snow. The singers sing 'We see how they freeze' as a group of people see a van of radiators off, waving happily.

Another SAIH video depicts the life of a child poverty star who is pampered by the film crew while perfecting his sad face for the cameras.[65] Satire may be a means to 'unmask' global justice projects for their extensive use of hyperbole and pathos. In the spirit of Naomi Klein's

---

[63] www.radiaid.com/about.
[64] Ibid.
[65] 'Let's Save Africa! – Gone Wrong', www.radiaid.com/.

analysis of branding in *No Logo*, the previous chapters have exposed the vacuum that arises through an excessive focus on marketisation, and the militarism and racial capitalism that can take the space of the vacuum created. Unmasking global justice means to highlight, perhaps to an extreme, the focus on image, both in its visual sense as well as in its reputational sense. Unmasked global justice does not shy away from making the object of attention look ridiculous, pathetic even. Irony may indeed be a means to open up new spaces of critique, 'chiding us to drop the straight faced moral seriousness that sometimes freezes ethical (self)-critique'.[66]

This seeming virtue can just as easily be seen as the greatest limitation. Unmasked global justice can be challenged for not taking seriously that which is serious. Lilie Chouliaraki describes the 'ironic spectator' in an age of post-humanitarianism as articulating 'detached knowingness, a self-conscious-suspicion vis-à-vis all claims to truth', marking the relationship between donors and 'distant others'.[67] When it comes to mass crimes, disaffection, cynicism, and irony are the symptoms of the distance and lack of feelings of solidarity. This distance, what Chouliaraki describes as 'narcissistic and increasingly corporate discourses of solidarity', is the ultimate result of 'brandicide of genocide'.[68]

Unmasking need not be comedic or ironic in a disaffected way; it can be provocative and political too. A 'strategy of rupture', for example, demonstrates an ironic stance towards the political power structures that constitute notions of legality, but is nevertheless focused on anti-imperial ends. A strategy of rupture has most successfully been pursued in the courtroom through the tactic of 'sacrificing' the defendant, where their defence is no longer an objective; instead, the exposure of the political power behind the court is the objective. Rather than the quietness of unplugged or de-spectacularised global justice, this type of tactic is *theatrical*. A famous lawyer who pursued the 'strategy of rupture' approach, and also coined it, was Jacques Vergès.[69] Invariably called 'terror's advocate' or 'devil's advocate', Vergès believed that some trials must 'shift the events to outside the courtroom and win over public

---

[66] Brassett, 'British Irony, Global Justice' 223.

[67] Lilie Chouliaraki, *The Ironic Spectator: Solidarity in the Age of Post-Humanitarianism* (Polity Press 2013).

[68] Ibid 203.

[69] Jacques Vergès, *De la stratégie judiciaire*, [1968] (Les Éditions de Minuit 1981).

opinion for the defendants'.[70] Vergès relished the opportunity of holding
a mirror to the powers constituting the court, unsettling impressions of
the neutrality of the court, and the bench. Later, when his anti-imperial
politics no longer appeared to drive his ambitions, Vergès relied on the
right to a fair trial, defending, among others, Nazi Klaus Barbie, Khmer
Rouge leader Pol Pot and former Serbian President Slobodan
Milosovic.[71] He was by no means the first to use the legal tactic of
rupture in and outside of the courtroom. Luxemburg and her lawyer,
too, used the public space of the courtroom and the attention of the
media as a political opportunity in the early twentieth century, when she
was accused of slandering the German army. Together with her lawyer
Paul Levi, Luxemburg utilised the attention on the trial as a means to put
the German minister of war on the spot, calling over a thousand witnesses to speak on army brutality.[72] The attendant public attention,
which Levi and Luxemburg courted and welcomed, allowed for the
debate about anti-militarism and anti-imperialism to spill over into a
broader domain. For Luxemburg, Levi and others in the SPD (before it
split precisely on the point of militarism), there was no neutrality of the
law or procedural even-handedness in the courtroom. Historian Henning
Grunwald observes that for them trials did not present a level playing
field – despite illusions of it – but presented a key arena of the class
struggle, a political battlefield.[73] The class struggle was presented in
various ways: through the hundreds of proletarian mistreated army
recruits called as witnesses before the bourgeois bench, the defence's
rejection of the presiding and assistant judges for bias on the grounds
that they had been army officers, and more generally the instrumentalisation of workers as soldiers for political ends, which undermined their
emancipation.[74] According to this position, trials (and war crimes trials
in particular) are always also 'show trials', whether undertaken by an
autocracy or a state of the 'free world'. The defence's strategy of rupture

---

[70] 'Interview with Notorious Lawyer Jacques Vergès: "There Is No Such Thing as Absolute
Evil', Spiegel Online, 21 November 2008, available at: www.spiegel.de/international/
world/interview-with-notorious-lawyer-jacques-verges-there-is-no-such-thing-as-abso
lute-evil-a-591943.html.

[71] Martti Koskenniemi, 'Between Impunity and Show Trials' (2002) 6 *Max Planck Yearbook
of United Nations Law* 1–35, 26, 27.

[72] Henning Grunwald, *Courtroom to Revolutionary Stage: Performance and Ideology in
Weimar Political Trials* (Oxford University Press 2012) 18.

[73] Ibid.

[74] Ibid 34–41.

resonates with Gerry Simpson's observation that '[w]ar crimes trials, then, may be show trials but they are shows for the defence, too'.[75] Interestingly, the use of Rosa Luxemburg's 1914 trial for purposes of shaping public opinion was at the very heart of the political disputes that followed. Levi used the case material for a number of public rallies, described as a 'veritable road-show which enthralled audiences all over Germany'.[76] These public displays were frowned upon by the more conservative, and later war-supporting, part of the SPD. Notably, the tensions within the party were played out in legal rather than political terms, with Hugo Heinemann, a senior figure in the party and 'figure-head of the old-style SPD lawyer' penning a formal opinion on the legal technicalities of the Levi rallies that more generally criticised the politi-cisation of the legal proceedings.[77] 'Underlying this attitude', Grunwald concludes, 'was an understanding of legal proceedings that strictly separ-ated "the political" from "the legal"'.[78] The strategy of rupture (a strategy in name, but a tactic in nature) theatrically seeks to *unmask* the assump-tion of the separation of the political and the legal in global justice.

9.3.4   Resistance Global Justice

Resistance global justice, which emphasises struggle, can be thought of as constituted by two guiding principles: agency and solidarity. Frantz Fanon, a revolutionary thinker and activist from the French colony of Martinique, is one of the key figures of resistance from and for the Global South. Fanon's refusal to follow Europe climaxes at the end of his book *The Wretched of the Earth* with the following appeal: 'Let us decide not to imitate Europe; let us combine our muscles and our brains in a new direction'.[79] Not averse to armed struggle as a means to fight the colon-isers, and influenced by his own revolutionary action in Algeria, Fanon warns of the pitfalls of imitating Europe. He describes how the United States sought independence through imitation, a former colony deciding it wanted to 'catch up with Europe'. Its success is, according to Fanon, evidenced in its monstrousness 'in which the taints, the sickness and the

---

[75] Gerry Simpson, *Law, War & Crime: War Crimes Trials and the Reinvention of International Law* (Polity Press 2007) 6.
[76] Grunwald, 'Courtroom to Revolutionary Stage' 37.
[77] Ibid 39, citing archive material.
[78] Ibid.
[79] Frantz Fanon, *The Wretched of the Earth* [1961] (Penguin 2001) 252.

inhumanity of Europe have grown to appalling dimensions'.[80] What does it mean for an anti-marketised global justice to 'forget Europe' to create something other than an imitation?

In the twentieth century, there were several episodes of resistance from the Global South that radically challenged the (neo-) imperial order. An early iteration of South-South solidarity was the Bandung conference of 1955;[81] another was the 1966 Solidarity Conference of the Peoples of Africa, Asia, and Latin America, also known as the Tricontinental Conference.[82] These conferences of solidarity among state representatives, guerrilla movements, and other radicals of the Global South were moments of resistance in which the oppressed and marginalised realised their power through collective action, eventually leading to the creation of the Non-Aligned Movement. They were also distinctly anti-capitalist. The link between colonialism and capitalism had long been identified by the resistance movements of the Global South. Often, these events, along with the New International Economic Order of the 1970s, are remembered as 'failures'. But this depends very much on what the time-frame is and what the markers of success are. The renewed interest in these events in fact mark them out as movements to be learned from and not dismissed.[83] Movements today – such as Black Lives Matter – still take inspiration from these events, what Adom Getachew calls 'world-making' events.[84]

The foregrounding of struggle in these episodes can be identified in the aesthetics of the projects, an aesthetics that refused to give in to the idea of the oppressed as weak. As a tactic of anti-marketised global justice, this aesthetics is relevant for its aim to disrupt dominant narratives not silently or quietly or through irony, but boldly. Building on the earlier 1955 Bandung Conference and 1964 UN Conference on Trade and Development (UNCTAD), the Tricontinental represented the extension, into the Americas, of Afro-Asian solidarity begun at Bandung. The Tricontinental Conference remains one of the largest global gatherings of anti-imperialists in history. More than 500 representatives from

---

[80] Ibid.
[81] Luis Eslava, Michael Fakhri, Vasuki Nesiah (eds.), *Bandung, Global History, and International Law: Critical Pasts and Pending Futures* (Cambridge University Press 2017).
[82] Anne Garland Mahler, *From the Tricontinental to the Global South: Race, Radicalism, and Transnational Solidarity* (Duke University Press 2018).
[83] Ibid.
[84] Getachew, 'Worldmaking after Empire'.

national liberation movements, guerrillas, and independent governments of some eighty-two countries gathered in Havana, Cuba, to discuss anti-imperial strategy.[85] The Organization of Solidarity with the People of Asia, Africa and Latin America (OSPAAAL) was founded in 1966 after the Tricontinental Conference.

From its foundation until the mid-1980s, OSPAAAL produced posters, folded and stapled into copies of the Tricontinental magazine, which had subscribers throughout the world. The Tricontinental posters adopted some of the distinct features of the pop art scene of the time (bright colours and stencilling), but also showed echoes of revolutionary Russian posters from around the time of the Russian Revolution. This is particularly evident in the depiction of women, which in stark contrast to the dominant imagery circulated through NGOs and international organisations today, are portrayed as strong workers and fighters.

Figure 9.2 'Day of Solidarity' by Berta Abelénda, Lincoln Cushing/Docs Populi

[85] Mahler, 'From the Tricontinental to the Global South'.

Third World actors more generally are depicted as agents. This is demonstrated in terms of confidence, action, and a readiness for violence. A report prepared for a subcommittee of the US Senate Committee on the Judiciary notes that the delegates at the Tricontinental Conference openly 'committed themselves to the overthrow by violence of all those governments which do not meet with their approval'.[86] Although perhaps purposefully over-emphasised for the Senate Committee, the report is not incorrect. However, resistance is not *necessarily* violent, but takes the *possibility* of violence seriously as a means for expressing equal agency with imperial powers. This agency, crucially, comes not from individual-ised experiences of suffering but from the connecting of personal experiences to global struggles as well as connections to previous iterations of global justice movements as anti-imperial movements. However, the display of agency in this way may also be the limitation of resistance global justice. Alexander Weheliye recently asked why 'formation of the oppressed are only deemed liberatory if they resist hegemony and/or exhibit the full agency of the oppressed?'[87] The question throws into relief whether in resistance we continue to consider the 'liberal humanist subject, Man' as the only agent. More generally, this regards the question of whether decolonisation can only ever occur through the gaze of the coloniser. This potential trap of decolonisation chimes with what Gayatri Spivak described as 'epistemic violence'. Indeed, such a trap or bind of decoloniality may be the reason why some movements continue to fail to create solidarity between the Global North and the Global South. Notably, the Global Justice Movement, which is most widely known for its mobilisation for the Seattle protests in 1999, appears to have failed to create this type of sustained solidarity. One book on the Global Justice Movement, tracking the collective action of various activists, NGOs, and other civil society organisations involved in so-called anti-globalisation protest, includes descriptions of the movement from Italy, Spain, France, Great Britain, Germany, Switzerland, and

---

[86] 'The Tricontinental Conference of Africa, Asian, and Latin American Peoples (A Staff Study)' Prepared for the Subcommittee to Investigate the Administration of the Internal Security Act and other Internal Security Laws of the Committee of the Judiciary, United States Senate (Washington 1966).

[97] Alexander G. Weheliye, *Habeas Viscus: Racializing Assemblages, Biopolitics, and Black Feminist Theories of the Human* (2014 Duke University Press) 2.

the United States.[88] Not a single study from the Global South, no mention of the civil rights movement, of the Black Panthers, or of anti-capitalist (and anti-North American Free Trade) demonstrations in Latin America.

Tactically, the debate around decolonisation, as already mentioned above, spans all the proposed forms of anti-marketised global justice. The questioning of epistemologies around global justice as a form of resistance is most aptly situated in places of knowledge production, such as the university. Since 2015, a lively debate around decolonising the curriculum as a means to question uneven epistemologies has emerged. Dalia Gebrial of the Rhodes Must Fall Oxford movement states: 'The university is a site of knowledge production and, most crucially, consecration: it has the power to decide which histories, knowledges and intellectual contributions are considered valuable and worthy of further critical attention and dissemination.'[89] The movement to decolonise the curriculum began in March 2015 when political science students at the University of Cape Town Chumani Maxwele emptied a container of faeces over the statue of Cecil Rhodes. This was followed by protests demanding that the statue of Rhodes (an imperialist and defender of the racist civilisational narrative) must fall. However, it was never only about the statue, which was removed on instruction by the University Council one month later.[90] It was about a broader debate about knowledge production and validation, despite various moves to anti-racism or diversity. Gebrial takes up Gilroy's diagnosis of revisionism through diversification, explained above, to highlight that universities tend to think of race only in terms of representation and admissions. She emphasises that the decolonisation movement must instead focus on the interrogation of wider systemic processes – how they came to be, and the inequalities that are engendered and reproduced by and within them.[91] The position of the Western university as a privileged site of knowledge production has institutionalised notions on who could be a competent 'knower' and who

---

[88] Donatella Della Porta (ed.), *The Global Justice Movement: Cross-National and Transnational Perspectives* (Routledge 2016).

[89] Dalia Gebrial, 'Rhodes Must Fall: Oxford and Movements for Change' in Gurminder K. Bhambra, Dalia Gebrial, and Kerem Nisancioglu (eds.), *Decolonising the University* (Pluto Press 2018) 19.

[90] Mahmood Mamdani, 'Between the Public Intellectual and the Scholar: Decolonization and Post-independence Initiatives in African Higher Education' (2016) 17(1) *Inter-Asia Cultural Studies* 68–83, 68.

[91] Gebrial, 'Rhodes Must Fall' 31.

'the known', who could speak for 'the universal' and whose knowledge was only ever 'local'. The West as the producer of the universal – including universalised ideas such as global justice – prompted Hamid Dabashi to ask provocatively 'Can non-Europeans think?'[92]

The decolonisation of global justice at the level of epistemology would at the very least need to be put into practice in ICL curricula. ICL is increasingly taught as a stand-alone module, although at some universities it is only a small part of the (public) international law syllabus. Predominantly, ICL is taught according to a canon of cases and opinions, with the 'core crimes' taking pride of place. The history of the discipline is mostly taught in the truncated and progressivist iteration of the story 'From Nuremberg to Rome'. This forecloses a mention of empire almost entirely as it not only begins with multilateralism after 1945 but also misses the struggles of decolonisation in the 1950s and 1960s. The elision of decolonisation precludes tensions that have been a critical context for the mass atrocities under the limelight in the late 1990s and 2000s. The omission of this period in ICL curricula may also explain the easy dismissal of the neo-colonial charge. It may also in part explain the continued sway of the idea of ICL as tempering rogue politics.

A decolonised ICL curriculum, which takes empire into account, would look decidedly different in the Global North to the Global South. The teaching of ICL in the Global North needs to be confronted with its role of knowledge production. The Western university's role in perpetuating divisions, as well as the compromises made due to histories of resistance, would play an overt role. Colonial histories, the slave trade, and unequal treaties would be studied for their value in understanding the condition of the discipline *today,* not merely as a part of history. This allows for a more nuanced view on coloniality as the continuation of suppression. A pedagogy of discomfort, which tackles questions of white privilege, would need to underlie the syllabus and teaching delivery.[93] Education does more than create critically minded, socially responsible citizens; it enables young people and others to challenge authority by connecting individual troubles to wider systemic concerns. A decolonised ICL syllabus would productively generate forgotten histories and voices, thereby provincialising Europe's standing within epistemologies of global

---

[92] Hamid Dabashi, *Can Non-Europeans Think?* (Zed Books 2015).
[93] Christine Schwöbel-Patel, 'Teaching International Law Critically – Critical Pedagogy and *Bildung* as Orientations for Learning and Teaching', Bart van Klink and Ubaldus de Vries (eds.), *Academic Learning in Law: Theoretical Positions, Teaching Experiments and Learning Experiences* (Edward Elgar 2016) 99–120.

justice.[94] This form of anti-marketised global justice seeks to dislodge the links between global justice, neo-colonialism and neoliberalism.

9.4 Conclusion

Resistance to marketised global justice has begun to destabilise the glue that sticks together the key themes of marketised global justice identified in this book. The tactics for occupying global justice in this chapter draw on these experiences of resistance and add to them. As structural inequality is becoming more evident, traditions of resistance are becoming increasingly pertinent. The promise of global justice lies in its anti-imperial roots, even if different iterations have failed to build on and draw on these roots. Occupying global justice is therefore not about sentimentality towards a past in which global justice was not marketised. Rather, it involves an active looking forwards.

Occupied global justice is about radical departures. In the decolonisation literature and praxis, this sentiment comes to the fore in a pedagogy of pursuing the irreconcilable and the incommensurable.[95] Decolonisation has recently become a buzzword, overlaid onto other struggles, or simply replacing critique. When Eve Tuck and Yang K. Wanyne insisted that 'decolonization is not a metaphor', they were articulating the danger of decolonisation as slogan, or as brand.[96] In this marketised form, decolonisation no longer generates discomfort for the existing structural inequalities. Decolonisation as struggle, however, remains uncomfortable, and unsettling. In order for it to maintain its distance and otherness to marketised global justice projects, any 'moves to innocence' of the dominating powers must be foreclosed.[97] Ultimately, decolonisation is incommensurable with reconciling a colonial past with the present. In this way, decolonisation as a tactic moves us closer to anti-imperialism as strategy.

---

[94] See Alexander Anievas and Kerem Nisancioglu, *How the West came to Rule: The Geopolitical Origins of Capitalism* (Pluto Press 2015).

[95] Eve Tuck and Yang K. Wayne, 'Decolonization is not a Metaphor' (2012) 1(1) *Decolonization: Indigeneity, Education & Society* 1–40.

[96] Ibid.

[97] Ibid, referencing Janet Mawhinney, '"Giving up the Ghost": Disrupting the (Re) Production of White Privilege in Anti-Racist Pedagogy and Organizational Change' (Masters' Thesis, Ontario Institute for Studies in Education of the University of Toronto 1998).

10

Conclusion

Recent literature on international law, neoliberalism, and empire has highlighted the profoundly de-politicising and de-historicising effects of universalising projects that emerged from Western notions of superiority and were forced onto the non-Western world. In this book, I have sought to contribute to this conversation by analysing the hegemonic understanding and institutionalisation of global justice as defined by international criminal law (ICL). I have particularly been interested in *how* ICL has gained such traction as a global justice project. To get to the question of *how?*, I introduced a so far under-researched, but crucially important mechanism: marketing. As one of capitalism's vital means of persuasion, distraction, and renewal, the alliance between marketing and ICL has narrowed and normalised a marketised idea of global justice. Mostly, this has evaded sustained scrutiny because of the normalisation of marketised language and practices. Contrary to common views on marketing being either benign or positive, I have shown that marketing has a deeply structuring effect on global justice. In its alliance with ICL, it has de-politicised and de-historicised global justice, thereby draining it of its radical potential. The effects of a de-politicised and de-historicised global justice are wide-reaching: The narrow version of global justice as concerning predominantly anti-impunity has adopted a crucial position for enabling and encasing the market, distracting from structural inequalities, and disabling or marginalising democratic contestation. Potential political action is reframed as consumption, whether this is the support for certain non-governmental organisation campaigns or the identity forged through allegiance with a particular place. This is marketing global justice as mass distraction. The focus on market values over social values explains the lack of redistributive functions for global justice.

When I began this research, I was not only interested in describing instances of the use of marketing in global justice projects, but also finding out what marketing *does* to global justice projects. No doubt, my interest in marketing was spurred through reading Naomi Klein's carefully researched and beautifully written critique of branding in *No Logo*, and shortly after that the story of disaster capitalism in *The Shock Doctrine*.[1] The books resonated with various fairly minor but perturbing experiences I had of the operation of ICL. One of them was when I was an intern at the ICC in the mid-2000s. As an intern, one of my main tasks was to create powerpoint presentations about the ICC, which we peddled at different events and organisations in The Hague. I trundled along with my powerpoint whilst an official from the ICC presented on the work of the ICC and how important it was. This peddling of the powerpoint presentations struck me as profoundly strange, but I could not articulate why. A further resonance was when several years later I was once again living in The Hague, this time employed on a fixed-term contract post-PhD with a research institute. My main task for the first weeks was to improve the institution's website. On one occasion, I was urgently sent to the print shop. A group of seasoned Ugandan judges had visited The Hague for a week for the purpose of 'being trained' in ICL. Uganda had fairly recently established a war crimes division of the High Court of Uganda. Here were specialists in their field, sent to be 'trained' by a group of mostly white, male, mid-30s ICL experts. At the printers, I was to get copies of certificates. The certificates stated that these Ugandan judges had been 'successfully trained in International Criminal Law'. A photo opportunity marked the occasion of the presentation of the certificates. The photo was sent to me to upload to the website with the headline 'Ugandan judges successfully trained'. Is this, I asked myself, ICL 'gone wrong'? or is this ICL as it was meant to be?

Throughout this book, I have sought to demonstrate that by constructing an alliance between marketing and ICL, global justice has been put to work in far-reaching ways. The most obvious purpose of employing marketing is that it *persuades*: identifying the use of marketing practices by global justice actors reveals the attempt to persuade donors, patrons, or investors to choose one conceptualisation of global justice over others. Linked to this, marketing is also a means of *distraction*. Indeed, I have argued that the *at*traction to spectacularised global injustice is a means of mass *dis*traction from structural violence and from redistributive interpretations of global justice. Connected to the structuring ability of spectacle is the ability of marketing to create *illusions*. The alliance between

---

[1] Naomi Klein, *No Logo* (10th anniversary edition, Fourth Estate, 2010); Naomi Klein, *The Shock Doctrine* (Penguin 2007).

marketing and ICL has created the illusion that anti-impunity is a counter-hegemonic tool, while in fact serving the interests of hegemonic powers. More generally, the illusion has been created that market values are social values. In response to the backlashes against marketisation and manipulation, marketing has a further useful power: It *renews*. Through re-brands and creating new demands, marketing responds to backlashes with enticing solutions. These market-based solutions strengthen rather than weaken the source of the problem. In its positioning of comparisons – 'the best', 'the most efficient', 'the newest' – marketing moreover restructures its objects into competitors. Such *foregrounding of competition* disrupts actions of solidarity. Related to this is the commodification process of marketing, whereby everything is 'on sale' – from the idea of community, to injustice, to justice. This commodification necessarily constructs a *prominence of private property* as private property concerns access to the market, and therefore seemingly access to freedom. Marketisation of global justice is, all in all, a mechanism of maintaining and renewing the status quo.

The critique of ICL has by no means been ignorant of marketing. It is common for ICL to be described as having been 'oversold' (much like neoliberalism itself).[2] However, the response to the overselling is most commonly a more 'humble' or 'modest' international criminal justice.[3] The problem with calling for a more humble ICL is that it assumes that marketing is simply used metaphorically. 'Overselling' is in quotation marks. In this understanding, marketing is simply a cosmetic feature, which can be readjusted. The dominant critique does not, then, take into account the deeply structuring capacities of marketing in its alliance with ICL. I have sought to show in the previous pages that this *matters*, it matters for the representation of victims of conflict, it matters for policy considerations for NGOs, it matters for how states conduct themselves in their dealings with one another, and it matters for the moral compass that is the contestation and struggle over social values.

---

[2] For example, see Birju Kotecha, 'The Art of Rhetoric: Perceptions of the International Criminal Court and Tribunals' (2018) 31 *Leiden Journal of International Law* 939–962, 956; William A. Schabas, Yvonne McDermott, and Niamh Hayes (eds.), *The Ashgate Research Companion to International Criminal Law: Critical Perspectives* (Routledge 2013) 541.

[3] Kotecha, 'The Art of Rhetoric' 962; Sara Kendall and Sarah Nouwen, 'Speaking of Legacy: Towards and Ethos of Modesty at the International Criminal Tribunal for Rwanda' (2016) 110(2) *American Journal of International Law* 212–232.

Of the greatest importance as far as global justice projects go is surely the burning issue of climate change. At times whilst writing this book, to neglect to write about climate disaster has itself felt like a distraction. The challenge of maintaining a habitable world for human and non-human animals and an environment in the rich diversity once known, is undoubtedly the greatest challenge yet. How to do this in the face of the devaluation of social values through thirty years of 'legalised neoliberalism' is an enormous question. Most definitely, it will require radical rethinking – or 'occupation'. Global justice as environmentalism brings into sharp relief many of the issues mentioned in this book. The Global South at the receiving end of injustice is, sadly, a consistent theme, not only when it comes to international criminal justice, but also more generally as a condition of the world in which we live. The starting point for considering global injustice and climate disaster together is no doubt the recognition of the causal effect between the legal-institutional construct of neoliberalism (the neoliberal order), capitalism, and environmental and social destruction. Indeed, given its profound limitations, there is real purchase in asking whether something so existential as the prevention of the destruction of the world that we inhabit should really be framed as 'climate *justice*'? The extraction of value from climate disaster has, predictably, already begun. It requires a great social effort to break through these structures and habits. I have suggested four possible tactics for breaking through structures and habits of marketised global justice: unplugged global justice, de-spectacularised global justice, unmasked global justice and resistance global justice. Represented in the bar-code art on the cover of this book is therefore the sentiment that marketisation keeps us *inside* a commodified and market-oriented understanding of global justice, a place of distraction where people can only act as 'consumers'. The time is ripe for a breaking *out* towards an anti-imperial global justice, where people can assume a role as political actors.

10.1   Postscript

After hold-ups concerning the intellectual property rights of images, I submit the final version of this book to the publisher in a changed world. News of the deadly coronavirus (COVID-19) reached us from China a few months ago, but with the habitual arrogance of Western nations, we failed to act quickly. Now those privileged enough not to be at the front-line of service obsessively watch the news about the global pandemic, tracking the daily death rate updates and the challenges facing chronically underfunded healthcare systems. In a matter of days, we stopped commuting to work, kids stopped going to school, and instead of socialising with family and friends, we are social distancing. Multiple countries are in lockdown, with borders closed and curfews enforced. Expansive state financial support packages have been announced in a bid to save economies, where it is already clear that an enormous global recession is inevitable. But, this is not socialism. Private companies are in a bid to persuade us to consume regardless. Some industries are indeed doing well, for example, the financially secure are purchasing home improvement materials and home exercise equipment. The precariousness of certain types of labour, and the divide between rich and poor has never been quite so palpable. The rich are able to purchase testing kits, self-isolate, and hoard food and medication. The poor often have no choice but to go to work, exposing themselves and others to increased risks, or face losing their jobs and homes. Never has the question of social justice been so burning. Self-identifying primarily as consumers, those who can afford to, panic-buy. It is the primary response we know to a crisis. Despite the inequalities in the effects of the pandemic, this is also an opportunity. As the labour of nurses, doctors, social carers, teachers, delivery drivers, farmers, and fruit-pickers becomes more valued than ever, imagining a better society becomes possible. But, social justice does not come from an emergency government package to support businesses or from compassionate consumption. In imagining a better post-pandemic world, it is crucial to confront the fact that we begin from a position of marketised justice, which is yet to be undone and unlearned.

SELECT BIBLIOGRAPHY

Books, Journals, Periodicals, Authored Newspaper Articles, Blogs, Web Articles

Aaker, David, *Managing Brand Equity: Capitalizing on the Value of a Brand Name* (Jossey Bass 1991)

Abrahamian, Atossa Abraxia 'Beyond the Wall: A Q&A With Wendy Brown', *The Nation*, 9 January 2019.

Ainley, Kirsten, 'Transitional Justice in Cambodia: The Coincidence of Power and Principle' in Renee Jeffrey (ed.), *Transitional Justice in the Asia-Pacific* (Cambridge University Press 2014) 125–156

Airault, Pascal and Walker, Brandice, 'Fatou Bensouda: The Victims Are African', Africa Report, 22 December 2011, available at: www.theafricareport.com/7894/fatou-bensouda-the-victims-are-african

Akhavan, Payam, 'The Lord's Resistance Army Case: Uganda's Submission of the First State Referral to the International Criminal Court' (2005) 99(2) *American Journal of International Law* 403–421

'The Rise and Fall, and Rise, of International Criminal Justice' (2013) 11 *Journal of International Criminal Justice* 527–536

Aksenova, Marina, 'The Al Mahdi Judgment and Sentence at the ICC: A Source of Cautious Optimism for International Criminal Justice', EJILtalk, 13 October 2016, available at: www.ejiltalk.org/the-al-mahdi-judgment-and-sentence-at-the-icc-a-source-of-cautious-optimism-for-international-criminal-justice/.

Al-Dabbagh, Amr, 'How to Run Your Non-profit like a Startup', *Fortune*, 2 February 2015

Anderson, Janet, 'The Hague, the ICC, and the Economic Benefits for Being a Centre for Justice', *The Guardian*, 25 September 2012

Anholt, Simon, 'Public Diplomacy and Place Branding: Where's the Link?' (2006) 2(4) *Place Branding* 271–275

Brand New Justice: The Upside of Global Branding (Butterworth Heinemann 2003)

'We've Just Started a New Country. Want to Join?', TEDx at Progressvideo, November 2018. Video available at: http://progressvideo.tv/videos/we-ve-just-started-a-new-country-want-to-join-simon-anholt-tedxprimorskipark.

Anghie, Antony, *Imperialism, Sovereignty, and the Making of International Law* (Cambridge University Press 2005)

Anievas, Alexander and Nisanciolglu, Kerem, *How the West Came to Rule. The Geopolitical Origins of Capitalism* (Pluto Press 2015)

Annan, Kofi, 'Africa and the International Court', *New York Times*, 29 June 2009

'Advocating for an International Criminal Court' (1997) 21(2) *Fordham International Law Journal* 363–366

Aronczyk, Melissa, *Branding the Nation: The Global Business of National Identity* (Oxford University Press 2013)

Arseneault, Michel, 'Congolese Warlord Thomas Lubanga Jailed', Radio France Internationale, 11 July 2012

Baars, Grietje, *The Corporation, Law and Capitalism* (Brill 2019)

'Capitalism's Victor's Justice? The Hidden Stories Behind the Prosecution of Industrialists Post-WWII' in Kevin Heller and Gerry Simpson (eds.), *The Hidden Histories of War Crimes Trials* (Oxford University Press 2013) 163–192

Balch, Oliver, 'The Rise of "Sadvertising": Why Social Good Marketing Works', *The Guardian*, 18 July 2014

Becker, Sven, Blasberg, Marian, and Pieper, Dietmar 'The Ocampo Affair: A Former ICC Chief's Dubious Links', Spiegel Online, 5 October 2017, available at: www.spiegel.de/international/world/ocampo-affair-the-former-icc-chief-s-dubious-libyan-ties-a-1171195.html

Beitz, Charles R., 'Justice and International Relations' in Thomas Pogge and Darrel Moellendorf (eds.), *The Global Justice Reader: Seminal Essays, Volumes I and II* (Paragon House 2008) 21–48

Benedict, Michael, 'Assembly of States Parties Side Event. Through the Looking Glass: Imagining the future of International Criminal Justice', Final Report, Wayamo Foundation, November 2016

Benjamin, Walter, *The Arcades Project*, trans. Howard Eiland and Kevin McLaughlin (Harvard University Press 1999)

Bensouda, Fatou 'Ceremony for the solemn undertaking of the Prosecutor of the International Criminal Court', 19 June 2012, available at: www.icc-cpi.int/NR/rdonlyres/561C232F-3C4F-47AC-91CB-8F78DCC6C3FD/0/15062012FBSolemnUndertaking.pdf.

van den Berg, Stephanie, 'ICC Declines to Refer South Africa to U.N. for Not Arresting Sudan's Bashir', Reuters, 6 July 2017, available at: https://uk.reuters.com/article/uk-warcrimes-sudan-safrica/icc-declines-to-refer-south-africa-to-u-n-for-not-arresting-sudans-bashir-idUKKBN19R1UE

Bergsmo, Morten and Buis, Emiliano J., (eds.), *Philosophical Foundations of International Criminal Law: Foundational Concepts* (Torkel Opsahl Academic EPublisher 2019)

Bernays, Edward L., *Propaganda* [1928] (IG Publishing 2004)

Public Relations [1945] (Kessinger Publishing 2002)

Bensouda, Fatou, 'Reflections from the International Criminal Court Prosecutor' (2012) 45(4) *Vanderbilt Journal of Transnational Law* 955–961

Biebricher, Thomas, 'Neoliberalism and Law: The Case of the Constitutional Balanced-Budget Amendment' (2016) 17(5) *German Law Journal* 835–856

Bigman, Alex, 'Three cool companies join the "No Logo" movement', 99 Designs (2013), at https://99designs.co.uk/blog/trends/beyond-branding-3-awesome-companies-with-no-logos/.

Binet, Les and Field, Peter, *The Long and Short of It: Balancing Short and Long-Term Marketing Strategies* (Institute of Practitioners in Advertising 2013).

Blaut, James Morris, *The Colonizer's Model of the World: Geographical Diffusionism and Eurocentric History* (Guilford Press 1993)

Bleiker, Roland, (ed.), *Visual Global Politics* (Routledge 2018)

'Mapping Visual Global Politics', in Roland Bleiker (ed.), *Visual Global Politics* (Routledge 2018) 1

Boulton, Christopher, 'In Defense of "Slacktivism": How KONY 2012 Got the Whole World to Watch' in Danielle Sarver Coombs and Simon Collister (eds.), *Debates for the Digital Age: The Good, the Bad, and the Ugly of Our Online World* (Vol. 1 ABC Clio 2016) 321–332

Bourdieu, Pierre, 'The Forms of Capital' in John G. Richardson (ed.), *Handbook of Theory and Research for the Sociology of Education* (Greenwood Press 1986) 241–258

Brabazon, Honor, (ed.), *Neoliberal Legality: Understanding the Role of Law in the Neoliberal Project* (Routledge 2016)

Brady, Leo, *The Frenzy of Renown: Fame and its History* (Vintage 1997)

Branch, Adam, 'Exploring the Roots of LRA Violence: Political Crisis and Ethnic Politics in Acholiland' in Tim Allen and Koen Vlassenroot (eds.) *The Lord's Resistance Army: Myth and Reality* (Zed Books 2010) 25–44

'Kony 2012 from Kampala', Critical Investigations into Humanitarianism in Africa, 11 March 2012, available at: www.cihablog.com/whats-wrong-with-the-kony-2012-campaign/.

Brannen, Kate, 'Blackwater's Descendants Are Doing Just Fine', *Foreign Policy*, 1 July 2014

Brassett, James, 'British Irony, Global Justice: A Pragmatic Reading of Chris Brown, Banksy and Ricky Gervais' (2009) 35(1) *Review of International Studies* 219–245

Breenetot, Arnaud, 'The Geographical and Ethical Origins of Neoliberalism: The Walter Lippmann Colloquium and the Foundations of a New Geopolitical Order' (2015) 49 *Political Geography* 30–39

Brough, Melissa M., '"Fair Vanity": The Visual Culture of Humanitarianism in the Age of Commodity Activism' in Roopali Mukherjee and Sarah Banet-Weiser (eds.), *Commodity Activism: Cultural Resistance in Neoliberal Times* (New York University Press 2012) 174–198

Brown, Wendy, *Undoing the Demos: Neoliberalism's Stealth Revolution* (Zone Books 2017)

Brunwasser, Matthew, 'Serbia's Brand of Reconciliation: Embracing Old War Criminals', *The New York Times*, 23 November 2017

Buchanan, Ruth, 'Perpetual Peace or Perpetual Process: Global Civil Society and Cosmopolitan Legality at the World Trade Organization' (2003) 16(4) *Leiden Journal of International Law* 673–699

Bueno, Olivia, 'Reconsidering Lubanga's Sentence: Views from Ituri', *International Justice Monitor*, 24 August 2015

Butler, Judith, *Frames of War: When is Life Grievable* (Verso 2010)

Carnoy, Martin and Castells, Manuel, 'Globalisation, the Knowledge Society, and the Network State: Poulantzas at the Millennium' (2001) 1(1) *Global Networks* 1–19

Carr, David, 'Citizen Bono Brings Africa to Idle Rich', *The New York Times*, 5 March 2007

Carroll, Rory, 'Kony 2012 Cover the Night Fails to Move from the Internet to the Streets', *The Guardian*, 21 April 2012

Cassese, Antonio, 'Reflections on International Criminal Justice' (1998) 61(1) *Modern Law Review* 1–10

Castile, George Pierre, 'The Commodification of Indian Identity' (1996) 98(4) *American Anthropologist* 743–749

Chandler, David, *A History of Cambodia* (2nd ed. Silkworm Books 1993)

Charlesworth, Hilary, 'International Law: A Discipline of Crisis' (2002) 65(3) *Modern Law Review* 377–392

Cheadle, Don and Prendergast, John, *Not on Our Watch: The Mission to End Genocide in Darfur and Beyond* (Hachette 2007).

Chiam, Madelaine et al., 'History, Anthropology and the Archive of International Law' (2017) 5(1) *London Review of International Law* 3–5

Chimni, BS, 'Teaching, Research and Promotion of International Law in India: Past, Present and Future' (2001) 5 *Singapore Journal of International & Comparative Law* 368–387

Chomsky, Noam, *Occupy* (Penguin 2012)

Chouliaraki, Lilie, *The Ironic Spectator: Solidarity in the Age of Post-Humanitarianism* (Polity Press 2013)

Christie, Nils, 'The Ideal Victim', in Ezzat A. Fattah (ed.), *From Crime Policy to Victim Policy: Reorienting the Justice System* (Palgrave Macmillan 1986) 17–30

Clark, Phil, *Distant Justice: The Impact of the International Criminal Court on African Politics* (Cambridge University Press 2019)

Clarke, Kamari Maxine, '"We Ask for Justice, You Give Us Law": The Rule of Law, Economic Markets and the Reconfiguration of Victimhood', in Christian De Vos, Sara Kendall and Carsten Stahn, *Contested Justice: The Politics and Practice of International Criminal Court Investigations* (Cambridge University Press 2015) 272–301

'The Rule of Law through its Economies of Appearances: The Making of the African Warlord' (2011) 18(1) *Indiana Journal of Global Legal Studies* 7–40

Fictions of Justice. The International Criminal Court and the Challenge of Legal Pluralism in Sub-Saharan Africa (Cambridge University Press 2009)

Clifford, Bob, *The Marketing of Rebellion: Insurgents, Media, and International Activism* (Cambridge University Press 2005)

Cole, Teju, 'The White Savior Industrial Complex', *The Atlantic*, 12 March 2012

Collini, Stefan, *Speaking of Universities* (Verso 2017)

Comaroff, Jean and John, *Ethnicity, Inc.* (Chicago University Press 2009)

'Millennial Capitalism: First Thoughts on a Second Coming' (2000) 12(2) *Public Culture* 291–343

Cooper, Helene, 'A Mission to Capture or Kill Joseph Kony Ends, Without Capturing or Killing', *The New York Times*, 15 May 2017

Cope, Zac, *The Wealth of (Some) Nations* (Pluto Press 2019)

Cormack, Patricia, '"True Stories" of Canada: Tim Hortons and the Branding of National Identity' (2008) 2(3) *Cultural Sociology* 369–384

Cox, Robert, *Production, Power, and World Order: Social Forces in the Making of History* (Columbia University Press 1987)

Crane, David, 'Dancing with the Devil: Prosecuting West Africa's Warlords – Current Lessons Learned and Challenges', in Edel Hughes, William Schabas and Ramesh Thakur (eds.), *Atrocities and International Accountability: Beyond Transitional Justice* (United Nations University Press 2007) 133–141

Craven, Matthew, 'Between Law and History: The Berlin Conference of 1884–1885 and the Logic of Free Trade' (2015) 3(1) *London Review of International Law* 31–59

Crenshaw, Kimberlé, 'Demarginalizing the Intersection of Race and Sex: A Black Feminist Critique of Antidiscrimination Doctrine, Feminist Theory, and Antiracist Politics' (1989) 1 *University of Chicago Legal Forum* 139–167

Crouch, Colin, *The Strange Non-Death of Neoliberalism* (2011 Polity)

Cryer, Robert, et al., *An Introduction to International Criminal Law and Procedure* (Cambridge University Press 2010)

Çubukçu, Ayça, *For the Love of Humanity: The World Tribunal on Iraq* (University of Pennsylvania Press 2018).

Curry Jansen, Sue, 'Designer Nations: Neo-liberal Nation Branding – Brand Estonia' (2008) 14(1) *Journal for the Study of Race, Nation and Culture* 121–142

Cutler, Claire, *Private Power and Global Authority: Transnational Merchant Law in the Global Political Economy* (Cambridge University Press 2003)

D'Amato, Anthony, 'International Law in the Curriculum' (1990) 2 *Pace Yearbook of International Law*, 83–91

Dabashi, Hamid, *Can Non-Europeans Think?* (Zed Books 2015)

Dahlén, Micael, Lange, Fredrik, and Smith, Terry, *Marketing Communications: A Brand Narrative Approach* (Wiley 2010)

Daley, Patricia, 'Rescuing African Bodies: Celebrities, Consumerism and Neoliberal Humanitarianism' (2013) 40(137) *Review of African Political Economy* 375–393

Danner, Mark, *Trapped in the Forever War* (Simon & Schuster 2016)

Dardot, Pierre and Laval, Christian (Gregory Elliott, trans.) *The New Way of the World: On Neoliberal Society* (Verso 2017)

Davenport, Thomas H. and Beck, John C., *Attention Economy: Understanding the New Currency of Business* (Harvard Business Review Press 2002)

De Vos, Christian M, 'Case Note: Prosecutor v Lubanga, "Someone Who Comes Between One Person and Another": *Lubanga*, Local Cooperation and the Right to a Fair Trial' (2011) 12(1) *Melbourne Journal of International Law* 217–236

Dean, Jodi, *Democracy and Other Neoliberal Fantasies: Communicative Capitalism and Left Politics* (Duke University Press 2009)

   Publicity's Secret: How Technoculture Capitalizes on Democracy (Cornell University Press 2002)

Debord, Guy, *Society of the Spectacle* [1967] (Black & Red 1984)

DeFalco, Randle, 'Accounting for Famine at the Extraordinary Chambers in the Courts of Cambodia: The Crimes against Humanity of Extermination, Inhumane Acts and Persecution' (2011) 5(1) *International Journal of Transitional Justice* 142–158

Del Ponte, Carla, 'The Dividends of International Criminal Justice', Goldman Sachs, London, 6 October 2005, available at: www.icty.org/x/file/Press/PR_attachments/cdp-goldmansachs-050610-e.htm.

Della Porta, Donatella, (ed.), *The Global Justice Movement: Cross-national and Transnational Perspectives* (Paradigm 2006)

Dinnie, Keith, (ed.), *Nation Branding: Concepts, Issues, Practice* (2nd ed. Routledge 2016)

Dinnie, Keith, *City Branding: Theory and Cases* (Palgrave 2011)

Dorobat, Carmen Elena, 'The WTO: Useless for Trade, Useful for the State', Mises Institute, 12 September 2017, available at: https://mises.org/wire/wto-useless-trade-useful-state.

Douglas, Lawrence, *The Memory of Judgment: Making Law and History in the Trials of the Holocaust* (Yale University Press 2001)

Doyle, Peter, 'Branding' in Michael J. Baker, *The Marketing Book* (Butterworth-Heinemann 1989)

Driscoll, David, 'The IMF and the World Bank: How Do They Differ?', International Monetary Fund, 1 June 1995

Drumbl, Mark, 'From Timbuktu to The Hague and Beyond: The War Crime of Intentionally Attacking Cultural Property' (2019) 17(1) *Journal of International Criminal Justice* 77–99

  'Victims Who Victimise' (2016) 4(2) *London Review of International Law* 217–246

  Reimagining Child Soldiers in International Law and Policy (Oxford University Press 2012)

  Atrocity, Punishment, and International Law (Cambridge University Press 2007)

Du Bois, W.E.B., *The Souls of Black Folk* [1903] (Penguin 1996)

Dubow, Saul, *South Africa's Struggle for Human Rights* (Ohio University Press 2012)

Duggan, Marian, (ed.), *Revisiting the 'Ideal Victim': Developments in Critical Victimology* (Bristol University Press 2018).

Dunoff, Jeffrey L. and Trachman, Joel P. (eds.), *Ruling the World? Constitutionalism, International Law, and Global Governance* (Cambridge University Press 2009)

Elliott, Stuart, 'When Products Are Tied to Causes', *The New York Times*, 18 April 1992

Elster, Jon, (ed.) *Karl Marx: A Reader* (Cambridge University Press 1986)

  (ed.) 'Theories of Surplus Value' in *Karl Marx: A Reader* (Cambridge University Press 1986) 321.

Engle, Karen, 'Anti-impunity and the Turn to Criminal Law in Human Rights' (2015), 100(5) *Cornell Law Review* 1069–1128

Enright, Michael, 'Marketing and Conflicting Dates for Its Emergence: Hotchkiss, Bartels, the "Fifties School" and Alternative Accounts' (2002) 18(5–6) *Journal of Marketing Management* 445–461

Eslava, Luis 'TWAIL Coordinates', (Critical Legal Thinking, 2 April 2019), available at: http://criticallegalthinking.com/2019/04/02/twail-coordinates/#fn-27281-2.

Eslava, Luis, Fakhri, Michael, and Nesiah, Vasuki, (eds.), *Bandung, Global History, and International Law: Critical Pasts and Pending Futures* (Cambridge University Press 2017)

Ess, Charles, 'The Political Computer: Democracy, CMC, and Habermas' in Charles Ess (ed.), *Philosophical Perspectives on Computer-Mediated Communication* (State University of New York Press 1996) 197–230

Evans, Brad and Forti, Simona, 'Who Is "Evil", and Who Is the Victim?', *The New York Times*, 16 September 2016

Evans, Brad and Spivak, Gayatri Chakravorty, 'When Law Is Not Justice', *The New York Times*, 13 July 2016

Fanon, Frantz, *The Wretched of the Earth* [1961] (Penguin 2001)

Fanon, Frantz, (Charles Lam Markmann, trans), *Black Skin, White Masks* [1952] (Pluto Books 2008)

Federici, Silvia, *Caliban and the Witch* (Autonomedia 2004)

Ferstman, Carla, 'The International Criminal Court's Trust Fund for Victims: Challenges and Opportunities' (2009) 6 *Yearbook of International Humanitarian Law* 424–434

Finnegan, Amy C., 'Beneath Kony 2012: Americans Aligning with Arms and Aiding Others' (2013) 59(3) *Africa Today*, 136–162

Fisher, Mark, *Capitalist Realism: Is There No Alternative?* (Zero Books 2009)

Fisher, Max, 'The Soft Bigotry of Kony 2012', *The Atlantic*, 8 March 2012

Flint, Adrian, 'The End of a "Special Relationship"? The New EU–ACP Economic Partnership Agreement (2009) 36(119)*Review of African Political Economy* 79–92

Foucault, Michel, *Discipline and Punish: The Birth of the Prison* (trans. Alan Sheridan) (Pantheon 1977)

Frank, Andre Gunder, *Capitalism and Underdevelopment in Latin America: Historical Studies of Chile and Brazil* (Monthly Review Press 1967)

Frederiksen, Lee, 'Elements of a Successful Brand 8: Messaging' Hinge Marketing online, 14 May 2018, available at: https://hingemarketing.com/blog/story/elements-of-a-successful-brand-8-messaging

Freedman, Jim, 'A Conviction in Question – Lessons from the International Criminal Court's Inaugural Trial', Justice in Conflict blog, 17 January 2018, available at: https://justiceinconflict.org/2018/01/17/a-conviction-in-question-lessons-from-the-the-international-criminal-courts-inaugural-trial/

A Conviction in Question: The First Trial of the International Criminal Court (University of Toronto Press 2017)

Freeland, Cynthia A., 'Realist Horror' in Cynthia A. Freeland and Thomas E. Wartenberg (eds.), *Philosophy and Film* (Routledge 1995) 126–142

Frick, Walter, 'As More People Worry About Monopolies, An Economist Explains What Antitrust Can and Can't Do', *Harvard Business Review*, 1 November 2017)

Fukuyama, Francis, 'The End of History?' (1989) 16 *The National Interest* 3–18.

Gathi, James Thuo, 'TWAIL: A Brief History of Its Origins, Its Decentralized Network, and a Tentative Bibliography' (2011) 3(1) *Trade, Law and Development* 26–64

Gebrial, Dalia, 'Rhodes Must Fall: Oxford and Movements for Change' in Gurminder K. Bhambra, Dalia Gebriel, and Kerem Nisancioglu (eds.), *Decolonising the University* (Pluto Press 2018)

Getachew, Adom, *Worldmaking after Empire: The Rise and Fall of Self-Determination* (Princeton University Press 2019)

Giannopoulos, Antonios A., Piha, Lamprini P., and Avlonitis, George J., '"Desti-Nation Branding": What for? From the Notion of Tourism and Nation

Branding to an Integrated Approach' (April 2011) Cultural Diplomacy, paper presented at the 2011 Berlin International Economics Congress, Berlin, Germany (March 15)

Gilroy, Paul, 'The End of Anti-Racism' 17(1) *Journal of Ethnic and Migration Studies* (1990) 71–83

'The End of Anti-Racism' in Wendy Ball and John Solomons (eds.), *Race and Local Politics* (Macmillan 1990), 191–209

Glissant, Édouard, *Poetics of Relation* (Betsy Wing, trans., University of Michigan Press 1997)

Goetz, Ariane, *Land Grabbing as Development?: Chinese and British Land Acquisitions in Comparative Perspective* (Transcript Verlag 2019)

Gráda, Cormac Ó, *Famine: A Short History* (Princeton University Press, 2009)

Gregory, Sam, '*Kony 2012* Through a Prism of Video Advocacy Practices and Trends' (2012) 4(3) *Journal of Human Rights Practice* 463–468

Green, Simon, 'Crime, Victimization and Vulnerability' in Sandra Walklate (ed.) *Handbook of Victims and Victimology* (Routledge 2007, 91–117)

Grotius, Hugo, *The Free Sea* [1609], (David Armitage (ed.), Richard Hakluyt (trans.) (Liberty Fund 2004)

Grunwald, Henning, *Courtroom to Revolutionary Stage: Performance and Ideology in Weimar Political Trials* (Oxford University Press 2012)

Guilfoyle, Douglas, 'This is not fine: The International Criminal Court in Trouble' Parts I, II, and III, *EJIL Talk*, 21–25 March 2019, available at: www.ejiltalk .org/part-i-this-is-not-fine-the-international-criminal-court-in-trouble/

Hafner-Burton, Emilie M., 'Sticks and Stones: Naming and Shaming the Human Rights Enforcement Problem' (2008) 64(4) *International Organization* 689–716

Hansler, Jennifer, 'US denying visas to International Criminal Court staff', CNN, 15 March 2019, available at: https://edition.cnn.com/2019/03/15/politics/ pompeo-icc-visa-restrictions/index.html

Haraway, Donna, 'Situated Knowledges: The Science Question in Feminism and the Privilege of Partial Perspective' (1988) 14(3) *Feminist Studies* 575–599

Harcourt, Bernard E., *Exposed: Desire and Disobedience in the Digital Age* (Harvard University Press 2015)

Hart, Susannah, 'The Future for Brands' in Susannah Hart and John Murphy (eds.), *Brands: The New Wealth Creators* (Palgrave Macmillan 1998), 206–214

Hart, Susannah and Murphy, John, *Brands: The New Wealth Creators* (New York University Press 1998)

Harvey, David, *Seventeen Contradictions and the End of Capitalism* (Profile Books 2014)

A Brief History of Neoliberalism (Oxford University Press 2007)

Hayek, Friedrich, *The Road to Serfdom* [1944] (Routledge 2001)

Hayes, Niamh, 'Sisyphus Wept: Prosecuting Sexual Violence at the International Criminal Court' in William A. Schabas, Yvonne McDermott, and Niamh Hayes (eds.), *The Ashgate Research Companion to International Criminal Law: Critical Perspectives* (Ashgate 2013) 7–44

Hazan, Pierre, *La justice face à la guerre, De Nuremberg à la Haye* (Stock 2000)

Heffernan, Richard, 'Media Management: Labour's Political Communications Strategy' in Gerald R. Taylor (ed.), *The Impact of New Labour* (Palgrave Macmillan 1999)

Hehir, Aidan, 'Lessons Learned? The Kosovo Specialist Chambers' Lack of Local Legitimacy and its Implications' (2019) 20(3) *Human Rights Review* 267–287 'Step towards Justice or Potential Timebomb?', *Report: Kosovo Specialist Chambers* (Balkan Investigative Reporting Network 2018).

Heller, Kevin Jon, 'ICC Labor Woes Part II: What's Two Million Euros Between Friends?', Opinio Juris blog, 30 July 2018, available at: http://opiniojuris.org/2018/06/30/the-iccs-labor-woes-part-ii/

Heller, Kevin Jon and Simpson, Gerry (eds.), *The Hidden Histories of War Crimes Trials* (Oxford University Press 2013)

Henley, Jon, 'Gaddafi's Wild Words Show He Hasn't Learned Anything' *The Guardian*, 22 February 2011

Herman, Edward S. and Chomsky, Noam, *Manufacturing Consent: The Political Economy of the Mass Media* (Vintage Books 1994)

Hirsch, Susan F., 'The Victim Deserving of Global Justice: Power, Caution, and Recovering Individuals' in Kamari Maxine Clarke and Mark Goodale (eds.) *Mirrors of Justice: Law and Power in the Post-Cold War Era* (Cambridge University Press 2009) 149–170

Hitchens, Christopher, *The Trial of Henry Kissinger* (Verso 2001)

Hohmann, Jessie and Joyce, Daniel, (eds.), *International Law's Objects* (Oxford University Press 2018

Holder, Alex, 'Sex Doesn't Sell Any More, Activism Does. And Don't the Big Brands Know It', *The Guardian*, 3 February 2017

Hong, Euny, 'Consultant, Consult Thyself: Why Gaddafi's Former Spin Doctor, the Monitor Group, Filed for Bankruptcy' Quartz, 11 November 2012, available at: https://qz.com/26285/once-prestigious-monitor-group-files-for-bankruptcy/.

Hopewell, Kristen, *Breaking the WTO: How Emerging Powers Disrupted the Neoliberal Project* (Stanford 2016)

Hopgood, Stephen, *The Endtimes of Human Rights* (Cornell University Press 2013)

Hours, Bernard, 'NGOs and the Victim Industry', *Le monde diplomatique* (November 2008)

Hughes, Chris, 'Libya: Brits Blitz Mad Dog Gaddafi', *The Mirror*, 22 March 2011

Huikuri, Salla, *The Institutionalization of the International Criminal Court* (Palgrave Macmillan 2019)

Hulleman, Bengt-Arne B. F. and Govers, Robert, 'The Hague, International City of Peace and Justice: A Relational Network Brand' in Keith Dinnie (ed), *City Branding: Theory and Cases* (Palgrave 2011) 150–156

Hurt, Stephen R, 'Co-operation and Coercion? The Cotonou Agreement between the European Union and ACP States and the End of the Lomé Convention' (2003) 24(1) *Third World Quarterly* 161–176

Iacono, Corey, 'Neoliberalism: The Left's Eternal Boogeyman', *Foundation for Economic Education*, (13 May 2016)

Jaffe, Eugene D. and Nebenzahl, Israel D., *National Image & Competitive Advantage: The Theory and Practice of Place Branding* (2nd ed. Copenhagen Business School Press 2006)

Jarvis, Helen and Fawthrop, Tom, *Getting Away with Genocide? Elusive Justice and the Khmer Rouge Tribunal* (UNSW Press 2005)

Jessop, Bob, 'The Heartlands of Neoliberalism and the Rise of the Austerity State' in, Simon Springer, Kean Birch, and Julie MacLeavy, *The Handbook of Neoliberalism* (Routledge 2016) 410–421

Johnson, Michael, *Branding in Five and a Half Steps* (Thames & Hudson 2016)

Kagumire, Rosebell and Smith, David, '*Kony 2012* Video Screening Met with Anger in Northern Uganda, *The Guardian*, 14 March 2012

Kapczynski, Amy, 'The Right to Medicines in an Age of Neoliberalism' (2019), 10 (1) *Humanity Journal* 79–107

Kapferer, Jean-Noël, *Strategic Brand Management: New Approaches to Creating and Evaluating Brand Equity* (Kogan Page 1992)

Kapoor, Ilan, *Celebrity Humanitarianism: The Ideology of Global Charity* (Routledge 2013)

Kapur, Ratna, *Erotic Justice: Law and the New Politics of Postcolonialism* (Glasshouse Press 2005)

Karlsgodt, Elizabeth, *Defending National Treasures: French Art and Heritage Under Vichy* (Stanford University Press 2011)

Kearon, Tony and Godfrey, Barry S., 'Setting the Scene: A Question of History' in Sandra Walklate (ed.), *Handbook of Victims and Victimology* (Routledge 2007) 17–36.

Kendall, Sara, 'Commodifying Global Justice: Economies of Accountability at the International Criminal Court' (2015) 13(1) *Journal of International Criminal Justice* 113–134

Kendall, Sara and Nouwen, Sarah, 'Speaking of Legacy: Towards and Ethos of Modesty at the International Criminal Tribunal for Rwanda' (2016) 110(2) *American Journal of International Law* 212–232

'Representational Practices at the ICC: The Gap between Juridified and Abstract Victimhood' (2014) 76(3) *Law and Contemporary Problems* 235–262

Kennedy, David, 'When Renewal Repeats: Thinking against the Box', 32 *New York University Journal of International Law and Politics* (1999–2000) 335–500

'Autumn Weekends: An Essay on Law and Everyday Life' in Austin Sarat and Thomas R. Kearns (eds.) *Law in Everyday Life* (University of Michigan Press 1993), 191–235

'International Legal Education' (1985) 26(2) *Harvard International Law Journal* 361–384

Khmomami, Nadia, '"It Was as if I Had Peered into Hell": The Man Who Brought the Nazi Death Squads to Justice', *The Guardian*, 7 February 2017

Killean, Rachel and Moffett, Luke, 'Victim Legal Representation before the ICC and ECCC' (2017) 15(4) *Journal of International Criminal Justice* (2017) 713–740

Klein, Naomi, *No Logo* (10th anniversary edition, Fourth Estate, 2010)
The Shock Doctrine (Penguin 2008)

Knox, Robert, 'Valuing Race? Stretched Marxism and the Logic of Imperialism' (2016) 4(1) *London Review of International Law* 81–126

'Strategy and Tactics' (2010) 21 *Finnish Yearbook of International Law* 193–229

Kohler, Lotte and Saner, Hans (eds.), Robert Kimber and Rita Kimber (trans.), *Hannah Arendt – Karl Jaspers, Correspondence 1926–1969* (Harcourt Brace Jovanovich 1992)

Koskenniemi, Martti, 'Foreword' in Immi Tallgren and Thomas Skouteris (eds.) *The New Histories of International Criminal Law: Retrials* (Oxford University Press 2019)

'Between Impunity and Show Trials' (2002) 6 *Max Planck United Nations Yearbook* 1–35

'The Lady Doth Protest Too Much: Kosovo, and the Turn to Ethics in International Law' 65(2) *Modern Law Review* (2002) 159–175

Kotecha, Birju, 'The Art of Rhetoric: Perceptions of the International Criminal Court and Tribunals' (2018) 31(4) *Leiden Journal of International Law* 939–962

Koulen, Sarah-Jane, 'Blind Justice and the Portraits on the Wall' in Lianne J. M. Boer and Sofia Stolk (eds.), *Backstage Practices of Transnational Law* 91–107

Krever, Tor, 'Dispensing Global Justice' (2014) 85 *New Left Review* 67–97

'International Criminal Law: An Ideology Critique' (2013) 26(3) *Leiden Journal of International Law* (2013) 701–723

Lang, Andrew, *World Trade after Neoliberalism: Reimagining the Global Economic Order* (OUP 2011)

Lanz, David, 'Save Darfur: A Movement and its Discontents' (2009) 108 *African Affairs* 669–677

Lawther, Cheryl, Killean, Rachel, and Dempster, Lauren, 'Transitional Justice at Sites of "Dark Tourism": The Case of Genocide Memorials in Cambodia', Justice in Conflict blog, 28 January 2019, available at: https://justiceinconflict.org/2019/01/28/transitional-justice-at-sites-of-dark-tourism-the-case-of-genocide-memorials-in-cambodia/.

Leary, John Patrick, *Keywords: The New Language of Capitalism* (Haymarket Books 2018)

Leeson, Robert, *The Eclipse of Keynesianism: The Political Economy of the Chicago Counter-Revolution* (Palgrave New York 2000)

Leong, Nancy, 'Racial Capitalism' (2013) 126(8) *Harvard Law Review* 2151–2226

Levy, Daniel and Sznaider, Natan, 'The Institutionalization of Cosmopolitan Morality: The Holocaust and Human Rights' (2004) 3(2) *Journal of Human Rights'* 143–157

Lippmann, Walter, *Public Opinion* [1922] (Greenbook Publications 2010)

    An Enquiry into the Principles of the Good Society (Little Brown 1937)

Luban, David, 'After the Honeymoon: Reflections on the Current State of International Criminal Justice' (2013) 11(3) *Journal of International Criminal Justice* 505–515

    'Carl Schmitt and the Critique of Lawfare' (2010) 43(1) *Case Western Reserve Journal of International Law,* 457–471

Lubin-Levy, Joshua and Shvarts, Aliza, 'Living Labor: Marxism and Performance Studies' (2017) 26(2–3) *Women & Performance: A Journal of Feminist Theory* 115–121

Lury, Celia, *Brands: The Logos of the Global Economy* (Routledge 2004)

Luxemburg, Rosa, *The Accumulation of Capital* [1913] (Routledge 2013)

    Junius Broschüre, Die Krise der Sozialdemokratie [1916] (Heptagon Verlag 2012)

    'The Mass Strike, The Political Party and the Trade Unions' [1906] in Helen Scott (ed.), *The Essential Rosa Luxemburg: Reform or Revolution and the Mass Strike* (Haymarket Books 2008).

Mabikke, Samuel B. 'Escalating Land Grabbing in Post Conflict Regions of Northern Uganda: A Need for Strengthening Good Land Governance in Acholi Region', conference paper presented at the International Conference on Global Land Grabbing (2011) *Land Deal Politics Initiative.*

MacKinnon, Ian, 'Prosecutor Wants to Indict Five More Khmer Rouge', *Financial Times,* 7 September 2009

Magubane, Zine, 'The Revolution Betrayed? Globalization, Neoliberalism and the Post-Apartheid State', 103 (4) *The South Atlantic Quarterly* 657–671

Mahler, Anne Garland, *From the Tricontinental to the Global South: Race, Radicalism, and Transnational Solidarity* (Duke University Press 2018)

Mamdani, Mahmood, 'Responsibility to Protect or Right to Punish?' (2010) 4(1) *Journal of Intervention and Statebuilding* 53–67

    Saviors and Survivors: Darfur, Politics and the War on Terror (Verso 2009)

    'Between the Public Intellectual and the Scholar: Decolonization and Post-Independence Initiatives in African Higher Education' (2016) 17(1) *Inter-Asia Cultural Studies* 68–83

Mandlebaum, Michael, *The Ideas that Conquered the World: Peace, Democracy, and Free Markets in the Twenty-first Century* (Public Affairs 2002)

Maquugo, Sivuyile, 'The African Contribution towards the Establishment of an International Criminal Court' (2000) 8(1) *African Yearbook on International Law* 333–350

Mark, Gloria, Gudith, Daniela, and Klocke, Ulrich, 'The Cost of Interrupted Work: More Speed and Stress', (Proceedings of the SIGCHI Conference on Human Factors in Computing Systems 2008).

Marks, Susan, 'Value' (2016) 4(1) *London Review of International Law* 1–3

'Human Rights and the Bottom Billion' (2009) 1 *European Human Rights Law Review* 37–49

The Riddle of All Constitutions (Oxford University Press 2000) 123

Marks, Susan and Clapham, Andrew, *'Victims' in International Human Rights Lexicon* (Oxford University Press 2005) 399–410

Marwick, Alice E., *Status Update: Celebrity, Publicity & Branding in the Social Media Age* (Yale University Press 2013)

Marx, Karl, *Das Kapital* [1867] (Regnery Publishing 2009)

Capital (Oxford World Classics 1999)

'Economic and Philosophic Manuscripts of 1844' in *Early Writings* (Penguin 2000)

Mawhinney, Janet, '"Giving up the Ghost": Disrupting the (Re)Production of White Privilege in Anti-Racist Pedagogy and Organizational Change' (Masters Thesis, Ontario Institute for Studies in Education of the University of Toronto 1998).

May, Christopher, *A Global Political Economy of Intellectual Property Rights: The New Enclosures?* (Routledge 2000)

Mazzucato, Mariana, *The Value of Everything: Making and Taking in the Global Economy* (Penguin 2018)

Mbembe, Achille, 'The Age of Humanism is Ending', *The Mail & Guardian*, 22 December 2016

Mcclintock, Anne, *Imperial Leather: Race, Gender and Sexuality* (Routledge 1995).

McDonald, Patricia, 'The Attention Economy and the Demise of the Middle Ground', *The Guardian*, 6 July 2016

McEvoy, Kieran and McConnachie, Sarah, 'Victimology in Transitional Justice: Victimhood, Innocence and Hierarchy' (2012) 9(5) *European Journal of Criminology* 527–538

McKinna, Anita, 'Haradinaj's Resignation 2.0: The Continued Politicisation of Transitional Justice in Kosovo', *Balkanist Magazine*, 31 July 2019

Mégret, Frédéric, 'What Sort of Global Justice is "International Criminal Justice"' (2015) 13(1) *Journal of International Criminal Justice* 77–96

'In whose name?' in Christian De Vos, Sara Kendall, and Carsten Stahn (eds.) *Contested Justice: The Politics and Practice of International Criminal Court Interventions* (Cambridge University Press 2015) 23–45

'International Criminal Justice: A Critical Research Agenda' in Christine Schwöbel (ed.) *Critical Approaches to International Criminal Law* (Routledge 2014) 17–53

Melamed, Jodi, 'Racial Capitalism' (2015) 1(1) *Critical Ethnic Studies* 76–85

Melissen, Jan (ed.), *The New Public Diplomacy: Soft Power in International Relations* (Palgrave Macmillan 2005).

Mendelsohn, Beniamin, 'The Origin of the Doctrine of Victimology' (1963) 3 *Excerpta Criminologica* 239–244

Mibenge, Chiseche Salome, *Sex and International Tribunals: The Erasure of Gender from the War Narrative* (University of Pennsylvania Press 2013)

Miers, David, *Responses to Victimisation: A Comparative Study of Compensation for Criminal Violence in Great Britain and Ontario* (Professional Books 1978)

Milanovic, Marko, 'An Eventful Day in The Hague: Channelling Socrates and Goering', EJIL: *Talk!*, 30 November 2017, available at: www.ejiltalk.org/an-eventful-day-in-the-hague-channeling-socrates-and-goering/

Milekic, Sven, 'Poison-Drinking War Criminal's Portrait Exhibited in Croatia', *Balkan Insight*, 27 August 2018

'War Criminal Praljak's Death Commemorated in Croatia', *Balkan Insight*, 11 December 2017

Moffett, Luke, 'Elaborating Justice for Victims at the International Criminal Court: Beyond Rhetoric and the Hague' (2015) 13(2) *Journal of International Criminal Justice* 281–311

Monbiot, George, 'Celebrity Isn't Just Harmless Fun – It's the Smiling Face of the Corporate Machine', *The Guardian*, 20 December 2016

Moor, Liz, *The Rise of Brands* (Bloomsbury 2007)

Moreno Ocampo, Luis, 'From Brexit to African ICC Exit: A Dangerous Trend', Just Security blog, 31 October 2016, available at: www.justsecurity.org/33972/brexit-african-icc-exit-dangerous-trend/.

'The International Criminal Court: Seeking Global Justice' (2007) 40(1) *Case Western Reserve Journal of International Law* 215–225

Mort, Frank, *Cultures of Consumption: Masculinities and Social Space in Late Twentieth Century Britain* (Routledge 1996)

Mostert, Tristan and Clulow, Adam, (eds.) *The Dutch and English East India Companies: Diplomacy, Trade and Violence in Early Modern Asia* (Amsterdam University Press 2018)

Moyn, Samuel, 'On a Self-Deconstructing Symposium' (2016) 110 *AJIL Unbound* 258–262

The Last Utopia: Human Rights in History (Belknap Press Harvard 2012)

Murai, Yasuko, "'Alive with Possibility": Brand South Africa and the Discursive Construction of South African National Identity', Dissertation, LSE Department of Media and Communications, 2011, Media@LSE Electronic MSc Dissertation Series

Murphy, John, *Brand Strategy* (Prentice Hall 1990)

Mushkat, Roda, 'State Reputation and Compliance with International Law: Looking through a Chinese Lens' (2011) 10(4) *Chinese Journal of International Law* 703–737

Mutua, Makau, 'Savages, Victims, and Saviors: The Metaphor of Human Rights' (2001) 42(1) *Harvard International Law Journal* 201–245

Navarro, Vincente, 'Neoliberalism as Class Ideology; or, the Political Causes of the Growth of Inequalities' (2007) 37(1) *International Journal of Health Services* 47–62

Nibbe, Ayesha Anne, 'The Effects of a Narrative: Humanitarian Aid and Action in the Northern Uganda Conflict', unpublished PhD thesis, Department of Anthropology, University of California Davis (2011)

Nichols Haddad, Heidi, 'The International Criminal Court was established 20 years ago. Here's How', *The Washington Post*, 17 July 2018

Nicholson, Rebecca, 'From Coke's Flower Power to Kendall Jenner's Pepsi Ad – How Ads Co-opt Protest', *The Guardian*, 5 April 2017

Nijman, Janne Elisabeth, 'Renaissance of the City as Global Actor. The Role of Foreign Policy and International Law Practices in the Construction of Cities as Global Actors' in Andreas Fahrmeir, Gunther Hellmann and Milos Vec (eds.), *The Transformation of Foreign Policy: Drawing and Managing Boundaries from Antiquity to the Present* (Oxford University Press 2016) 209–239

Nixon, Rob, *Slow Violence and the Environmentalism of the Poor* (Harvard University Press 2013)

Nouwen, Sarah and Werner, Wouter, 'Monopolizing Global Justice: International Criminal Law as Challenge to Human Diversity' (2015) 13(1) *Journal of International Criminal Justice* 157–176

'Doing Justice to the Political: The International Criminal Court in Uganda and Sudan' (2010) 21(4) *European Journal of International Law* 941–965

Nussbaum, Martha, *Not for Profit: Why Democracy Needs the Humanities* (Princeton University Press 2010)

O'Brien, James, 'The International Tribunal for Violations of International Humanitarian Law in the Former Yugoslavia' (1993) 87(4) *American Journal of International Law* 639–659

O'Grady, Siobhán, 'Gambia: The ICC Should be Called the International Caucasian Court', *Foreign Policy*, 26 October 2016

Ociepka, Baeta, 'Public Diplomacy as Political Communication: Lessons from Case Studies' (2018) 33(3) *European Journal of Communication* 290–303

Olugbuo, Benson Chinedu, 'Implementing the International Criminal Court Treaty in Africa: The Role of Nongovernmental Organizations and Government Agencies in Constitutional Reform' in Kamari Maxine Clarke and Mark Goodale (eds.), *Mirrors of Justice: Law and Power in the Post-Cold War Era* (Cambridge University Press 2010) 106–130.

O'Neill, Onora, 'Lifeboat Earth' in Thomas Pogge and Darrel Moellendorf (eds.), *The Global Justice Reader: Seminal Essays, Volumes I and II* (Paragon House 2008) 1–20

Orford, Anne, *Reading Humanitarian Intervention: Human Rights and the Use of Force in International Law* (Cambridge University Press 2003)

'Muscular Humanitarianism: Reading the Narratives of the New Interventionism' (1999) 10(4) *European Journal of International Law* 679–711

Osborne, Simon, 'Bosnia War Commander DIES After Drinking POISON in United Nations Courtroom', *Express*, 29 November 2017

Ostry, Jonathan D., Loungani, Prakash, and Furceri, Davide, 'Neoliberalism: Oversold?' (2016) 53(2) *Finance & Development*, available at: www.imf .org/external/pubs/ft/fandd/2016/06/ostry.htm.

Owen, John M., 'How Liberalism Produces Democratic Peace' (1994) 19(2) *International Security* 87–125

Pahuja, Sundhya, *Decolonising International Law: Development, Economic Growth and the Politics of Universality* (Cambridge University Press 2011)

Palmer, James, '"Skull Map" of Killing Fields is Laid to Rest', *The Independent*, 11 March 2002

Parker, Gillian and Perry, Alex, 'Gambia's Fatou Bensouda: The New Face of Global Justice', *Time Magazine*, 18 June 2012

Pashukanis, Evgeny B, *Law & Marxism: A General Theory* [1929], trans. Barbara Einhorn (Pluto Press 1989)

Pauwelyn, Joost, 'WTO Dispute Settlement Post 2019: What to Expect?' (2019) *Journal of International Economic Law* 22(3) 1–25

Perry-Kessaris, Amanda, 'The Pop-Up Museum of Legal Objects Project: An Experiment in "Sociolegal Design"' (2017) 68(2) *Northern Ireland Legal Quarterly*, Special Issue on the Pop Museum of Legal Objects, 225–244

Petersmann, Ernst-Ulrich, 'The WTO Constitution and Human Rights' (2000) 3 (1) *Journal of International Economic Law* 19–25

'How to Promote the International Rule of Law? Contributions by the World Trade Organization Appellate Review System (1998) 1(1) *Journal of International Economic Law* 25–48

The GATT/WTO Dispute Settlement System: International Law, International Organizations and Dispute Settlement (Kluwer 1997)

Petras, James, 'NGOs: In the Service of Imperialism' (1999) 29(4) *Journal of Contemporary Asia* 429–440

Pilkington, Ed, 'US firm Monitor Group Admits Mistakes over $3m Gaddafi Deal', *The Guardian*, 4 March 2011

'UN general assembly: 100 Minutes in the Life of Muammar Gaddafi', *The Guardian*, 23 September 2009

du Plessis, Carien, 'Withdrawing from International Criminal Court May Hurt SA as Investment Destination', Fin24, 30 August 2018, available at: www.fin24 .com/Economy/World/withdrawing-from-international-criminal-court-may-hurt-sa-as-investment-destination-20180830.

du Plessis, Max, 'The International Criminal Court and Its Work in Africa: Confronting the Myths' (2008) Institute for Security Studies, paper 173

Pogge, Thomas, and Moellendorf, Darrel, (eds.), *The Global Justice Reader: Seminal Essays, Volumes I and II* (Paragon House 2008)

Power, Samantha, *A Problem from Hell: America and the Age of Genocide* (Flamingo 2010)

Quashie, Kevin, *The Sovereignty of Quiet: Beyond Resistance in Black Culture* (Routledge 2012)

Quelch, John, 'Global Brands: Taking Stock' (1999) 10(1) *Business Strategy Review* 1–14

Raad Al-Hussein, Prince Zeid, Stagno Ugarte, Bruno, Wenaweser, Christian, and Intelman, Tiina, 'The International Criminal Court Needs Fixing', Atlantic Council, 24 April 2019, available at: www.atlanticcouncil.org/blogs/new-atlanticist/the-international-criminal-court-needs-fixing/

Rajagopal, Balakrishnan, 'Counter-Hegemonic International Law: Rethinking Human Rights and Development as Third World Strategy' in Richard Falk, Balakrishnan Rajagopal and Jacqueline Stevens (eds.) *International Law and the Third World: Reshaping Justice* (Routledge 2008) 767–783

Rancière, Jacques, *The Politics of Aesthetics*, trans. Gabriel Rockhill (Bloomsbury 2004)

Rasmussen, Rasmus Kjærgaard and Merkelsen, Henrik, 'The New PR of States: How Nation Branding Practices Affect the Security Function of Public Diplomacy' (2012) 38(5) *Public Relations Review*, 810–818

Rawls, John, 'The Law of People' in Thomas Pogge and Darrel Moellendorf (eds.), *The Global Justice Reader: Seminal Essays, Volumes I and II* (Paragon House 2008) 421–460

Reinhoudt, Jurgen and Audier, Serge, *The Walter Lippmann Colloquium: The Birth of Neo-Liberalism* (Palgrave MacMillan 2018)

Reisman, Michael W. , 'The Teaching of International Law in the Eighties' (1986) 20(3) *The International Lawyer* 987–995

Remnick, David, 'Trump's Cruelty and the Crying Children at the Border', *The New Yorker*, 19 June 2018

Reynolds, John and Xavier, Sujith, '"The Dark Corners of the World": TWAIL and International Criminal Justice' (2016) *Journal of International Criminal Justice* 14(4) 959–983

Ricardo, David and Hartwell, Ronald Max, (eds.) *Principles of Political Economy and Taxation* [1817] (Penguin 1971)

Richards, Thomas, *The Commodity Culture of Victorian England: Advertising and Spectacle 1851–1914* (Stanford University Press 1991)

Richey, Lisa Ann and Ponte, Stefano, *Brand Aid: Shopping Well to Save the World* (University of Minnesota Press 2011)

Rigney, Sophie, 'Postcard from the ICTY' in Jessie Hohmann and Daniel Joyce (eds.) *International Law's Objects* (Oxford University Press 2018) 366–376

Ritson, Mark, 'Mark Ritson: The Lessons We Can Learn from Kony 2012', *Marketing Week*, 15 March 2012

Rossi, Christopher R., 'Hauntings, Hegemony, and the Threatened African Exodus from the International Criminal Court' (2018) 40(2) *Human Rights Quarterly* 369–405

Rozenberg, Joshua, 'ICC Prosecutors Should Not Be Grandstanding Their Own Cases', *The Guardian*, 18 August 2010.

'Prosecutor Luis Moreno-Ocampo Is the Best Asset of Those Opposed to the International Criminal Court', *The Guardian*, 21 April 2011.

Safire, William, 'On Language; Worth a Thousand Words', *The New York Times*, 7 April 1996

Said, Edward, 'Grey Eminence' (1981) 4(4) *London Review of Books* 7.

Orientalism [1978] (Penguin 2003)

Sands, Philippe, *East West Street: On the Origins of "Genocide" and "Crimes against Humanity"* (Alfred Knopf 2016)

Lawless World: Making and Breaking Global Rules (Penguin 2006)

Sarkar, Christian and Kotler, Philip, *Brand Activism: From Purpose to Action* (IDEA BITE PRESS 2018)

Sassen, Saskia, *The Global City: New York, London, Tokyo* (Princeton University Press 2001)

Schabas, William, *The UN International Criminal Tribunals: The Former Yugoslavia, Rwanda and Sierra Leone* (Cambridge University Press 2012)

Schabas, William A., McDermott, Yvonne, and Hayes, Niamh (eds.), *The Ashgate Research Companion to International Criminal Law: Critical Perspectives* (Routledge 2013)

Scheffer, David, *All the Missing Souls: A Personal History of the War Crimes Tribunals* (Princeton University Press 2013).

'The United States and the International Criminal Court' (1999) 93(1) *American Journal of International Law* 12–22

Schneiderman, David, 'Investment Arbitration As Constitutional Law: Constitutional Analogies, Linkages and Absences' in Thomas Schultz and Frederico Ortino (eds.), *Oxford Handbook of International Arbitration* (Oxford University Press, 2020)

Schwöbel-Patel, Christine, 'Spectacle in International Criminal Law: The Fundraising Image of Victimhood' (2016) *London Review of International Law* 4(2) 247–274

'The Comfort of International Criminal Law' (2013) 24(2) *Law & Critique* 169–191

'The Core Crimes of International Criminal Law' in Kevin Jon Heller et al. (eds.) *The Oxford Handbook of International Criminal Law* (Oxford University Press 2020)

'The "Ideal" Victim of International Criminal Law' (2018) 29(3) *European Journal of International Law* 703–724

'The Market and Marketing Culture of International Criminal Law' in Christine Schwöbel (ed.), *Critical Approaches to International Criminal Law: An Introduction* (Routledge 2014) 264–279

'The Re-branding of the International Criminal Court (and Why African States Are Not Falling for It)', Opinio juris blog, 28 October 2016, available at: http://opiniojuris.org/2016/10/28/the-re-branding-of-the-international-criminal-court-and-why-african-states-are-not-falling-for-it/.

Schwöbel-Patel, Christine and Werner, Wouter, 'Screen' in Jessie Hohmann and Daniel Joyce (eds.), *International Law's Objects* (Oxford University Press 2018) 419–430

Seaton, A. V., 'Guided by the Dark: From Thanatopsis to Thanatourism' (2007) *International Journal of Heritage Studies* 2(4) 234–244

Sharp, Byron, *How Brands Grow: What Marketers Don't Know* (Oxford University Press 2010)

Shklar, Judith, *Legalism: Law, Morals, and Political Trials* (Harvard University Press 1986)

Shringarpure, Bhakti, 'The Rise of the Digital Saviour: Can Facebook Likes Change the World?' *The Guardian*, 18 June 2015

Shultz, Howard, *Pour Your Heart Into It* (Hyperion 1997)

Sikkink, Kathryn, *The Justice Cascade: How Human Rights Prosecutions are Changing World Politics* (W. W. Norton & Company 2011)

Simpson, Gerry 'Unprecedents' in Immi Tallgren and Thomas Skouteris, *The New Histories of International Criminal Law: Retrials* (Oxford University Press 2019) 12–29

Law, War & Crime: War Crimes Trials and the Reinvention of International Law (Polity Press 2007)

Great Powers and Outlaw States: Unequal Sovereigns in the International Legal Order (Cambridge University Press 2004)

Simon, H. A., '*Designing Organizations for an Information-Rich World*' in Martin Greenberger (ed.), *Computers, Communication, and the Public Interest* (The John Hopkins Press 1971)

Simons, Marlise, 'International Criminal Court Issues First Sentence', *The New York Times*, 10 July 2012

Simons, Marlise and Cowell, Alan, 'A War Criminal Drank Poison in Court, and Died. How Could This Happen?', *The New York Times*, 1 December 2017

Great Powers and Outlaw States: Unequal Sovereigns in the International Legal Order (Cambridge University Press 2009).

Singer, P. W., *Corporate Warriors: The Rise of the Privatized Military Industry* (Cornell University Press 2011)

Skouteris, Thomas, *The Notion of Progress in International Law Discourse* (T. M. C. Asser Press 2010)

'The New Tribunalism: Strategies of De-Legitimation in the Era of International Adjudication' (2008) 17 *Finnish Yearbook of International Law* 307–356

Skuba, Charles, 'Branding America' (2002) 3 *Georgetown Journal of International Affairs* 105–114

Slobodian, Quinn, *Globalists: The End of Empire and the Birth of Neoliberalism* (Harvard University Press 2018)

'Neoliberalism's Populist Bastards: A New Political Divide between National Economies', Public Seminar, 15 February 2018, available at: https://publicseminar.org/2018/02/neoliberalisms-populist-bastards/.

Slosson, Mary, 'ICC Prosecutor courts Hollywood with Invisible Children', Reuters, 2 April 2012, available at: https://af.reuters.com/article/commoditiesNews/idAFL2E8F203020120402.

Smeulers, Alette, Weerdesteijn, Maartje, and Hola, Barbora, 'The Selection of Situations by the ICC: An Empirically Based Evaluation of the OTP's Performance' (2015) 15(1) *International Criminal Law Review* 1–39

Smith, Adam, *Wealth of Nations* [1776] (Penguin 1982)

Smith, David, 'New Chief Prosecutor Defends International Criminal Court', *The Guardian*, 23 May 2012.

Snyder, Bill, 'Nike Co-founder: Why I Approved the Controversial Colin Kaepernick Ad', *Fast Company*, 6 March 2019

Sontag, Susan, *Regarding the Pain of Others* (Penguin 2004)

On Photography (Penguin 1979)

de Sousa Santos, Boaventura, *The End of the Cognitive Empire: The Coming of Age of Epistemologies of the South* (Duke University Press 2018)

Epistemologies of the South: Justice against Epistemicide (Routledge 2014)

Beyond Abyssal Thinking: From Global Lines to Ecologies of Knowledges, 30(1) Review 45–89 (2007)

Spalek, Basia, *Crime Victims: Theory, Policy and Practice* (Palgrave Macmillan 2006)

Springer, Simon, *Cambodia's Neoliberal Order: Violence, Authoritarianism, and the Contestation of Public Space* (Routledge 2010)

Stedman, Stephen John, 'The New Interventionists' (1992–1993) 71(1) *Foreign Affairs* 1–16

Steel, Ronald, *Walter Lippmann and the American Century* (Bodley Head 1981)

Steinke, Ronan, *The Politics of International Criminal Justice: German Perspectives from Nuremberg to The Hague* (Hart 2012)

Stevenson, Burton, *MacMillan Book of Proverbs, Maxims and Famous Phrases* (Macmillan 1965)

Stigler, George J., 'The Economics of Carl Menger' 45(2) *Journal of Political Economy* (1937) 229–250

Stolk, Sofia, 'A Sophisticated Beast? On the Construction of an 'Ideal' Perpetrator in the Opening Statements of International Criminal Trials (2018) 29(3) *European Journal of International Law* 677–701

'A Solemn Tale of Horror: The Opening Statement of the Prosecution in International Criminal Trials' (doctoral thesis on file at Vrjie Universiteit Amsterdam 2017)

Stracey, Frances, *Constructed Situations: A New History of the Situationist International* (Pluto Press 2014)

Strachey, Lytton, *Queen Victoria* [1901], (Chatto & Windus 1921)

Streek, Wolfang, 'The Return of the Repressed' (2017) 104 *New Left Review* 5–18

Stoddard, Ed, 'Uganda Expects First Oil Production in 2021, Refinery by 2023, *Reuters* (8 November 2018), available at: https://uk.reuters.com/article/africa-oil-uganda/uganda-expects-first-oil-production-in-2021-refinery-by-2023-idUKL8N1XJ3VR.

Subramanian, Samanth, 'How to Sell a Country: The Booming Business of Nation Branding' *The Guardian*, 7 November 2017

Suddath, Claire , '"Kony 2012": Guerrilla Marketing', *Bloomberg*, 31 August 2012

Sunkara, Lavanya, '*From Auschwitz To Chernobyl: Tips on Respectfully Visiting Dark Tourism Sites*', Forbes, 1 August 2019

Swart, Mia, 'Layers of Coloniality: How to Navigate the Political Nature of the International Criminal Court', (draft paper on file with the author).

Szondi, György, 'Public Diplomacy and Nation Branding: Conceptual Similarities and Differences' (2008) *Discussion papers in Diplomacy, Netherlands Institute of International Relations 'Clingendael'*

'The Role and Challenges of Country Branding in Transition Countries: The Central European and Eastern European Experience' (2007) 3(1) *Place Branding and Diplomacy* 8–20

Tadlock, Tara, 'Dark Tourism in Cambodia: Exploitation and Cultural Insensitivity', World Foot Prints, 17 February 2019, available at: https://worldfootprints .com/dark-tourism-in-cambodia-exploitation-and-cultural-insensitivity/

Tallgren, Immi, 'Voglio una donna!': On Rewriting the History of International Criminal Justice with the Help of Women Who Perpetrated International Crimes' in *Immi Tallgren and Thomas Skouteris, The New Histories of International Criminal Law: Retrials* (Oxford University Press 2019) 110–129

'Come and See? The Power of Images and International Criminal Justice' (2017) 17(2) *International Criminal Law Review* 259–280

'The Sensibility and Sense of International Criminal Law' (2002) 13(3) *European Journal of International* 561–595

Tallgren, Immi and Skouteris, Thomas, 'Editor's Introduction' in Immi Tallgren and Thomas Skouteris (eds.), *The New Histories of International Criminal Law: Retrials* (Oxford University Press 2019)

Taylor, Adam, 'Was #Kony2012 a failure?', *Washington Post*, 16 December 2014

Taylor, John, *Body Horror: Photojournalism, Catastrophe and War* (Manchester University Press 1998)

Thomas, Chantal, 'Globalization and the Reproduction of Hierarchy' (2000) 33 *University of California, Davis Law Review* 1451–1501

Tomlinson, Alan, 'Introduction: Consumer Culture and the Aura of the Commodity' in Alan Tomlinson (ed.), *Consumption, Identity and Style: Marketing, Meanings and the Packaging of Pleasure* (Routledge 1990) 1–40

Tomuschat, Christian (ed.), *Kosovo and the International Community: A Legal Assessment* (Brill 2002)

'The International Community' in *Collected Courses of the Hague Academy of International Law* (Brill/Nijhoff, 1993)

Tooze, Adam, *The Deluge: The Great War and the Remaking of Global Order 1916–1931* (Penguin 2015)

Touissant, Eric, *Your Money or Your Life: The Tyranny of Global Finance* (Haymarket Books 1999)

Tuck, Eve and Wayne, Yang K., 'Decolonization Is Not a Metaphor' (2012) 1(1) *Decolonization: Indigeneity, Education & Society* 1–40

Tuck, Richard, *The Rights of War and Peace: Political Thought and the International Order from Grotius to Kant* (Clarendon Press 1999)

Tushnet, Rebecca, 'Worth a Thousand Words: The Images of Copyright (2012) 125(3) *Harvard Law Review* 683–759

Tzouvala, Ntina, 'Neoliberalism as Legalism: International Economic Law and the Rise of the Judiciary' in Ben Golder and Daniel McLoughlin (eds.), *The Politics of Legality in a Neoliberal Age* (Routledge 2017) 116–133

Upshaw, Lynn, *Building Brand Identity: A Strategy for Success in a Hostile Marketplace* (Wiley 1995)

Valier, Claire, 'Punishment, Border Crossings and the Powers of Horror' (2002) 6 (3) *Theoretical Criminology* 319–337

Van Schaak, Beth and Slye, Ron, 'A Concise History of International Criminal Law' in Beth van Schaak, and Ron Slye (eds.), *International Criminal Law: Essentials* (Aspen Publishers 2009)

Vaughan, Shannon K. and Arsneault, Shelly, 'Kony 2012, A Cautionary Tale about Social Media' in *Managing Nonprofit Organizations in a Policy World* (Sage Publishing 2013)

Vergès, Jacques, *De la stratégie judiciaire*, [1968] (Les Éditions de Minuit 1981)

Verini, James, 'The Prosecutor and the President', *New York Times Magazine*, 22 June 2016.

Vladisavljevic, Anja, 'Praljak's Courtroom Suicide Anniversary Marked in Croatia', *Balkan Insight*, 29 November 2018

Walklate, Sandra, 'Introduction and Overview' in Sandra Walklate (ed.), *Handbook of Victims and Victimology* (Routledge 2007) 1–10

'Perspectives on the Victim and Victimisation', in Sandra Walklate (ed.), *Handbook of Victims and Victimology* (Routledge 2007)

Walsh, Catherine E. 'The Decolonial For Resurgences, Shifts, and Movements' in Walter D Mignolo and Catherine E. Walsh, *On Decoloniality: Concepts, Analytics, Praxis* (Duke University Press 2018)

Walsh, Catherine E. and Mignolo, Walter D., 'Introduction' in Walter D. Mignolo and Catherine E. Walsh, *On Decoloniality: Concepts, Analytics, Praxis* (Duke University Press 2018)

Wark, McKenzie, *Fifty Years of Recuperation of the Situationist International* (Princeton Architectural Press 2008)

Webb, Malcolm, 'Ugandans React with Anger to Kony Video', *Al Jazeera*, 14 March 2012

Webber, Alan M., '*What Great Brands Do*', *Fast Company*, 31 August 1997

Weheliye, Alexander G., *Habeas Viscus: Racializing Assemblages, Biopolitics, and Black Feminist Theories of the Human* (2014 Duke University Press)

Werner, Wouter 'Justice on Screen – A Study of Four Documentary Films on the International Criminal Court' (2016) 29(4) *Leiden Journal of International Law* 1043–1060

White, Michael, ' Blair Defines New Labour', *The Guardian*, 5 October 1994

Whyte, Jessica, '*The Morals of the Market*': *Human Rights and the Rise of Neoliberalism* (Verso 2019)

Williams, James, *Stand out of Our Light: Freedom and Resistance in the Attention Economy* (Cambridge University Press 2018)

van Wijk, Joris, 'Who is the 'Little Old Lady' of International Crimes? Nils Christie's Concept of the Ideal Victim Reinterpreted' (2013) 19(2) *International Review of Victimology* 159–179

Wolff, Ernst, *Pillaging the World: The History and Politics of the IMF* (Tectum Wissenschaftsverlag 2014)

Wu, Tim, *Attention Merchants: The Epic Scramble to Get Inside Our Heads* (Vintage Books 2016)

Zamfir, Ionel, 'International Criminal Court: Achievements and Challenges 20 Years after the Adoption of the Rome Statute', *Briefing of the European Parliament*, (European Parliament Research Service July 2018)

Zarbiyev, Fuad, 'From the Law of Valuation to the Valuation of Law? On the Interplay of International Law and Economics in Fair Market Valuation' in

Theresa Carpenter, Marion Jansen, and Joost Pauwelyn (eds.), *The Use of Economics in International Trade and Investment Disputes* (Cambridge University Press 2017)

Zelno, Kevin, 'On Slacktivism: Lessons from #Kony 2012', *Scientific American*, 14 March 2012, available at: https://blogs.scientificamerican.com/evo-eco-lab/on-slacktavism-lessons-from-kony2012/.

Zuboff, Shoshana, *The Age of Surveillance Capitalism: The Fight for a Human Future at the New Frontier of Power* (Profile Books 2019)

International Materials

'Action Plan to Follow-Up on the Decision on the International Criminal Court' and Annex (Council of the European Union) 12080/11 (12 July 2011)

Agreement on Trade-Related Aspects of Intellectual Property Rights, Annex 1C Marrakesh Agreement (15 April 1994), 319–350

At O'Hare, President Says "Get On Board"', Remarks by the President to Airline Employees, 27 September 2001, *The White House, President George W. Bush Archives*

Case Concerning Arrest Warrant of 11 April 2000 (*Democratic Republic of the Congo v. Belgium) Judgment [2002] ICJ Rep* 3

'Case Information Sheet, Situation in the Democratic Republic of the Congo', *Prosecutor v. Thomas Lubanga Dyilo*, ICC-01/04-01/06 (October 2016)

'Dutch Authorities Conclude Criminal Investigation into Slobodan Praljak's Death', United Nations Residual Mechanism for Criminal Tribunals, (Press Release) (2 November 2018)

'Establishment of a Fund for the Benefit of Victims of Crimes within the Jurisdiction of the Court, and of the Families of Such Victims' ICC-ASP/1/Res. 6 (9 September 2002)

Extraordinary Chambers in the Courts of Cambodia Internal Rules (adopted 12 June 2007)

'Extraordinary Session of the Assembly of the African Union', African Union, Ext/Assembly/AU/Dec.1–2 (12 October 2013)

'Facing Political Attacks, Limited Budget, International Criminal Court Needs Strong Backing to Ensure Justice for Atrocity Crimes, President Tells General Assembly', General Assembly Plenary 73rd Session, GA/12084 (29 October 2018)

'Foreign Relations Authorization Act, Fiscal Years 1994 and 1995', United States Congress, PL 103–236, (30 April 1994), 108 Stat 486; 22 USC 2656, Sec. 571–574

House of Representatives (Expressing Support for Robust Efforts by the United States to see Joseph Kony, the Leader of the Lord's Resistance Army, and Its Top Commanders Brought to Justice and the Group's Atrocities Permanently Ended') H.Res.583, 112th Congress (13 March 2012)

ICC Assembly of States Parties Resolution, 'Strengthening the International Criminal Court and the Assembly of States Parties', ICC-ASP/3/Res.3 (10 September 2004)

ICC Office of the Prosecutor, 'Policy Paper on the Interests of Justice' (September 2007), available at: www.icc-cpi.int/NR/rdonlyres/772C95C9-F54D-4321-BF09-73422BB23528/143640/ICCOTPInterestsOfJustice.pdf

ICC Statement on the Philippines' Notice of Withdrawal: State Participation in Rome Statute System Essential to International Rule of Law', (Press Release), ICC-CPI-20180320-PR1371 (20 March 2018)

Independent International Commission on Kosovo, *The Kosovo Report: Conflict, International Response, Lessons Learned* (Oxford University Press 2000)

'Integrated Strategy for External Relations, Public Information and Outreach', ICC Registry, (18 April 2007)

'International Conference on Military Trials: London 1945, Report to the President by Mr. Justice Jackson, October 7, 1946', available at http://avalon.law.yale.edu/imt/jack63.asp

'International Criminal Court Marks Opening of Judicial Year 2019' (Press Release) ICC-CPI-20190118-PR1430 (18 January 2019)

'International Criminal Court Promises Universal Justice, Secretary-General Tells International Bar Association' (Press Release) United Nations Secretary General/SM/6257 (12 June 1997)

International Criminal Court Rules of Procedure and Evidence, ICC-PIDS-LT-02-002/13

'International Organisations in the Netherlands: An Overview', Ministry of Foreign Affairs, The Netherlands, May 2014

'Introductory Statement by Justice Louise Arbour, Prosecutor ICTY and ICTR at the Launch of the ICC Coalition's Global Ratification Campaign', (Press Release) JL/PIU/401-0E (13 May 1999)

"Justice Matters": Multimedia Exhibit Opening in The Hague to Commemorate the ICC's 10th Anniversary' (Press Release) ICC-CPI-20121115-PR853 (15 November 2012)

'Justice Matters Social Media Campaign Launched to Commemorate 17 July: International Criminal Justice Day', (Press release), ICC-CPI-20140619-PR1018 (19 June 2014)

'Policy Paper on Case Selection and Prioritisation', The Office of the Prosecutor, ICC, 15 September 2016

'President of Uganda Refers Situation Concerning the Lord's Resistance Army (LRA) to the ICC' (Press Release) ICC-20040129-44-En (29 January 2004)

Prosecutor v Ante Gotovina and Mladen Markač (Appeals Judgment) ICTY-IT-06-90-A (16 November 2012)

Prosecutor v Jadranko Prlić et al (Judgment) ICTY-IT-04-74-A (29 November 2017)

Prosecutor v Kaing Guek Eav alias Duch, (Appeal Judgment) 001/18-07-2007-ECCC/SC (3 February 2012)

'Records of the United States Information Agency (RG 306)', USA National Archives, available at: www.archives.gov/research/foreign-policy/related-records/rg-306

Regulations of the Court, International Criminal Court, The Hague, 26 May 2004, ICC-BD/01-01-04

'Representing Victims before the International Criminal Court: A Manual for Legal Representatives', The Office of Public Counsel for Victims, (5th ed.) ICC-OPCV-MLR-005/19

Rome Statute of the International Criminal Court (signed 17 July 1998, entered into force 1 July 2002) A/CONF.189/9

'Security Council Refers Situation in Darfur, Sudan, to Prosecutor of International Criminal Court' (Press Release) SC/8351 (31 March 2005)

Situation in Georgia, (Decision on the Prosecutor's Request for Authorization of an Investigation) ICC-01/15 (27 January 2016)

Situation in the Islamic Republic of Afghanistan (Decision Pursuant to Article 15 of the Rome Statute on the Authorisation of an Investigation into the Situation in the Islamic Republic of Afghanistan) ICC-02/17 (12 April 2019).

Situation in Uganda (Pre-Trial Chamber II, Warrant of Arrest for Joseph Kony Issued on 8 July 2015 as Amended on 27 September 2005) ICC-02/04-01/05 (27 September 2005)

Statement by Luis Moreno-Ocampo, Chief Prosecutor of the International Criminal Court, Press Conference in relation with the surrender to the Court of Mr Thomas Lubanga Dyilo, The Hague, 18 March 2006

'STL Requests that the Lebanese Authorities Take Further Steps to Advertise New Accused', Special Tribunal for Lebanon (Press Release) (11 October 2013), available at: www.stl-tsl.org/en/media/press-releases/2549-media-advisory-stl-requests-that-the-lebanese-authorities-take-further-steps-to-advertise-new-accused

'Strategic Plan 2019–2021', Office of the Prosecutor, 17 July 2019

The 28th Ordinary Session of the Assembly of the African Union', African Union, (30 January 2017) link available at: https://au.int/web/en/newsevents/20170130/28th-ordinary-session-assembly-african-union

The Cotonou Partnership Agreement (signed 23 June 2000, revised 25 June 2005) European Commission, Directorate-General for Development and Relations with African, Caribbean and Pacific States

The Prosecutor v. *Ahmad Al Faqi Al Mahdi* (Judgment and Sentence) ICC-01/12-01/15 (Trial Chamber VIII, 27 September 2016)

The Prosecutor v. *Bosco Ntaganda*, (Pre-Trial Chamber II, Decision on Common Legal Representation of Victims) ICC-01/04-02/06-160 (2 December 2013)

The Prosecutor v. *Dominic Ongwen*, (Trial Chamber IX, Decision on Registry's Request for Clarification on the Issue of Legal Assistance Paid by the Court for the Legal Representatives of Victim) ICC-02/04-01/15-591 (14 November 2016)

(Trial Chamber IX, Decision on the 'Request for a Determination Concerning Legal Aid' Submitted by the Legal Representatives of Victims) ICC-02/04-01/15 (26 May 2016)

(Pre-Trial Chamber II, Decision on the Confirmation of Charges against Dominic Ongwen) ICC-02/-4-01/15 (23 March 2016)

(Pre-Trial Chamber II, Decision on Contested Victims' Application for Participation, Legal Representation of Victims and Their Procedural Rights), ICC-02/04-01/15 (27 November 2015)

The Prosecutor v. Germain Katanga (Judgment) ICC-01/04-01/07-3436-tENG (Trial Chamber II, 7 March 2014)

The Prosecutor v Germain Katanga and Mathieu Ngudjolo Chui, (Pre-Trial Chamber II, *Opening of the Trial*) ICC-01/04-01/07, (24 November 2009)

The Prosecutor v Germain Katanga and Mathieu Ngudjolo Chui, (Trial Hearing) ICC-01/04-01/07, (24 November 2009), transcript available at: www.icc-cpi .int/Transcripts/CR2009_08585.PDF.

The Prosecutor v. Jean-Pierre Bemba Gombo, Aimé Kilolo Musamba, Jean-Jacques Mangenda Kabongo, Fidèle Babala Wandu and Narcisse Arido (Judgment) ICC-01/05-01/13-1989-Red (Trial Chamber VII, 19 October 2019)

The Prosecutor v. Jean-Pierre Bemba Gombo (Order on the Conduct of the Proceedings Related to 'Mr Bemba's claim for compensation and damages') ICC-01/05-01/08 (14 March 2019)

The Prosecutor v. Jean-Pierre Bemba Gombo (Judgment on the Appeal of Mr Jean-Pierre Bemba Gombo against Trial Chamber III's 'Judgment pursuant to Article 74 of the Statute'), ICC-01/05/08 A (8 June 2018)

The Prosecutor v. Laurent Gbagbo and Charles Blé Goudé (Transcript, Trial Chamber I) ICC-02/11-01/15-T-232-ENG (15 January 2019)

The Prosecutor v. Omar Hassan Ahmad Al Bashir (Pre-Trial Chamber I, Warrant of Arrest for Omar Hassan Ahmad Al Bashir) ICC-02/05-01/09-1 (04 March 2009)

The Prosecutor v. Thomas Lubanga Dyilo (Judgment) ICC-01/04-01/06-2842 (14 March 2012)

(Opening Statement) ICC-01/04-01/06 (26 January 2009)

(Decision Regarding the Practices Used to Prepare and Familiarise Witnesses for Giving Testimony at Trial) ICC-01/04-01/06, (Trial Chamber I, 30 November 2007)

(Pre-Trial Chamber I, Request Submitted Pursuant to Rule 103(1) of the Rules of Procedure and Evidence for Leave to Participate as Amicus Curiae in the Article 61 Confirmation Proceedings), ICC-01/04-01/06 (7 September 2006)

The Prosecutor v. Uhuru Muigai Kenyatta (Decision on the Withdrawal of Charges against Mr Kenyatta) ICC-01/09-02/11 (13 March 2015)

(Trial Chamber V, Status Conference Transcript) ICC-01/09-02/110 (5 February 2014)

The Prosecutor v. William Samoei Ruto, Henry Kiprono Kosgey and Joshua Arap Sang, (Pre-Trial Chamber II, Decision on the Motion from Victims a/0041/

10, a/0045/10, a/0051/10 and a/0056/10 Requesting the Pre-Trial Chamber to Reconsider the Appointment of Common Legal Representative Sureta Chana for All Victims) ICC-01/09-01/11-330 (9 September 2011)

Trial of the Major War Criminals before the International Military Tribunal, Nuremberg 14 November 1945-October 1946, Official Text in the English Language, Volume II (Nuremberg Tribunal 1947)

UK Cabinet Office, *Ministerial Code: A Code of Conduct and Guidance on Procedures for Ministers*, July 1997

'UK Statement to the Assembly of States Parties 17th Session', Assembly of States Parties 17th Session, 5 December 2018

United Nations Declaration of the Basic Principles of Justice for Victims of Crime and Abuse of Power (adopted 29 November 1985) A/CONF.121/22/Rev.1

United Nations General Assembly Resolution 44/23, 'United Nations Decade of International Law', 60th plenary meeting at the 44th session, (17 November 2019) UN Doc A/RES/44/23

'United Nations Guidelines on the Use of the UN Emblem', Publications Board Secretariat New York, June 2007

United Nations Office for the Coordination of Humanitarian Affairs, 'Consolidated Appeal for Uganda 2006', 30 November 2005

United Nations Security Council Resolution 678 (29 November 1990)

United Nations Security Council Resolution 794 (3 December 1992)

United Nations Security Council Resolution 808 (22 February 1993)

United Nations Security Council Resolution 827 (25 May 1993)

United Nations Security Council Resolution 940 (31 July 1994).

United Nations Security Council Resolution 955 (8 November 1994)

Films

General. Directed by Antun Vrdoljak, Kiklop Film & Croatian Television 2019

Hotel Rwanda. Directed by Terry George, United Artists 2004

Invisible Children: Rough Cut. Directed by Laren Poole and Jason Russell, Invisible Children and People Like You Productions 2006

La société du spectacle. Directed by Guy Debord 1973

No Logo: Brands, Globalization and Resistance. Directed by Sut Jhally, Media Education Foundation 2003

Peace versus Justice. Directed by Klaartje Quirijns, Submarine Channel 2012

Prosecuting Evil: The Extraordinary World of Ben Ferencz. Directed by Barry Avrich, Melbar Entertainment Group 2019

Prosecutor. Directed by Barry Stevens, White Pine Pictures 2010

The Court. Directed by Marcus Vetter and Michele Gentile, Filmperspektive GmbH 2012

INDEX

Lightning Source UK Ltd.
Milton Keynes UK
UKHW020847120921
390429UK00003B/33